EARLY MESSAGES TO THE WEST

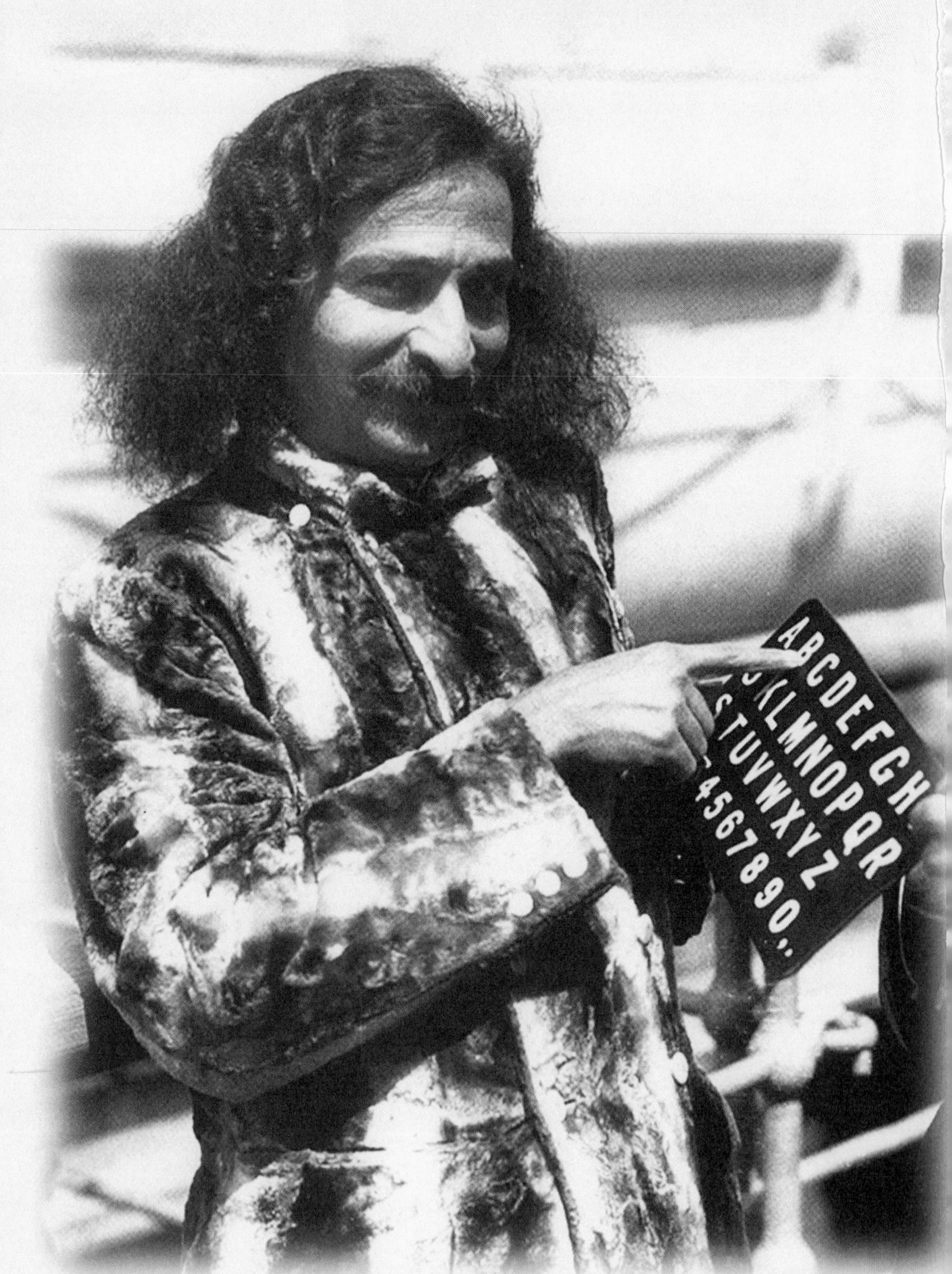

Meher Baba on the S.S. Bremen arriving in New York, May 19, 1932.

MEHER BABA'S

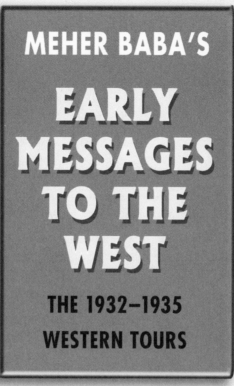

EARLY MESSAGES TO THE WEST

THE 1932–1935 WESTERN TOURS

EDITED FOR PUBLICATION
UNDER THE AUSPICES OF THE
AVATAR MEHER BABA PERPETUAL
PUBLIC CHARITABLE TRUST
AHMEDNAGAR, INDIA

Sheriar Foundation
NORTH MYRTLE BEACH, SOUTH CAROLINA

Cover photographs: (TOP) Meher Baba aboard the S. S. Esperia about to sail from Genoa to Alexandria, December 1932. Photographer unknown. (CENTER RIGHT) Meher Baba in the New York Harbor on the S. S. Bremen, 1932, courtesy of the Hermes Reiter Collection. (CENTER LEFT) Meher Baba with Tallulah Bankhead in Hollywood, 1932, courtesy of the Hermes Reiter Collection. (BOTTOM) Meher Baba photographed at Devonshire Retreat in England in 1932. Photograph by R. L. Knight. Reproduced from the original photograph. From the Beloved Archives Collection, Princeton, New Jersey. (BACK COVER) Meher Baba in Hollywood, 1935, photographed by Elizabeth Patterson. Courtesy of ECP Archives.

Photograph on page 2 of Meher Baba sitting in bunk on an ocean liner en route to the West is from the Meher Desai Collection, courtesy of Meher Baba Trust's Archive Collection. © 2009 by Avatar Meher Baba Perpetual Public Charitable Trust, Ahmednagar, India. Used with permission.

Photograph on the bottom of page 116 of Meher Baba and Herbert Davy by an unknown photographer, courtesy of Avatar Meher Baba Trust Archives. © 2009 by Avatar Meher Baba Perpetual Public Charitable Trust, Ahmednagar, India. Used with permission.

All other photographs reproduced from the Hermes Reiter Collection. Used with permission.

Reproduction of diagrams, charts, illustrations and letters on pages 169, 170, 174, 175, 186, 191, 193–5, 198, 356–64, courtesy of Avatar Meher Baba Trust Archives. © 2009 by Avatar Meher Baba Perpetual Public Charitable Trust, Ahmednagar, India. Used with permission.

Reproduction of letters on pages 58 and 197, courtesy of the Meher Spiritual Center, Myrtle Beach, South Carolina. Transcriptions of letters on pages 317–18, 324–27, 329–31, 334–42, courtesy of the Meher Spiritual Center, Myrtle Beach, South Carolina. Transcriptions of the letters on pages 318–25, 327–29, 331–36, courtesy Columbia University Rare Book and Manuscript Library, New York City, New York.

Library of Congress Cataloging-in-Publication Data Meher Baba, 1894-1969.
Early messages to the West / Meher Baba.
p. cm.
ISBN 978-1-880619-35-3
1. Spirituality. 2. Spiritual life. I. Title.
BP610.M43128 2009
299'.93—dc22

2009039484

Introduction

On September 11, 1931, for the first time in recorded history, the Avatar of the Age set foot in the Western world. Disembarking that morning from the S. S. Rajputana at Marseilles, Meher Baba proceeded by train to England, where he stayed for three weeks. Continuing his tour, Baba traveled on to Istanbul and then New York, which he reached on November 6. For about a month he was hosted in a house thirty miles up the Hudson River from the city. Here in Harmon-on-the-Hudson, as in London and Devonshire the month before, Meher Baba made his first acquaintance with a new country, giving interviews with interested newcomers, and establishing links with that select group of individuals who over the following decades proved to be among his closest Western disciples.

And thus was inaugurated a major new phase in this Avataric advent. For unlike the previous Avatars known to us, Meher Baba in his travels and activities encircled the globe. Mohammed, Jesus, Buddha, and the others all moved within circumscribed geographic limits; and while the archetypal character of what they did became evident over time, outwardly their lives were played out within the arenas provided by their local environments. Meher Baba, by contrast, was born into an age when the great world civilizations, long separated by seas and mountains and disparate cultural histories, had at last come into direct contact with each other. His work spanned these intercultural divides and distances; and when he spoke, it was in a universal language that could immediately be understood by all. One of the most significant of these divisions was the line between "East" and "West." The integration of East and West indeed defined one of the major thrusts of Baba's Avataric mission; and though it continued throughout the following decades until he dropped his physical form in 1969, this aspect of his work was launched in real earnest during his Western tours in the early 1930s.

Meher Baba's 1931 Western tour was the first of thirteen during his lifetime, ten of them between 1931 and 1937. But the fertile period in the arena of public communication, that is, in the Avatar's work towards the conveyance of his message to the world through the various public media, took place between April 1932 and January 1935; and this present collection for the most part centers on that period. For Baba's 1931 voyage to England and America passed largely "beneath the radar" in the sense that he avoided public meetings and contacts with the press, concentrating rather on personal interviews and the establishment of links with disciples. During his round-the-globe tour from March to July of 1932, however, Meher Baba attracted all kinds of media attention, some of it sensationalist, and gave a series of major public addresses in which for the first time he presented himself and his mission to the Western world. Though the media hullabaloo soon subsided, during Baba's subsequent Western visits in the next year and a half his disciples, under his direct supervision, began to prepare literary materials with a view to presenting Baba's message through the print medium. The culmination of this phase seems to have arrived in 1934–35 when Baba visited America for the last time in that decade, ostensibly to participate in discussions with Hollywood filmmakers that aimed at the creation of a film depicting spiritual themes. Though the film work had an afterlife that continued on as late as his visit to Cannes in 1937, the main thrust of Baba's energies from 1935 onward turned elsewhere—particularly towards his work with the masts and the training of his Western disciples in residence in his ashrams in India.

This greater three-and-a-half year span (from 1931–35) stands out, then, as a phase in which communications in various aspects and through various media occupied much of Meher Baba's attention. And when one looks back in retrospect, amid the breathless whirl of Baba's ceaseless activities during this period, a clear pattern emerges. His focus seems to have progressed from personal interviews (in 1931) to formal live statements before the press and other large audiences (in 1932), to books (in 1933), and at last to films (in 1934–35): that is, from the most intimate, personal, informal kind of communication to the most complexly developed and technologically dependent. None of these efforts came fully to fruition during these years; indeed, each time Baba seems to have shifted gears and moved on to another sphere of activity before this could happen. Yet it seems possible that, in some archetypal fashion, the Avatar was carrying out deep preparation and foundation laying in the consciousness of humanity.

The purpose of this book is to bring back into print the major statements, published messages, interviews, booklets, and creative narrative intended for film, that Meher Baba gave out in the early 1930s, since all of these collectively constitute the first serious self-presentation to the world public by the Avatar of the Age. The book's primary text subdivides into five parts. The first includes the six messages that Meher Baba conveyed in May–June 1932 during his round-the-world tour. The second section republishes some of the more noteworthy interviews with Baba and other articles that appeared in the mainstream press. The third and fourth parts bring back into print books prepared under Baba's own close supervision and published by the Circle Editorial Committee, a group of his disciples, in London in late 1933. Released in September, *Shri Meher Baba, the Perfect Master: Questions and Answers* compiles Baba's responses to, in its original edition, fifty-eight, and in its intended second edition, sixty-three questions, carefully edited and organized under major headings. *The Sayings of Shri Meher Baba* collects 136 pithy comments and aphorisms, probably gleaned from Baba's earlier discourses to the Indian mandali and previously published in the *Meher Message,* an Indian magazine that appeared on a monthly basis from 1929 through 1931.

Finally, part five publishes a body of material intended for a major film that would convey the fundamentals of Baba's philosophy and cosmology to the world. The narrative centerpiece, which Meher Baba dictated to his hostess Margaret Mayo during his first visit to America in 1931, describes the careers of three individuals, X, Y, and Z, through five lifetimes. This narrative was somewhat expanded upon, and set in the greater cosmological context of creation, evolution, reincarnation, spiritual advancement, and God-realization, through dictations that Baba gave to the mandali at Meherabad in May of 1934. *How It All Happened,* as this concept came to be called, was at the heart of Baba's undertakings in the film world during his two Western tours of 1934 and 1935.

Since Meher Baba personally observed silence and did not handwrite his own statements and explanations, naturally the question arises whether or in what way the messages, sayings, and other verbal content attributed to him are truly his. While the interviews in the second part of this book are as reliable as the journalists whose handiwork they represent, the main substance of the first, third and fourth sections issued directly from Baba himself and was published with his approval under his name; and the content of section five, while unpublished during Baba's lifetime, was based on his dictation. Throughout his lifetime Meher Baba's usual authorial method was to dictate essential points, the gist of a communication, to close disciples, who would write this content up and read it back to him for checking and correction. Though we do not know with certainty which disciples took the dictation, composed the drafts, incorporated the rewrites, typed the fair copies, proofread, and performed other relevant literary tasks and services, all available evidence suggests that Meher Baba used this same general process in creating what is collected in this book. There is no reason to doubt, in other words, that these primary materials are as fully his as *God Speaks* and the *Discourses* are.

Nonetheless, for those who interest themselves in these matters, this present volume incorporates a supplement with information relating to the historical and literary backgrounds to the various primary texts. The essay on this subject (pp. 203–76) explores in further detail important information relating to each of this book's major parts. This book also incorporates into its appendices selections from the newspaper and magazine coverage of

Baba's 1932 tour, passages from the correspondence of his disciples, and other materials relevant to problems of sources, editorship, and publication history. Meher Baba's literary productions, like the work of any author, emerged out of specific contexts, biographical, literary, and historical. Yet Baba's statements in this particular period of the early 1930s are, to an unusual degree, linked to and embedded within the environment and circumstances in which he was moving at the time. For this reason students of the Avatar's life and the unfoldment of his work in the world may find some of this contextual information to be especially illuminating.

In the preparation of this edition great pains have been taken to ensure that the texts of Baba's words as republished here are as reliable and authoritative as possible. Further information on the textual sources and editorial procedures can be found, again, in the essay that begins the supplement. By thus bringing together between a single pair of covers these early materials long scattered through various publications and in some cases out of print, it is our hope to enable Meher Baba's lovers and the general public to meet the Avatar as, in the early 1930s, he came forward to meet them. Though he did not fully declare himself at the time, many even then recognized him as the Christ; and the words he delivered, though tailored to the specific circumstances in which he "spoke" them, still carry the power and resonance and fragrance of that universal working that will one day transform the world.

Ward Parks
on behalf of the Avatar Meher Baba
Perpetual Public Charitable Trust

Table of Contents

PART THREE. *QUESTIONS AND ANSWERS:* THE FIRST WESTERN BOOKLET

PART FOUR. *THE SAYINGS:* ANOTHER EARLY COMPILATION

PART FIVE. *HOW IT ALL HAPPENED:* NOTES FOR A FILM

SUPPLEMENT

PART ONE

Six Messages: The Avatar Presents Himself to the Western World

During his 1932 global tour, Baba met with press representatives and gave public addresses explaining his mission to the West. Taken in Devonshire, this photo shows Baba with some of the key disciples on this tour, notably Meredith Starr and Quentin Tod.

(LARGE PHOTO) Baba sitting in bunk on an ocean liner en route to the West
(TOP INSERT) Baba in China on the final leg of his 1932 world tour
(BOTTOM INSERT) Baba in Hollywood with Tallulah Bankhead

INTRODUCTION TO PART ONE

Meher Baba's second world tour—the first in which he encircled the globe—was carried out between March and July 1932 amidst great media fanfare. The major broadcast networks and mainstream press corps pursued him in England, New York, and across the continent to Los Angeles. There the Hollywood film world, at that time in its golden age, feted and celebrated his arrival as a new celebrity. Promising that he would return from China to break his silence over the radio in the Hollywood Bowl on July 13, during his Pacific cruise Meher Baba canceled this engagement. And with this apparent letdown, the frenzy of publicity subsided.

During the English and American legs of the tour Meher Baba gave out six major messages, most of them in the form of addresses read out by his disciples at receptions in his honor or before representatives of the press. During this period the Western world was plunged into the depths of an economic depression; at the same time it was afflicted by social unrest following the legal prohibition of alcohol in America, the rise of organized crime there, the specter of emergent racial and ideological conflict in Europe and around the world, and other problems. In his six messages Meher Baba spoke to these world conditions, explaining that their true solution lay in the domain of spirituality, and indicating his own role in bringing about the needed transformation.

The primary source for these six messages is the compilation published by Baba's secretary, Messages of Meher Baba Delivered in the East and West *(Ahmednagar, India: Adi K. Irani for the Publication Committee, Meher Baba Universal Spiritual Centre, 1945), pp. 81–101. But since this text is at points defective, it has been corrected and emended through reference to other sources. For further details,* *see pp. 266–70.*

Message to the West
Given for the "Paramount Newsreel" by Shri Meher Baba on his Arrival in London, April 8, 1932[1]

(Read out by Mr. C. B. Purdom, Editor, *Everyman,* London)

My coming to the West is not with the object of establishing new creeds or spiritual societies and organizations, but is intended to make people understand religion in its true sense.

True religion consists of developing that attitude of mind which should ultimately result in seeing One Infinite Existence prevailing throughout the universe; when one could live in the world and yet be not of it and, at the same time, be in harmony with everyone and everything; when one could attend to all worldly duties and affairs and yet feel completely detached from all their results; when one could see the same Divinity in art and science and experience the Highest Consciousness and Indivisible Bliss in everyday life.

I see the structure of all the great and recognized religions and creeds of the world tottering. The West particularly is more inclined towards the material side of things which has, from untold ages, brought in its wake wars, pestilences and financial crises.[2] It should not be understood that I discard and hate materialism. I mean that materialism should not be considered an end in itself, but a means to the end.

Organized efforts, such as the League of Nations, are being made to solve world problems and to bring about the millennium. In some parts of the West, particularly America, intellectual understanding of Truth and Reality is attempted, but without the true spirit of Religion.

It is all like groping in the dark. I intend to bring together all religions and cults like beads on one string and revitalize them for individual and collective needs. This is my mission to the West. The peace and harmony that I talk of and that will settle on the face of this worried world are not far off.

Message to Reporters and Press Representatives Given on Board the "S. S. Bremen" in New York, May 19, 1932[3]

I am not come to establish any cult, society or organization, nor even to establish a new religion.

The Religion I shall give teaches[4] the knowledge of the One behind the many. The Book that I shall make people read is the Book of the Heart which holds the key to the mystery of life. As for ritual, I shall teach humanity to discriminate, express and live rather than utter it. I shall bring about a happy blending of the head and heart.

Societies and organizations have never succeeded in bringing Truth nearer. Realization of the Truth is solely the concern of the individual.

Every being is a point from which a start could be made towards the limitless Ocean of Love, Bliss, Knowledge and Goodness already within him. No spiritual Master brings religion to the world in the form which it eventually assumes. His very presence is a blessing and radiates spirituality. He imparts it to others by personal contact.

The so-called religions are an effort to commemorate the association with a great spiritual Master and to preserve his atmosphere and influence. It is like an archeological department trying to preserve things which only resuscitate the past. The living spirit being absent, religions or organizations gradually lose their glamour. The result is a mental revolt against the established order. Something more substantial and practical is required which expresses the life of the spirit. There exists at the moment a universal dissatisfaction and an indescribable longing for something that will end the chaos and misery that is holding the world in its grip. I will satisfy this craving and lead the world to real happiness and peace by making people look more deeply[5] into things than hitherto.

As a rule, Masters help individually according to temperament and fitness of the aspirant; but this being an "Avataric" period (which means the end of the previous cycle and the beginning of a new one), my spiritual help to humanity will be both individual and collective.

The period of junction of the old and new cycle usually connotes the advent of a Master who rejuvenates religious thought, infusing new life and meaning into the old order of things.

Besides imparting the highest state of spirituality to a select few, he gives a general spiritual push to the whole world.

The West looks at things only from the standpoint of reason and logic and is sceptical about things which baffle the intellect.

Intellect is the lowest form of understanding and is developed by reading, hearing, reasoning and logic. These processes create an illusion of real knowledge. The higher[6] state of understanding is permanent illumination through which one experiences and sees things as they are. In this state, one feels at harmony with everyone and everything, and realizes Divinity in every phase of life, and is able to impart happiness to others. Here, one attends to all duties and material affairs and yet feels mentally detached from the world. This is true renunciation. The last and highest state of understanding is the merging of the soul into the limitless Ocean of Infinite Bliss, Knowledge and Power. One who has himself attained this Freedom can make thousands perfect like himself. I intend bringing about a great spiritual revival in the near future, utilizing the tremendous amount of energy possessed by America for the purpose. Such a spiritual outpouring that I visualize usually takes place at the beginning or end of a cycle and only a Perfect One who has reached the Christ State of Consciousness can make such a universal appeal. My work will embrace everything. It will permeate every phase of life. Perfection would fall far short of the ideal if it were to accept one thing and eschew another. The general spiritual push that I shall give to the whole world will automatically adjust problems such as politics, economics and sex, though these are not directly connected with the original theme. New values and significance will be attached to things which appear to baffle solution at the moment.

The benefits that shall accrue to different nations and countries, when I bring about the spiritual upheaval, will be largely determined by the amount of energy each one possesses. The greater the energy, however misapplied, the greater the response. The Master merely diverts the current into the right channel. It will be one of my greatest miracles to bring together and blend the realistic West with the idealistic East, and the West at the zenith of its intellectual and material attainment and the East at the height of its spiritual manifestation in the shape of a Perfect Master will meet without shaming or looking down upon each other. I repeat, materialism and spirituality must go hand in hand. The balance of head and heart must be maintained (the head for discrimination, the heart for feeling), whereby it is possible to realize Infinite Consciousness in art, science, nature and every phase of life.

I have become one with the Infinite Source of everything. This is the state of Christ Consciousness. If people call me Messiah, Savior or Redeemer, it does not affect me. Terms and names do not matter. What really matters is the state of Christ Consciousness that I eternally enjoy and towards which I shall lead all who come to me. When I speak, my original message will be delivered to the world and it will have to be accepted.

The ability to perform miracles does not necessarily connote high spirituality. Anyone who has reached the Christ Consciousness can perform them. People must not come to me merely for help in their physical infirmities or for material purposes. I shall perform miracles when the time and situation demand, and not to satisfy mere idle curiosity. Spiritual healing is by far the greatest healing, and this is what I intend to give. The Highest is latent in everyone but has to be manifested.

Message at the Residence of Mr. Graham Phelps Stokes Given by Shri Meher Baba at a Reception in his Honor New York, May 22, 1932

(Read out by Mr. Meredith Starr)

I am so very pleased to see you again. Among you are many of the first Americans I met last time I was here: so I regard you as old friends.

No doubt, some of you have seen various newspaper reports about myself and my work.[7] Many of these are misleading. But it is not to be wondered at if journalists do not understand my work or pander to the desire for sensation.

I do not intend to found any religion, cult, creed or society. There are already far too many of these organizations. I have come to help people realize their ideals in daily life. The wide-spread dissatisfaction in modern life is due to the gulf between theory and practice, between the ideal and its realization on earth. The spiritual and material aspects of life are widely separated instead of being closely united. There is no fundamental opposition between spirit and matter, or if you like, between life and form. The apparent opposition is due to wrong thinking, to ignorance. Hence the remedy lies in the continuous practice of right thinking, to permanent illumination resulting from the balance between the head and heart. This is the illumination which I intend to give.

The greatest mystics have realized through personal experience that God alone is real and everything is God. This means that (though you may not be aware of it) the Highest is latent in each one of you. But in order for it to be lived and experienced in consciousness, it must be manifested.

Intellectual conviction of this truth is not enough. True knowledge consists in illumination which finally culminates in union with the Ultimate Reality. This last is the state of Christ Consciousness which is my permanent condition.

The obstacles to illumination are certain mental tendencies and desires connected with egoism which, in the East, are called "sanskaras." The sum total of these tendencies and desires creates the illusion of a separate self at war with or isolated from other selves. Evolution, or the fall into matter, made the creation of such a separate self necessary—otherwise, spiritual consciousness could never be attained in the flesh.

In the beginning, before evolution began, we were united with the source of all,[8] but unconsciously, as the fish lives in the sea without being aware of the sea, because it has never left it. Evolution involved a separation from the source of all and a consequent conscious longing to return to it through a succession of lives and forms. The conscious return to the Source during physical incarnation only became possible when consciousness became equilibrated in gross matter.

America represents the vanguard and synthesis of the white races and hence forms the best foundation for the spiritual upheaval I will bring about in the near future. America has tremendous energy, but most of this energy is misdirected. I intend to divert it into spiritual and creative channels.

I am now going to California for a few days. From there, I must go to the Far East for one day for spiritual reasons; but I will be back in California by the end of June and then I will speak on June 29. But if I should be delayed, I will return on July 12 and speak on July 13.[9]

When I speak, there will be many proofs of my spiritual power and of my ability to bestow illumination. People will then realize that Truth, which is the source of all love and existence, rules supreme in all departments of life.

My work and aims are intensely practical. It is not practical to overemphasize the material at the cost of the spiritual. It is not practical to have spiritual ideals without putting them into practice. But to realize the ideal in daily life, to give a beautiful and adequate form to the living spirit, to make brotherhood a fact—not merely a theory as at present—this is being practical in the truest sense of the word.

My work will arouse both great enthusiasm and a certain amount of opposition. That is inevitable. But spiritual work is strengthened by opposition, and so it will be with mine. It is like shooting an arrow from a bow. The more you pull the bow-string towards you, the swifter the arrow speeds to its goal.

Message to Reporters in Hollywood Given by Meher Baba on his Arrival in California May 29, 1932[10]

So much has been said and written about the "Highest Consciousness" and God-realization that people are bewildered as to the right process and immediate possibility of attainment. The philosophical mind wading laboriously through such literature only ends by learning a few intellectual gymnastics. The highest state of consciousness is latent in all. The Son of God is in every man, but requires to be manifested. The method of attaining this great consciousness must be very practical and must be adapted to the existing mental and material conditions of the world.

Rituals and ceremonies instituted by the priest-ridden churches have made the process of attainment too dry; and that accounts for the lack of interest felt all over the world towards religious things in general. India, in spite of its high state of spirituality,[11] at the present moment is very caste-ridden because of the enforcement by various cults of a plethora of rituals and ceremonies, which maintain the form but kill the spirit. Forms and ceremonies, instead of diminishing the ego, strengthen it. The stronger the ego, the more aggressive it becomes. In the anxiety to become conscious of a separate self through thinking thoughts such as "I am in the right," "I am the favored one," "I only have the right to live," one becomes destructive. The furious race for armaments by the Christian world, evincing an utter disregard for the commandment of Jesus that if one cheek is smitten, the other should be offered, shows clearly what I mean by the ego.[12]

In the evolutionary ascent from the mineral, vegetable and animal life, the latent mind gradually expands and develops till full consciousness is reached in the human form. To create this very consciousness, the universe emanated from the Infinite Ocean of Knowledge and Bliss, i.e., God the

Absolute. In the human form, however, a difficulty is confronted, to remove which, prophets and spiritual Masters have periodically visited this earthly plane. Besides full consciousness in the human form, as a result of previous conditions of life, the ego, the "I," is evolved.

The ego is composed of fulfilled and unfulfilled desires and creates the illusion of feeling finite, weak and unhappy. Henceforth, the soul can only progress through the gradual suppression of this finite ego and its transformation into the Divine Ego, the One Infinite Self, but retaining in full the consciousness of the human form. When man realizes this state of Divine Consciousness, he finds himself in everyone and sees all phenomena as forms of his own Real Self. The best and also the easiest process of overcoming the ego and attaining the Divine Consciousness is to develop love and render selfless service to humanity in whatever circumstances we are placed. All ethics and religious practices ultimately lead to this. The more we live for others and less for ourselves, the more the low desires are eliminated, and this, in turn, reacts upon the ego, suppressing and transforming it proportionately. The ego persists to the end.[13] Not till all the six out of the seven principal stages on the Path (culminating in the God-conscious state)[14] are traversed is the ego completely eliminated, to reappear on the seventh plane as the Divine "I," the state of Christ Consciousness to which Jesus referred when he said, "I and my Father are One," and which corresponds to the state of living in the Infinite and finite at one and the same time.

The above is the normal procedure for one who works on his own initiative without having come across a living Master. With the help of a Perfect Master, the whole affair, however, is greatly simplified.

Complete surrender to the Divine Will of the Perfect One, and[15] an unflinching readiness to carry out his orders, rapidly achieve a result not possible even by rigidly practising all the ethics of the world for a thousand years. The extraordinary results achieved by a Perfect Master are due to the fact that being one with the Universal Mind, he is present in the mind of every human being and can therefore give just the particular help needed to awaken the Highest Consciousness latent in every individual. Perfection, however, in order to achieve the greatest result on the material plane, must possess a human touch and a keen sense of humor.

I eternally enjoy the Christ State of Consciousness, and when I speak, which I intend doing in the near future, I shall manifest my true Self.[16]

Besides giving a general spiritual push to the whole world, I shall lead all those who come to me towards Light and Truth. This, in short, is my mission in the world.

The ability to perform miracles does not necessarily connote high spirituality.[17] Anyone who has reached the Christ Consciousness can perform them. People must not come to me merely for help in their physical infirmities or for material purposes. I shall perform miracles when the time and the situation demand, and not to satisfy mere idle curiosity. Spiritual healing is by far the greatest healing, and this is what I intend to give. The Highest is latent in everyone, but is to be manifested.

Message at the Knickerbocker Hotel Given by Shri Meher Baba at a General Reception in his Honor Hollywood, May 31, 1932

Since arriving in America, I have been asked many times what solution I brought for the social problems now confronting you—what did I have to offer that would solve the problems of unemployment, prohibition, crime—that would eliminate the strife between individuals and nations and pour a healing balm of peace upon a troubled world?

The answer has been so simple that it has been difficult to grasp. I will elaborate it now in order that it may be more easily understood.

The root of all our difficulties, individual and social, is self-interest. It is this, for example, which causes corruptible politicians to accept bribes and betray the interests of those whom they have been elected to serve; which causes bootleggers to break, for their own profit, a law designed, whether wisely or not, to help the nation as a whole; which causes people to connive, for their own pleasure, in the breaking of that law, thus causing disrespect for law in general and increasing crime tremendously; which causes the exploitation of great masses of humanity by individuals or groups of individuals seeking personal gain; which impedes the progress of civilization by shelving inventions which would contribute to the welfare of humanity at large, simply because their use would mean the scrapping of present, inferior equipment; which, when people are starving, causes the wanton destruction of large quantities of food, simply in order to maintain market prices; which causes the hoarding of large sums of gold when the welfare of the world demands its circulation.

These are only a few examples of the way self-interest operates to the detriment of human welfare. Eliminate self-interest and you will solve all your problems, individual and social.

But the elimination of self-interest, even granting a sincere desire on the part of the individual to accomplish it, is not so easy and is never completely achieved except by the aid of a Perfect Master, who has the power to convey Truth at will. For self-interest springs from a false idea of the true nature of the Self, and this idea must be eradicated, and the Truth experienced, before the elimination of self-interest is possible.

I intend, when I speak, to reveal the One Supreme Self which is in all. This accomplished, the idea of the self as a limited, separate entity, will disappear, and with it will vanish self-interest. Co-operation will replace competition; certainty will replace fear; generosity will replace greed. Exploitation will disappear.

It has been asked why I have remained silent for seven years, communicating only by means of an alphabet board, and why I intend to break my silence shortly; and it might be asked, in view of what has just been stated, what relation my speaking will have to the transformation of human consciousness which has been predicted.

Humanity, as at present constituted, uses three vehicles for the expression of thought, and experiences three states of consciousness. These three vehicles are: (1) the Mental Body, in which thoughts arise as the result of impressions from past experiences. These thoughts may remain latent in the mental body as seeds, or they may be expressed. If they are expressed, they take first the form of desire, and pass first through (2) the Subtle or the Desire Body, which is composed of the five psychic senses. They may rest here, as in the case of dreams or unfulfilled desire, or they may be further expressed in action through (3) the Physical Body, with five physical senses.

The three states of consciousness corresponding to the three vehicles mentioned above are: (1) unconsciousness, as in deep, dreamless sleep, (2) sub-consciousness, as in dreams, or obscure, unformed and unfulfilled desires, and (3) waking consciousness, as in active daily life.[18]

The process by which thought passes from the mental through the subtle into physical expression may be called the expression of human will.

In order that thought may be expressed effectively, all three of the vehicles used in its expression must be perfectly clear, and the interaction between them must be harmonious. The head and the heart must be united; intellect and feeling must be balanced; material expression must be understood to be the fruit of spiritual realization.

The God-man neither thinks nor desires. Through him, the Divine Will flows inevitably into perfect manifestation, passing directly from the spiritual body, which in the ordinary human being is undeveloped, into physical expression. For him, the super-conscious is the normal state of consciousness. From him there flows continuously infinite love and wisdom, infinite joy and peace and power.

In order to convey thought to others, man uses speech, or writing, or some other physical means of expression; or in some cases, as in telepathy, thought is transmitted and received through and by the subtle body.

The God-man does not convey thought, but Truth, which he either awakens in the individual whom he is helping through deep, inner experience, or which he transmits directly from the super-conscious to the conscious, from the spiritual to the physical, by means of either the physical eye, the physical touch or the spoken word.

When he speaks, Truth is more powerfully manifested than when he uses either sight or touch to convey it. For that reason, Avatars usually observe a period of silence lasting for several years, breaking it to speak only when they wish to manifest the Truth to the entire universe. So, when I speak, I shall manifest the Divine Will, and a world-wide transformation of consciousness will take place.

Message at Pickfair House
Given by Shri Meher Baba at a Reception at the Residence of Douglas Fairbanks and Mary Pickford
Beverly Hills, Hollywood, June 1, 1932

I was particularly glad to come to California because of the opportunity which it afforded to contact those who made or appeared in the moving pictures, and I am delighted that this gathering could be arranged for tonight.

I do not need to tell you, who are engaged in the production and distribution of moving pictures, what a power you hold in your hands; nor do I doubt that you are fully alive to the responsibility which the wielding of that power involves.

He who stimulates the imagination of the masses can move them in any direction he chooses, and there is no more powerful instrument for stimulating their imagination than the moving pictures. People go to the theatre to be entertained. If the play is strong, they come away transformed. They surrender their hearts and minds to the author, producer, director, stars, and they follow the example which they see portrayed before their eyes more than they themselves realize.

Both the press and the radio influence thought, but both lack the power of visible example, which is the greatest stimulant to action and which the moving pictures offer better now than any other medium.

We find ourselves today in the midst of a world-wide depression which affects everyone, rich and poor alike, and from which all are groping blindly for deliverance. The film companies, the picture theatres and the stars have also suffered from it. If they could help to end the depression, I am sure, they would be glad to. How could the moving pictures help in this respect?

First, it must be understood that the depression is not an accident, nor is it purely the result of overproduction and inflation. Those, although the immediate causes, are merely the instruments which were used to bring the depression about. The depression itself was caused by those entrusted with the evolution of humanity. Man has to be stripped of his material possessions in order that he may realize, through actual experience, that his true base is spiritual, and not material. Then he will be ready to receive the Truth which I have come to bring.

This Truth consists in the knowledge that man, instead of being a limited, separate individual, completely bound by the illusion of time and space and substance, is eternal in his nature and infinite in his resources. The world-illusion is a dream of his imagining—a play enacted in the theatre of his consciousness—a comedy of which he is at once author, producer, director, star. But his absorption in the role which he has chosen to enact has made him forgetful of his true Self, and he stumbles now as creature through the part he has created.

He must be awakened to his true nature. He must see that all material expression depends upon and flows from spiritual being. Then he will be steadfast and serene under all circumstances. There will be no further need, then, for the depression, and it will disappear.

Now how can the moving pictures help man to attain to this realization? The character of the pictures exhibited need not be changed. Love, romance, adventure are fundamental things.[19] They should be portrayed as thrillingly, as entertainingly, as inspiringly as possible. The wider the appeal, the better.

What needs to be changed is the emphasis, or stress. For example, courage is a great virtue, but it may, if misapplied, become a vice. So it is with love, the mainspring of our lives, which may lead to the heights of Realization or to the depths of despair. No better example can be given of the two polarities of love and their effects than that of Mary Magdalene, before, and after meeting Jesus.

Between these two extremes are many kinds of love all of which are good, but some of which are better than others. I use the terms "good" and "better" simply to designate the degrees of liberation which they lead to, or confer. Even the love which expresses through physical desire is good to the extent that it frees one from the thralldom of personal likes and dislikes and makes one want to serve the beloved above all other things.

Every human relationship is based on love in one form or another, and endures or dissolves as that love is eternal or temporal in character. Marriage, for example, is happy or unhappy, exalting or degrading, lasting or fleeting, according to the love which inspires and sustains it. Marriages based on sex attraction alone cannot endure; they lead inevitably to divorce or worse. Marriages, on the other hand, which are based on a mutual desire to serve and inspire, grow continually in richness and in beauty, and are a benediction to all who know of them.

To lead men and women to the heights of Realization, we must help them to overcome fear and greed, anger and passion. These are the result of looking upon the self as a limited, separate, physical entity, having a definite physical beginning and definite physical end, with interests apart from the rest of life, and needing preservation and protection. The self in fact is a limitless, indivisible, spiritual essence, eternal in its nature and infinite in its resources. The greatest romance possible in life is to discover this Eternal Reality in the midst of infinite change. Once one has experienced this, one sees oneself in everything that lives, one recognizes all of life as his life, everybody's interests as his own. The fear of death, the desire for self-preservation, the urge to accumulate substance, the conflict of interests, the anger of thwarted desires, are gone. One is no longer bound by the habits of the past, no longer swayed by the hopes of the future. One lives in and enjoys each present moment to the full. There is no greater romance in life than this adventure in Realization. There is no better medium to portray it than the moving pictures.

Plays which inspire those who see them to greater understanding, truer feeling, better lives, need not necessarily have anything to do with so-called religion. Creed, ritual, dogma, the conventional ideas of heaven and hell and sin, are perversions of the truth and confuse and bewilder, rather than clarifying and inspiring. Real spirituality is best portrayed in stories of pure love, of selfless service, of truth realized and applied to the most humble circumstances of our daily lives, raying out into manifold expression, through home and business, school and college, studio and laboratory—evoking everywhere the highest joy, the purest love, the greatest power—producing everywhere a constant symphony of bliss.

This is the highest practicality. To portray such circumstances on the screen will make people realize that the spiritual life is something to be lived, not talked about, and that it—and it alone—will produce the peace and love and harmony which we seek to establish as the constant rule of our lives.

PART TWO

Selected Articles from the Mainstream Press: The West Responds to the Avatar

Sunday Express

SLEEPING BADLY? GENASPRIN

DARKALINE

LATE FINAL

A TALK WITH THE STRANGE MESSIAH.

What He Told JAMES DOUGLAS In A Kensington Bedroom.

"MY MISSION WILL LAST FOR 33 YEARS."

THREE HOURS' SLEEP A DAY.

SILENT INTERVIEW WITH AN ALPHABET.

By JAMES DOUGLAS.

FRENCH DOLLAR PLOT, TO DRIVE US OFF THE GOLD STANDARD.

SENATE INQUIRY.

WALL STREET CHIEF CALLED IN.

ARSENAL'S PROBLEMS.

SHOTS AT DR. LUTHER.

LINDBERGH DRAMA IN BRITAIN.

Girl Of 18 Shows The Tennis Stars How.

LUCKIEST WOMAN.

BETTER TIMES ON THE WAY!

A PENSION OF £400 A YEAR FOR LIFE

Indian Mystic Arrives Soon

HARMON (N. Y.) May 25. (AP)—Shri Meher Baba, Indian mystic, will leave tomorrow for California to visit Hollywood and other cities. He will be accompanied by nine disciples.

Baba, called Messiah by his followers, will stay in Hollywood for five days and will go to San Francisco, whence he will sail for Shanghai. He plans to return to California July 12 and break his seven-year silence the following day.

Meher Baba's 1932 world tour precipitated an avalanche of coverage in the era's leading newspapers and magazines. Front-page articles featured Baba's silence and trumpeted the "New Messiah." While many journalists opted for sensationalism and derision, others portrayed the "Indian seer" responsibly and sometimes insightfully.

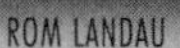

ROM LANDAU

CHARLES PURDOM

CHRISTMAS HUMPHREYS

JAMES DOUGLAS

(TOP LEFT) Rom Landau, author of *God Is My Adventure*, a 1935 bestseller
(TOP RIGHT) Charles Purdom, editor of *Everyman*
(BOTTOM LEFT) Christmas Humphreys, founder of the Buddhist Society and one of England's leading barristers
(BOTTOM RIGHT) James Douglas, a senior editor for the *Daily Express*, one of London's leading newspapers

INTRODUCTION TO PART TWO

While Meher Baba's first visit to Europe and America in the autumn of 1931 was conducted privately, without public meetings or interviews with the press; his second tour, from March to July 1932, precipitated nothing less than a media extravaganza. High-profile articles about the "New Messiah" bloomed on the pages of many of the leading newspapers and magazines of the period. Appendix 1 reproduces a hefty selection of these in facsimile.

Part two culls from this bumper harvest six items that are especially distinctive in one way or another. The first, Charles Purdom's "A Perfect Master," published in the September 24, 1931 issue of Everyman, *pp. 272 and 274, could be characterized as the original literary introduction of the Avatar of the Age to the British public at the historical moment when he first set foot on Western soil. Purdom's initial contact led him to become a follower and disciple, and he remained so until his death in 1965. At the same time, as the editor of* Everyman *and the author of numerous books, he was and remained a strong voice in the cultural commentariat during the decade before World War II and the two decades thereafter.*

The second and third items in part two pertain to an interview that Meher Baba had with James Douglas, a leading writer and religious editor for the Daily Express *in London, on April 9, 1932, at the outset of Baba's second, highly publicized world tour. Approaching the much ballyhooed "Messiah" with deep reservations, planning indeed to "trap" him with carefully prepared and challenging questions, Douglas was quite astonished when he met Baba in person. His interview, "A Talk with the Strange Messiah," appeared as a major spread with photographs on the front page of the April 10 issue of the* Sunday Express, *one of the leading London newspapers of that time.*

The disciple who interpreted Baba's dictation on the alphabet board on that occasion was Framroze Dadachanji; and eleven years later, in his Gujarati biography, "Chanji" (as he is generally known) gave his own full account of this interview. While Chanji's record includes most of the exchanges from the published article, it provides other backgrounds as well which make for interesting reading. Chanji's narrative was translated (and slightly abridged) by Naosherwan Anzar in the February 1980 issue of Glow International, *pp. 13–17; we quote from that translation here.*

During this same 1932 London visit Meher Baba was interviewed by another writer with interests in spirituality and mysticism, Rom Landau, who recalled his experience in God is My Adventure: A Book on Modern Mystics, Masters, and Teachers *(London: Ivor Nicholson and Watson, 1935), pp. 130–48 (the selection quoted here is taken from pp. 131–34). In fact, by the time the book was published three years after the actual interview, Paul Brunton's highly critical account of Meher Baba in* A Search in Secret India *(based on his meetings with Baba in Nasik and Meherabad in late 1930 and early 1931) had already reached the literary marketplace, and Landau's own point of view reflects this influence. It seems, moreover, that Meher Baba had declined to answer Landau's questions during their meeting. Baba did have answers sent to him several days later, however, in the form of a letter; and Landau quotes extracts. These passages seem to be authentic; and Landau's account on the whole is representative of some of the adverse, though on the whole journalistically responsible, press coverage of the period.*

Sailing from London, on May 19, 1932 Meher Baba arrived in New York for a three-week cross-continental America tour that, again, was extensively covered by the press. While in New York, Baba was interviewed by Frederick Collins, a well-published author who evinces no special spiritual orientation but seems to have approached the "Perfect Master" merely as an interesting, and perhaps somewhat exotic, journalistic subject. Much to his own surprise, Collins, like Douglas, was profoundly affected by what he found. His interview, which records Baba's comments on "non-spiritual" topics such as divorce and prohibition, was published in the August 27 issue of Liberty *magazine, pp. 26–27, at that time one of the foremost weekly magazines in America.*

Part two closes with two paragraphs from a short article that Christmas Humphreys published in Buddhism in England, *vol. 16, no. 4 (November–December 1941), p. 77, entitled "The Man of Love." By this time the forty-year-old British barrister had become, and for the rest of his long life remained, probably the best-known Buddhist convert in England. His article recalls vivid memories from his meeting with Baba ten years earlier during Baba's first visit to the West in 1931.*

A Perfect Master

by Charles Purdom

I interrupt the sequence of these articles to relate something of importance. My object in this series has been to give an outline of practical thought and action that would be of use to those who desire to get rid of the aimlessness of their lives.[20] For that reason I have considered the individual in relation to the actual circumstances of life today and have avoided generalizations as much as possible. When I started I proposed to draw on my own experience, using also the knowledge I had of what the philosophers have said and what religion has taught us. I had not, however, been in personal contact with a great Teacher. I did not know where such a Teacher was to be found. There were books, of course, of Scripture and poetry, and the wise things that some people of our own time had written; but there is no one to whom I could have gone, or could have recommended others to go, for wisdom. Now, quite unexpectedly, and partly as a consequence of what I have already written, I have actually met a Teacher, and it is about him that I wish to write this week.

What we want, all we modern men and women, is not sound advice or original ideas or profound thought, but experience. We want what will help us to live. We do not want someone who can help us to think more clearly or even one who can tell us what to do. We want something done. We want, exhibited as a reality, the life that we are deeply conscious ours ought to be. We want, that is to say, not an intellectual demonstration of the truth, but the truth itself. We know what science teaches, or can get that knowledge, and we know what the sages say. We do not need to know any more. We want the evidence of knowledge put into practice.

It is here that the need of a teacher is felt. Only someone with a consciousness greater than ours can take us the necessary step further. The world has always had its teachers, of that we can be sure. What the poets and philosophers have said and the great men of action have done have not sprung simply from nothing. Our greatest Master in the West has been Christ. He was more than a teacher, and I do not dispute that; but a teacher He was. There have been other lesser teachers among us since. In the East, which is God-conscious to an extent that is completely foreign to the West, there have been a number of great teachers. Buddha was one. There have been others, most of them unknown. For the Perfect Masters of the spiritual life do not always show themselves to the world. Their work is done in secret.

I have been brought by what seemed to be chance, but no doubt deserves some other name, into personal contact with a Perfect Master from the East. He has come to Europe because of the grave troubles of the time, and because he has something to do in the crisis upon which we have just entered. He knows that we are ready for a great spiritual outburst. I said a moment ago that we do not need more knowledge: but there is one knowledge that we do need. That is knowledge of God or the ultimate reality. In that knowledge everything else is contained. If we had it our lives would be lifted to their highest level. The Perfect Masters have that knowledge. The Perfect Master of whom I speak has that knowledge. He is a Perfect Master because He is united with the Unconscious—that is with God. He has conscious knowledge of God. He has come to the West, leaving his seclusion in India to get men and women to turn their minds in these times of great anxiety from the outer world of material things to the inner world of the spirit, where all problems of the material world are solved. This Perfect Master arrived in England quietly twelve days ago and went to an isolated place in the country where only a few people know of his presence. The driver of the taxi which took him through London said to the friend who accompanied him as he received his fare, "That was a remarkable gentleman. I felt it was a privilege to drive him." Yet Shri Sadguru Meher Baba, for that is this

Perfect Master's name, had not spoken a word. In fact, he has not spoken a word for seven years, and does not propose to speak now.

Meher Baba has not come to this country with a "message" or to give lectures, or to found a new sect or a new religion. There is too much talking, he says, and there are plenty of religions. He has come to impart his knowledge of God to those who wish to receive it. His method is simple. He says to the inquirer, "What I am, you are." This seems nothing at all; but coming from him with the unmistakable spiritual certainty that he possesses, it comes as a shock. What he does is to get the seeker after truth to look into his own heart to find it. And, what is more significant, he gives him the power to find it. For from Meher Baba there flows power. He has no startling things to say. All that he does say is communicated by signs and pointing to letters on a board. It is sufficient to be in his presence to know the truth. He does not need to speak: he has the power of truth in him.

In appearance, Meher Baba is rather under medium height, his skin is not very dark, he has dark brown hair, which he wears long, and a full moustache. He is thirty-eight years old. His eyes are large and beaming, lighting up his face, which irradiates happiness. He has a great sense of fun, and is said to be a first-rate cricketer. He combines the simplicity of a child with the wisdom of the ages.

He is willing at present to receive anyone who comes to him with a sincere mind; but he does not care to exhibit himself. It is not to be thought that he is an impracticable mystic, out of touch with everyday affairs. His knowledge includes even the concerns of ordinary men and women. He is one who brings into the conscious world of commonplace things, experience of the Unconscious. He has, that is to say, a balanced existence.

I have had several "conversations" with him. But as I have said, to talk truth with him is not the important matter. It is sufficient to be in the same place. He asked me if I knew the poems of Kabir, the fifteenth-century Mohammedan mystic. I was able to tell him that I did, and I quote from Rabindranath Tagore's translation of one of the poems, the description of a perfect master:[21]

He is the real Sadguru, who can reveal the form of the Formless
to the vision of these eyes:
Who teaches the single way of attaining them, that is other than
rites and ceremonies:
Who does not make you close the doors, and hold the breath, and
renounce the world:
Who makes you perceive the Supreme Spirit wherever the mind
attaches itself:
Who teaches you to be still in the midst of all your activities:
Ever immersed in bliss, having no fear in his mind, he keeps the
spirit of union in the midst of all enjoyments.
The infinite dwelling of the Infinite Being is everywhere: in earth,
water, sky, and air:
Firm as the thunderbolt, the seat of the seeker is established
above the void.
He who is within is without: I see Him and none else.

That describes Meher Baba better than anything I, or perhaps anyone else, could write.

He makes no demands on anyone; but those who come to him for help have to be prepared to do what he says, which may be severe. The way to truth is simple, but it is very hard; for the way to know God is to know oneself, to face oneself in one's own inner consciousness, and then, renouncing everything, to let God flood the soul. Meher Baba is master of one knowledge, which is God, but that knowledge includes everything else. The rules that he gives, so far as he gives any at all, are meditation, selfless service and pure intention. He does not ask the Christian to cease being a Christian, but to be a true follower of Christ, that is, to do what Christ said. He does not ask the sceptical man or woman of today to accept any dogma, but in the spirit of humility to obey the God in his heart. What Meher Baba says the mystics of the Western world have said: he also lives it. What he says, the psychologists of the West have also said in part; but he interprets their theories in practical life.

It may be strange to find a great spiritual teacher from the East speaking in terms that belong to our scientific text-books; but it is stranger still, and this is the overwhelming fact about Meher Baba, that he is the one whose word is alive with the spirit.

In my articles continuing "A Plan of Life," I shall explain what I have learned from him.

A Talk with the Strange Messiah

by James Douglas[22]

Shri Sadguru Meher Baba received me yesterday afternoon in his bedroom in a Kensington house.

He has been described as the Indian Christ or Messiah. He arrived in England on Friday.

His mission, his disciples declare, is to save mankind, East and well as West.

He is a saint and a mystic, a Mahatma and or spiritual superman. It is said that he can perform miracles.

When I arrived a procession of his disciples filed out. First a bevy of beautiful young white girls passed me, then several young Indians departed.

Meher Baba was sitting on a sofa. He wore a dressing gown, and a soft blue silk scarf round his neck.

What He Is Like

He is a slender man of thirty-eight, but he looks ten years younger. He wears his dark brown hair very long. It flows down to his shoulders. He reminded me of the young [unreadable].

He has a brown moustache. His face is ascetic. The chin is rather pointed and most powerful. His forehead is lined.

His eyes are large and radiant. They sparkled with happiness and serene joy. His smile is charming. It is gay and humourous and childlike.

I am told that he is a brilliant cricketer. He is ebulliently healthy and natural in his manner. His hands are eloquently artistic. They are the hands of a virtuoso. They talk. They are hypnotic.

He has immense magnetism. As I entered the room I felt a rush of personal fascination and force. It seemed to fill the chamber with his warmth.

As he grasped my hand I felt a strange thrill. He made me sit close to him on the sofa, and during our talk he perpetually caressed me, laying his hand on mine, or touching me on the back. A very magnetic personality.

He Does Not Speak

As a rule I shrink from the human touch, so I guarded myself against physical hypnotism. I armoured myself with skepticism, but I melted under his enchantment in spite of my caution.

Meher Baba does not speak. He says he has not spoken for seven years. Our talk was conducted through a young Indian, who rapidly interpreted the Master's signs.

On his knee rested a small board with the letters of the Roman alphabet painted on it. His slim fingers flickered from letter to letter. He does not spell words. His telegraphy is too rapid for that.

His interpreter reads the alphabet upside down. I do not know how he does it, for the pace is as swift as speech.

I had prepared a questionnaire with the help of Sir Denison Ross, the Oriental scholar. It was designed to trap the teacher, but he smilingly threaded his way through it without stumbling. His mastery of dialect[ic] is consummate. It was quite Socratic in its ease.

He frequently put questions to me which startled me by their penetration. But he never evaded a direct question. His simplicity is very subtle.

"I am a Persian," he said. "I was born in Poona, but my father and mother were Persians."

He is above races and religions. He is universal. He is one with God, and God is everywhere and in every one.

"Do you know Gandhi?" I asked.

"Yes. I met him in the steamship Rajputana. He is not as far advanced as I am. He asked me to help him. But I will not help him until he abandons politics. I have no politics."

"Are you a Mahatma?" I asked. He smiled.

"What is a Mahatma?" he replied. "I know the truth. You live in London. You know it. I know."

"Are you divine?" He smiled.

"I am one with God. I live in Him, like Buddha, like Christ, like Krishna. They knew Him as I know Him. All men can know Him.

"There Is No Evil"

"Have you solved the problem of evil?"

"There is no evil," he said. "There are only degrees of good."

"The world is perplexed with disaster. Is there any way out of the world crisis?"

"Yes."

"How long will it last?"

"Only another year. Then there will be recovery and deliverance."

"Christ's mission was accomplished in three years. How long will your mission last?"

"Thirty-three years," he replied.

"What is your secret?" I asked.

"The elimination of ego," he replied.

Then I put my questionnaire.

"Have you a Scripture, a Bible, a Koran, an inspired book?"

"No, I teach. I am a teacher."

"Do you believe in Buddha and the Eight-Fold path?"

"Yes. All religion is ascent by stages to perfect union with God."

"What God do you believe in?"

"There is only one God for all men."

"What religion is nearest to yours?"

"All religions are revelations of God."

"Is there a future life?"

"Yes. The soul does not die. It goes on from life to life till it is merged in God."

"Nirvana?"

"Yes. But not the loss of the self."

"Does the self survive?"

"Yes. But it is merged in God. The soul is not the brain. It functions the brain. The brain is its instrument."

"Who has sent you to save mankind?"

"I know. It is my whole life. My ecstasy is continuous. It is unbroken."

"Do you sleep much?"

The Sadguru smiled. He held up three fingers.

"Three hours," said the interpreter.

"Are you married?" He smiled in wonder.

"Sex does not exist for me."

"Is God a Person or a Power?"

"God is both personal and impersonal. He is in art, in literature, in everything."

"Are you a Pantheist?"

"You Are Lucky"

"No," he smiled. "When you know God it is plain. The Self is one with Him at the height of experience."

"Why am I not happy?"

"You have not grown out of self," he smiled.

He had said that he would give me a minute, but the minute lasted an hour.

"You are lucky," said a disciple. "He likes you."

The Sadguru is going to a rest house or Ashram at Combe Martin in Devonshire for a few days. Then he goes to New York.

He is serenely certain that he can redeem mankind and end its discords.

I wonder.

A Disciple's Account of the Interview between James Douglas and Meher Baba

by Framroze Dadachanji

I now introduce to the reader a well-known English journalist and public figure Mr. James Douglas and narrate his experience on meeting Meher Baba. The report of this experience was published in the *Sunday Express* of London. The freedom of the English press and its right to discuss every question of public interest without let or hindrance is universally known. During his second visit to the West in 1932, when Baba stayed for a few days in England, the English papers gave him wide publicity. Several articles based on personal interviews and even imaginary stories, were published and a great deal of public opinion was generated in England, especially in London. Before publishing his account Mr. Douglas consulted the well-known Oriental scholar, Sir Denison Ross.

The day this journalist planned to meet him, Baba was preparing to visit a home for the poor in East London.

Baba when indoors wore his long white robe, but when going out, he would wear European clothes and cover his long hair under a felt hat or a small beret.

Baba was about to leave when someone brought the news that a gentleman wanted to meet him for a moment to discuss an important matter. He had been told that he could not see Baba without prior appointment. The person insisted and was adamant on seeing Baba. Saying this, he produced his visiting card and said, "Please go and tell him that Mr. James Douglas would like to see him for a moment."

His card was shown to Baba, and without any inquiry or hesitation Baba consented, "All right, call him in." As Baba was observing silence, I was present to interpret the alphabet board. It is essential to note that what follows is my personal experience.

Before entering the room Mr. Douglas stood at the threshold gazing all around and glancing for a while at the opposite wall, hesitating to step in. I was obliged to say, "Please come in."

Without giving any reply he looked around again. Very hesitatingly he put one foot on the threshold. The other foot was still outside and he stood in that position for a moment. I witnessed all these movements with surprise. Why should such a robust man hesitate to come in, I wondered. The next moment he entered the room.

He stood startled as if in shock. Beads of perspiration appeared on his face. His body began to tremble. It was a cold day in April, we were all dressed in warm clothes, and I was surprised to see Mr. Douglas perspire. He tried to speak, but his throat was choked. He tried again and while wiping the perspiration from his face, he asked, "What is happening to me? Will you please tell me?"

Baba gestured pointing to a chair near the sofa, and I said, "Do not fear, come forward, sit here." He did not move and said, "I feel a tremendous power here. Will you please tell me what is happening to me and from where that power comes?" Baba again pointed to the chair in front of him and conveyed, "Come forward, sit here."

But the visitor hesitated, stood near the door and asked, "Will you please tell me what is happening to me? What is that power, where does it come from?"

Again pointing to the chair Baba gestured, "Come and sit down."

He again pleaded, "But will you tell me first?"

Baba smilingly gestured, "I will tell you," and put a question, "Have you anything else to ask?"

He again repeated pleadingly, "Before I ask you anything, will you not explain this to me. I am eager to know."

Baba began moving his finger on the board, "I shall explain all that to you, but tell me why have you come here and what do you want to ask?"

He moved closer and came near Baba and said, "I have come with the intention of having a long discussion with you and get some answers to my questions." "You can ask whatever you want," Baba reassured him.

"Your original name?"

As Baba's finger moved on the board, I read, "Merwan—Merwan Sheriar Irani." Here he got the urge to read Baba's board for himself and requested me, "Would you please let me read the board?"

"Most willingly," I replied.

I stood watching this new experiment. He sat on the edge of the chair and tried to read the board looking at Baba's fingers move on the board.

Baba slowly pointed his name with his finger on the board, "M. S. Irani," but Mr. Douglas could not read it.

It was necessary for me to interrupt and say, "He is pointing out his name to you with his finger."

He said, "Please let me try again," and bending over the board, requested Baba to move his finger again. Baba again spelt, "M. S. Irani," but Mr. Douglas could not decipher it. "But why can I not understand?" he asked dejectedly, and suggested, "Let me take some other letters and see whether I can read them."

Baba patiently agreed. Another sentence was pointed on the board —"My name is . . . ."

He read the first two letters, and failed to read the rest. I read the letters again.

He began to look at me rather perplexed.

"How can you read from there?" he asked, coming up to me. "And that too from the opposite side?"

I explained, "It requires only a little practice, it is not at all difficult." Baba at this stage rather solemnly interrupted, "Please come to your original topic."

At this hint from Baba the visitor began his interview, which I recorded in my diary.

Q. Your nationality.

A. I am Persian.

Q. Where were you born?

A. In Poona.

Q. That is India? How can you be then called a Persian?

A. My parents have a Persian lineage.

Q. Are you a Zoroastrian?

A. I was born to Zoroastrian parents.

Q. Which is the best religion today?

A. I consider all religions equal, because all religions are different paths leading to one God.

Q. What is your opinion about the Christian religion?

A. Jesus Christ had realized God. Therefore the religion based on his divine teachings should be good.

Q. What religion do you profess?

A. I am beyond caste and religion. All religions belong to me, though I do not belong to any religion, caste, or creed. I am one with God, and God resides everywhere and in everything.

Q. Are you a Mahatma?

A. What does Mahatma mean? Whom would you call a Mahatma? He who realizes Atma, the final Truth, is a Mahatma. I know truth, I experience it personally, as you know London by staying here for years. If those who have not lived in London or seen it, want information about London, they must get it from outside or through other means. But living in London you have personal knowledge of it; so you have no need to acquire that information through other means. Do you understand!

He nodded and replied "Absolutely."

Q. Do you know Gandhi?

A. Yes, we met on the steamer "Rajputana."

Q. Do you believe in politics?

A. I mix with no ism, so not in politics either, because spirituality includes everything. One who has acquired self-knowledge, has acquired everything.

Q. What is your opinion about him?

A. He is a good soul, a learned scholar of the Gita and a seeker after spiritual knowledge.

Q. Are you divine?

A. I am merged in God. As Buddha, Christ, merged and lived in God, I am also merged and living in Paramatma. As they had realized God, I have also realized Him. You and all others can also similarly know and be one with God.

Q. Is there evil in the world?

A. No, there is nothing like evil.

He was taken aback for a moment.

Q. What do you mean?

A. There is nothing but Bliss all around, everywhere.

Q. Wonderful. How can it be?

A. It is so, a fact.

He got up from the chair and asked his questions more forcefully.

Q. Then how do you explain theft, fraud, faithlessness, dishonesty, immorality, slaughter and a host of other evils spreading round the world? Are they not evils?

A. Not necessarily.

Q. Then what would you call them?

A. It is all a degree of good.

He heaved a sigh, rubbed his forehead with his hand; and said, "O God, how astonishing! Why did poets and philosophers not explain this fact so simply?"

Baba continued, "As I said earlier there is nothing except bliss all around in the world. What the world calls evil is a degree of good."

"Sure, sure. How easy and straightforward? It is a wonder why the world cannot understand such a simple matter."

Q. Will you please tell me when the world will understand this simple principle?
A. When its angle of vision changes.
Q. But when?
A. That working has begun from within.

"Thank God," sighed Mr. Douglas.

Q. What have you to say about the present critical period of the world? The monetary crisis prevailing today, everyone ready to throttle everyone else, turmoil all around, when will these calamities subside?
A. Not till there is a change of heart.

"Change of heart? What a solution?"

Q. But when will that change come?
A. The beginning will be made within a year.
Q. Christ took three years to finish his mission. How long will your mission last?
A. 33 years.
Q. What is your silent message or special discourse?
A. Elimination of the ego.
Q. You desire salvation of mankind. Have you any Bible, Koran or some such Book of Revelation?
A. Though I give discourses and people take me to be a teacher, I do not give much importance to superficial book knowledge and learning, because I awaken the latent divinity within.
Q. Do you believe in Buddha and his Eight-fold path?
A. Yes, any religion is a stage-by-stage path to achieve complete unity with God. You wish to ask th[a]t same question about Christ, Krishna, for which also this is the answer.

He got up at this and began to gaze at Baba's face in bewilderment.

Q. Which God to you believe in? Christian or . . .

A. God is one for all.

Q. Which religion could be called nearest to your own religion or a belief that has the greatest similarity?

A. All religions are revealed by God, so all are equal.

Q. Is there any life after death?

A. Yes, only not for the body. Because the Atma is immortal. It never dies. It takes incarnation again and again till it becomes one with God.

Q. That is Nirvana?

A. Yes, but not after losing the original real self.

Here he was about to interrupt and put a question when Baba gestured to him to remain silent and continued.

"Though the original Atma keeps its identity till the very end, it becomes one with Infinite Existence or God, in the end. That original existence which is Atma, should not be mixed up with intelligence. Atma guides intelligence but nothing guides Atma. Atma is independent. Intelligence relies on Atma, but Atma does not rely on anything. Intelligence becomes an instrument of Atma in realizing that self and has its personal experience. Atma can realize Paramatma through love, service, devotion and surrender."

Q. Where did you acquire all this knowledge? How do you know the questions before I even ask you?

A. I can understand all that easily.

Q. You did not reply to my last question, as to how you understand and know all this?

Baba smilingly replied,

A. Because I am one with the Infinite.

Mr. Douglas was taken aback. This was a divine assertion, but was substantiated by divine knowledge. He carried the subject further in order to test Baba's unique powers.

Q. What is your mission?

A. Spiritual salvation of mankind; in the East, the West, everywhere.

Q. Are you sure you will be able to do so, especially in the West?

A. Certainly. With as much conviction as you are talking with me now. In fact that is the reason for my incarnation.

Q. Who sent you here or ordained you to bring salvation to mankind?

A. I know that. It is my life.

He had conviction in his heart about Meher Baba's divine powers, but intellect did not accept that fact. It was a fight between the head and the heart. Baba placed his hand in his and both sat quiet for a moment.

The fire of struggle between the head and the heart within James Douglas was calmed by Baba's touch. His face reflected inner joy and he lifted his eyes and glanced at Baba's beautiful face, and asked,

Q. Do you always remain in bliss like this?

A. I enjoy bliss eternally. That is my eternal existence.

Q. Why am I not blissful like you are?

A. Because you have not stepped out of the false ego. Similarly the people of the world remain unhappy on account of ignorance. In fact, nothing exists except bliss, everywhere.

Q. Is God a person or a power?

A. God is both personal and impersonal. He is present in every person and everywhere, in all walks of life—in art, literature, beauty.

He was about to ask some question at this juncture, but Baba stopped him with the gesture of his hand and asked him to listen.

"You must not believe that I am a pantheist. In fact I do not believe in any particular ism. I know everything by personal experience. When you realize God you understand everything easily. The highest experience is to know the self, that is merging in God."

Q. Are you married?
A. I am beyond sex.
Q. How much do you sleep?
A. Three hours.
Q. What are your future plans?
A. To stay a few days in Devonshire Ashram; then go to America.
Q. Well Sir, will you please bring an end to my hour's anxiousness by replying to my first question?

Baba's face beamed with a beautiful smile. He good humouredly gestured to me to convey to him, "you are very fortunate."

"Thank you, Sir."
Q. What is the reason for the "Power" pervading the room, where does it come from?

With a smiling face, Baba replied on the board,

A. It is due to my presence.

He took Baba's hand in his own hand and pressed it to his eyes. Mr. Douglas thanked Baba and asked his permission to leave.

It is indeed possible to scale the dizzy heights of greatness by humility. Real greatness lies in acknowledging humbly the greatness of a person superior to us. That is true moral courage.

Saints and Mahatmas never enter into discussion with any person. Meher Baba had never entered into such a long conversation with any visitor. He gave a few minutes' audience to those who came to meet him in Europe and America. The meeting would end with a handshake or a bow, but it was sufficient for inner recognition and exchange of love. Baba would say, "Those who have love and understanding do not need talk or discourse."

It is for this reason that I have considered the lengthy interview of an hour with Mr. James Douglas important and have narrated it in detail.

The group of lovers gathered in the house were naturally curious to know as to what was discussed and eagerly looked at Mr. Douglas as he was on his way out. Before anyone could ask anything, Mr. Douglas said, "Really a wonderful person. I have never come across such a powerful man, I have never been thus defeated. He seems to be an unusual Master. I have doubts whether any of you can know him completely."

One of them asked, "Are you satisfied with him?"

"Satisfied? I am amazed and bewildered."

"We are pleased to hear that," some one said and again asked, "Is he not marvellous?"

"No doubt, he is."

"What do you think about him?"

"I cannot say that at length at this stage, but I must say that it does not matter what he says, but it does matter what he is."

Having said this he departed hastily.

The article was published in *Sunday Express* on Sunday, April 20, 1932.[23]

From *God is My Adventure*

by Rom Landau

A few weeks after the publication of Mr. Douglas's article I had an interview with Shri Meher Baba. It had been arranged by one of his chief British disciples.

I arrived on a chilly spring morning at one of those large houses off Lancaster Gate, which might once in opulent Edwardian days have been attractive but had become gloomy and uncared for since they had been transformed into understaffed lodgings, boarding houses and residential hotels. I was received by a somewhat forbidding domestic who said that she would call "one of them Arabs" for me; but after a few minutes a more presentable young woman appeared, only to assure me that nothing was known to her about an interview—if, however, I maintained that an interview had been arranged, it was probably so, and she would immediately inquire. A few minutes later a little Indian with a kind face appeared. He wore European clothes and had a black moustache. "Oh yes, Mr. Shri Meher Baba will be delighted to see you; he knows all about you, and it won't be a moment." After he went, I counted for about twenty minutes the number of leaves in the pattern of the wallpaper in the narrow entrance hall. Eventually, however, another lady appeared and asked me to follow her upstairs.

I climbed five flights of stairs, and was received on the top landing by another little man with a black moustache. He, too, had an inviting smile, and he said: "Please do come in. Mr. Shri Meher Baba has been expecting you." He opened the door, and I found myself in a small bedroom. The bed had not been made yet, and the furniture was simple and typical of the smaller residential hotels in the district.

Shri Meher Baba (whom I shall call for simplicity's sake Baba) was sitting in the middle of the room in an easy chair. He corresponded in his appearance exactly to the description of Mr. James Douglas, but I waited in vain for the "rush of personal fascination and force"; I missed the "strange thrill" when he grasped my hand, and though he "caressed me, laying his hand on mine," I could not make myself "melt away under his enchantment." He was wearing a dressing gown, bedroom slippers and a woolen scarf round his neck. He was holding in his hands the little blackboard with the white letters of the Roman alphabet written upon it. Two Indian interpreters were placed behind him, and they interpreted to me each of the many quick movements of Baba's flickering fingers.

Unfortunately my questions must have been badly prepared, or awkwardly presented, for the answer was almost invariably: "This question requires a more elaborate answer and a longer discussion. I shall have to write this answer to you in a day or two." After this had been going on for about three-quarters of an hour I decided that it would be unfair to trespass any longer on my host's time. I had been informed that Baba was leaving for America in a few days' time, and I was certain that he had a lot to do before his departure. But, after I had turned towards the door, Baba suddenly began making more signs on his board. One of his two interpreters stopped me: "Baba says that he is going to help you in the future." I was taken by surprise, and though I tried to express thanks for this unsought promise, I must have done so not without embarrassment.

A thick letter from Baba arrived a week after my interview, containing a number of sheets of paper, covered with the handwritten answers to my questions.

"The spiritual revival that you ask about," said the letter, "is not very far off and I am going to bring it about in the near future, utilizing the tremendous amount of misapplied energy possessed by America for the purpose. Such a spiritual outburst as I visualize usually takes place every seven or eight hundred years, at the end or beginning of a cycle, and it is only the Perfect One, who has reached the Christ state of consciousness, that can appeal and work so very universally. My work will embrace everything; it will affect and control every phase of life. . . . In the general spiritual push that I shall impart to the world, problems such as politics, economics and sex . . . will all be automatically solved and adjusted. All collective movements and religions hinge round one personality who supplies the motive force—without this centrifugal force all movements are bound to fail. . . . Perfect masters impart spirituality by personal contact and influence, and the benefit that will accrue to different nations, when I bring about the spiritual upheaval, will largely depend upon the amount of energy each one possesses."[24] There followed several passages about the possibility of performing miracles, and on the last page I found the following sentences: "I now take orders from no one; it is all my supreme will. Everything is, because I will it to be. Nothing is beyond my knowledge; I am in everything. There is no time and space for me, it is I who give them their relative existence. I see the past and the future as clearly and vividly as you see material things about you."

I Can Hardly Believe It, Myself

by Frederick L. Collins[25]

"I want you to come to tea," said my friend, "with Shri Sadguru Meher Baba."

"With what?"

My friend smiled in her most superior manner.

"With the new perfect master from India."

I am not much on perfect masters, myself. Or on tea. But my friend was insistent. So off we went to visit her globe-trotting Parsee. But in the taxicab my reluctance grew into a sort of terror.

"What language does this friend of yours speak?" I asked.

"He doesn't speak at all," was the reply. "He hasn't spoken for seven years."

The interview was looking sourer and sourer to me.

"What did you say his name was?" I asked in desperation.

My companion was very patient. "Shri," she said, "which means Sir. Sadguru, which means perfect master. Meher, which means compassionate. And Baba, which means father."

Sir Perfect Master Compassionate Father! This was a large order. But I must say that Shri Sadguru Meher Baba, in spite of the fact that he had dressed up for tea in an imitation-chinchilla coat and a light-gray flannel pants, looked every inch the part. Not very many inches, to be sure; for Baba—that's what I decided to call him—was small, in the Oriental fashion; yet somehow strangely impressive.

How, in such a get-up, he managed to be anything but funny was more than I could see. Certainly it was not the sartorial or tonsorial effect of Shri Sadguru Meher Baba, as he sat draped over the soft red upholstery of Mrs. Phelps Stokes' best square-backed couch, that kept me from laughing out loud. It must have been—though I was loath to admit it—the man himself.

A stunning yellow-headed, ruddy Englishwoman was pouring Baba's tea—on her knees by a small tabouret in front of the Sadguru. Baba is not married. At thirty-seven, he even flirts tentatively with the doctrine of celibacy as a sort of worldly sedative. But his disciples made it clear that he did not prescribe celibacy for his followers.

"Sex for me," he said, "does not exist."

Of course, he did not *say* it; but he communicated it to me by a method I'll explain in a minute.

"Modern marriage is too much of a business affair," he continued. "No wonder it so often results in divorce. Husband and wife should put each other first. It is essential for a happy family life that selfless love should predominate over lust."

I ventured to suggest that we who live in America had a good many problems right now besides sex problems. Baba smiled sympathetically, humorously. His smile was like an open fire in a cold house.

"Things *have* been messed up a good deal here," he said, "by lack of understanding."

The fact that this Parsee messiah was discussing our American problems in American language as naturally as if he had lived here all his life didn't seem so strange as you might think.

And the fact that he was discussing them, not with his perfectly good voice but by means of letters which he pointed to on a small blackboard which he held on his lap, did not seem strange, either.

Seven-year silences, it seems, are not uncommon events among the holy men of India. The uncommon thing about Baba's was that he made you forget it so soon and so completely. He could "talk" in seven different languages on his little board, and could spell out his words in any of the seven faster than human eye could follow. He was articulate in many other ways, this odd little man who had come out of the East to save the world. He talked with his eyes, which I must say are the largest and softest and shiningest and smilingest I ever saw; and with jolly little grunts; and with affectionate pats of approval and agreement. Then there was his smile.

"What are you going to do," I asked, "for this 'messed-up' country of ours?"

"It is my country, too," he said simply.

Apparently he feels that way about every country. When Gandhi came to him and asked him to help him, Baba replied:

"Not until you abandon politics. I have no politics."

Baba is not an Indian in the sense that Gandhi is. He is a Persian, born in Poona, South India, on February 25, 1895.[26] He was by birth a racial internationalist. And by profession a religious one. He tolerated, he said, all cults and all faiths. His aim was to make those who professed faith worthy of the faith they professed. It happened that he himself was born in the religion of Zoroaster, but he was apparently no proselytizer for any creed or dogma.

"I intend to bring together all religions and cults like beads on one string and revitalize them," he said, "for individual and collective needs. This is my mission to the West."

His special reason for visiting *us* for the purpose of breaking his seven-year silence was, he said, that America, being most deeply engrossed in material things, and suffering most in consequence, was the soil in which a new spiritual rebirth would first take place.

"When you break your silence," I asked, "how will you do it? By radio?"

"Surely not by radio!" exclaimed one of his London disciples in his most horrified British manner.

"Why not?" spelled out Baba on his board.[27]

Skeptic that I was, I could not doubt his sincerity. Or his courage. When I asked him to particularize about the kinds of messing up to which we in America had been subjected, he might easily have sought refuge behind one of the general, vague assertions of principle with which all Eastern writings are filled.

"AMERICA has great energy," he said, "but a great deal of it is misdirected; and misdirected energy produces destructive complexes, and these in turn produce fear, greed, lust, and anger, which result in moral and spiritual decay."

"Those are strong words," I protested.

He smiled reassuringly. He certainly could do wonders with that smile!

"Is your aim to help us with our spiritual problems or our practical problems?" I asked.

"Our spiritual problems *are* our practical ones."

"And just how do you intend to help?"

"The help I will give will produce a change in heart in thousands, and then right thinking and living will result automatically."

"Will that solve the depression problem?"

"It will solve *every* problem."

"Prohibition?"

"Yes—and the problem behind prohibition," he said. "I do not believe in drink, and none of my followers drink. But I know that prohibition should never have been put in effect the way it was."

"All at once?"

"Yes. Spirits should have been barred, but not beer and wine. Then we might have had a law that could be enforced. As it is, we have a law which makes money for dishonest officials and increases all vices everywhere."

You may not agree with this opinion. But, at least, it *is* an opinion. I had to admit that, for all his seven-year silence, Meher Baba had said more in those few spelled-out sentences than many a senator or party platform maker had mouthed in seven-hour speeches.

"I believe in self-control," he continued, "not in coercion. Coercion is based on oppression, and results in fear and hatred. Self-control requires courage, and may be induced by love. We will do many things for those whom we love which we would not ordinarily do—which we would not ordinarily have the strength of mind and power to do. How many habits have we been able to break, through love, which we would never have had the strength to break without love? And when the love is universal love, all habits which are detrimental, either to the individual or to the social order, will be dissolved in its light.

"It is the same way with this economic situation you were asking me about," he added. "There is a very close connection between a man's character and his circumstances, between his internal environment of thoughts and desires and his external environment. 'As within, so without,' is the law.

"If we are dissatisfied with our environment, it is usually because we do not know how to adjust ourselves properly to the environment. Instead of thinking, 'How can I get out of this?' and becoming discouraged and depressed, we should think, 'What is the lesson I should learn from this experience?'

"Poverty, if cheerfully endured, provided one does one's best to find work, develops humility and patience, and can greatly assist spiritual progress. It is a test of character. I know it is difficult to be cheerful when starving, but all the worth-while things are difficult.

"Even millionaires are unhappy unless they have learned to think and live rightly."

I asked him if he thought a general acceptance of his doctrine of love would bring about a more equable distribution of what you and I need every day—money.

"It must," he replied. "Suppose we all loved each other as deeply as we now love the one whom we love best. The most natural desire of love is to share what one has with the beloved. The desire to share with everyone would produce a condition under which it would be a disgrace rather than an honor for anyone to possess more than anyone else."

Sex. Prohibition. Poverty. All were to be banished by love!

"Do you expect to do this all at once?" I asked.

"No. But sooner than you think. People will respond."

"Why?"

"They will have to."

He did not explain. But he didn't need to: I knew that he would say that the compelling force would be love.

"What are you going to do first?" I asked.

"Go to China. But I shall come right back. I am only staying there a day."

I knew he had recently come sixteen thousand miles from his native India by way of Port Said, Marseilles, Southampton, and Greenwich Village. And now he was planning to go to China just for a day. To China, by way of Hollywood and Honolulu!

"I want to lay a complete cable," he said, "between the East and the West."

I did not laugh. I might have, half an hour before. I am sure I would have three years before, when the gospel of acquisitiveness was saving, or enslaving, the world. But now, God knows, we need a cable layer, a Sadguru, perfect master—someone to lead us out of the slough of materialistic despond—and if he comes in the guise of a mustachioed Parsee in an imitation-fur pyjama jacket and gray flannel pants, who cares?

"AND, after all, why shouldn't he? In his *ashram* in India—an *ashram* is a sort of retreat—Baba is treated almost as a god. Listen to the words of a disciple:

"The devotion inspired by Shri Meher Baba has to be seen to be believed. Practically everyone in the *ashram* would have laid down his life for the master. A glance or a touch from him was more esteemed than a handful of jewels. *Even at a slight reproof men have been known to sob for days.*"

"Oh, that's all right for India," you say; "but this—"

Well, here he was, this "perfect master," in his doubtful chinchilla jacket, on Mrs. Phelps Stokes' square-backed sofa. And here was I, the unbeliever, sitting joyously beside him.

He just looked at me and smiled. I think I smiled, too. We sat that way a long time. I know you will laugh, but we *did!* Baba believes in meditation; and when you are with him you believe as Baba does. I can hardly believe it now, but I distinctly remember I was having a good time.

Everybody does have a good time with Baba; for he is that rare being, a happy man!

From "The Man of Love"

by Christmas Humphreys

It must be ten years ago since I was taken to a room in London to visit Meher Baba, and the recent receipt of literature about his life and work, and a copy of Mr. C. B. Purdom's book, *The Perfect Master,** has reminded me of one of the three most remarkable men I have ever met. I sat beside him cross-legged on a sofa while we talked—by means of an alphabet board, for he had taken a vow of silence—of love, and the use of love and, if I remember rightly, of the doctrine of transmitted merit, whereby, it is said, the Bodhisattva hands over for the benefit of all mankind the karmic benefit of all his noble deeds.[28] For the first time in my life, and I have not met another like him, I found myself in the aura of a man who literally radiated love. Like all great mystics, he combined the profundity of mystical experience with the guileless candour of a child, and his smile was as infectious as the words he used were immaterial. For I found, as I found with the Abbot Tai Hsü and Nicholas Roerich, that after a while there is no need of words, and one can speak from mind to mind in silence. And all the while he radiated such a pure affection that one wondered why, when all religions praise the value of pure love, it should be a memorable experience to meet one man who practised it. . . .

The cause of war is hatred, born of desire, born of ignorance, and "hatred ceases not by hatred, hatred ceases but by love." If there were more Meher Babas in the world today war would end for want of causes. This man of love sets all men an example. Let us who invoke the name of the All-Compassionate One at least make further attempts to follow it.

* Williams and Norgate, 1937.

PART THREE

QUESTIONS AND ANSWERS: THE FIRST WESTERN BOOKLET

SHRI MEHER BABA

A mirage attracts the thirsty, but soon it is discovered to be an illusion and not the life-giving water. A *false* Messiah may attract the attention of the people through outward appearances, by force of personality, or by intellectual dissertations about spirituality, but he cannot do that which the *true* Messiah can do i.e. arouse the highest ideals in men and touch th hearts of millions.

See also Question **21.**

3. *Was Christ the only Son of God?*

Christ, and not Jesus, was the only Son of Go By Christ is meant He who is at One wi Infinite, and so all those who come to reali Ultimate Reality may be said to be in the State."

By Jesus is meant "the historical Man Nazareth," who attained to the Christ Con i.e. who gained *perfection*.

See also Questions **14, 15, 20.**

4. *What is his opinion concerning the ritua observances of religion?*

Dogmas, creeds, and conventional ide *hell* and of *sin* are perversions of Tru and bewilder the mind.

Rituals and ceremonies, institute ridden Churches, have concentrated

12

SHRI MEHER BABA

THE PERFECT MASTER

QUESTIONS AND ANSWERS

Published by
THE CIRCLE EDITORIAL COMMITTEE
50 Charing Cross
London, S.W.1
1933

During the summer of 1933 Meher Baba created the Circle Editorial Committee, charged with disseminating Baba's message through the print media. Headed by Herbert Davy, the Committee's first undertaking was *Questions and Answers,* a 60-page booklet published in London that September.

Posted at Port Said 6/11/33

P & O.S.N.Co.
S.S. Viceroy of India

My dearest Herbert -

I am sending the answers to the questions we had discussed about in Madrid. I have dictated them almost word by word. You may make alterations & additions and change the language & phraseology, but retain the sense. You need not send it to me for approval as that would take too much time, but print it, sticking strictly to the original sense.

I miss you very, very much. Remember all my instructions & try best to follow them and not to worry.

All my love

M S Irani

Written from an ocean liner in the eastern Mediterranean, Baba's note *(LEFT)* accompanied a draft of five new questions and answers intended for the second edition of the recently published booklet.

These Answers to Questions dictated by Shri Meher Baba have to be translated into German, French, and Italian.
A publication ought to be arranged in book form. Further publications of it can appear in journals, reviews and magazines.
The Editorial Committee retains the copyright.
The book price should not exceed 1 lira in Italy, threepence in England, one franc in France, and in Germany.
The Editorial Committee does not claim any profit until the publisher has covered the expenses for printing and distribution. After this has been covered future terms concerning royalties, price, and future editions will be discussed between the Editorial Committee and the publisher.
In Catholic countries we must consider the opposition of the Catholic Church (Index of heretical books)
It is advisable to handle this matter in a quiet and tactful way before publication.
Possibly a publisher in London could handle the matter for the whole world.

Editorial Committee: Norina Matchabelli.
Graham Phelps Stokes.
Charles Purdom.
Kitty Davy.
H. R. Davy.

M S Irani

(RIGHT) Probably taken down in Portofino in July 1933, this Circle Editorial Committee memorandum records decisions concerning *Questions and Answers*, a work in progress at that time.

INTRODUCTION TO PART THREE

During 1933 Meher Baba turned much of the focus of his work towards the literary domain, encouraging Western disciples with literary aptitudes to help disseminate his message through this medium. Under Baba's direction, in July–August a "Circle Editorial Committee" was formed, with an office in Charing Cross, London. Herbert Davy headed the committee and appears to have done the major editorial work in 1933 and early 1934; but Norina Matchabelli and Will Backett played significant roles as well. Also during this period Charles Purdom, a member of the English group and a distinguished writer and editor, began the research that culminated in the publication of The Perfect Master *in 1937.*

Herbert Davy oversaw the compilation of fifty-eight questions, with Meher Baba's answers to them, in a booklet, Shri Meher Baba, the Perfect Master: Questions and Answers, *which Circle Editorial Committee published in September 1933. Though the sources for much of this material remain unknown, some of it at least came from messages and communications that Baba had given during his Western tours of the previous two years. Baba himself took great interest in the book and encouraged its translation into a number of languages, both European and Indo-Iranian.*

The text of this original edition of Questions and Answers *has been reproduced with only a few emendations; except in the case of inconsistencies and a few other slight problems, the original stylistic decisions and editorial judgments have been left untampered with. The footnotes have been replicated from the original; they are the handiwork of Circle Editorial Committee.*

Records of correspondence show that, by early December of 1933, Herbert Davy had envisioned, and perhaps drafted, a new edition of the book, enhanced by the incorporation of five new questions and answers. No copy of that second edition can be found, either in print or manuscript form. Yet the translator responsible for the French translation of the book Shri Meher Baba, le Maître Parfait: Questions et Réponses *(Paris: Éditions de la Revue Mondiale, 1934) must have had access to this material, since it contains five additional questions and answers, nos. 59–63. (This French text is reproduced in appendix 6.) Two identically titled articles in the* Meher Baba Journal, *"Questions Baba Answers," vol. 2, no. 6 (April 1940), pp. 353–55 (containing questions nos. 59–61), and vol. 2, no. 7 (May 1940), pp. 415–16 (containing questions nos. 62–63), provide a translation into English from this French source. That English translation, adjusted and corrected by Françoise and Daniel Lemetais and Ward Parks and reformatted to conform to the style of the main English booklet* Questions and Answers, *is reproduced in this section under the title "Five Additional Questions and Answers."*

For further details on the history of Questions and Answers *in its English and French versions, see pp. 227–36 and 271–73.*

Shri Meher Baba, Perfect Master: Questions and Answers

Preface

Shri Meher Baba was born thirty-nine years ago of Persian parents in Poona, India. He is a Parsee Zoroastrian by birth, and is unmarried.

When he was nineteen years old he met a Mohammedan saint, Hazrat Babajan, and had a profound spiritual experience that made him aware of his high spiritual destiny. Then after years of close contact with a Hindu saint, Shri Upasni Maharaj, he consciously became "One with the Infinite." He began his spiritual work, and now has followers all over the world.

Since July 10, 1925, he has observed complete silence.

During the following two years he wrote a book on Spiritual Truths, but since 1927 he has stopped all writing. He reads and can speak five languages fluently. He now communicates by pointing to the roman letters and digits printed on a small board.

During the last two years he has visited the West five times and has travelled round the world. His eight years' silence is the prelude to his manifestation.

Many questions relating to Shri Meher Baba have been asked by Western people, and in this small book a number of these questions has been gathered together with the answers to them which Shri Meher Baba has himself given to enquirers. Since he neither speaks nor writes, his answers, usually in English, are spelt out letter by letter on the board. After watching his fingers the followers have to write down the words and sentences. The continuity that is required for good prose is thus interrupted.

Contents

The fifty-eight Questions are grouped under seven headings.

I

QUESTIONS ABOUT CHRIST

II

QUESTIONS ABOUT THE SPIRITUAL PATH

III

QUESTIONS ABOUT MESSIAH OR AVATAR

IV

QUESTIONS ABOUT SPIRITUAL MASTERS

V

QUESTIONS ABOUT SHRI MEHER BABA'S MISSION

VI

"PERSONAL" QUESTIONS

VII

MISCELLANEOUS QUESTIONS: WORLD PROBLEMS, PHILOSOPHICAL PROBLEMS

The answers to Questions 10, 12, 26, 31, 35, 41, 49, 51 were previously given in his *Messages to London, New York, Hollywood, and India.*[29]

The answers to Questions 27 and 49 were written in America, and the answer to Question 19 was suggested by an English writer.[30]

I
QUESTIONS ABOUT CHRIST

1 Will Shri Meher Baba explain Christ's words concerning the Second Coming?

2 There have been and still are so many false Messiahs. How can we recognize the *true* Messiah?

3 Was Christ the only Son of God?

4 What is his opinion concerning the ritual or ceremonial observances of religion?

5 What is the right way to attain "Christ Consciousness"?

I
ANSWERS

1 ***Will Shri Meher Baba explain Christ's words concerning the "Second Coming"?* (St. Mark xiii. 21, 26, 27.[31])**

> "And then if any man shall say to you, Lo, here *is* Christ; or lo, *he is* there; believe *him* not . . . ."
>
> "But in those days, after that tribulation . . . then shall they see the Son of man coming in the clouds with great power and glory. And then shall he send his angels, and shall gather together his elect from the four winds, from the uttermost part of the earth to the uttermost part of heaven."

The gathering of the elect refers to the reincarnation and final assembling of His close disciples and followers at the time of His Second Coming. It is wrong to associate the Second Coming with the imprisonment of the Devil and a thousand years' peace, or with a literal interpretation of the Last Day of Judgment.

All the great mystics have understood the word "clouds" as a symbolic expression for states of consciousness or spiritual planes. When the Christ descends from the Infinite, i.e. Seventh Plane, He brings with Him to earth the Infinite Goodness, Wisdom, Power, and Love, and also the powers, signs, and experiences of the six lower planes. In the words of a great Sufi saint:

> "Behold the sky, and clouds and the world:
> First is God, then the planes, the last is earth; but all three are linked."*

* *"Asman o Abro dunya basta been*
Avvalin Haq bad manzil pus zamin."

We read in St. Mark ix. 2 and 7 that the Transfiguration of Jesus occurred when He ascended into a mountain: "And there was a cloud that overshadowed them: and a voice came out of the cloud saying, This is my beloved Son: hear him."

> Brother Leo relates the Vision of St. Francis in Mount Alvernia that he "saw coming down from Heaven a torch of flame exceeding beautiful and light, which, descending, rested on the head of St. Francis; and out of the flame there came a voice. . . ." St. Francis explains to Brother Leo: "Then was I in a light of contemplation, in which I saw the abyss of the infinite goodness and wisdom and power of God. . . . And in the flame that thou sawest was God, who also spake in such a manner unto me, even as in old time He had spoken unto Moses."
>
> On Mount Sinai God appeared in a thick cloud and with fire.[32]

Therefore we see that "clouds," "the house of clouds" *(manzil*[33]*)*, is a symbolic expression among mystics for "the six planes."

See page 77 note 2, "The Seven Planes."

2 ***There have been and still are so many false Messiahs. How can we recognize the "true" Messiah?***

The feeling and inspiration for things sublime and the Divine Love are imparted by a *real* Messiah to anyone who comes in contact with Him. A *false* Messiah cannot do this.

Through His Divinity the *true* Messiah gradually attracts the world to Himself, and people come to know and feel that He is REAL. The knowledge and feeling of confidence in His words grow gradually into certainty, and masses follow Him, drawn by an irresistible force.

A mirage attracts the thirsty, but soon it is discovered to be an illusion and not the life-giving water. A *false* Messiah may attract the attention of the people through outward appearances, by force of personality, or by intellectual dissertations about spirituality, but he cannot do that which the *true* Messiah can do, i.e. arouse the highest ideals in men and touch the hearts of millions.

See also Question 21.

3 *Was Christ the only Son of God?*

Christ, and not Jesus, was the only Son of God.

By Christ is meant He who is at One with the Infinite, and so all those who come to realize the Ultimate Reality may be said to be in the "Christ State."

By Jesus is meant "the historical Man-God of Nazareth," who attained to the Christ-Consciousness, i.e. who gained *perfection.*

See also Questions 14, 15, 20.

4 *What is his opinion concerning the ritual or ceremonial observances of religion?*

Dogmas, creeds, and conventional ideas of *heaven* and *hell* and of *sin* are perversions of Truth, and confuse and bewilder the mind.

Rituals and ceremonies, instituted by the priest-ridden Churches, have concentrated on outward forms, and have ignored the essence of spiritual life. The elementary virtues—love, obedience, humility, and sincerity—are represented by allegorical statues, and the way to Eternal Life is forgotten in their sumptuous and magnificent temples. Man seeks life and is given a stone.

India is, at the moment, ridden with caste prejudices, innumerable cults and ceremonies, which ignore and contradict the spirit of their religious teachings. And this in a country which has wonderful spiritual traditions stretching back thousands of years!

See also Questions 7, 15, 16, 26, 54.

5 ***What is the right way to attain "Christ Consciousness"? In other words, How can we overcome or escape from our "Ego"?***[34]

So much has been said and written about God-realization and "The higher Consciousness" that people are bewildered as to the right way to, and the immediate possibility of, its attainment. The *enquiring* mind, after wading laboriously through such mystical and theosophical literature, only succeeds in learning some pseudo-philosophical terms that confuse and puzzle it. The highest state of consciousness is latent in all. The Son of God is in every man; but He has to be manifested.

The best and easiest way of overcoming the "Ego" and of attaining the "Divine or Christ Consciousness" is to purify and deepen our love, and widen continually the circle of those we love, and to render selfless service to humanity in whatever circumstances we are placed. All the ethical and religious practices ultimately lead up to this. Our animal desires are gradually sublimated if we live more for others and less for ourselves; slowly our crude sense of "Ego" is transmuted. The "Ego" persists till the last stage of the Path. Not until the seventh stage of the Path, when the "God or Christ Conscious" state is reached, can the "Ego" be completely transmuted from finite to Infinite, reappearing again on the seventh plane as the Divine "I." This is that state of "Christ Consciousness" to which Jesus referred when He said, "I and my Father are one," and which implies living simultaneously in the Infinite and in the finite. This is the right way for the independent aspirant.

The shortest and the easiest way is that of the seeker, who has the good fortune (Karma) to be accepted as a disciple by a Perfect Master. Certain pitfalls are avoided by the Master's love and prevision.

It is absolutely impossible for the independent aspirant to pass from the sixth to the seventh plane without the help of a Perfect Master.

See page 77, note 2, "The Seven Planes."

II
QUESTIONS ABOUT THE SPIRITUAL PATH

6 What way of approach does Shri Meher Baba recommend for those who aspire to Perfection?

7 Which is the right way to attain "Wider Consciousness"? (Do religions help or hinder spiritual development?)

8 What is the right way to attain "Christ Consciousness"?

9 What discipline or qualification is necessary to enter the Path?

10 Do *intellectual* attainments help or hinder man's progress on the Spiritual Path?
(Intellectual and Spiritual *understanding* compared.)

11 Does renunciation help a man's progress on the Spiritual Path?

12 *(a)* How does a Master help an aspirant and how does a Master help mankind?
(b) Why is it necessary to have the aid of a Perfect Master in order to attain Perfection?

13 Why is meditation on a Perfect Master the most effective form of meditation?

II
ANSWERS

6 ***What way of approach does Shri Meher Baba recommend for those who aspire to Perfection?*** [35]

All ways: Divine Love, the various yogas, Religion, Science, Art, household duties. But after a certain point the usefulness of each ceases.

And then the aid of a Perfect Master is needed if further progress is to be made.

See also Question 13.

7 ***Which is the right way to attain "Wider Consciousness"? (Do religions help or hinder spiritual development?)***

No general rule or process can be laid down for the attainment of the Ultimate Reality or, as you term it, the "Wider Consciousness."

Every individual has got to work out his or her own salvation, and for that end he himself has to create and choose the *path,* which is mostly determined by the total effect or momentum of impressions (called *sanskaras* in Sanskrit*) acquired in previous life. The panaceas the world hears about, the pseudo-religions for the guidance of humanity, do not go far towards solving the problem. As time goes on, the Founder, the One who supplied the motive force, is relegated more and more to the background of time and obscurity. The aftermath of his manifestation, usually a religion or an organization, gradually loses its glamour and attractiveness.[36] Finally, a mental revolt against

* See Question 58.

the old order of things arises, and with it is felt a thirst for the Way, the Truth, and the Life. This thirst or demand has to be met, and will be met.

See also Questions 4, 15, 16, 26.

8 ***What is the right way to attain "Christ Consciousness"?***

(See answer to Question 5.)

9 ***What discipline or qualification is necessary to enter the Path?***

To say that decent living is the only requisite for attaining "Wider Consciousness" is but giving one side of the picture. What you are today is the result of both your decent and your indecent living in the past. Occult, religious, or spiritual training serves merely as means to an end, and is only the threshold to entering the Path.

But when you are accepted as a disciple by a "Perfect Master," no such disciplinary process is necessary. The only requirements then are complete surrender to his supreme will, perseverance, love, courage, and trust in the Master.

10 ***Do intellectual attainments help or hinder man's progress on the Spiritual Path?***
(Intellectual and Spiritual "understanding" compared.)[37]

It is impossible to reach Spiritual Truth and Realization by talks, arguments, or by reading books. It can be reached by the *heart* alone; but that would be a very slow process. But when the *heart* and the *head* are equally developed and balanced, then man's progress is much quicker.

The man in whom the *head* (intellect) is more developed than the *heart* is liable to get fixed ideas, and he becomes attached to his own intellectual achievements.

The man with a warm *heart* is more likely to have *faith,* and for Love and Truth to give up all.

Intellect is the *lowest* form of *understanding,* and is developed by reading, listening, reasoning, and logic. These processes create an *illusion* of the real knowledge.

The *higher* form of *understanding* is "permanent illumination," through which one experiences and sees things *as they are.* In this state one feels in harmony with everyone and everything and realizes Divinity in every phase of life, and one is able to impart happiness to others. And although performing efficiently and intelligently all duties and material affairs, one feels mentally detached from the world. This is *true renunciation.*

The last and *highest* state of *understanding* results from the merging of the soul into the limitless Ocean of Infinite Knowledge, Bliss, and Power. One who has himself attained to this can enable thousands to attain Perfection.

11 ***Does renunciation help a man's progress on the Spiritual Path?***

Shri Meher Baba does *not* believe in *external* renunciation. For the West particularly, it is impracticable and inadvisable.

Renunciation should be mental. One should live in the world, perform all legitimate duties, and yet feel mentally detached from everything. One should be *in* the world, but *not* of it.

See also Questions 46, 53, 57.

12 ***(a) How does a Master help an aspirant and how does a Master help mankind?***[38]

As a rule, Masters help individually according to the temperament and preparedness of the aspirant. But this being the Avataric period, i.e. the end of the previous cycle and the beginning of the new one (it usually occurs every seven to eight hundred years), Shri Meher Baba's spiritual help to humanity will be both individual and collective. He rejuvenates and infuses new life into the old order of things, and imparts the highest state of spirituality—the state of Oneness with the Infinite Ocean of Bliss, Knowledge, and

Power to his close disciples. He gives a general *spiritual push* to the whole universe.

See also Question 51.

12 ***(b) Why is it necessary to have the aid of a Perfect Master in order to attain Perfection?***[39]

Only a Perfect Master, who is the veritable incarnation of Divinity, can awaken in the individual the fire of Divine Love, which consumes in its flames the lesser desires of the body, mind, and world, all of which must be completely relinquished before Perfection can be realized.

13 ***Why is meditation on a Perfect Master the most effective form of meditation?***[40]

By meditating on a Perfect Master, who is Divine and fully conscious of his Divinity, the individual who is divine but not fully conscious of his divinity is led into Divine Self-consciousness.

(There are two aspects of the Infinite One—Personal and Impersonal. The *Impersonal* aspect lies beyond the domain of creation and transcends even the mental plane. The *Personal* aspect of God is the Perfect Master who, having attained to the *Impersonal* aspect, lives in the world and helps others towards Truth.)[41]

Editor's Note.—"The Perfect Master of the Age" is called by Hindus and Buddhists the Avatar; by Jews and Christians he would be called the Messiah. The terms "saint," or even "Mahatma," do not imply the absolute spiritual perfection or Christ Consciousness which is experienced continually by the Perfect Masters.

III
QUESTIONS ABOUT MESSIAH OR AVATAR

14 What is the theory of the manifestation of an Avatar?

15 Why, when so many inspired religions already existed, were additional revelations of God as Avatar required?

16 *(a)* Will the new Avatar replace existing organized religions by something else?
(b) Will any changes take place in the existing religions when Shri Meher Baba imparts the *spiritual push* to the world?

17 Will an Avatar ever appear in feminine form?

18 Will the West ever give birth to an Avatar?

Editor's Note.—(1) In several of these answers a knowledge of the doctrines of Reincarnation and of Karma is assumed: Reincarnation means rebirth of the Spirit in another physical body; Karma is that law of Cause and Effect which governs every detail of our present lives and also of our subsequent rebirths.
(2) The Seven Planes of Consciousness are often referred to. They are intellect, lower inspiration, intuition, insight, higher inspiration, illumination (the Sixth Plane which is only experienced by the greatest saints), and Christ Consciousness. The Seventh Plane is separated by a great gulf from the Sixth and no one can cross it and attain Christ Consciousness without the aid of a Perfect Master.

III
ANSWERS

14 ***What is the theory of the manifestation of an Avatar?***

God-realized Masters always do exist on the physical as well as other planes, but are not always known and seen physically. After cycles of years, when spirituality reaches its lowest ebb and materialism is at its highest point, when there is chaos and confusion everywhere, the impersonal aspect of Divinity assumes personality, and the world sees the physical manifestation of an Avatar.

It is the same Divine personality who manifested as Avatar in past times in different physical bodies and under different names. These Avatars (the world usually recognizes them as *prophets*), after completing their mission of giving a great *spiritual push* to humanity, abandon the physical body, and assume once more the original impersonal aspect of Divinity. But even in their impersonal aspect they remain always self-conscious of their Divinity.

See also Questions 15, 20.

15 ***Why, when so many inspired religions already existed, were additional revelations of God as Avatar required?***

At the time of the manifestation of an Avatar the force of the new spiritual impulse is so tremendous that it creates quite a new awakening of consciousness. This, combined with the teachings and activities of the Avatar on the physical plane during the life in which he manifests himself, is given outward form by his followers, who call it a new religion.

As the force of the *spiritual push* gradually weakens with the lapse of time, spirituality also recedes until it almost sinks into insignificance;

religion, or rather the outward form of it, becomes like a dry crust, ready to crumble at any moment, and world conditions reach a climax. It is at this critical juncture that an Avatar appears, and manifests on the physical plane, to give once again the *spiritual impulse* that the world then requires. The force of this *spiritual push* is again adopted as a new outward religious form according to the existing circumstances. The Avatar, after completing his mission, abandons his physical body and assumes the impersonal aspect of Divinity as before, till he is compelled once more by force of circumstances to take the human form and reappear and manifest as an Avatar; and thus the process goes on and on.

This is why contemporary religions have apparently different forms, owing to the different times and circumstances in which they were established, and they are known after the name of the Avatar of that particular period, though in essence they contain the same ideal of life taught over and over again by the same Divinity, who appeared and manifested on earth at different times and under different circumstances.

See also Question 20.

16 ***(a) Will the new Avatar replace existing organized religions by something else?***

The new "awakening of the spirit" and the new "consciousness" that will accompany his manifestation will synthesize all existing sects, castes and creeds and religions, which will automatically find a new outward expression.

16 ***(b) Will any changes take place in the existing religions when Shri Meher Baba imparts the "spiritual push" to the world?***

All collective movements and religions have hinged round one personality who supplied the motive force. Without this centrifugal force all movements are bound to fail. Societies and organizations have never succeeded in making people attain spiritual perfection.[42]

See also Questions 26, 29.

17 ***Will an Avatar ever appear in feminine form?***

Never has there been a female Avatar, nor will there ever be one. The Avatar has always possessed a male form and always will. Yet he comprises in himself both the male and female aspects.

18 ***Will the West ever give birth to an Avatar?***

Asia is the "Garden of Eden," the starting-place of the evolution of the universe, and because of its direct link with the source of creation and on account of its geographical position it will always be the birthplace of the Divine personality as Avatar.

IV
QUESTIONS ABOUT SPIRITUAL MASTERS

19 How may one recognize a Perfect Master?

20 What does Shri Meher Baba say about the Masters of the Past?

21 Are persons who can perform miracles necessarily spiritually perfect?

22 Why and when do Masters perform miracles?

23 If a Master is God Incarnate, why does he allow his disciples to be ill?

24 How is it that a Master, being superhuman, still has hunger, thirst, and the need of sleep?

25 Why, if he knows everything, does the Master ask questions?

IV
ANSWERS

19 ***How may one recognize a Perfect Master?***

Kabir has rightly said:

"When you meet the true Guru, He will awaken your heart;
He will reveal to you the secret of love and detachment;
Then you will know indeed that He transcends this universe."

"He is the real Guru, who reveals the form of the formless to the vision of these eyes:
Who teaches the simple way of attaining Him, that is other than rites and ceremonies:
Who does not make you close the doors, and hold the breath, and renounce the world:
Who makes you perceive the Supreme Spirit wherever the mind attaches itself:
Who teaches you to be still in the midst of all your activities:
Ever immersed in bliss, having no fear in his mind,
He keeps the spirit of union in the midst of all enjoyments."

(From a translation by Rabindranath Tagore of the fifteenth-century saint and poet Kabir.[43]*)*

20 ***What does Shri Meher Baba say about the Masters of the Past?***

Christ, Buddha, Mohammed, Zoroaster, Krishna, and other Masters were all, in reality, the embodiment of the same Divine Self-consciousness, manifesting according to the needs of different periods and of different countries.

See also Questions 13, 14, 15, and footnote to Question 35.

21 ***Are persons who can perform miracles necessarily spiritually perfect?***

In the West people are very interested in the problem of *miracles.*

Shri Meher Baba has explained that the ability to perform miracles does not necessarily imply high spirituality. Anyone who has attained perfection and enjoys the "Christ Consciousness" can perform miracles.[44] Healing the sick, giving sight to the blind, and even raising the dead are quite simple for a Perfect Master. Even those who have not become One with the Infinite, but who are only traversing the planes, can perform miracles and are able to make and unmake things.

22 ***Why and when do Masters perform miracles?***

Spiritual Masters do not perform miracles to order, just to satisfy idle curiosity. Miracles were performed, and will be performed, according to the existing circumstances. Masters have sometimes performed miracles when they intended to give a universal spiritual push.

See also Question 40.

23 ***If a Master is God Incarnate, why does he allow his disciples to be ill?***

Although spiritually the Master of everything, he never consciously interferes with the Laws of Nature and of Karma—laws governing all existence, and which he himself established for the universe.

The terrible sufferings that the past Masters (who had of course the powers to avert these sufferings) and their disciples underwent were due, on the one hand, to these laws of nature, and on the other hand to the reason that by their vicarious sufferings they were able to help spiritually all humanity.

24 ***How is it that the Master, being superhuman, still has hunger, thirst, and the need of sleep?***

The Master works on different planes—spiritual, mental, astral, and physical. And in order to work with different individuals at different stages of evolution he comes down to their level. Even when in the physical body he can aid highly advanced souls on the mental plane, less advanced souls on the astral[45] plane, and ordinary human beings on the physical plane. He uses the appropriate body—spiritual, mental, subtle (astral), or physical—as the medium for his work on the required plane.*

It is rightly said that the best teacher is he who can come down to the level of his student. The Master comes down to the level of this world for its upliftment. This physical body, now his medium for work, has its physical needs†—food and rest—which must usually be attended to physically. If necessary, he could live without food or water for weeks together.[e]

The problem of the Divine and human elements in the God-man is difficult to comprehend, except for those who have had long personal contact with a Master. This attention to the requirements of the physical body of the Master, although outwardly similar, is inwardly different. It is not, as with ordinary men, actuated by any desire to satisfy hunger, thirst, or sleep, nor for the pleasure that gross men derive from eating, drinking, and other enjoyments. He tends to the physical needs of the body merely to preserve it as a medium for the great work that he has to do on this physical plane.

Similarly, people are puzzled by the everyday details of his material or physical life and activities; his natural, spontaneous manner; his appearance and dress; his long travels and frequent movements from place to place; his visits to theatres, cinemas, and places of amusement; and so on. Though he may seem to enjoy them for themselves, they are necessitated by his work. The Master has no desires, and can have none to gratify. His only desire, if it-

---

* See Question 35—description of the different bodies.

† Shri Meher Baba has often fasted for long periods.

could rightly be called a desire, is to enable every human being to realize the "Self" and drink of the well of everlasting life.[46]

25 ***Why, if he knows everything, does the Master ask questions?***

The impressions of the experiences of the innumerable past lives of an individual remain in his mental body in the form of thoughts, which lie, like seeds, latent and unmanifested. When faced with suitable circumstances and environments, these thoughts are expressed in the subtle body as desires and emotions. And these, when expressed more fully, develop into the physical actions in the gross body.

The Master knows the expressed as well as the unexpressed thoughts of everyone. Yet he sometimes asks questions. While asking questions he acts, through his working on the inner planes, upon the expressed and unexpressed impressions of the individual or individuals with whom he is speaking, and renders them impotent while they are still in the mental body, so that they cannot develop and eventually be expressed in the form of desires and actions.

In short, the Master, through his subtle working, checks certain evil thoughts in their very growth, eradicates the unexpressed desires, and thus prevents them developing into the corresponding actions, which might cause harm to the individual and hinder his spiritual progress.

See also Questions 35, 58.

V
QUESTIONS ABOUT SHRI MEHER BABA'S MISSION

26 (a) What is it that Shri Meher Baba has come into the world to teach?
(b) What is his *object* in coming to the West?
(c) What is his *mission?*

27 Does Shri Meher Baba claim to be the Avatar of the new dispensation?

28 Whence does he derive his authority? How does he know that he is God- realized?

29 (a) When will the *spiritual revival* take place?
(b) When does it usually occur?
(c) In what sphere of life will its effect be most obvious?

30 Why does he intend speaking in England instead of in America?

31 Will his work create opposition?

32 Will he bring peace and happiness to the world?

33 How can he bridge the gulf between East and West?

V
ANSWERS

26 *(a) What is it that Shri Meher Baba has come into the world to teach?*[47]

Apparently his message pertains to Divine Love, Universal Brotherhood, right living, and the elimination of the motive of self-interest.[48]

But in reality Shri Meher Baba has not come to teach. He has come to awaken. By the power of the Divine Love, which flows from him continually, he transforms the consciousness of those who come to him for liberation, that they may know, through experience, what the philosophers have tried to teach theoretically through the ages.

26 *(b) What is his* **object** *in coming to the West?*[49]

His coming to the West is not with the object of establishing new creeds or spiritual societies or organizations, but for the purpose of making people understand religion in its true sense.

He will revitalize all religions and cults, and bring them together like beads on one string.

26 *(c) What is his* **mission?**[50]

It is to make mankind realize, not only through intellect, but by actual experience, the One Infinite Self which is in all.

Before we can attain to everlasting peace and experience constant joy, we must realize the God within ourselves and in everything we see and meet.

Shri Meher Baba has attained to that realization. The whole purpose of his incarnation is to help others to attain to a like realization.

See also Questions 4, 16.

27 ***Does Shri Meher Baba claim to be the Avatar of the new dispensation?*** [51]

Such a claim would have no value until it were substantiated, and once it were substantiated there would be no need of claims. What Shri Meher Baba is, and the nature of his *mission,* will be abundantly demonstrated at the time of his public manifestation.

Note*—It may be said, however, that some of Shri Meher Baba's closest disciples have come to believe, not through words or explanations, but through deep inner experience, that Shri Meher Baba is such a Being as Jesus was, and that he has come into the world now to effect that transformation of consciousness which is a necessary prelude to the establishment of the new civilization.

It may also be said that to those with whom he lived during his recent visits to this country, Shri Meher Baba gave ample proofs of being able to extend the consciousness of other individuals at will.

28 ***Whence does Shri Meher Baba derive his authority? How does he know that he is God- realized?***

Just as an individual, from the actual experience that he has of being a human, can authoritatively say that he is a human being, so does he, from his own continuous conscious experience of Oneness with the Infinite, know of his Godhood.

29 ***(a) When will the "spiritual revival" take place?***
(b) When does it usually occur?
(c) In what sphere of life will it be most obvious?

The *spiritual revival* that you ask about is not far off, and his approaching manifestation will be the signal. He will utilize the tremendous amount of energy—often misapplied—possessed by the West, particularly by America, for the purpose.

* This article was written in America.

Such a spiritual outburst usually takes place every seven or eight hundred years, at the end or beginning of a cycle, and it is only the Perfect One who has reached the state of "Christ Consciousness" who can appeal to all and work universally.

Shri Meher Baba's *working* will embrace everything. It will penetrate into every phase of life. Perfection would fall far short of the ideal if it were to accept one thing and eschew another.[52]

See also Question 51.

30 ***Why does Shri Meher Baba intend speaking in England instead of in America?***

Owing to the postponement of his speaking and the change of circumstances, Europe is better suited for breaking his silence than America. Yet, as he has said before, America will be the centre of his great spiritual working in future, and will play a prominent part in the organization and development of his plans for the upliftment of humanity.

England has a special spiritual significance for many reasons: his first emissary to the West was sent there; the first Western disciples to come to him in India were English; his first visit to the West was to England; there his first Western Ashram or Spiritual Retreat was established; and in England the plans for his Western work were prepared.

This spiritual value, added to the change in circumstances and time, makes England the more suitable place for the breaking of his silence. And since his first place of residence and association with his close disciples was in *London,* it will be there that his first public speech will be delivered.

31 ***Will his work create opposition?***[53]

His work will create both great enthusiasm and a certain amount of opposition. This is inevitable. But all spiritual work is eventually strengthened by opposition, and so it will be with his. It is like the shooting of an arrow from a bow: the more you pull the bowstring the farther the arrow flies.

32 *Will Shri Meher Baba bring "peace and happiness" to the world?*[54]

There exists at the present moment a universal dissatisfaction and an indescribable longing for something that will end the terrible chaos and misery that overshadows the world just now. He is going to satisfy this longing, and will lead the world to *real happiness.*

The disorders in the world without are a reflection of the disorders within. Shri Meher Baba will enable mankind to solve their *inner* problems by awakening the Divine elements in them.

33 *How can he bridge the gulf between East and West?*

He is doing this in many ways, internally as well as externally.

Recently, he has travelled from East to West and from West to East. He has visited Europe five times, Italy four times, England thrice, America twice, Africa twice, China once, and he has encircled the globe. He has explained that these journeys were for the purpose of "laying *cables* between East and West."

He has taken some of the Eastern disciples to the West; has brought some of his Western disciples to the East. Thus the impressions of the East are brought to the West and vice versa.

This external or physical action of bringing together East and West has its personal side. Every one of his disciples looks upon the others, whether Eastern or Western, as "members of the same family, of which the beloved and revered Master is at once the father, mother, friend, guide and Guru." And while this intimate feeling is now confined to the circle of his close devotees, the great gulf of religious and social differences will also be truly bridged, and a healthy and happy reunion of all brought about. For when he speaks and manifests his Divinity,[55] a world-wide transformation of consciousness will then cause all ideas of superiority and inferiority concerning race, colour, caste and creed to disappear.

The East has been the place of his birth, of his realization of Godhood from manhood, and thereafter of his long, silent activities for the upliftment of humanity. He has many times withdrawn to mountains or caves for his spiritual working. In India and Persia he has established Ashrams (spiritual retreats) to prepare and lead seekers after Truth towards their ideal.

And now he has decided to break his "vow of silence" in the West, which will be the scene of his manifestation and the principal centre of his activities for humanity. These will all help "to bridge the gulf" between East and West, and lead to a clearer mutual understanding.

His teachings are largely concerned with forming a lasting union of all existing races and religions into a harmonious whole.

VI
"PERSONAL" QUESTIONS

34 (a) What work has he done in this life to help humanity?
(b) What sort of work does he do in India?
(c) How does he work in the West?

35 What relation will his *speaking* have to the transformation of human consciousness, which has been predicted?

36 Why has he been silent for eight years?

37 Why does he keep changing his plans and postponing his promises of healing?

38 Who pays for all his travels? Has he money of his own?

39 Was he, during his boyhood, conscious of his own high spiritual destiny?

40 Will he perform miracles when he speaks?

41 In what religion does he believe?

42 Will his work, like Christ's, be missionary in character?

43 What sort of work will his followers do?

44 How can he have both Buddhic and Christ Consciousness?[56]

45 Is he interested in politics?

46 Why does he encourage vegetarianism?

47 Why does he not help his own country first?

VI
ANSWERS

34 ***(a) What work has Shri Meher Baba done in this life to help humanity?***

Most of the people who came to him have benefited, some internally, some externally.

The *internal* benefits have been in the form of spiritual experiences, glimpses and visions of life beyond this material existence, which have transformed their lives and changed their outlook.

The *external* advantages of coming in contact with and having faith in him, too, have been many and varied; to some, in miraculous recoveries from diseases declared incurable by doctors; to others, in overcoming their personal troubles and solving their intricate problems in everyday life. Some of his disciples were saved from fatal accidents and actually owe their lives to him.

And but for the Master's dislike to attach any importance to what by many would be called *miracles,* the practical and subjective instances of these experiences would fill volumes.

Quite apart from these individual subjective experiences, his other *external* activities in the social and religious spheres of life have benefited the masses. Through the Ashrams (spiritual retreats) that he has established in India, he has brought about a wonderful unity of all races and religions, particularly that of the high-class Brahmins with the most depressed class, who are called "untouchables" and are the *most neglected* class of people, and whose upliftment he has ever at heart.

This work was begun some years ago. Shri Meher Baba also maintained a boarding-school, where boys of all castes and creeds and races lived, studied, and played together under his personal guidance. Scholarships covering all expenses were even offered to enable English boys to attend this spiritual and educational school.

He also established a hospital, supervised by a Western-trained doctor, to give free treatment to the poorest peasants of the neighbouring districts, who had never before had access to Western medical treatment, and to whom it was a blessing. With his own hands he washed lepers, and healed five of these afflicted persons.

Sincere seekers after Truth and Knowledge (no matter what their religious creed or agnostic attitude) have found in him their true guide and Guru who led them to the Light they had been trying to find. His benign grace and guidance on the spiritual path have helped many to advance towards Perfection. The lives of others who were on the verge of ruin and degradation have been redeemed by his timely advice and help.

34 ***(b) What sort of work does Shri Meher Baba do in India?***

In whichever part of the world he may be, his *internal* working is one and the same; but his *external* workings vary in accordance with the situation and needs of the place where he is.

In India, his external working is mainly devoted to the running of Ashrams (spiritual retreats); giving *darshana* (i.e. accepting homage and worship) to thousands of his devotees, who worship him as God-man, and who journey hundreds of miles in order to offer their homage and devotion.*

34 ***(c) How does he work in the West?***

In the West, his *external* working is chiefly concerned with teaching and explaining; giving answers to questions; issuing messages and statements concerning spiritual life.

* "I never wish to be called Redeemer, Saviour, Divine Majesty. The disciples through their love, faith, and enthusiasm give such titles; there are many who misunderstand me, who call me Satan Devil, Anti-Christ; but to me it is all the same—I know who I am."—*Shri Meher Baba*

Sometimes he gives private interviews and explains individually; at other times he explains to multitudes at receptions and meetings.

35 ***What relation will his "speaking" have to the transformation of human consciousness, which has been predicted?*** [57]

Humanity, as at present constituted, uses three vehicles for the expression of thought, and experiences three states of consciousness. These three vehicles are:

(1) The mental body, in which thoughts arise as the result of impressions from past experiences. These thoughts may remain latent in the mental body as seeds, or they may be expressed. If they are expressed, they take first the form of *desires* and pass through:

(2) The subtle body, or desire body, which is composed of the five psychic senses. They may rest there, as in the case of dreams or unfulfilled desires, or they may further be expressed through:

(3) The physical body, with its five physical senses.

The three states of consciousness corresponding to the three vehicles mentioned above are:

(1) Unconsciousness, as in deep, dreamless sleep.
(2) Subconsciousness, as in the dreaming state, or obscure, unformed, unfulfilled desires. Everything is experienced through the subtle (astral) body.
(3) Waking consciousness, as in active daily life.

The process by which thought passes from mental through the subtle into physical expression may be called "the expression of human will."

In order for thought to be expressed effectively, all three of the vehicles used in its expression must be perfectly clear, and the interaction between them must be harmonious. The *head* and the *heart* must be united; intellect and feeling must be balanced; material expression must be understood as dependent on spiritual realization.

The God-man neither thinks nor desires. Through him the Divine Will flows inevitably into perfect manifestation, passing directly from the spiritual body (which in the ordinary human being is not developed) into physical expression. For him the superconscious is the normal state of consciousness. From him there flows constantly Infinite Love, Wisdom, Joy, Peace, and Power.

In order to convey thought to others man uses speech, or writing, or some other physical means of expression; sometimes, as in telepathy, thought is transmitted and received through and by the subtle body.

The God-man does not convey thought, but Truth, which he either awakens in the individual whom he is helping, through a deep inner experience, or which he transmits directly from the superconscious to the conscious, from the spiritual to the physical, by means of either the physical eye, the physical touch, or "the spoken word."

Extract from Shri Meher Baba's Message to India[58]

> In the conscious (awake) state all that you experience by seeing, hearing, eating, walking, etc., is done through the gross body.
>
> In the subconscious (dream) state, everything is experienced through the subtle body. In this state the mortal mind, with the help of the desire-body, may see past events recur, or may foresee future happenings, and sometimes past, present, and future events may appear together in confusion (this would be a nightmare). This all depends upon the impressions on the mind received through the physical body in accordance to the proportion of its attachments to gross activities.
>
> In the unconscious (deep sleep) state you are unaware of either[59] the physical or astral happenings, and so experience nothingness.
>
> One who transcends these three states of consciousness and gains illumination[60] experiences the superconscious state. This is the Christ-Buddha-Krishna state, the God-man state, in which one attains to perfect manhood and perfect Divinity. To be one with the source of all Love, Knowledge, Power, Light, and Existence is to enjoy infinite bliss and feel in harmony with everyone and everything. Art,

science, beauty, nature appear as one's own manifestation.

This is all well and good for the individual, but what about the multitudes? In the present state of world depression and economic strife the supreme thought of the people at large is about their daily bread. How can they think of or aspire to spiritual illumination? And it is self-interest (caused by low selfish desires) that is at the root of this universal condition of misery. Material desire is misery. When you want a thing, you crave for it until you get it—this is suffering. And when you do get it, you don't experience the happiness you expected—this is disappointment, which is also suffering.

And this self-interest cannot be eliminated by means of religious piety, nor can sermons or the fear of heaven or hell help. Only when the atmosphere of selfless love and universal brotherhood prevails throughout the world will this self-interest be annihilated. Then only will people realize that the true aim of life is not merely to eat, drink, sleep, or seek for pleasure—in other words to gain material welfare—but to attain real happiness in every phase of life: material, social, and spiritual. And this time is drawing near.

See also Questions 24, 25, 56.

36 *Why has he been silent for eight years?*

When he speaks, Truth is *more powerfully* manifested than when he uses either sight or touch to convey it. For that reason Avatars usually observe a period of silence lasting for several years, breaking it to speak only when they wish to manifest the Truth to the entire universe.

So when Shri Meher Baba speaks he will manifest the Divine Will, and a world-wide transformation of consciousness will result.

37 *Why does he keep changing his plans and postponing his promises of healing?*

Although he seems to change his plans, and apparently does not keep his promises about the dates of his speaking and healing, etc., in reality it is not so. For, as a Perfect Master and the Avatar of the age,[61] he knows all that is to happen in future, and everything is planned and arranged by him beforehand. Although he really knows when he is destined to speak and heal, he postpones the dates from time to time in order to give greater force to his final workings, and in order also that all that he has planned during these past years will be revealed fully on the day of his manifestation.

38 ***Who pays for Shri Meher Baba's travels? Has he money of his own?***

Amongst his numerous disciples, in the East as well as in the West, there are many who are rich and who voluntarily contribute money towards his cause, for the maintenance of Ashrams, and for the travels that his work necessitates. There are a few who have dedicated all their possessions, and even their lives, to him.

From the spiritual point of view it may be expressed in his own words: "The whole universe is mine."

From the material standpoint he is sometimes wealthy and sometimes penniless, but always equally unattached.

See also Question 53.

39 ***Was he, during his boyhood, conscious of his own high spiritual destiny?***

Yes, at certain times he had glimpses of his Divinity and of his future work and mission.

40 ***Will he perform miracles when he speaks?***

He will perform miracles when the time and situation demand. He will perform them to draw towards him the sceptical, unbelieving people who would never believe in Truth unless it were proved by some extraordinary phenomena.

Miracles are not necessary for *understanding* persons because spiritual healing is by far the greatest healing, and this is Shri Meher Baba's real work. He will not perform miracles to satisfy mere idle curiosity.

See also Questions 21, 22.

41 ***In what religion does he believe?***

He belongs to no religion in particular, and yet to every religion. Love is his principal agent.

The Infinite One can be attained only through Love and Selfless Service. Dogmas and doctrines, rites and ceremonies, do not constitute *true religion.* To realize God in every phase of life—in art, science, beauty, nature—that is his religion.

This question is more fully answered in Questions 16, 20, 26.

42 ***Will his work, like Christ's, be missionary in character?***

He will establish no new religion, yet his work will embrace all religions in their essence and spirit, particularly in their *mystical* and *spiritual* aspects, and be absolutely unconcerned with their ceremonial side and dry dogmas. His work, therefore, will not be *missionary* in the narrowest sense of the word, but will permeate through all religions.

See also Questions 4, 15, 16, 26.

43 ***What sort of work will his followers do?***

The duties allotted to each of his disciples will vary in form and character according to the inner experiences of each.

A certain number will attain the realization of the One Divine Self, and a large number will have *illumination.*

Both groups will know inwardly what to do through the spiritual experiences that they in their highly advanced states will then have, and they will work spontaneously without further instructions.

And the duties of one and all his disciples, whether in an advanced or in a normal state, will always concern the spiritual upliftment of humanity.

See also Question 33.

44 *How can Shri Meher Baba have both the Buddhic and Christ Consciousness?*

There is but one Divine Infinite "Consciousness," whether realized by Christ or experienced by Buddha, and the external expression of this Divine Consciousness varies according to the circumstances confronting (at the moment of historical time) the God-men who have attained to this superconscious state.

Once gained, the Cosmic Consciousness is gained for eternity, and is continually present either on the spiritual plane or as "The Word" made flesh for the upliftment of humanity.

See also Question 20.

45 *Is he interested in politics?*

Spirituality touches all the problems of religion, politics, sociology, and economics. It concerns each and every phase of life, and as Shri Meher Baba is spiritually perfect, he, directly or indirectly, is interested in *all* the various aspects of life.

46 *Why does he encourage vegetarianism?*

He advises vegetable food for spiritual reasons, and also for reasons of health. Animal food stimulates excitement, lust, passion, and evil desires, which are all detrimental to spiritual progress. Vegetable food helps one to keep the feelings, emotions, and desires balanced and normal, and hence assists the aspirant on the spiritual path. Also it improves health, aids digestion, and is free from certain poisons contained in animal food.

47 *Why does he not help his own country first?*

The whole universe is his country and home, and he responds to the call of any part of the universe which he sees to be in need of his help.

VII
MISCELLANEOUS QUESTIONS: WORLD PROBLEMS, PHILOSOPHICAL PROBLEMS

48 What, in his opinion, is the real meaning and purpose of life?

49 How will he be able, by speaking, to ease the world depression, to solve the problems of unemployment, prohibition, and crime?

50 Has he any solution for the problems of politics, economics, morals, and sex?

51 Which individuals and nations will benefit most by the new spiritual impulse?

52 What, in his opinion, is the characteristic mental attitude of the West?

53 What is his opinion concerning money?

54 How does he explain *good* and *evil, heaven* and *hell?*

55 How did evolution begin and work?

56 Does he deny *matter?*

57 What is his opinion about marriage and celibacy?

58 What are *sanskaras?*

VII
ANSWERS

48 ***What, in his opinion, is the real meaning and purpose of life?***

It is to become identified with the Universal Self, and thus to experience Infinite Bliss, Power, and Knowledge; and finally, to be able to impart this experience to others, and make them see the One Indivisible Infinity existing in every phase of life.

49 ***How will Shri Meher Baba be able, by speaking, to ease the world depression, to solve the problems of unemployment, prohibition, and crime?*** [*] [62]

The root of all our difficulties, individual and social, is *self-interest.* It is this, for example, which causes corrupt politicians to accept bribes and betray the interests of those whom they have been elected to serve; which causes bootleggers to break, for their own profit, a law designed, whether wisely or not, to help the nation as a whole; which causes people to connive, for their pleasure, in the breaking of that law, thus causing disrespect for law in general and increasing crime tremendously; which causes the exploitation of great masses of humanity by individuals or groups of individuals seeking personal gain; which impedes the progress of civilization by shelving inventions which would contribute to the welfare of humanity at large, simply because their use would mean the scrapping of present inferior equipment; which, when people are starving, causes wanton destruction of large quantities of food simply in order to maintain market prices; which

* Written in United States of America, 1932.

causes the hoarding of large sums of gold when the welfare of the world demands its circulation.

These are only a few examples of the way *self-interest* operates to the detriment of human welfare. Eliminate *self-interest* and you will solve all your problems, individual and social.

But the elimination of *self-interest,* even granting a sincere desire on the part of the individual to accomplish it, is not easy, and is never completely achieved except by the aid of a Perfect Master, who has the power to convey Truth at will. For *self-interest* springs from a false idea of the true nature of the Self, and this idea must be eradicated and the Truth experienced before this elimination is possible.

Shri Meher Baba intends, when he speaks, to reveal the One Supreme Self (God) which is in all. This accomplished, the idea of the Self as a limited separate entity will disappear, and with it will vanish *self-interest.* Co-operation will replace competition; certainty will replace fear;[63] generosity will replace greed; exploitation will disappear.

Refer to footnote, Question 35 ("Message to India").

50 ***Has Shri Meher Baba any solution for the problems of politics, economics, morals, and sex?***

In the general *spiritual push* that he will impart to the world, the problems of politics, economics, and sex, although they are subsidiary to the primary purpose,[64] will automatically be solved and adjusted, and new values and significance will be attached to matters which appear to baffle solution at the present moment.

51 ***Which individuals and nations will benefit most by the new spiritual impulse?***[65]

Perfect Masters impart spirituality by personal contact and influence, and the benefit that will accrue to different nations when Shri Meher Baba brings about the spiritual upheaval will largely depend upon the amount of energy each possesses. The more the energy, however misapplied, the greater the response.

The Master merely directs the current into the right channels.

52 ***What, in his opinion, is the characteristic mental attitude of the West?***

The West looks at life from the standpoint of reason and logic, and is sceptical about things which baffle the intellect. This trend of thought has brought about some great achievements: Political Ideals and a conception of Social Responsibility; Mathematics and Science. It has also led her towards *materialism,* which has brought about wars, political and economic crises.

Organized efforts such as a League of Nations, World Conferences, and Peace Pacts are made in the hope of solving the world problems which face all nations today. But all such efforts have only a very partial success on account of the prevailing *materialism,* and because these efforts ignore the spiritual character and potentialities of man.[66]

53 ***What is his opinion concerning money?***

It entirely depends upon the way in which we use our money, whether it is good or bad. Money earned and utilized as a means of livelihood for oneself and those who depend on one is good. Given as charity for the benefit of humanity, it is *better.* But to give anonymously and yet carefully for the intelligent service and spiritual upliftment of humanity, without dictating as to how it shall be administered or spent—this is the *best* use of money. But very, very few selfless souls can do that.

When money, gained by fair means or foul, is spent in order to gratify one's desire for pleasure and enjoyment, it makes the spender pleasure-loving and selfish. And if the same person suddenly loses that money, he naturally feels miserable and curses life and fate. Worse still is it when he wastes money, earned or inherited, in speculation and gambling, or on wine and women.

Whether it is good or bad for us to possess money depends entirely on the use we make of it. Fire can serve and warm man; fire can burn and destroy man.

54 *How does he explain "good" and" evil," "heaven" and "hell"?*

In the general sense of the word, *evil* is merely *perverted good,* a lower stage of the ladder of evolution, an obstacle the overcoming of which enables man to test and strengthen his character.

Looked at from the personal point of view, *evil* is the result of ignoring the Law of Karma and of indecision or weakness of the personal character.

The Master is beyond *good* and *evil.*

Virtue or goodness is the antithesis of evil or sin in an individual character. Virtue, then, is due to co-operation with the Karmic Law, and sin is due to conscious or unconscious failure to co-operate with the Karmic Law.

As separate worlds, or as separate planes, *heaven* and *hell* do not exist. They are states of mental peace or torture. The person who lives in accordance with the Law of Karma experiences happiness and may be said to be in the *heaven state;* while the person who ignores and disobeys the Law of Karma suffers spiritually, mentally, and physically, and may be said to be undergoing the tortures of *hell.*

The individual's possession of strength of mind or weakness of character, of the rudiments of *virtue* and *vice,* and the various experiences of *heaven* and *hell,* are all due to the past impressions (*sanskaras* as they are termed) of previous lives. And every human being must pass through the dual aspects of both *good* and *evil* before attaining Perfection. The Master is beyond *good* and *evil.* Removing past impressions by his Love, he can truly say, "Thy sins be forgiven thee."

See also Question 4.

55 *How did evolution begin and work?* [67]

The fish lives in the sea without being aware of the sea, as it has never left the sea. So in the beginning, before *evolution* started, we were united with the Source of All, but *unconsciously.*

Evolution involved a separation from the source of all and a consequent longing to return to it through a succession of lives and forms. The conscious return to the source is possible only during physical incarnation, when consciousness becomes equilibrated in the gross matter. The unconscious soul, through evolution, gradually gains consciousness by means of successive related forms.

56 *Does Shri Meher Baba deny "matter"?*

He denies nothing because for him *duality* does not exist. To a God-realized personality, matter and spirit seem both to be merged in the Ocean of Divinity. He sees the "Divine One" playing simultaneously the different rôles of the soul, spirit, mind, and body.

(a) The *soul* exists independently of nature and matter, it is infinite, everlasting, and pure.

(b) The *spirit,* though having the same Divine essence as the *soul,* differs in that it is attached to the matter, the body, the world and the affairs of the world, but is unconscious of the Infinite Self. "Until it is realized, the spirit has to reincarnate."

(c) The *mind* is the medium by which the spirit's experiences of matter are expressed.

(d) The *body* is the medium through which the *mind* puts its desires, emotions, and thoughts into action on the physical plane.[68]

The God-man teaches us the Truth that to realize the oneness of everything we must realize that *spirit* and *matter,* or the spiritual life and material life go hand-in-hand. When *intellect* and *feeling,* or *head* and *heart,* are equally developed and balanced, the apparent antithesis is resolved into the One Divine Consciousness.

See also Questions 35, 24.

57 ***What is Shri Meher Baba's opinion about marriage and celibacy?***

Every human relationship is based on *Love* in one form or another, and endures or dissolves as that love is eternal or temporal in character.

Marriage, for example, is happy or unhappy, exalting or degrading, lasting or fleeting, according to the love which inspires and sustains it. Marriages based on sex attraction alone cannot endure. They lead inevitably to divorce or worse. Marriages, on the other hand, which are based on a mutual desire to serve and inspire grow continually in richness and beauty, and are a benediction to all who know of them.

Celibacy is good for progress in the spiritual path, for those who can control their sex emotion. Contact with a Perfect Master helps one to gain that control, but as very few people have the very strong will-power to control themselves, marriage for most men and women is advisable. Indeed, it is much better to marry and devote your attention to one person than to remain a bachelor, and like a bee pass from flower to flower in search of new experiences.

58 ***58. What are "sanskaras"?***

The veil of darkness that covers one's inner vision and the obstacles to *illumination* are certain mental impressions of actions, desires, and tendencies bound up with our *egoism.* In the East they are called *sanskaras.* Some of these impressions were formed during countless past lives; others may have been formed during this present life.

These tendencies and desires create two illusions: first, of a separate self, at war with our own higher self, and the second, of being isolated from other selves.

"Evolution" or the "Fall" into matter involved the creation of this lower self. But without the physical body *realization* could never be consciously attained.

See also Question 25.

Five Additional Questions and Answers

Translated from the French

59 ***What is the difference between Destiny and Chance?***[69]

Destiny is the divine law which guides us through our numerous existences. Every soul must experience happiness and unhappiness, vice and virtue, from the commencement of evolution up to that goal which is the Realization of God.

Chance is based on Karma,[70] that law of Cause and Effect which governs the events of our present life as well as those of our future lives. Through evolution the soul receives, by means of the spirit, the impressions or sanskaras.[71] The processes which create the experiences and later the elimination of those impressions, can be called Chance. Destiny, or the goal that souls have to attain, is Realization of God; but actually[72] Chance is different for every individual. We can compare Destiny to a load of (let us imagine) seven hundred tons of happiness and unhappiness, vice or virtue, which every soul has to carry throughout its existence. One soul carries seven hundred tons of iron, another soul the same weight in steel, others—lead or gold; the weight is always the same. Only matter changes. The impressions of each individual vary and the acquired sanskaras from the structure and the condition of the future life of every individual.

60 ***What is the difference between the inner and the outer work of an Avatar?***[73]

His inner work is executed for the good of humanity by the means of his spiritual body and divine will, on the spiritual and the subtle planes directly, or through the intermediary of his agents. The work that he accomplishes through his physical body, in making personal contact with individuals while passing through different countries, is his outer work. He turns their minds towards spirituality, enhancing their progression towards the subtle planes and from these towards the spiritual planes.*

See also Questions 12, 15, 24, 25, 33, 34, 35.

61 ***Why were certain Avatars married and why was Jesus not married?***

The exterior way of living of an Avatar is regulated by the habits and the customs of the times, and he adopts that attitude which is most suited to serve as an example to his contemporaries. But, in essence, all the Avatars incarnate the same ideal of life. At the epoch of Mohammed[74] the Arabs were very sensuous and it was not considered bad or illegal to live with several wives. If, like Jesus, he had not married, and had advocated celibacy, or if he had imposed absolute continency, it would have produced dangerous and inevitable reactions. Few people would have followed his teaching and fewer still would have been attracted towards such an ideal. Mohammed had nine wives,[75] but he had no physical contact with them; it was legal to have several wives.

At the time of Krishna, the Hindus were fighting amongst each other. Envy and greed predominated;[76] the real conception of spiritual life and love was unknown to them. Krishna based his teachings on the laws of love and pure and innocent merriment. So,[77] human beings were directed joyfully towards a disinterested ideal of love.

At the time of Zoroaster, humanity was hesitant and lacked equilibrium. They were neither complete materialists nor really attracted towards the spiritual light. He taught them to be good householders, to marry, and to abstain from desiring the wife of another, and to worship God. His own life was

* The two ways of working can be used simultaneously.

based on this principle, "Good thoughts, good words, good actions." Zoroaster was married.

At the time of Buddha, humanity was deep in materialism. In order to demonstrate that their conception of values was wrong and that they were victims of the goddess Illusion, or *Maya,* Buddha renounced his wife, his family, the riches of the world in order to establish his teachings on *Sannyas,* or renunciation.[78]

At the time of Jesus, arrogance, imperiousness, pride, cruelty were the characteristics of the people. Nevertheless they possessed a conception of justice regarding women and marriage, and it was not necessary, as it was in Arabia, to make marriage an example. Jesus lived the life of humility,[79] simplicity and poverty, and he endured suffering in order to direct humanity towards the purest ideal—God. All the prophets were the incarnation of God; therefore they stand beyond desire and temptation;[80] they were the manifestation of the same divine element.

62 ***Why do the teachings of the Avatars differ from each other?***

The Avatars are the manifestation of the same divine element incarnate in this world at different times; therefore their teachings have to be adapted to the mentality of their epoch. At times the Avatar bases his teaching on the search of the personal God; and at another time, on the search of the impersonal aspect of God. At one time he will prohibit the eating of pigs' meat, drinking of wine, or the eating of cows' meat. It is like in a hospital where the sick complain about their thirst. The doctor will prescribe tea or coffee in the morning, water or a refreshing fruit juice in the afternoon, and in the evening sour milk; then before sleeping hot milk. God, manifesting through the Avatar of different periods, quenches the thirst of man in different ways. All human beings, whether consciously or unconsciously, have the same thirst for Truth.

63 ***What does Shri Meher Baba think about life after death? What is his attitude regarding spiritualism?***[81]

The semi-subtle sphere is the chain that links the physical material world to the subtle plane. During our habitual dreams we make use of the subtle body and in a sub-conscious way we perceive sensations belonging to the physical material world. In certain conditions it is possible to make conscious use of the physical senses in such a way that we can contact the semi-subtle sphere. We can, through this fact, enter into communication with the spirits of the dead. These spirit communications have nothing to do with the spiritual life, nor with the subtle spirit, nor with the spiritual planes. There is a vast difference between the subtle sphere and the semi-subtle sphere.

After death the spirits of human beings (except for those who have sufficiently progressed on the spiritual path and are beyond the fourth plane) reach the semi-subtle sphere. According to their sanskaras they go to "heaven" or to "hell," and when they achieve the point they had to attain they can return to earth with a new body (reincarnate), or otherwise they return to the semi-subtle sphere for a certain time. These spirits are, so to say, in the ante-chamber of the semi-subtle sphere and one can enter into contact with them through the means of spirit[82] communication, whether they have achieved their period of joy or pain, and wait for a new rebirth, or whether they are on the point of going to "heaven" or "hell."[83]

The semi-subtle sphere, "heaven" or "hell," with their respective experiences have no reality; they are merely joys and pains experienced through the organs of the subtle body. It is advisable to attribute only relative importance to certain descriptions of life after death, although they may be exact.[84]

Spiritually evolved persons can communicate with high spirits, but it is preferable if they abstain. Human beings can never enter into communication with the high spirits who belong to the subtle, mental or spiritual planes, because even if they have to reincarnate, they do not sojourn in the ante-chamber of the semi-subtle sphere.

True spirituality has nothing in common with spiritualism and communications between the living and the dead.† [85]

---

† Planes are briefly described in note 2. p. 77.

The states pertaining to dreams as well as to the mind and the subtle body are described in questions 24, 35 and 56.

Concerning "heaven" and "hell," see question 54.

"Sanskaras" are not synonymous with "sin." See questions 25, 58, 59.

This response has been taken from "Philosophical Fragments" of Shri Meher Baba.

PART FOUR

The Sayings: Another Early Compilation

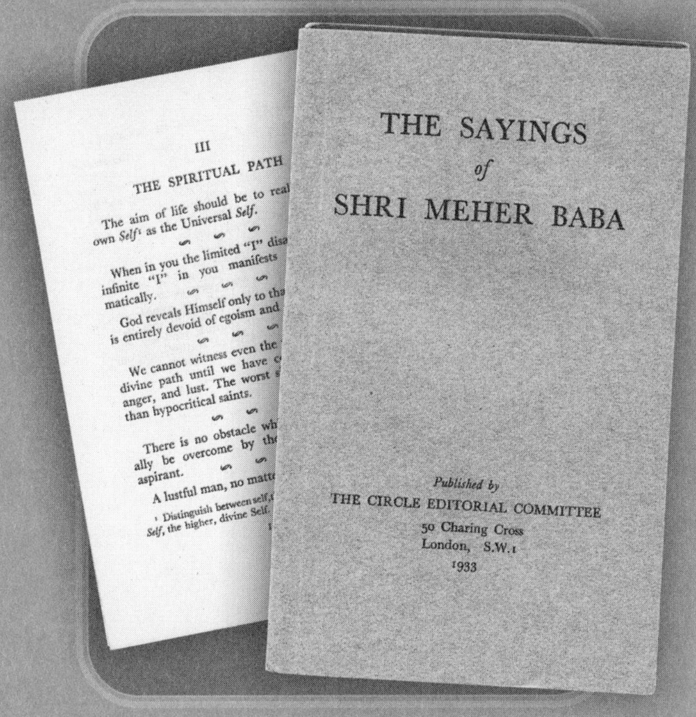

III
THE SPIRITUAL PATH
THE SAYINGS
of
SHRI MEHER BABA
Published by
THE CIRCLE EDITORIAL COMMITTEE
50 Charing Cross
London, S.W.1
1933

In December 1933 Circle Editorial Committee in London published its second booklet, *The Sayings of Shri Meher Baba,* a collection of 136 sayings organized under seven headings. Its editor, Herbert Davy, probably based his work on manuscripts from India.

(LEFT) Baba with Herbert Davy in Portofino June–July 1933. At this time Baba established the Circle Editorial Committee, headed by Herbert, which oversaw the publication of Baba's words.

(RIGHT) Despite the signal service he had rendered, Herbert found himself in the throes of wrenching conflicts between head and heart, and wound up severing his connection with Baba during 1934.

INTRODUCTION TO PART FOUR

In December of 1933, three months after the release of Shri Meher Baba, the Perfect Master: Questions and Answers, *the Circle Editorial Committee published a second booklet,* The Sayings of Shri Meher Baba. *Probably edited once again by Herbert Davy, its fifty pages organized 136 sayings, ranging in length from a sentence to a short paragraph, into seven thematically defined sections.* The Sayings *was somewhat more fully annotated than* Questions and Answers; *and it was enhanced through the incorporation of an excellent glossary.*

Actually, all of these sayings had been published before, though the Committee might not have been aware of this fact. An Indian monthly magazine issuing out of Nasik from 1929 through 1931 under the editorship of K. J. Dastur, Meher Message *began each of its first twenty-eight issues with five "Sayings of His Divine Majesty Sadguru Meher Baba," as the editor liked to call them. Though some of the sayings in the 1933 booklet have been slightly revised, for the most part they are identical to their* Meher Message *counterparts. (The four sayings in* Meher Message *that somehow did not find their way into* The Sayings of Shri Meher Baba *have been reproduced in appendix 7.)*

The probable source for both the periodical and the booklet, however, is a typed manuscript entitled "Sayings of Shri Sadguru Meher Baba" and dated "January 1929" that has been found among the J. Graham Phelps Stokes papers in the Columbia University Rare Book and Manuscript Library. In other words, the two sets of sayings (in the magazine and booklet) were probably published independently of each other. For fuller discussion of these matters, see pp. 237–45 and 273.

The text republished here follows that of the 1933 booklet with only a few slight emendations; the care evident in the original editorship has rendered recourse to the other versions of these sayings unnecessary. All notes and footnotes are reproduced from the booklet and are the handiwork of the Circle Editorial Committee.

The Sayings of Shri Meher Baba

Contents

Preface

Shri Meher Baba was born thirty-nine years ago of Persian parents in Poona, India. By birth he is a Parsee Zoroastrian. He is unmarried.

In 1913, while he was attending college at Poona, he met an ancient woman, Hazrat Baba Jan, a Perfect Master. As a result he entered the state of Superconsciousness. In 1921, through another Perfect Master, Shri Upasni Maharaj of Sakori, he gained normal consciousness. That is, to The Superconscious state was added the gross, and the subtle consciousness.[86] He then wrote an account[*] of his spiritual experiences, but ceased writing altogether in 1923.[87] He began his spiritual mission in 1921 and now has followers throughout the world.

Since July 10, 1925, he has observed complete silence; he communicates by means of an English alphabet board. During the last two years he has visited America, China, Egypt, France, Italy, Spain, Turkey; he has visited England six times. Despite his silence he leads an active life, administers Ashrams in India and Persia, and continues his spiritual mission throughout the world.

The use of the alphabet board imposes severe limitations on style and on the composition of longer prose passages. It was by means of the alphabet board that these Sayings were delivered by Shri Meher Baba.[†]

---

* This book which has not hitherto been seen by anyone will be published shortly.

† Shri is an Indian title of respect meaning saintly or holy; Meher means compassion or grace; Baba means father or friend.

THE SAYINGS OF SHRI MEHER BABA

I
Divine Love

GOD, THE REAL BELOVED, is ever ready to enter your house, the mind, but he cannot because it is occupied by your numberless unreal beloveds—desires, and there is no room for Him.

You yourself are the cause of your separation from the Beloved. Annihilate that which is called self* and you will thereby gain union with Him.

True Love means the dedication of one's self or the complete surrender of one's self to the Beloved. It seeks the happiness of the Beloved without the least desire of obtaining happiness from the Beloved.

The highest divine knowledge is attained through love (which has in it the spiritual faculties, intuition, and inspiration), and is opposed to the intellectual faculty. It is love that makes one transcend the dominion of intellect and gain the state of complete self-annihilation. It is this state that ends in union with God.

* "Self" means lower self.

Revenge follows hatred and forgiveness follows love. Without love none can cultivate the noble habit of forgetting and forgiving. You forgive a wrong done to you in the same measure in which you love the wrong-doer.

You can counteract a disease only by its antidote. Love is the only antidote to hatred. When you feel like hating a man try to remind yourself that he is a form of your own *Self.*[*]

There is a greater valour in conquering the heart of a single enemy than in gaining victory over the bodies of thousands of enemies. The mind is capable of turning the bitterest enemy into the sweetest friend by constantly thinking well (charitably) of him.

Jealousy is not born of love, but of petty-mindedness, and dies simultaneously with the death of petty-mindedness.

Real happiness lies in Oneness; wherever there is duality there is trouble.

Love resembles death in that it annihilates snobbery, vulgarity, and all distinctions.

[*] Distinguish between self, the ordinary lower self, and *Self,* the higher divine Self.

The trinkets of this world cannot tempt the true divine lover. He does not feel the appetites and cannot enjoy sound sleep. He resembles a fish just taken out of water. He is restless until he is united with the Beloved.

Divine love causes its captive to forget his own individual existence by making him feel less and less bound by the trammels of human limitations on his onward march, till he reaches a point where he can raise himself to the realization of the highest in himself.

II
Religions Or Shariat*

THE ACT OF WORSHIP should spring from the heart. Let it be born in mind that worship from the heart presupposes great efforts. It cannot be evoked by a mere wish. If one decides upon practicing true Bhakti,† one has to make heroic efforts in order to achieve fixity of mind, for contrary thoughts are very likely to disturb one's mind.

Profound worship based on high ideals of philosophy and spirituality, and prompted by divine love, constitutes true mysticism (Bhakti Yoga‡). It follows, then, that the various ceremonies and rituals which are the part and parcel of every creed (the Shariat of every religion) constitute only its shadow.

Do not be afraid of God, for how can you love Him if you fear Him? Fear and love do not go hand in hand. The truly religious man is he who is God-loving and not God-fearing.

Upon the altar of humility we must offer our prayers to God. Humility is spiritually of greater worth than devotion. It is easier to be devout than to be humble, but devotion in many instances proves to be a stepping-stone to humility.

---

* Shariat means the outward forms and ceremonies of religion.

† Worship or devotion.

‡ The practice of devotion.

True Bhakti (worship or devotion) does not necessarily mean the observance of religious rites and the muttering of mantras or bhantras.* But it certainly means the continual repetition of any one name of God, or the continuous thinking and remembrance of God.

Though millions say that there is nothing but God, to most men this gross world is all in all, and God is unreal or a phantom.

To pray to God for material prosperity is not a prayer but a farce.

On the day of Jarthoshtno-diso[88] many Parsees fervently pray, "May the soul of Zoroaster rest in peace." Surely these Parsees are utterly ignorant of the spiritual position of their Prophet or are impudent to the last degree. No greater insult can be hurled at Yazdan Zoroaster than by offering such a prayer.

You will not be saved by accepting any theological dogmas or by regarding a Prophet who lived hundreds or thousands of years ago as the only God-incarnate, as the only genuine Saviour, as the last real messenger of God. If you want to be saved, conquer your mind, lead a pure life, renounce low desires, and follow One who has realized God and in whom you have sound faith.

---

* A mantra is a sacred verse or formula, a prayer written in a rhythmical form. A bhantra is the chanting aloud of a mantra.

Most of the so-called religious ceremonies performed by the Parsees, the Hindus, and followers of other creeds are unnecessary and worthless. For these useless ceremonies it is the avaricious and worldly priests who are responsible. Prophets, Sadgurus, and Saints are not bound by them.

Worldly-minded priests, though they may mutter prayers throughout the day and may perform this and that ceremony, can confer no spiritual benefits on anyone. Poison trees may be watered with nectar, but they will not produce edible fruits.

The so-called religious leaders who repeatedly quarrel over rites and dogmas can only lead their followers into the deep pit of ignorance. Only the blind will follow the blind. What light can be thrown by him who is himself in the dark? What knowledge can he impart who has not experienced Truth?

The priest, whose principal motive is to serve himself and not others, should be called a minister, not of God, but of his lower self. Disinterestedness and eagerness to serve others should be the characteristics of a genuine priest, to whatever creed he may belong. He should be like a river that does not drink its own waters but is useful to others, irrespective of their caste, creed, and colour.

Many of the so-called Christian missionaries are the followers of Judas and not of Jesus. The object of a true Christian missionary should be not merely to baptize the so-called pagans, but to render unselfish service to others, regardless of their creed and colour.

If a so-called religious leader comes forth and proclaims that marriages* between brothers and sisters are quite lawful, he will immediately have a large following; but if a God-realized personage proclaims that renunciation is indispensable to the attainment of Truth, only a few will care to follow him.

High spiritual Truth has nothing to do with creeds, religions or Shariat. It is far beyond the limited dogmas and doctrines of every creed. You will attain to this truth if you give up worldly Maya—lust, anger, and greed (kama, krodh, and lobh).

To change our outward religion for another is like going from one cage to another. Either cross the boundary of Shariat (outward forms of religions) and enter Tarikat (the spiritual path) or remain within the cage of the creed of your birth.

A man becomes wise by practicing, not by preaching virtue. Ability in advising others about virtue is no proof of saintliness, nor is it a mark of wisdom.

In order to realize God and to gain the original state from which everything emerged, we should follow the creed that accords with our own conscience and stick to that path which best suits our spiritual tendency, our mental attitude, our physical aptitude, and our external surroundings and circumstances.

---

* 3,500 years ago there lived a so-called religious leader who taught this.

III
The Spiritual Path

THE AIM OF LIFE should be to realize one's own *Self*[*] as the Universal *Self.*[89]

When in you the limited "I" disappears, the infinite "I" in you manifests itself automatically.

God reveals Himself only to that mind which is entirely devoid of egoism and egotism.

We cannot witness even the threshold of the divine path until we have conquered greed, anger, and lust. The worst sinners are better than hypocritical saints.

There is no obstacle which cannot eventually be overcome by the genuine spiritual aspirant.

A lustful man, no matter what good qualities he may possess, cannot move along the spiritual path; he is like a cart with one wheel.

---

[*] Distinguish between self, the ordinary lower self, and Self, the higher, divine Self.

Do not get disheartened and alarmed when adversity, calamity, or misfortunes pour in upon you. Thank God, for He has thereby given you the opportunity of acquiring forbearance and fortitude. Those who have acquired the power of bearing with adversities can easily enter the Spiritual Path.

Beware of pride, not only because it is hydra-headed, but because it is deceptive. So deceptive is it that, more often than not, it puts on the apparel of humility.

Do not try to find excuses or extenuating circumstances for your misdeeds. Unless you repent of your wickedness you cannot improve. To attempt to justify your misdeeds is to smother your conscience and to make virtues out of vices.

Take good care of your body, but do not be a slave to it. If you think constantly of its welfare, you are like the miser who thinks constantly of his gold.

Vegetarian food and milk assist the development of the divine nature in man, whereas eggs, meat, alcoholic drinks, and fish tend to excite the animal nature in man.

Service

That is real service where there is no thought of self at all.

Selfless service may not only bring you to the foot of that mystical mountain whose summit is Self-realization, but it may enable you to climb far on the path. Finally, it may bring you in contact with a Perfect Master and cause you to surrender to him.

True Karma (Service) means the rendering of service to others without any thought of gain or reward, and also without the least intention of putting others under an obligation.

Never think that by helping another you have put him under any obligation to you. On the contrary, believe that the recipient of your generosity gives you an opportunity to serve yourself.

Renunciation or Sanyas

It is praiseworthy to be a genuine sanyasin (spiritual pilgrim) but honest householders are far better than hypocritical sadhus. And there are today many false sadhus.*

* Ascetics.

Wearing the yellow robe,[*] begging for bread, visiting the holy places, do not necessarily prove Sanyas or Renunciation. The true sanyasin is he who has renounced his lower self and all worldly desires.

From the materialistic standpoint it may seem cowardly to forsake the world, but it requires great heroism to lead the spiritual life.

He who does not act according to the dictates of his lower self and who resists all worldly temptations is a true sanyasin.

True Yoga[†] means detachment from the world and leading a life of total renunciation or self-abnegation.

For those who insist from the very depths of their souls and from the innermost cores of their hearts on seeing Reality face to face, at all costs and consequences, there is only one way—that of complete renunciation.

Meditation

Just as a random thought can manifest force in the shape of a bodily action,

[*] The symbol of renunciation in the East.

[†] A spiritual discipline.

so meditation or deep and properly organized thinking produces a force of its own which is very useful to the spiritual aspirant. The manifestation of this force may not become evident immediately, or in a short time, but meditation is sure eventually to bear fruit.

It is unnecessary to lay down hard and fast rules regarding the posture in meditation. The sitting posture* which you find most convenient should be adopted. But once it is adopted you must stick to it and sit in the same way daily.

There is no length of time which can be called too long for meditation, and every hour of the night and the day is suitable; but the best period for meditation is the early hours of the morning, 4 to 7 a.m.

To attain the state of the highest, three different routes have to be chalked out. They are Bhakti, Dnyan, and Karma (devotion, spiritual knowledge,† and service). The aspirant has to pass through three principal stages: they are the gross or physical, the subtle or astral, and the mind spheres.[90]

* Or kneeling posture.

† Dnyan or Real Knowledge is usually attained as the fruit of Meditation or Prayer.

IV
INTELLECT,* [91] MIND, AND MAYA

Intellect

INTELLECTUAL DISPUTATIONS ABOUT GOD will not bring you any nearer to Him, and may take you farther away. But persistent, heartfelt prayers to Him will lower the veil that now envelops you in darkness.

God-realization is not to be confused with intellectual convictions regarding God and Creation, just as the head is not to be confused with the hair, nor the thing itself with its shadow.

True knowledge is that knowledge which makes man after *Self*-realization or union with God assert that his real *Self* is in everything and everybody.

To realize the Supreme Being as your own *Self* is to realize Truth. The universe is the outcome of imagination. Then, why try to acquire knowledge of the imaginative universe instead of plumbing the depths of your real *Self*?

---

* The mind is the medium by which the spirit accumulates impressions of its experiences, and works out and expresses these as thoughts and desires.

The mind (Mun) must not be confused with the intellect (Anddhai).

The mind has everything to do with desires, the intellect has nothing to do with them. A savage and a great scientist both have mind, the former's comprises more desires and little intellect, and the latter's contains a larger proportion of intellect or thought power. The mind might be compared to a cup containing the lusts, ambition, and intellect.

Though the heart cannot take the place of the head nor the head that of the heart, they are not necessarily enemies of each other. Intellect counts for very little in the Spiritual Life. When the heart and the head are equally developed and balanced, man's progress on the path is more rapid.

Many young persons today think that they are wise when they are only proud, and clever when they are only self-conscious.

Whereas atheism is generally born of intellectual vanity, agnosticism is often the outcome of intellectual humility. Humble, honest agnosticism will eventually be converted into a firm conviction of the Reality of God.

Mind

He who gets control over the mind gets everything under control.

The existence of almost all persons is under the control of the mind, but scarcely one out of every ten thousand persons controls the mind, and thus masters the very existence itself.

Happiness and misery, virtue and vice, pleasure and pain, heaven and hell, birth and death, are the creations of the mind and depend on the mind.

He who has completely brought his mind under control is a true yogi.*

It is the mind that makes us slaves to worldly desires. The mind also can enable us to become the masters of destiny and to realize the Supreme *Self.*

It is only in the super-conscious state that the mind is conscious of the Real *Self.*

Maya or Illusion†

A human being comprises Godhead plus Maya. When man liberates himself from the chains of Maya completely, he is sure to realize his original pure Godhead.

The chief props and agents of Maya are kama, krodh, and lobh (lust, anger, and greed). Unless and until you subjugate them it is impossible for you to enter upon the path that leads to union with God.

* A semi-advanced spiritual aspirant, one who practices a spiritual discipline.

† The world seems so real, all its phenomena so true that the average man simply cannot conceive of it as Maya. He knows the nothingness of the world only when he is in sound sleep. When he is in sound sleep, he knows not his family, wealth, profession, body, or mind; in short, he knows nothing. But when his sound sleep is disturbed, and he enters the dreaming state, he considers all his dreams real and true. He knows not that he is actually dreaming. Whatever he does and sees in dreams he considers real and true. But as soon as he wakes up he realizes the illusory nature of the phenomena he witnessed in dreams. In just the same way when one enters the divine realm, one realizes the nothingness of the world.

The body is but the outer covering of your soul. It is Maya that makes you identify yourself with the body and which makes you forgetful of your eternal, indivisible, resplendent Divinity.

Maya signifies ignorance. It is Maya that drives man to think of the universe and its charms as realities.

As a single object seems to multiply itself to him who is drunk to excess, so Unity appears as plurality to those who are intoxicated with the wine of egoism.

If worldly desires and anger take hold of your mind, then no matter how much you may practice tapa-japa[*92] and meditation, you are still entangled in the toils of Maya. Maya is the source of all worries, anxieties, and troubles.

Illusion is the basis of the juggler's tricks. Through Maya, the world, which is no more substantial than a mirage, appears to be real. Children admire the juggler and think that his tricks are realities, but adults know that he is a trickster and that his tricks are illusions. Ignorant men regard the world as the ultimate reality, but dnyanis[†] know that it is only illusion.

All those who experience the gross world as real are asleep. Only those who experience it as unreal can realize God and become awakened.

---

* Austerity and asceticism.

† Sages, possessors of spiritual knowledge.

Just as darkness becomes invisible in sunlight, so to those who are in the darkness of Maya, God, who is present in all places and at all times, is still invisible.

As soon as the clouds of sanskaras* pass away we begin to see the Sun of God in His pristine glory.

Do not be angry with him who backbites you, but be pleased, for thereby he serves you by diminishing the load of your sanskaras; also pity him because he increases his own load of sanskaras.

In order to enter upon the divine path it is necessary to purify the mind, to abstain entirely from carnal pleasures or sense enjoyments, and to love truth. He is a real aspirant who escapes the snares of Maya, speaks the truth, holds by the truth, and seeks truth only.

"Cast not your pearls before swine." Materialistic people are like swine because they prefer the filth of the world to the pearl of liberation from the chain of births and deaths.

The Supreme Soul—Paramatman—God, is nowhere to be searched for. For He is very near you; He is with you. Seek Him within. You could easily see Him were it not for the four big "Devils" that stand in your way. They are Egoism, lust, anger, and greed.

* Sanskaras are impressions on the mind body of actions, desires, tendencies, thoughts bound up with our egoism; they may be good or bad, important or unimportant.

Notes.[93]—There are three bodies—mind body, subtle body, and physical body. (In the ordinary human being the spiritual body is not developed.) They are the vehicles by which the spirit, through the mind, experiences existence.

(1) *The Mind Body,* in which thoughts arise as the result of impressions from past experiences. These thoughts may remain latent as seeds; if they are expressed they take first the form of desires, and pass through (2) the *Subtle Body,* which is composed of the five psychic senses. They may rest there as dreams, or they may be further expressed through (3) the *Physical Body,* with its five physical senses.

Corresponding to the three bodies there are three states of consciousness: unconsciousness, sub-consciousness, and waking consciousness. (See page 135, note †)

The Mind Sphere comprises the fifth and sixth planes; the Subtle Sphere comprises the first, second, third, and fourth planes.

The seven planes of consciousness are: (1) Intellect; (2) Lower Inspiration; (3) Intuition; (4) Insight, or the fourth plane, which tempts the aspirant with its supernatural powers from drawing nearer to God; (5) Higher Inspiration, or the fifth plane, where the aspirant "feels the Infinite"; (6) Illumination, the sixth plane, where the aspirant "sees God in everything" (still dualism); (7) the seventh plane, where there is no longer dualism and man becomes "One with God"—this is the state of Christ Consciousness, and of *The Perfect Master.*

V
THE SPIRITUAL PLANES
THE MIND AND SUBTLE SPHERES

YOU HAVE WITHIN YOUR SELF—the Paramatman—the planes, the planets, and the entire universe, but you do not know it. They are within you, but you do not see them there, because you see only *without* and not the Real *Self within.*

Three curtains—the gross, the subtle, and the mind—intervene between man and the Real Truth or Paramatman. When you remove the subtle curtain you act through the mind alone; when you are free of the mind curtain you become One with the Paramatman.

The difference between Antar-Drashti, Spiritual *Insight,* and Atman-Drashti, Spiritual *Sight,* is great indeed. The former means seeing the subtle universe, but Spiritual *Sight* means seeing God and seeing Him everywhere.

With the gross eye gross things are seen; with the subtle or internal eye the subtle world and the planes are seen; and with the spiritual eye God is seen.

The Jivatman, the individual or unrealized soul, is in the bindings of the mind, the subtle, and the gross bodies. Its bindings are both of the mind and of the body. But when the Jivatman crosses these bindings and becomes Shivatman, the realized soul, *One with God,* there are no desires left.

It is only when you rise above the Mind sphere that you can realize the nothingness of the gross world. Those who say that God is real and that the world is also real are ignorant. It is because they have very hazy notions about the divine realm that they say that the world is real.

In the ordinary sense of the word it is correct to call very fine substances, such as ether, atoms, vibrations, light, and space, subtle. They are unquestionably matter, though in a very fine form. In talking of spiritual concerns, *subtle* means something completely contrary to material or physical, however fine or attenuated these gross things may be.

Although the gross sphere is the outcome of the subtle sphere and is dependent upon it, the subtle sphere is completely independent of the gross or physical world.

Spirit communication is the experience of the semi-subtle[*] by the physical senses in the conscious state. It is not a sign of advancement on the divine path and has nothing to do with its goal (Gnosis).

Semi-advanced spiritual aspirants, Yogis, see Truth through multi-coloured glasses; Sadgurus or Perfect Masters need no glasses at all because they are Truth-incarnate.

---

[*] The ante-room of heaven, hell, and rebirth.

The superhuman powers which Yogis* seem to possess are not really their own; they are borrowed by them from the Sadgurus, whose powers are their own. To exercise these gifts the Yogis have to make tremendous efforts, but Sadgurus exercise them automatically, whenever the need arises.

Miracles, whether performed by Perfect Masters or by Yogis, are mere illusions in comparison with the everlasting truth, and are not more real than the shadows of this world.

Miracles† performed by Yogis are essentially selfish, as they are invariably based on personal (egotistic) motives; whereas the miracles‡ of Sadgurus or Perfect Masters are absolutely selfless, as they are based on the principle of giving a spiritual push to humanity.[94]

Just as the unreality of a dream is only appreciated on waking from sleep, so to experience the gross creation with all its apparent realities and tangibilities as a mere vacant dream, one has to be fully conscious of the subtle and mind spheres.

* The fourth plane is also called the Yogic Plane, because those that reach it can perform wonders. It is a snare. Yogis should not be confounded with true Saints.

† Karamats.

‡ Mojezas.

When a person is in Yoga Samadhi his mind is temporarily dead but his intellect and egoism are there just the same, and no sooner does the state of Samadhi pass than his egoism begins to work. Nirvikalpa Samadhi is higher than, and quite different from the Yoga Samadhi. Before a person can expect to enjoy Nirvikalpa Samadhi his intellect and egoism must disappear in order to make room for Dnyan or Real Spiritual Knowledge.*

Proverbs

(Twelve Miscellaneous Sayings)

To be virtuous out of vanity is little better than to be virtuous out of perversity.

He is indeed a brave man who in time of adversity feels the happiness of prosperity, and who, though oppressed on all sides, remains calm and balanced.

As a tree is judged not by the size but by the quality of its fruits, so a man's worth should be judged not by his talents but by the use he makes of them.

Mere description of a medicine will not cure you of any disease, nor will mere hearing about saints make you saintly. To be cured you must take medicine, and to become saintly you must practice virtue.

* (1) Samadhi, absorption, contemplation, or Mind merged in complete stillness.
(2) Unconscious Samadhi as in normal sound sleep.
(3) Yoga Samadhi brought about by Yogis through concentration or pranayam.
(4) Nirvikalpa Samadhi is a state of perfect forgetfulness, and realization of Truth, enjoyed by One who is on the Seventh Plane.

The virtue that is the outcome of vanity is not real virtue; the valour that is prompted by desperation is not real courage.

What food is to the body, the body, to some extent, is to the soul. When food is thrown off in the form of refuse you do not lament, neither should you mourn when the body is given up at death.

Nature never has been, never will be, and never is at war with man. It seems as if she is at war with man because he violates her laws. No individual and no nation can break her laws with impunity.

Humanity should be considered the greatest test of civilization. He who is devoid of humanity should be considered a barbarian. Though a man may be very learned, very up to date in the worldly routine of life, and advanced in scientific knowledge, yet, if he lacks humanity he is still a barbarian.

Make use, when necessary, of modern civilization, but do not let it dominate you. Neither despise it nor be repelled by it.

India became depressed with the establishment of the depressed classes. When the depressed classes are raised up, India will find herself to be one of the greatest countries, if not the greatest, in the world.

Do not mistake verbosity for wisdom. A great flow of words is not necessarily an indication of great intelligence.

Who would set a fine jewel in lead? Who would shoot a butterfly with a rifle? Who would exchange a cuckoo for a crow? Every worldly minded person does such actions every day of his God-forsaken life.

VI
THE PERFECT MASTER OR SADGURU

ONE'S GURU MUST BE SPIRITUALLY MORE ADVANCED than oneself—better if he is spiritually perfect. If you are in bonds and wish to be free, to whom should you go? Certainly to one who is quite free, and not to one whose hands are tied. Similarly, if a person wishes that Maya should no longer bewitch him, he must go to One for whom Maya does not exist and who has completely subjugated his passions.

God-realized personages, whether conscious[*] or unconscious[†] of the gross world, are above sanskaras, and so they have no egoism whatsoever. The cause of egoism is sanskaras, whether good or bad. Egoism disappears forever when all sanskaras are wiped out. In short, no sanskaras, no egoism.

The grace of a God-realized master works wonders, but one must extort this grace from him.

You surrender your head to a barber, when you want to get your hair cut, till the work is done; similarly you must surrender yourself to a Sadguru if you want God-realization.

---

* Sadgurus, Kutubs, or Perfect Masters.

† Majzoobs.

If the mind is regarded as a hand and the body as a spoon, the difference between the Shivatman or God-realized person and the Jivatman or unrealized person is this—the former eats only with the aid of the "spoon" or body, the latter eats with the hand or mind as well as with the spoon or body.

God-consciousness means to be mentally, emotionally, and spiritually conscious of the One *Self* at all times and in all places. The God-conscious man radiates spirituality even as a cheerful man radiates joy. And He can impart spirituality even as a wealthy philanthropist parts with money to help others.

Even as copper is glossed by tamarind, so a wicked man can be polished by a true saint. But even as tamarind cannot make copper glossy without friction, so a saint can do nothing for a wicked man unless he comes in contact with him.

To be in "sat-sang" means not merely to keep company with a Sadguru, but to follow him and carry out his orders cheerfully and lovingly.

Never hesitate to show the recesses of your heart to one whom you consider to be your spiritual master.

He who loves his spiritual master for the sake of love, ever intent on giving it and never desirous of receiving it, is a true lover.

Maya is too powerful to allow your mind to be attracted by anything else. But with the grace of a real saint or a Perfect Master you can turn your eyes away from it and towards Paramatman.

The average person's stock of sanskaras may be appropriately compared to an Augean stable, which is impossible for him to cleanse. But just as Hercules cleans the stable of Augeas by turning the river Alpheus through it, so a Sadguru can destroy the sanskaras of any person with the fire of his spirituality.

Truth or Sat uses Maya neither for carrying on the world nor for making others free from Maya. The Creator, Ishwar, uses Maya for carrying on the world, but the Sadguru uses Maya to make others free from Maya.

What does it mean to be super-conscious? It means to be fully conscious of unconsciousness, that is, to be conscious of nothing but the Divine *Self.*

Do nothing even to please Me,* or the world, against the dictates of your own conscience. Unhesitatingly do what you think to be right and proper, despite the opposition of the world. Let your mind be as firm as a rock that resists strong blasts of wind from all sides.

---

* The Perfect Master has annihilated *self,* and is One with The *Self.*

No matter what vicious qualities you may be possessed of, you should neither hesitate to come, nor feel any shame in coming before Me.* I am for all. The wicked have as much right to approach Me as the virtuous. Indeed, my main concern is to improve the vicious.

* See Note on Shivatman, page 151.

VII
GOD

GOD IS TO BE LOVED and not feared. As a matter of fact nobody fears God. What many fear is hell or some punishment which they expect to undergo for their sins, just as schoolboys fear the cane and not the teacher himself.

Although the one sun, God, who is without a second, shines at all times without a moment's break on all forms, animate as well as inanimate, you are unable to see Him even for a moment, because you are imprisoned in a cell of ignorance coated with desires.

It is one and the same Universal Being, God, who plays the different roles of stone, metal, vegetable, dumb animal, and human being, and, through the existence of each of these, experiences His own gross and subtle manifestations. It is the same indivisible Being who through the existence of a realized or spiritually perfect person experiences His own Real State which is beyond the gross and subtle planes.[95]

Do not be afraid of the *Self*. You do not only possess but actually are Soul, which is but one with Paramatman. If you fear the *Self*, you become aloof and separated from God.

If you look at distant objects through binoculars they seem to be brought nearer; if you reverse the binoculars the objects seem to be removed farther away. God seems far off because we look with the gross eyes which are but the outer lenses; the real eye is within.

Pain and evil are only real in the sense in which dreams are real. Considered absolutely, only God is real; all other things, including pain and evil, are unreal. Pain and pleasure, good and evil, are all relative and illustrate the law of polarity (the law of opposites).

To see God means to cease seeing everything except God.

Just as your shadow is not separate from you, so God is not outside of you, but is within you; and just as you cannot grasp at your shadow, so you cannot take hold of God in an ordinary way. Only a few out of millions realize God.

God is one, not in the numerical sense, but He is the One that remains for ever One, without a second. He was always infinite, is infinite, and always will remain infinite.

Paramatman does not know that He is Paramatman and is unconsciously experiencing and sustaining infinite powers. Paramatman is fully conscious in the Shivatman state.

Man is in the "had"* state; to become "an-had"† the "bi-had"‡ state must be realized. Paramatman is in the "bi-had" state.

God is one, is everything, and alone is real; whereas the Universe is full of the Many, is the outcome of nothing, is under the influence of Maya and, consequently, unreal. As long as the Many are seen, the One cannot be seen. For the One to be seen the Many must go. The One God is seen when the phantom of the Universe disappears; and the Universe ceases to exist for him whose lower self is annihilated.

Note[96]

There is nothing but God.—

Only three things are of Real Worth: God, Love, and the Perfect Master. These three are almost one and the same.

It is the same One Paramatman or Supreme Soul who is playing the different parts of The Almighty, The Creator (Ishwar), Shivatman, and Jivatman.

The Almighty, The Supreme Soul, God, is beyond even the super-conscious state. He is infinite; He is the shoreless ocean of Truth. As Ishwar, He is the creator, preserver, and destroyer of the Universe.

The individual, or ordinary consciousness that has not *realized* God is finite and limited.

The Shivatman—or God-realized man—knows Himself as the Almighty, the One Infinite Ocean of Truth; He has attained the Christ-conscious state. Shivatman is the Sadguru or Perfect Master. He knows that He is in every man (Jivatman) and that every Jivatman is in Him. The Perfect Master is Love, Lover, and the Beloved.

---

* Limited.

† Beyond limits.

‡ Without limits.

Glossary

Antar-Drashti	=	*Spiritual Insight,* high inspiration, or the ability to see the Subtle Sphere.
Astral Body	=	Subtle or Desire Body.
Atman-Drashti	=	*Spiritual Sight,* high revelation, means seeing God and seeing Him everywhere.
Bhakti	=	Worship or devotion.
Bhakti Yoga	=	The practice of Devotion.
Dnyanis	=	Sages, those who possess spiritual knowledge.
Gnosis	=	Knowledge, see Tarikat.
Intellect	=	Thought power, anddhai.[97]
Ishwar°	=	The Creator, Khalik.
Jivatman	=	Individual Soul, Makhlook, man who has not yet *realized* God.
Kama	=	Lust, passion, desire.
Karma	=	Service. (Cause and effect.)
Krodh	=	Anger.
Lobh	=	Greed.
Majzoob	=	One who has reached the seventh plane, but who, unlike the Sadguru or Kutub, has not retained gross and subtle consciousness. (See pages 120 and 145)
Mantra	=	A sacred verse or formula, a prayer written in a rhythmical form. A Bhantra is the chanting aloud of a Mantra.
Maya	=	*Not that,* It *is* but is an illusion. Compared with the reality of God the Universe is unreal (see Section IV).

Mind	=	Mun (see Section IV).
Mind Sphere	=	The fifth and sixth planes are within the Mind Sphere (see Section IV, final note). (The seventh plane is beyond the Mind and Subtle spheres.)
Paramatman	=	God, the supreme Soul (see page 151).
Sadguru	=	A Perfect Master, Kutub, Acharya—one who has attained to the Christ Conscious State (see Majzoob).
Samadhi	=	Mind merged in complete stillness (see page 142).
Sanskaras	=	A'mal, impressions on the Mind body (see page 137).
Sanyas	=	Renunciation, Tyaga.
Sanyasin	=	A spiritual pilgrim, one who practices renunciation.
Shivatman	=	God-man, Perfect Master, Sadguru, Kutub, Acharya, One who has *realized* God.
Soul		(a) The Soul is the infinite Self and is infinite in its individuality. It exists independently of nature and matter.
Spirit		(b) The soul, when experiencing the subtle and gross worlds through the mind, subtle, and physical bodies, has an illusion of limitation and is called the Spirit. Though of the same essence as the Soul, it differs in that is it attached to the body, the world, and the affairs of the world. It is unconscious of the infinite Self, and owing to its delusion of being limited appears to be finite. Until "Realization" the spirit has to reincarnate.
Subtle Sphere	=	The first four planes of consciousness (see end of Section IV) are within the Subtle Sphere.
Tarikat	=	Gnosis, spiritual or esoteric knowledge, Adyatman Marga.
-Yoga	=	A spiritual discipline.
-Yogi	=	A semi-advanced spiritual aspirant.

Hollywood, May–June 1932

PART FIVE

How It All Happened: Notes for a Film

Indian Mystic Plans to View 'Grand Hotel'

One of the Southland's most colorful visitors in some time, Shri Meher Baba, Indian mystic who has not spoken for several years, will be the guest of honor at the Chinese Theater Thursday evening, when he will witness "Grand Hotel" and the Sid Grauman prologue.

Meher Baba, who is declared to be spiritual adviser to Mahatma Gandhi, has announced that he will break his long self-imposed silence over a national broadcast from Hollywood on the 13th inst.

The attendance of the mystic at the Chinese will be one of his few personal appearances during his sojourn in Southern California.

"Grand Hotel" features Greta Garbo, John Barrymore, Joan Crawford, Wallace Beery and Lionel Barrymore.

A new definition of Hollywood was given this week when Shri Meher Baba, Indian mystic who hasn't spoken for seven years, visited Tallulah Bankhead at Paramount. When the star asked him why he had chosen Hollywood at which to break his silence July 13, Shri Baba spelled on his alphabet board: "Because of the equal balance which exists here between the spiritual and the material forces."

During 1934–35 Baba turned his attention to the medium of motion pictures. In preparation for meetings with representatives of the Hollywood film world, Baba and his mandali created a variety of literary and artistic materials to be used in *How It All Happened,* a film conveying Baba's cosmology and the story of the soul's journey.

At Paramount movie studio with Adi Jr., Quentin Tod, Beheram,
Tallulah Bankhead, Chanji and Kaka.
Hollywood, May–June 1932

INTRODUCTION TO PART FIVE

Though Meher Baba's work in the domain of film came to a head in 1934–35, its seeds were sown during his first trip to America in 1931. While staying in Harmon, at the behest of his hostess Margaret Mayo, on December 3, 1931, Baba dictated a story of three individuals, X, Y, and Z, over five lifetimes, through the course of which they progress from utter barbarism and cannibalism to the heights of spiritual realization. Dramatizing reincarnation and spiritual advancement as stages in the soul's journey, the X-Y-Z narrative held its place at the core and center of Baba's undertakings in the domain of film during the next four years.

During 1932 and 1933 Meher Baba made many further contacts in the world of motion pictures; and by the beginning of 1934 work in the film medium had emerged as his major focus. In late May, Baba with several of his mandali prepared a body of material—narrative, metaphysical, scientific, and artistic—to be incorporated into a film that would dramatize what Baba later called the "Divine Theme." That is, the film would depict the original creation of the universe out of the Ocean of God's Infinite Light; the evolution of form and consciousness from ether and atom to the advanced ape; the cycle of reincarnation in human form; spiritual advancement through the planes of consciousness; and the fulfillment of the Goal of creation in the soul's Realization of God. The stages of creation and evolution were explained through material that Baba dictated and that his mandali gleaned from scientific textbooks. Reincarnation and spiritual advancement were to be illustrated through the X-Y-Z narrative.

The materials from this period preserved in the Archives of the Avatar Meher Baba Trust are essentially notes for a film—literary and artistic sketches, as it were, to be used in presenting the film concept to representatives of the motion picture industry. The surviving textual documents take the form of rough drafts; and none of them presents a scenario of How It All Happened *in its developed entirety. Moreover, while some of this material clearly records points of Meher Baba's own dictation, other content represents extracts from the evolutionary and physical sciences of the 1930s. We would misconstrue the nature of this material, then, if we took it simply to be another compilation of "Meher Baba's words." It is better understood as an assemblage of pointers and gleams and promptings that were to be used and consummated through the combined efforts of a team of writers, visual artists, scientists, philosophers, mystics, actors, film technicians, and producers in a major motion picture.*

In fact, Baba paid two visits to the West, one to Europe in June–July 1934, and one to Hollywood in December–January of 1934–35, in an effort to translate How It All Happened *from a concept into an actualized film. The meetings and plans and undertakings of the period proved to be inconclusive, however. Though Baba continued to encourage efforts among his followers and disciples over the next few years, no film eventuated. All that descends to us today is a residue of documents in the Trust Archives.*

The text that we have assembled here under the title How It All

Happened *brings together passages from three principal documents in the vision and sequence that Baba clearly had in mind. The sequence of elements is indeed spelled out in the first page of a document entitled "Scenario," reproduced on pp. 191–92. Since the original prose is rough, it has been edited here in the interests of readability. The story of X-Y-Z, that constitutes the second movement of* How It All Happened, *reproduces the edited text that Filis Frederick published in the* Awakener, *vol. 22, no. 1 (1986), pp. 1–4 under the title "'A Touch of Maya': A Scenario by Meher Baba." Yet though* How It All Happened *has been prepared editorially for presentation in this book, readers can be assured that all of its content is directly based on the prose of original documents. Nothing of substance has been added and nothing deleted, except passages that are essentially digests of information from scientific reference sources. (Those who would like to read these excised passages will find them, in their complete raw form, in appendix 8).*

We have also reproduced, in "Other Notes and Dictations," a selection of other materials of interest in the Trust Archives. For further description of these original documents, see pp. 250–55 and 274–76. Part five concludes with reproduction of assorted visual materials from the Trust Archives. Outstanding among them is what we are calling the Film Master Chart, an enormous diagram (or pair of diagrams) that Adi Sr. prepared under Baba's instructions. Intended as an aid to the screenwriters, the chart is a global representation of the Divine Theme explicitly linked to the written content of How It All Happened. *The archival collection also includes a pair of drawings of exotic creatures, illustrations clipped out from a scientific manual, sample pages of documents, and other selections from the body of materials Baba had compiled for this film work.*

This is the only section of this book collecting material that never found its way to publication during the phase of Meher Baba's early Western tours in the 1930s. This particular assemblage is being published here for the first time. One presumes that the grand cosmological vision of How It All Happened, *left uncompleted during Meher Baba's own lifetime, will one day flower into full expression in the world of cinema, perhaps as a single master film, or perhaps as a line and tradition of movies, exploring, through the talents of creative artists in generations to come, this great legacy that the Avatar bequeathed to humanity.*

How It All Happened

INTRODUCTION

PRELIMINARY COMMENTS

This film will command world-wide appeal. It depicts four phases in the spiritual journey: (1) creation; (2) evolution; (3) reincarnation; and (4) spiritual advancement.

From the film's treatment of creation, astronomers will learn something new. Up till now, their knowledge and discoveries have extended only so far as the nebula.[98] But where did the nebula come from? This, as well as the source and beginning of creation itself, will be explained in the picture.

The film's treatment of evolution will interest and prove useful to scientists. Organic evolution is explained, so far as possible, in terms and a manner familiar to Western scientists, because terms and treatments foreign to them would only confuse matters. These notes do provide some original explanations, however. The beginning of life even before the amoeba is explained through reference to *bhanchua,*[99] about which scientists know nothing. Also, these notes describe the *subtle gases* created prior to the first appearance of protons and electrons.

The film will show three previously unknown species of creatures, which will throw open a window of fresh light for scientists. One of these species is half fish and half reptile; the second is half bird and half bat; and the third is the so-called "missing link" between the advanced apes and man.

The part of the film concerned with reincarnation will give new hope to the depressed and suffering people of today, because it will help them to understand that this present life, weighed down with unhappiness, does not give the whole picture. Life seen in its totality consists of a series of innumerable lifetimes spent gathering experiences of good and bad, happiness and misery—experiences which ultimately lead to Bliss.

The explanation of "spiritual advancement," a phase which subdivides into seven planes or stages, will appeal to, and provide food for, mystics, occultists, seekers of Truth, and spiritually minded people in general.

Finally, the stories of three characters passing through five lifetimes will thrill and stir the emotions of the sensation-loving masses of humanity.

Overall, the world will glean some idea of how, through these phases of creation, organic evolution, reincarnation and Realization, the gradual advancement of the soul and the development of its consciousness take place.

One of the special features of the film will be the spirit dance, which occurs on one of the planes of consciousness. This will fascinate the film's viewers.

The first and fourth phases of the journey, that is, creation and the spiritual advancement, will have to be shown through trick photography. Evolution will be depicted through animated drawings and cartoons.

A detailed chart illustrating and explaining evolution has already been prepared.[100] We may choose to follow it closely, tracing the course of evolution in detail. Or then again, we may prefer to show only the main species on the principal stem of evolution: that is, a single figure representing one particular species evolves into a figure representing the next main species, and so on. (This effect can be achieved by an animated figure that represents one species dissolving into a figure representing the next main species in the order of evolution, and so forth.)

The transformation of the physical forms between the first four lifetimes (in the story dramatizing reincarnation) is to be shown thus.

When a person dies (i.e., when the gross body falls off), the subtle body still attached to the person lingers in the spirit world for three days. Thereafter, the mental body enjoys or suffers in the spirit world, according to the impressions it has gathered during the lifetime of the person who has physically passed away. After a time, according to the imprint of the spent-out impressions of the mental body, a new subtle body is created, exactly similar to the gross body in which the soul subsequently reincarnates.[101]

I think it would be best to begin with the last life in the story, that is, the lifetime in which the soul of X gains God-realization. From that state he can then look back and "see" creation, evolution, the previous four lifetimes, and the multifarious experiences (of reincarnation, progress through the planes, and so forth) that he has gone through.

Of course, the three souls in the story passed through innumerable lifetimes besides these principal five. Only the last two are consecutive; otherwise, the souls incarnated many times between each of their first four lives. From the fourth lifetime, however, the soul progressed directly to the fifth, without any intermediate incarnation.

THE THREE TRACKS

"The evolution of the soul" really means the evolution of the soul's consciousness, through the course of which the soul itself remains unmodified. The soul itself does not evolve; it is consciousness that evolves. The purpose of the evolution of body or form is to facilitate the evolution of consciousness; body or form cannot evolve independently of consciousness. Now it is still to be seen how forms evolve. Because consciousness must evolve for the achievement of union with the Divine, forms must evolve also.

In overview, the entire cycle of evolution, which begins when consciousness emanates from God and concludes when it merges into God again, is divided into three distinct parts or sections, as illustrated in the diagram on the following page.

> The first part can be called the Descending Track, which commences with the original emergence from God and ends with the creation of the first human form. The Descending Track comprises all the different evolutionary stages of form and consciousness, which, as explained, run parallel to one another.

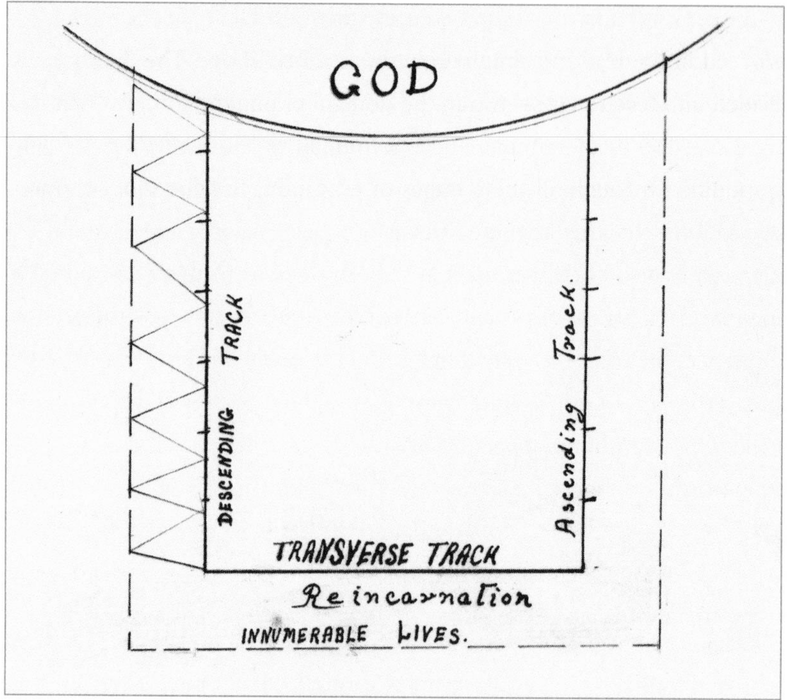

Diagram 1: Original drawing illustrating the three tracks in the soul's journey.

The second part, or the Transverse Track of the evolutionary cycle, begins when consciousness achieves the first human form and ends when it gains admission into the Divine Path. The Transverse Track comprises the rounds of births and deaths, that is, the innumerable human incarnations in the course of reincarnation.

The third part is represented by the Ascending Track through the planes of consciousness, which begins with entry into the first plane and concludes with attainment of the seventh, which is the plane of God-realization.

Now let us see how evolution manifests on the passage down this first track, which is the Descending Track.

The evolution of consciousness and the evolution of forms and bodies proceed in tandem and simultaneously, as noted above. The first track is divided into seven stages—two in the domain of mineral forms, two in the vegetable, two in the animal, and one human.[102] The soul itself remains unmodified through all these stages of evolution. But the soul contracts impressions through the medium of consciousness, and accumulates consciousness through the medium of body or form; that is, consciousness evolves, and form evolves alongside. With each new step in the evolution of consciousness and form, new impressions are created. These impressions, in turn, serve as means or stepping stones for the evolution of new consciousness and a new body. The consciousness and body thus created, in other words, are the result of newly gathered impressions, and these, in turn, give rise to yet another set of impressions. And so on and on it goes—consciousness and body breeding impressions, and impressions creating new consciousness and forms. They are interdependent. This process of evolution as described here stands good only to the human form, however. It can roughly be visualized as a zigzag course drawn in the Descending Track on the left hand side of the diagram.

The second part of the journey of evolution, depicted in the diagram as the Transverse Track, consists of a series of innumerable *human* incarnations in the cycle of reincarnation.

The third and final part, called the Ascending Track, consists of seven planes, that is, the seven internal spheres of high and higher experience, culminating in the state of ultimate Union with God.

The story written by Baba, which plots its course across five different lifetimes in the career of three souls, illustrates the second and third parts—that is, the Transverse and Ascending Tracks—in the evolutionary journey.

LIGHT AND DARKNESS

God is the real, Infinite Light, and the infinite, subtle gas is real, Infinite Darkness.[103]

The nebula, which is created by the compact of Space and Energy[104] and subtle gas, is false light. The indescribably huge and innumerable pieces into which the nebula breaks up are so dazzlingly bright that each of them surpasses the light of billions of suns put together. But they are not hot.

Each piece of the nebula is so dazzlingly brilliant that it equals the light of ten crores[105] of suns combined, and its size equals that of a thousand millions of suns. And there are millions and billions of such pieces of nebula, all originating from the tiniest Creation Point!

To sum up: God is the Real Infinite Light; the infinite subtle gas is the Infinite Real Darkness; the nebula is false light; the sparks or heavenly bodies are the shadows of the false light; and our world is false darkness.

First Movement. The Descending Track of Creation and Evolution

Chapter I. Creation

God Infinite	=	Existence
	=	Intelligence
	=	Light
	=	Bliss

God is an Indivisible Entity without limit,
without beginning, without end.

Show a calm, still, Shoreless Ocean of most dazzling light. Limitless, it has no space above it.

God in this state is infinitely unconscious. Suddenly the Infinite Existence of this Shoreless Ocean moved, and simultaneously with the movement there appeared the Creation Point (or the Cosmos Point, or the Point of Universal Mind). From this Point bulged out Infinite Space and Energy. Note that this Space and this Energy are quite distinct from and unlike the dynamic or static energy of Western science. Rather, they fall under, and are encompassed in, the subtle sphere, and as such are entirely imperceptible and incomprehensible by the physical senses.

This original Space was infinite and *hollow,* while the original Energy was infinite and *latent.* They were set apart from each other by the movement of the Point which caused their projection out of the Limitless Ocean. With this same movement of the Point, Space and Energy clashed; and the flash of this clash produced what can only be described as a subtle, infinite gas. This gas impacted with the infinite hollow Space and the infinite latent

Energy, creating a thin, misty, cloud-like substance called *nebula.* This nebula, though exceedingly fine, was nonetheless a substance that falls in the category of the gross, and it belongs to the gross sphere. Nebula was the primordial gas evolved. Although limited, it was vast and thin, and as such, could not be grasped by or made perceptible to the human senses.

The evolution of the universe starts from the nebula.

When movement stirred in the nebula, it condensed and broke into pieces. These pieces were of uneven dimensions and not necessarily round. Some of the pieces clashed with each other, producing millions of round, extremely hot and rotating sparks or heavenly bodies. These sparks or heavenly bodies, again, are nothing but the gas of nebula in heated form. They are huge, weighing hundreds of thousands of millions of tons. In short, this process has resulted in billions of huge, immensely hot, round globes of gas, all spinning at a tremendous speed.

Once again, these sparks clashed among themselves, creating millions of suns. These suns, in turn, clashing with the original sparks, produced other round, hot bodies, one of which is our Earth. At this point in the creation story, everything is exceedingly hot.

Through all these early evolutionary stages, from the appearance of the original infinite Space to the emergence of our world, infinite God is always present, with a most limited and most finite consciousness.

These early developments in the creation of the universe are illustrated in diagram 2 on the right.

There follow two pages devoted to a brief characterization of the Earth's solar system. The text names the nine planets, describes their axial revolutions and orbits around the sun, and gives the sizes, distances from the sun and each other, and other interesting facts about certain planets (especially the Earth, Jupiter, and Saturn). The discussion is followed by a diagram depicting the solar system as a series of concentric rings, representing planetary orbits, around the sun; the planets themselves are indicated, along with the rings and moons (if any) associated with each.

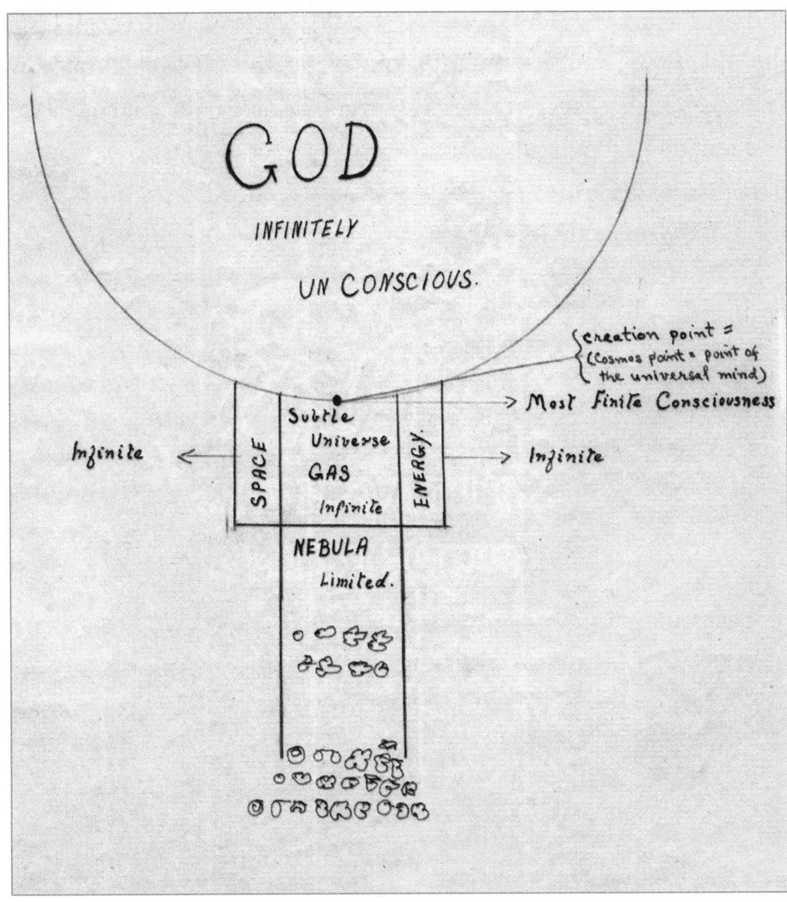

Diagram 2. An original figure illustrating the earliest stages of creation. For a related artistic rendering, see the Film Master Chart (p. 194).

The complete text that we have deleted here is reproduced in appendix 8, pp. 355–57. Our story resumes with an account of the formation of the earth, as follows.

It took millions of years for the Earth to cool down. As the gas slowly cooled, it shrank into a solid mass at the planet's outer edge, thus forming the Earth's crust as shown in diagram on the following page. Below the crust, the gas began to solidify into huge mountains and rocks. These rose and fell in uneven ridges, leaving deep gaps and fissures between. Since the earth all the while had been cooling, by this time the gas in the center was only somewhat hot. Slowly it condensed into water, which rushed up and around the rocks, filling the gaps and fissures created by the emerging mountain ridges. Thus the oceans were formed. This primal process brought the oceans into existence.

In short, we have seen the formation[106] of the Earth first in the solidification of its crust, then in its rocks and mountains, and finally in the appearance of its oceans. The diagram illustrates this process.

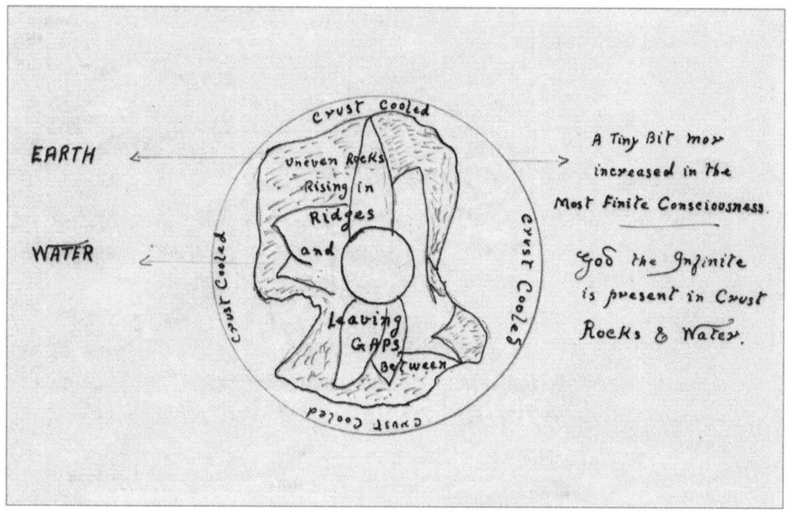

Diagram 3. An original figure illustrating the earth in its evolution. A similar detail appears in the Film Master Chart (p. 194).

Concurrent with the evolution of the Earth that we have been describing was the evolution of consciousness. Infinite God prevails throughout the crust, the rocks, the ocean, and the center of the Earth—indeed, throughout the entire universe—with the most finite consciousness evolving only slightly. This new consciousness, with its tiny bit of increase, did not differ much from the original finite consciousness, in that it remained unconscious even of the existence of the Earth itself—that is, its own form.

Chapter II. The Evolution of Atom, Stone, and Mineral

Subtle gas existed between Space and Energy, which, as we have seen, emerged from the Creation Point. This subtle gas is imperceptible to the human eye and undetectable by instruments. Yet between the subtle and the gross, gas has evolved in 276 stages—which again, since they are fundamentally subtle in nature, the eye cannot see nor instruments measure. These stages of gas evolved as the original, primary gas gradually became denser and denser, or as might more appropriately be said, less and less subtle, until this evolution culminated in the gross. The 277th stage, which is the first gross stage, could be represented by the particle called "ether." The 276 gaseous stages before ether, as we say, were subtle, and thus they elude perception even with the aid of scientific instruments.

Next in the order of gross substances comes the proton (278th overall). The electron (279) follows the proton. Ether, having density, can be classified in the gross sphere. Protons and electrons have weight, so they too can be classified among the gross particles. But the atom (280) is entirely in the domain of gross matter.

The atom is succeeded by the stone form and then the mineral. The evolutionary order progresses from hydrogen to helium, lithium, oxygen, iron, zinc, silver, tin, platinum, gold, mercury, radium, and uranium.

We think it better to explain the different stages in the evolution of consciousness by following a particular individual case. This would be more practical for our purposes; the major stages in evolution could thus be more effectively shown. Accordingly, we focus on the soul—who is no one other than God, since soul is a drop in the Divine Ocean. The soul has been ever present throughout all the different forms of evolution enumerated in this chapter. Through the course of these different stages, the consciousness of the soul has grown by tiny bits, by increments so infinitesimally small that, to outward appearances, no consciousness has evolved at all! In minerals, the consciousness is as finite as the mineral is dense. In mineral form, the soul is absolutely unconscious of its form and surroundings.

CHAPTER III.
THE EVOLUTION OF VEGETATION

Millions of years have elapsed since the first form of water vegetation evolved into existence. Back when the water in the seas was still warm, it gave rise to the first vegetative form, which resembled the soft, green, slippery sea weed that is called "leel"[107] in the vernacular.

This leel-like substance was produced through the combined action of water with its varied properties, the warm temperatures that still prevailed then, and wind blowing across the water's surface. Pervading throughout the vast volumes of water, this leel is imperceptible to the ordinary human eye or gross instrument, but can be discerned by the spiritual eye only. The process of its formation could be likened to the accumulation of rust on a piece of iron through the effect of moisture. The primal leel so formed could be called the "rust" of water.

After this first vegetative form, there followed sea weeds proper. It happened like this. The original, primary, greeny substance continued and extended itself from the surface of the ocean right down to the sea bed. Coming into contact with the bottom of the sea with its terrestrial properties, through a natural process it acquired the provision of growth. Sea weeds are the result. The vegetable kingdom begins from the time when sea weeds came into existence.

We shall now see how these sea weeds gradually transformed into land vegetation. The ebb and tide of the oceans were responsible for transferring the original leel onto the land. When the waters of the sea receded during the hours of ebb tide, the leel left ashore was laid bare and exposed to the sun. It took root on the land, developing into the first land-based plant resembling primal mushrooms. Thus from the original leel grew sea weeds, and from these sea weeds there sprang into being a vegetable kingdom such as we have at present.

The succession of plants in the order of evolution is as follows.

1. Leel
2. Sea weeds
3. Mushrooms
4. Grass
5. Neem trees
6. Spinach, etc. (i.e., edibles)
7. Alvi plants

From the very first vegetable form through all its successive various stages of development, the soul—Infinite God—was always and invariably present. The most finite original consciousness, which had developed to some tiny degree in the evolution of forms up to the mineral, enjoyed an additional slight progress in the vegetable kingdom. Consciousness here reached that stage where life and its movements have begun.

Chapter IV. The Evolution of Animals

The last vegetable forms (alvi plants) contain finite chaitanya,[108] finite consciousness, soul, and energy. They also contain life sparks—which are themselves made up of chaitanya, energy, and the gross essence of vegetables. These life sparks are so minute in their form that they are visible only to the eye of spiritual insight. If millions and billions of these sparks muster together, they would hardly form one-millionth part of a pin point. If thousands of such millionth parts were combined, they would collectively constitute the *very first gross form of life,* which is called "bhanchua." Bhanchua has special importance as the first manifestation of gross life from the subtle. Nonetheless, even though it has emerged into the gross sphere, bhanchua is hardly perceptible through scientific instruments.

There follow two pages of text that review the general course of evolution and name major phyla and individual species of particular interest. The discussion regularly refers to page numbers and figures from the reference source; a number of these figures and their accompanying text, clipped out from their source volume, are preserved among the papers in the Trust Archives. The exposition traces the evolution of vertebrates and invertebrates, varied species of fish, and amphibians. (The full text that we are summarizing here has been reproduced in appendix 8, pp. 357–60.)

At this juncture the account digresses from standard science to the description of an unusual species at the cusp between fish and reptile forms, as in the description below and illustration on the following page.

Prior to the evolutionary formation of reptiles proper, there emerged a weird, three-headed animal, half fish and half reptile. This species has its own distinct importance, since it shows how some of the reptiles evolved from the fishes directly, just as reptiles evolved from amphibians. Its length runs to **HALF BAT, HALF BIRD.** By this time, there appeared on earth this wonderful animal. It was a huge creature, fifteen feet high. It had two legs like an
ostrich's, each seven feet long; it had a neck two feet in circumference and four feet in length. Its beak, bent like

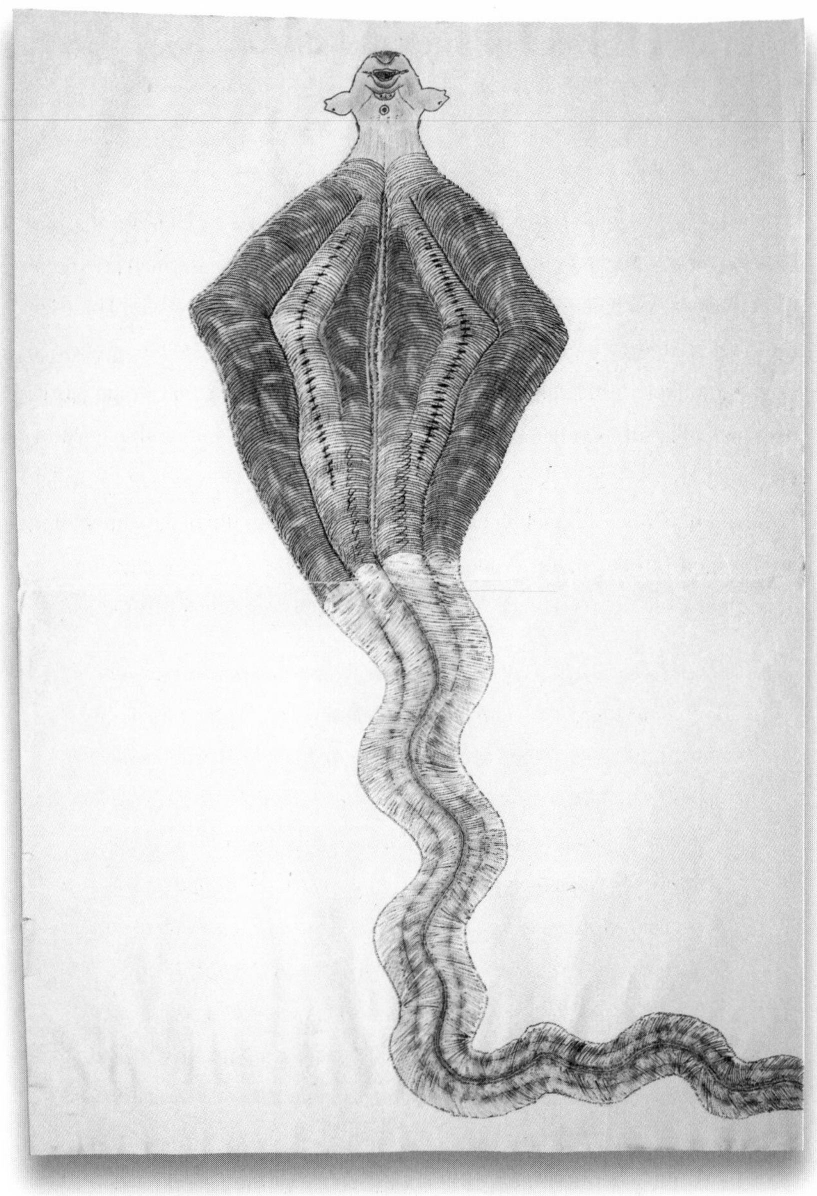

Two illustrations probably drawn by Baba's mandali in May 1934.
(ABOVE) A three-headed creature on the cusp between fish and reptile.
(RIGHT) Half bat and half bird, this strange creature stands fifteen feet tall.

175 feet. Its central head is six feet in circumference, and the two protruding heads on either side are one foot each in circumference. These side heads branch off from the central head. This strange animal is fourteen feet wide in the middle of its body, while its reptilian hind portion slowly tapers to a tail that is six feet in breadth and ten feet long. The three heads resemble that of a fish. The central head has jaws and teeth, but the other two have no teeth but holes connected with the gills of the central head. All three heads are provided with only a single windpipe, and they breathe together. Each head has a single, fish-like eye. It is very likely, therefore, that the third, pineal eye that is so prominent in the sphenedon[109] (ancestor of the reptile) first exhibited itself in this three-headed creature.

The exposition continues with a review of reptiles and various classifications and species of mammals. (For the complete original text, again see appendix 8, pp. 360–62.) At this juncture our account devotes special attention to another unusual form, shown below.

HALF BAT, HALF BIRD. By this time, there appeared on earth this wonderful animal. It was a huge creature, fifteen feet high. It had two legs like an ostrich's, each seven feet long; it had a neck two feet in circumference and four feet in length. Its beak, bent like that of a vulture, ran to a foot in length, broad but tapering down at the outer end. It could both walk and fly, but it ran much faster than it flew. It could attain a running speed of about 60 miles per hour.

The bat that we see today is the form that has evolved out of this half bat, half bird animal.

> *Now the review reverts to dinosaurs and other reptiles, certain birds, and primates (for the complete original text, see appendix 8, pp. 362–64). After enumerating some of the higher apes, the exposition comes to the emergence of man.*

The most wonderful fact is that, while scientists have failed until this point to formulate the correct idea about the missing link, and while the fossil record remains incomplete in this respect, the following description supplies the wanted information.

The missing link is similar to the gorilla, but it has a small tail like the tcheli's—and unlike those of other tailed apes. His gait of walking partly resembles the gorilla's and the tcheli's. His mouth is like that of a chimpanzee. In short, then, he has a tail like a tcheli's, a face like a chimpanzee's, a figure like the gorilla's, and a gait of walking that is half a gorilla's and half a tcheli's. Possibly fossils will be found in Java and Sumatra, or in the jungles of the Central Provinces of India.

THE BUSHMAN. The first primitive man who came to earth belongs to one of those ancient African tribes called the bushmen. His face resembled that of an ape, and his figure and gait that of a gorilla. He had no tail and walked erect.

THE CANNIBAL. Cannibalism was almost the first state in primitive man; but we can classify the cannibal nonetheless as the stage that followed the bushman.

And now we have reached the beginning of our story of the five lifetimes in the careers of X, Y, and Z.

Before continuing, we should say a further word about *consciousness.* It was the soul that gained sufficient consciousness in the vegetable forms to manifest the first stage of life and movement. That same soul went on to acquire more and more consciousness of the world and its surroundings in the animal forms, whose greater evolutionary chain is headed by the bhanchua and reaches its terminus with the first manifestation of the human form. As the gross form evolves, consciousness evolves with it proportionately, and thus the soul in human form gains full consciousness of the world and its surroundings. In short, through the course of organic evolution, the soul's consciousness of the universe went on increasing step by step alongside the evolution of gross bodies, until the process culminated in the human.

Even as its consciousness went on growing and progressing, the soul had to face another situation. Through its experience in the world of gross forms, the soul kept contracting impressions or *sanskaras.* These impressions were instrumental in creating new forms, which provided the mediums for the gathering of fresh impressions, and so on. Thus consciousness went on increasing while the bodies evolved and transformed.

SECOND MOVEMENT. THE TRANSVERSE AND ASCENDING TRACKS OF REINCARNATION AND SPIRITUAL ADVANCEMENT

"A TOUCH OF MAYA": A SCENARIO BY MEHER BABA[110]

First Life: CAST OF CHARACTERS

X: Cannibal man who wins the woman

Y: Cannibal woman

Z: Jealous cannibal man who is killed

Scenario: Cannibals are eating a corpse around a fire in the jungle. One man (X) catches the eye of a young woman (Y). They smile at one another, and he throws her a tasty bit of human flesh. She eats. Another man (Z) is jealous, and a fight ensues between the two men. X wins and kills Z.

Second Life: CAST OF CHARACTERS

Z: (The murdered cannibal becomes) The cruel king

X: (The lover of the cannibal woman becomes) A foreigner

Y: (The cannibal woman becomes) The cruel king's wife who pities X and asks her husband to spare him

Scenario: A great and cruel king (Z) is reigning in Turkey; he kills all foreigners who fall into his hands. X, a Persian, is captured by the king and is tortured in every way: he is bound to a tree and lashed; long pins are thrust down his finger nails; he is hanged upside-down while the soles of his feet are lashed; etc. The king's wife, Y, pities the Persian and asks her husband to forgive X for her sake. Z loves his wife greatly and forgives X, who then becomes a court favorite. Later Queen Y falls in love with the foreigner. The king discovers this and kills them both.

Third Life:	CAST OF CHARACTERS Y: (The queen killed by her husband becomes) An honest merchant in China Z: (The cruel king becomes) The merchant's son, a profligate X: (The foreigner and queen's lover becomes) The merchant's wife, who loves her son
Scenario:	Y, a merchant in China, and his wife, X, have three daughters and one son. They are millionaires and live lavishly. The merchant is very honest. His son Z is a corrupt rogue, interested only in drink and drugs; secretly, he uses his father's money for his own advantage. Z forges Y's check for a large amount, and Y comes to know about it. Instead of protecting his son, Y imprisons him. The merchant's wife, X, loves Z and sorrows deeply. Gradually she pines away. Soon Y, the merchant, becomes disgusted with the world, and he too dies. Z suffers much in prison, and after being freed, he leads a good life and repents, then eventually dies.
Fourth Life:	CAST OF CHARACTERS X: (The Chinese merchant's wife becomes) A reigning prince in India Y: (The Chinese merchant becomes) The prince's wife Z: (The rakish son becomes) The prince's spiritually minded slave
Scenario:	X is now a reigning prince in India, with Y as his wife. Z is his slave, who is very spiritually minded and who daily goes to sit at the feet of a great Yogi who sits under a tree in Benares. The prince and princess love each other dearly. One day, the slave loses his wife to death, but remains calm throughout it all. The prince wonders and asks him, "How can you be serene now?" Z replies, "My Master has made me

understand the secret of life and death." When he hears this, X longs to see the master, and the slave takes him. On seeing the master, the prince is deeply impressed and says "O Master, I surrender myself to you and will obey you implicitly." The master replies, "Leave all and come to me." Prince X renounces his kingdom and everything in it, dons the yellow robe, and goes with his wife Y to the master's retreat to await his order. The master orders X to beg from his own subjects, and the prince obeys. Next, the master orders X to wander through the jungle for one year. X and Y go together; they live on fruits and nuts and continually meditate on the master. One day, a tiger approaches them, but X merely looks at him and utters the master's name. Immediately the tiger is transformed into the master who blesses them and disappears. After the blessing, the prince enters a trance and passes through the following cosmic planes unto the fifth:

The prince in the **first plane** finds his gross body disconnected and set apart, and through his subtle body (which is exactly like the gross body in every detail, except that it is smoke-like, vapory and transparent) gets the subtle experience. Into his subtle ears are poured forth streams of sweet melodious, enchanting, thrilling and exquisite sound rhythms and beautiful tunes, the like of which he never had dreamt of; his subtle nose smells such a sweet, refreshing scent that he feels rejuvenated completely. His subtle eyes see different luminous ultra colors and innumerable small circles of steady light, with his master's figure looming large in the circles. He now finds his gross body attached to him and so comes to the gross consciousness. But the tremendous impressions of the subtle experiences had such an effect on him as to leave him in a dazed condition.

In the **second plane** the prince, as in the first plane, sees his gross body lying aloof, and gets more subtle experiences through his subtle body. He sees the innumerable, small circles of steady light becoming one, limitless mass of shattered light. He experiences his subtle body traversing through the shattered mass of light which he feels always near him and with him during his travel, and feels inexpressible thrills of ecstasy during this sojourn. At times, he finds his subtle body merged in light. He sees millions of spirits without a dense body—vapory, smoke-like, transparent forms—moving about very rapidly and making signs to each other. He then sees these spirits dancing. This dancing of the spirits is so weird, so wonderful, so fantastic that he is completely dumb-founded and enthralled. He now gets full knowledge from within of all that happens in the world. Through his subtle senses he now exists, and sees all the world affairs whenever he likes. From one corner of the world, he knows what is happening in the other corner of the world during the traversing of his subtle body.

Eventually he feels his gross body attached to him, and so comes down to the normal consciousness amongst other gross-minded people. But the deep impressions of the second plane have given him such powers as to be able to read the mind of anyone he likes if the person be near him.

In the **third plane** he again finds his gross body set apart, and his subtle body so engulfed in the shattered mass of light as to find it a piece of that light. His ecstasy is more intensified than it was in the second plane. He here sees millions of mental bodies of other advanced souls in the form of vapory seeds, and with his subtle body, tries to make signs to them and to understand their signs. He feels inexpressible thrills all through his subtle senses. Again, in time he finds his gross body attached to him and comes down to the gross consciousness. The supernatural impressions of the third plane have now given him such powers as to be able to perform miracles of healing with touch, or thought or sight, and of reading the mind of anyone irrespective of the distance, as also the minds of other souls on the subtle plane.

In the **fourth plane** the prince again finds his gross body dislinked, and sees with his subtle eyes the unlimited mass of shattered light as one whole undivided ocean of steady light. He finds his subtle body traversing on the surface of the ocean of light. He sees other innumerable subtle bodies of other souls and millions of mental bodies. He reads the minds of these subtle-bodied souls and also holds direct communication with the mental-bodied souls.[111] The ecstasy is now much, much more intensified. When his gross body reattached to him, he comes down to the level of other gross-conscious souls, but the super impressions of the fourth plane have now given him such supernatural powers as to enable him to raise the dead, give sight to the blind and also create other temporary gross forms.

In the **fifth plane** the prince finds both his gross and subtle bodies set aside and his mental (seed-like, vapory) body as the medium of his experiences. (In the four planes, he sets aside his gross body and experiences his subtle body traversing in the light, and in the fifth, he sets aside both his gross and subtle bodies, experiencing everything through his mental body.) He now finds his mental body traversing the ocean of light, and living on the same level as the mental plane spirits. He not only has direct communication with them, but also feels attached to and linked with them. The ecstasy is now immensely intensified, and he finds in his existence a regular flow of Divine happiness. Once again, he resumes both his gross and subtle bodies, and the lasting impressions of the fifth plane have given him such powers as to be able to know all the affairs and thoughts of the gross, subtle, and mental worlds. But he does not use his powers as when coming out of the fourth plane.

Finally, the prince (X) and his wife (Y) die.

Fifth Life: CAST OF CHARACTERS
X: (The prince)
Y: (The prince's wife)
Z: (The prince's slave) all become brothers

Scenario: X, Y, and Z are now brothers, sons of a grand multi-millionaire in America. They are all well educated. X is the leader of the three. He is spiritually minded, always studies spiritual subjects (the lives of the Masters, etc.), and is a great

> benefactor of the poor. His two brothers, also spiritually minded, always obey his wishes. A Perfect Master comes to America from India. People are deeply impressed by Him; they flock to Him, are transformed by Him. (Insert sayings of Meher Baba as samples of the Perfect Master's lectures.[112]) X hears of the Master and seeks Him out. The Master, on seeing X, is very pleased and exclaims, "Here is my man at last!" The Master embraces X and gives him Illumination. He experiences the following:

On the **sixth plane**, he find his gross, subtle and mental bodies set apart, and his spiritual body as a dot of unfathomable light. With this spiritual body (which has eyes, ears, nose all in one) he sees the Real Ocean of Light that is God. His ecstasy is now at its zenith. He does not resume his gross, subtle and mental bodies, and being thus regardless of the world and its affairs, he is conscious of God and God alone. His gross, subtle and mental bodies are all merged in the spiritual existence.

X lies in trance in the superconscious state for four days, and then regains his consciousness of the universe with partial illumination.

X goes home permanently transformed. His parents and others do not understand and think him mad. His brothers understand and sympathize. X does not sleep or eat but is always radiantly happy. His parents call in physicians who give him injections and other treatment, but X remains the same.

One day the two brothers tell their father about the Master from the East, and beg him to take X to Him. X is taken to the Master. The Master embraces him the second time and gives him the Divine Knowledge **(seventh plane consciousness).** Here, he is One with this Divine Ocean of Infinite Light. He is now God, the Infinite.

He becomes a Perfect Master. His two brothers become his most devoted disciples.

Other Notes and Dictations

EXTRACTS FROM MEHER BABA'S DICTATION TO MARGARET MAYO

DEC. 3, 1931
POINTS FOR SHRI MEHER BABA'S FILM

A. Creation.

(1) Deep darkness.

(2) The darkness gradually to vanish into (hollow) space.

(3) In the hollow space a tiny point of light appears.

(4) From the point comes forth *Akasha* and *Prana.*[113]

[see drawing in letter below]

A (Full Space) — P (Primal Energy)

Dec. 3, 1931.

POINTS FOR SHRI MEHER BABA'S FILM

A Creation (1) Deep darkness

(2) The darkness gradually to vanish into empty (hollow) space.

(3) In the hollow space a tiny point of light appears.

(4) From the point comes forth Akasha and Prana.

A (full space) — P (Primal Energy)

(5) These come together like this with a clash (chaos)

(6) And from this whirling chaos the primal elements of fire, water, air and earth come forth.

(7) From these four begins evolution ⊕ rotating starting with the electron. . . . Describe this process according to typed copy up to the appearance of the monkey. . . The final monkey form is the gorilla (to look half man, ... cannibal, and now begins the STORY.

(5) These come together like this with a clash (chaos). [see drawing in typed scenario on facing page]
(6) And from this whirling chaos the primal elements of fire, water, air and earth come forth.
(7) From these four begins evolution [see drawing] rotating starting with the electron. . . . Describe this process according to typed copy up to the appearance of the monkey. . . . The final monkey form is the gorilla (to look half man, half ape).
(8) Next to gorilla, appears the cannibal, and now begins the STORY.

There follows the story of X-Y-Z recounted earlier under the title "A Touch of Maya." The text of Margaret Mayo's version is virtually identical to that of the Awakener *article (the source of "A Touch of Maya" as reproduced in this book) up through the fourth lifetime. And even at that juncture, the life narrative accounts for the fourth and fifth lifetimes are the same. What Baba's 1931 dictation lacks are the vivid and detailed descriptions of the planes of consciousness. Instead, it provides a final page with a much shorter and sparser description of the first five planes (the sixth and seventh planes go entirely undescribed in this document), as follows.*

Planes of Consciousness

(1) **First plane**

He sees visions (as if in a mirror) of great Masters of the past with circular auras of light around their forms; and then the forms disappear. (Groups of forms appear at a time.) Then he sees clairvoyantly different luminous colours (ultra colours, all colours) dazzling, and hears exquisite sound-rhythms.

(2) **Second Plane**

Here he sees millions of spirits without a dense body, smokelike, transparent forms, vapoury, moving about very rapidly and making signs to each other. He then gets full knowledge from within of all that happens in the world—sees at will any part of the world, hears all sounds and so on with the other senses. (This must be shown in pictures.)

(3) **Third Plane**

He sees an ocean of fluctuating light, giving impression of extreme restlessness, flickering continually—but is himself aloof from the light.

(4) **Fourth Plane**

He sees the ocean of light, but now it is steady—a smooth white sheet of light, but he still remains aloof from it. He obtains full control of his physical body, and can use it as a coat, put it on and off at will. He feels he has tremendous powers at his command, and works miracles. (Working miracles must be shown—raising the dead, giving sight to the blind, curing the sick.) A Voice speaks to him—"Oh Son, Truth lies far beyond all this."

(5) **Fifth Plane**

He sees the steady ocean of light with himself in it—i.e. he is no longer aloof but is conscious of living in the light. He experiences great ecstasy and a great extension of consciousness. A Voice speaks: "Oh Child: I am beyond even this! Only those who love Me, lead a pure life, serve humanity selflessly and obey a Perfect Master can come to Me!"

Introduction to the Planes

These five lives have in them the themes of Reincarnation, Experiences of the Planes, Illumination and Realization.

The Soul in the First Life (i.e. the human form) has gained full consciousness of the world and the body. This soul in the innumerable consequent human forms (which it has to adopt according to the impressions of the world gained through its previous mental, subtle and gross bodies) through this full consciousness gets every kind of experience of good, bad, virtue, vice, happiness, suffering. This state of its experiencing we name M.

Later comes a state when it directs its consciousness towards Self, and not only world and body, not as it had done before. This state of its directing consciousness a bit towards Self, we will name P.

The Three Lives in our story (which comprises of innumerable lives) is of the M state.

In the Fourth Life of our story the Soul is in the P state. It experiences the five planes of the spiritual domain. It has full ordinary human consciousness, plus sub-superconsciousness.[114] In every consequent plane, the sub-superconsciousness increases step by step till the fifth plane, and here we show what it experiences in each plane.

There follow several typed pages of detailed description of the planes of consciousness. This constitutes the first draft of the material that was later rewritten in the document entitled "Scenario," which in turn provided one of the direct sources for "A Touch of Maya." "Introduction to the Planes" concludes with a description of the seventh plane, as below.

The seventh plane where the Seer, Sight and the Seen are all one. Here, the pilgrim is One with the Divine Ocean of Infinite Light. He is now God, the Infinite.

It is the same Soul which was unconscious of either the universe or the Self when in the original God Unconscious state. The same Soul, passing through the process of organic evolution, gains the consciousness of the universe bit by bit, till in the human form it becomes fully conscious of the universe, but unconscious of the Self.

The same Soul then, through the process of Reincarnation till Illumination, gains Self-consciousness step by step and so on, and finally, the same Soul gains full Self-consciousness in the state of Realization.

SCENARIO

1. God (show still ocean of most dazzling Light without any shore or space).

2. Point of projection.

3. Space and Energy.

4. Gas (subtle sphere).

5. Gas coming in contact with Space and Energy becomes nebula.

6. Nebula (gross sphere).

7. Billions of sparks (heavenly bodies).

8. To show billions of huge, enormous, immensely hot, round forms of gas all rotating at tremendously high speed.

Scenario.

1. God (Show still ocean of most dazzlingly Light without any shore or space).
2. Point of Projection.
3. Space and Energy.
4. Gas (Subtle sphere).
5. Gas coming in contact with Space and Energy becomes Nebula.
6. Nebula (Gross sphere).
7. Billions of Sparks (Heavenly Bodies).
8. To show billions of huge, enormous, immensely hot, round forms of Gas all rotating at tremendously high speed.
9. To show incalculable Sparks, billions of suns, millions of bodies (one of which is our Earth) very, very hot.
10. Solar system, Worlds and Planets.
11. Show World having crust, uneven rocks with gaps as shown in the diagram and gas in the centre.
12. Show World having crust, uneven rocks filled in with water coming out of the liquidated gas, thus forming oceans.
13. Show 276 stages between Subtle Gas and Nebula.
14. Show evolution of Minerals beginning from Electron.
15. Show evolution of Vegetables, original "Leel" to sea-weed to vegetable kingdom, and a few major vegetable species.

1. "Leel", 2. Sea-weeds, 3. Mushrooms,
4. Grass, 5, Neem Tree, 6. Spimach etc. (eatables). 7. Alvi plants.

16. Show Animal evolution according to Chart.

17a. Show the Four Lives and Five Planes as under:

17b. Show the Fifth Life and Sixth and Seventh Planes as under:

P.T.O.

This original manuscript page gives a complete sequential outline of elements in *How It All Happened*.

9. To show incalculable sparks, billions of suns, millions of bodies (one of which is our Earth) very, very hot.

10. Solar system, worlds and planets.

11. Show world having crust, uneven rocks with gaps as shown in the diagram and gas in the centre.

12. Show the world having a crust, uneven rocks filled in with water coming out of the liquidated gas, thus forming oceans.

13. Show 276 stages between subtle gas and nebula.

14. Show evolution of mineral beginning from electron.

15. Show evolution of vegetables, original "leel" to seaweed to vegetable kingdom, and a few major vegetable species.

16. Show animal evolution according to the chart.

17a. Show the four lives and five planes as under.

17b. Show the fifth life and sixth and seventh planes as under.

Though the papers have been disordered and scattered over the decades, it appears that "Scenario" contains several more pages. The immediate sequel to the preceding, which ought to comprise the story of X-Y-Z through their first three lifetimes, is missing. The story picks up, however, with the story of the prince (X in his fourth lifetime) just as he is starting to experience the first plane of consciousness. From this point the manuscript constitutes the clear and immediate source for "A Touch of Maya" up through the sixth plane. The final page appears to be missing, however; and "A Touch of Maya" concludes as in the Margaret Mayo dictation on December 3, 1931.

Explanation of the 1934 Film Master Chart*

In May of 1934, as a part of his work in the film medium, and in preparation for his upcoming visit to the West, Meher Baba had his disciple Adi K. Irani (and perhaps others among his mandali) prepare what we are calling the "Film Master Chart." This chart serves specifically to illustrate the points Baba had been conveying in his dictations during that same period, as recorded in the document "Creation and Evolution" and incorporated into the text of How It All Happened *in this book.*

Five feet wide and seven and a half feet high, the Film Master Chart divides into two sections, a top half and a bottom half. The top half displays the entire Divine Theme in a complexly developed form. The bottom half selects out and expands upon the earlier stages of this process, that is, the original creation through subtle gases, the emergence of rocks and minerals, and the origins of life in the vegetable kingdom.

TOP HALF. *The top half of the chart presents the Divine Theme as a cycle that moves counter-clockwise. Starting from "God Unconscious" at the top left, the journey begins with a movement down the Descending Track represented through two columns on the left, continues with a horizontal progress from left to right along the Transverse Track at the bottom, and concludes with the vertical climb up the Ascending Track to the right.*

The upper left-hand section immediately beneath the "Projection Point" (which in Infinite Intelligence *Baba called the "Creation Point" or "Om Point") displays visually the early stages of creation as described in chapters 1–2 of* How It All Happened. *Evolution proper begins when the drop-soul identifies with the*

* For an enlarged (17" x 22") print of the Film Master Chart, see insert inside the back cover.

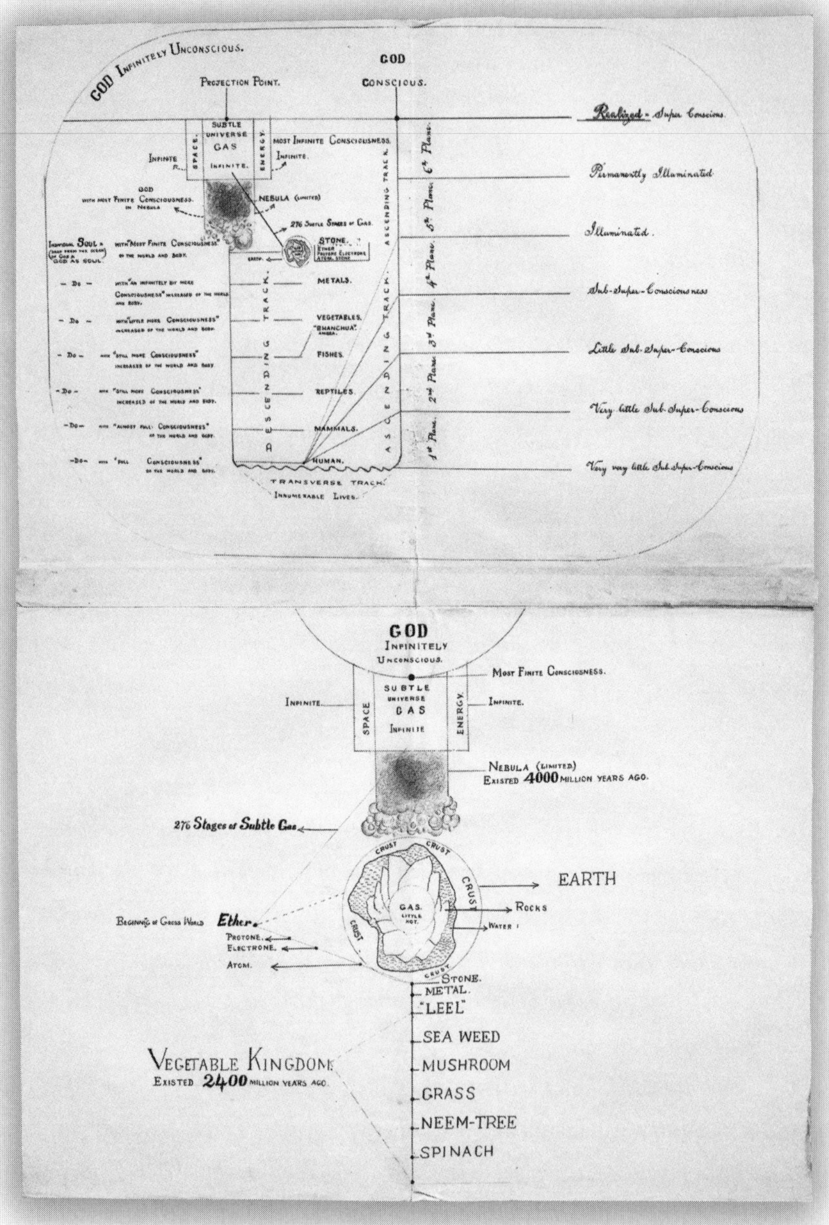

A replication in miniature of the Film Master Chart, depicting the processes of creation, evolution, reincarnation, spiritual advancement, and God-realization. An enlarged foldout can be found inside the back cover. The original, 5' x 7 1/2' chart is housed in the Trust Archives at Meherabad.

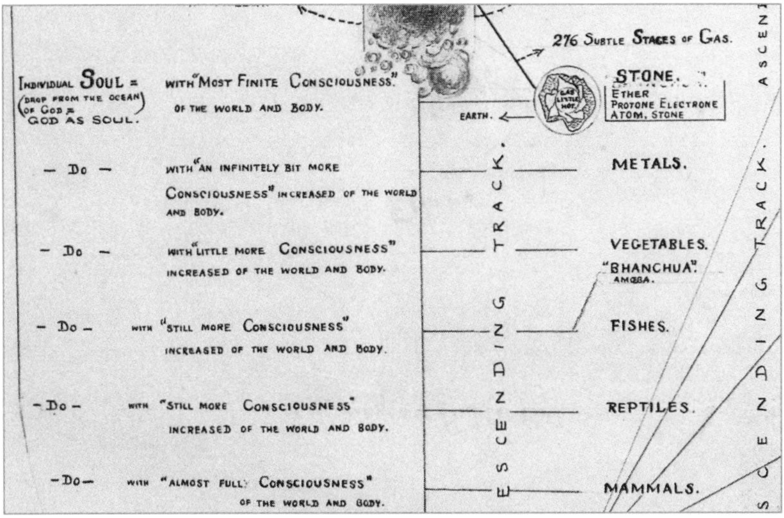

Detail from the top left portion of the Film Master Chart depicting the Descending Track in which form and consciousness evolve concurrently.

most primitive stone forms. The far left-hand column describes evolution as a process of gradual accumulation of consciousness. (The abbreviation "Do" repeating in that column is evidently an acronym for "Drop from the Ocean.") The parallel descending vertical column to the near right (with the kingdoms of stones, metals, vegetables, etc.) represents this same process as an evolution of form. *As* How It All Happened *emphasizes (see esp. the introduction), form and consciousness evolve concurrently and interdependently. This interdependence of form and consciousness is represented in the diagram on p. 164 as the zigzag line in the Descending Track. In the Film Master Chart, each aspect, consciousness and form, is given its own column.*

The Transverse Track of reincarnation, which the chart associates with the human form at the bottom of the evolutionary descent, is said to involve "innumerable lifetimes." In God Speaks, *Meher Baba fixes the number at 8,400,000. (In the film narrative of* How It All Happened, *the phase of reincarnation is dramatized through the first three of the five lifetimes that the three characters, X, Y, and Z, pass through.)*

The right hand column shows the Ascending Track by means of which the drop-soul climbs through the planes of consciousness towards its final reunion with God. In later years Meher Baba called this process "involution"; at this stage in the 1930s he characterized it as "spiritual advancement." Each step is described in terms of a progress from a lower degree of sub-Superconsciousness towards the full achievement of Superconsciousness in the Realization of God. Standing at the head of the Ascending Track is "God Conscious." The entire evolutionary cycle of the Divine Theme in this chart could be characterized as a movement from "God Infinitely Unconscious" (at the top left) to "God Conscious" (at the top right).

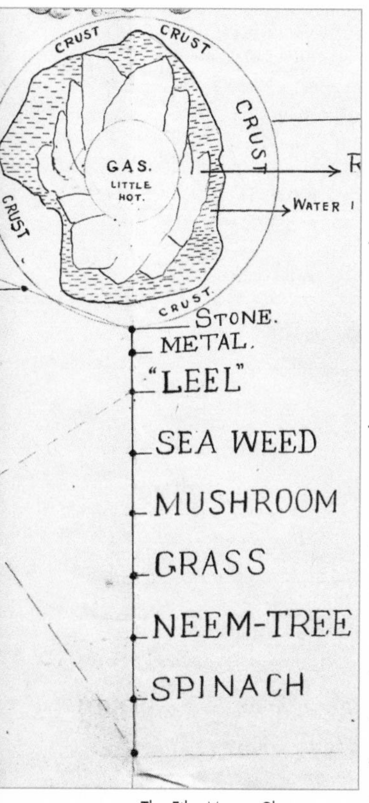

The Film Master Chart showing evolution of stone and plant forms.

BOTTOM HALF. *The bottom half of the chart could be described as an expansion and development of material from the chart's top left sections as described earlier. Indeed, many of the elements repeat: the origination of the universe in Unconscious God; the Creation Point; the domain of subtle gases dividing space and energy; the nebula; and the 276 subtle gaseous stages.*

Below this, however, we find a visual presentation of the stone and mineral forms of evolution that links with Baba's description of the gradual formation of the planet Earth in How It All Happened *(pp. 169–70). The downward movement in this portion of the chart extends as far as the vegetable kingdom with its several named representative species (leel, sea weed, mushroom, etc.). At this juncture the chart seems to be based specifically on pp. 173–74 of* How It All Happened. *That text includes alvi plants as the seventh representative form in the vegetable kingdom, an item of information which the chart has omitted, though the vertical line through the vegetable kingdom ends with an unlabeled point that was perhaps intended for it.*

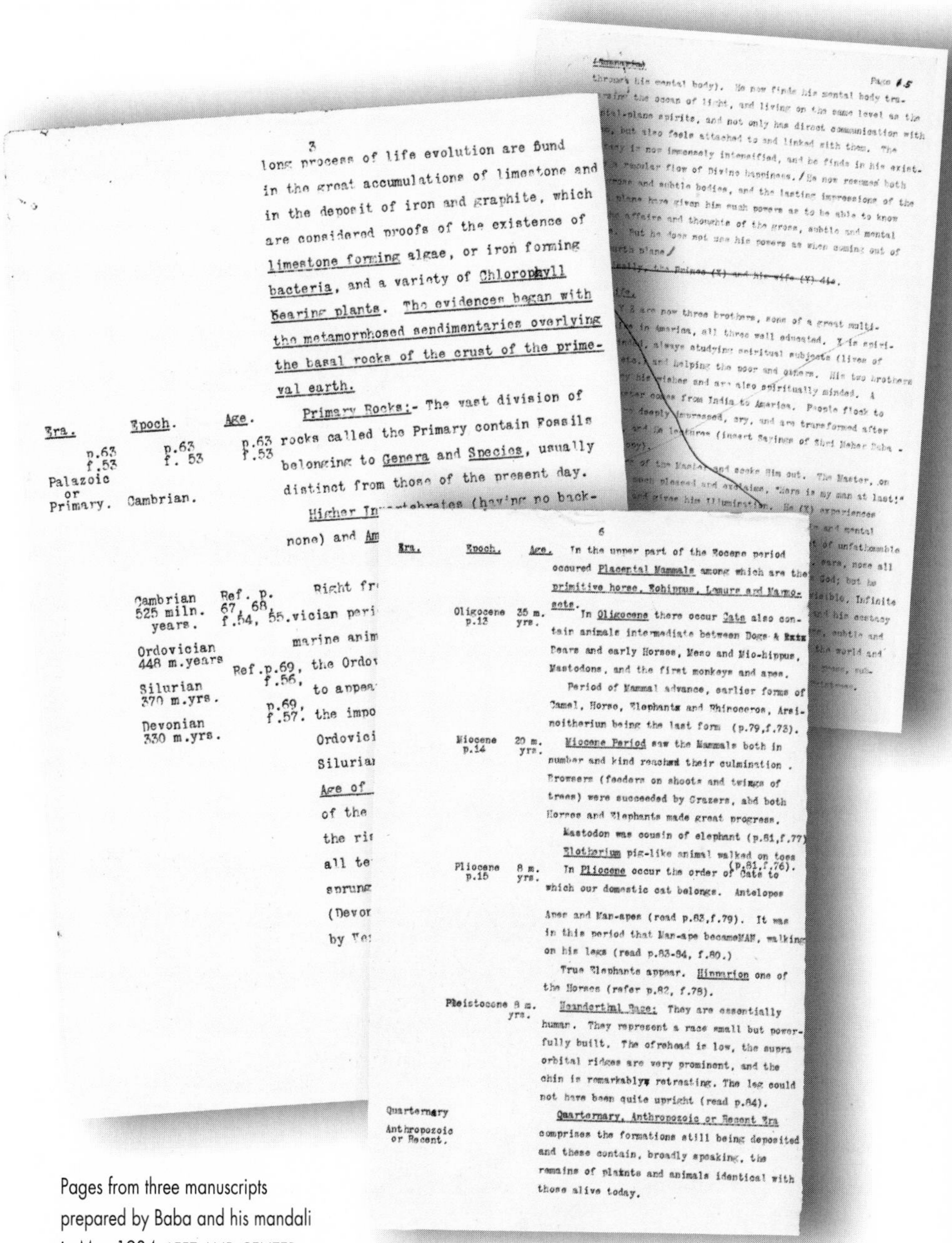

3

long process of life evolution are fund in the great accumulations of limestone and in the deposit of iron and graphite, which are considered proofs of the existence of limestone forming algae, or iron forming bacteria, and a variety of Chlorophyll Bearing plants. The evidences began with the metamorphosed sendimentaries overlying the basal rocks of the crust of the primeval earth.

Era.	Epoch.	Age.	
p.63 f.53 Palazoic or Primary.	p.63 f. 53 Cambrian.	p.63 f.53	Primary Rocks:- The vast division of rocks called the Primary contain Fossils belonging to Genera and Species, usually distinct from those of the present day. Higher In[illegible]tebrates (having no back-none) and Am[illegible]

Cambrian 525 miln. years. — Ref. p. 67, 68, f.54, 55.

Ordovician 448 m.years — Ref. p.69, f.56.

Silurian 370 m.yrs. — p.69, f.57.

Devonian 330 m.yrs.

Right fr[illegible] [illegible]vician peri[illegible] marine anim[illegible] the Ordo[illegible] to appea[illegible] the impo[illegible] Ordovici[illegible] Siluria[illegible] Age of [illegible] of the [illegible] the ri[illegible] all te[illegible] sprung[illegible] (Devor[illegible] by Ve[illegible]

(Summary)

Page #5

through his mental body). He now finds his mental body tra- [illegible] the ocean of light, and living on the same level as the [illegible]tal-plane spirits, and not only has direct communication with [illegible], but also feels attached to and linked with them. The [illegible] is now immensely intensified, and he finds in his exist- [illegible] regular flow of Divine happiness. / He now resumes both [illegible] and subtle bodies, and the lasting impressions of the [illegible] plane have given him such powers as to be able to know [illegible] affairs and thoughts of the gross, subtle and mental [illegible]. But he does not use his powers as when coming out of [illegible] plane /

~~[illegible], the Prince (X) and his wife (Y) die.~~

[illegible]

[illegible] are now three brothers, sons of a great multi- [illegible] in America, all three well educated. X is spiri- [illegible], always studying spiritual subjects (lives of [illegible]) and helping the poor and others. His two brothers [illegible] also spiritually minded. A [illegible] comes from India to America. People flock to [illegible] deeply impressed, cry, and are transformed after [illegible] lectures (insert Sayings of Shri Meher Baba - [illegible]).

[illegible] of the Master and seeks Him out. The Master, on [illegible] pleased and exclaims, "Here is my man at last!" [illegible] gives him Illumination. He (X) experiences [illegible]

6

Era.	Epoch.	Age.	
			In the upper part of the Eocene period occured Placental Mammals among which are the primitive horse, Eohippus, Lemurs and Marmosets.
	Oligocene p.13	35 m. yrs.	In Oligocene there occur Cats also contain animals intermediate between Dogs & ~~Rats~~ Bears and early Horses, Meso and Mio-hippus, Mastodons, and the first monkeys and apes. Period of Mammal advance, earlier forms of Camel, Horse, Elephants and Rhinoceros, Arsinoitherium being the last form (p.79,f.73).
	Miocene p.14	20 m. yrs.	Miocene Period saw the Mammals both in number and kind reached their culmination. Browsers (feeders on shoots and twigs of trees) were succeeded by Grazers, abd both Horses and Elephants made great progress. Mastodon was cousin of elephant (p.81,f.77). Elotherium pig-like animal walked on toes (p.81,f.76).
	Pliocene p.15	8 m. yrs.	In Pliocene occur the order of Cats to which our domestic cat belongs. Antelopes Apes and Man-apes (read p.83,f.79). It was in this period that Man-ape becameMAN, walking on his legs (read p.83-84, f.80.) True Elephants appear. Hipparion one of the Horses (refer p.82, f.78).
	Pleistocene	8 m. yrs.	Neandertal Race: They are essentially human. They represent a race small but powerfully built. The ofrehead is low, the supra orbital ridges are very prominent, and the chin is remarkably retreating. The leg could not have been quite upright (read p.84).
Quarternary Anthropozoic or Recent.			Quarternary, Anthropozoic or Recent Era comprises the formations still being deposited and these contain, broadly speaking, the remains of plants and animals identical with those alive today.

Pages from three manuscripts prepared by Baba and his mandali in May 1934. *LEFT AND CENTER* compile geological and evolutionary information from a scientific text; *TOP RIGHT* is an early draft of "A Touch of Maya."

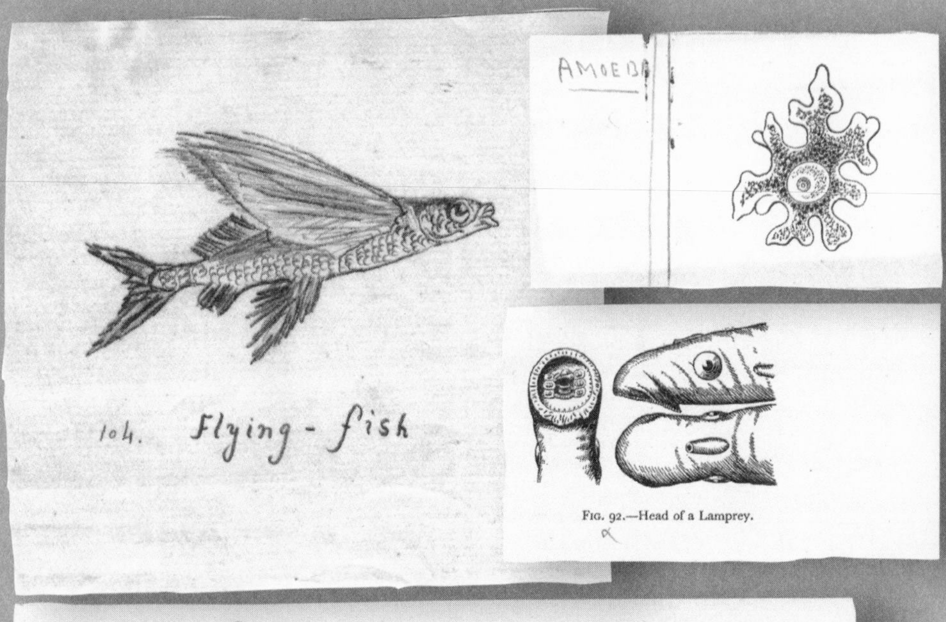

104. Flying-fish

Fig. 92.—Head of a Lamprey.

Fig. 57.—A Fish in the Making.

Fig. 108.—Sphenodon.

Fig. 142.—Orang sitting in its nest.

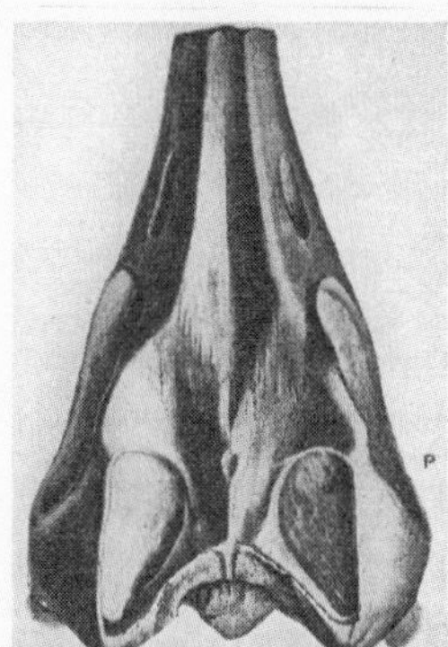

From Sir Ray Lankester's "Extinct Animals" (Constable).

Fig. 112.—Photograph of the upper surface of the Skull of an Ichthyosaurus.

Fig. 123.—A Flying Mammal—the Bat.

Several folders in the Archives of the Avatar Meher Baba Trust contain typed manuscripts drafted by Meher Baba and his mandali and illustrations of life forms cut out from a text in evolutionary science. This material was prepared and compiled in May 1934 with a view towards presenting the film concept for *How It All Happened* to Hollywood executives. As these images illustrate, the film was to integrate the discoveries of modern science into its greater spiritual and cosmological vision.

Fig. 119.—Duck-billed Platypus, or Duckmole.

SUPPLEMENT

Historical and Textual Backgrounds

The primary materials collected and republished in this book comprise the major statements and messages that Meher Baba gave out to the world, and other creative materials that he was preparing to disseminate through the medium of film, during the period of his early tours to the West.[1] As it happens, during Meher Baba's very first Western visit in 1931, he avoided publicity, declined interviews with press representatives, and issued no significant public communications. His second tour during the next year, however, was quite a different matter. It took place amidst great media fanfare; and for the first time the Avatar of the Age presented himself and his mission and message to a global audience. Over the next twenty months Baba's new Western disciples, acting under his instructions and supervision, began to edit a variety of literary materials; and this effort bore fruit in the form of two short booklets of Baba's words released in London in late 1933. Meanwhile, Baba had inaugurated preparations towards the creation of films

---

[1] For brief summaries of Meher Baba's thirteen tours to the West, starting with the first (which ran from August 29, 1931 through January 1, 1932), see appendix 10.

The principal source for most of the historical-biographical information in this essay is Bhau Kalchuri, *Lord Meher: The Biography of the Avatar of the Age, Meher Baba* (Hyderabad, A.P., India: Meher Mownavani Publications, 2005). This Indian edition republishes in eight volumes, with certain corrections, the complete text of the original twenty-volume series, whose first volumes were entitled *Lord Meher: The Biography of Avatar Meher Baba* (North Myrtle Beach, South Carolina: Manifestation, Inc., 1986–2001). David Fenster, editor of *Lord Meher,* is currently preparing another edition, far more comprehensively corrected and revised. He has graciously made available a preliminary (January 2009) draft, and I have used it whenever relevant in the preparation of *Early Messages to the West.* When these editions of *Lord Meher* diverge from each other, this current edition in progress is taken as most authoritative.

Since this essay relies on *Lord Meher* so extensively, no attempt is made to provide citations for every detail but only on major points. In what follows, the Indian edition will be cited in the abbreviated form *LM* (Mownavani), the American edition as *LM* (Manifestation), and the January 2009 revised draft in progress as *LM* (in progress).

on spiritual themes; and this work came to a head during his two Western tours of 1934–35.

While almost none of this content can be called "new," in the sense that most was published back in the 1930s and most of the rest since Meher Baba dropped his physical body in 1969, much of it has gone out of print, languished in obscurity, or been scattered through periodicals now available only to collectors. The main purpose of this book, then, is to gather these materials and present them in a single volume. For all of these items originated in a coherent and circumscribed phase of Meher Baba's life when a main thrust of his work involved communications through various media to the general public. The significance of these individual messages, in other words, emerges more fully when they are seen in their relation to each other.

Such is the rationale for the book's assemblage of primary texts. The reason for the inclusion of this supplement is to flesh out and detail more fully some of the history out of which this efflorescence of literary and creative materials arose. Students of Meher Baba's life and work may find their readings enriched by an understanding of the circumstances that he was responding to when he issued these communications to a Western public unacquainted with the idea of "Avatar" and the living spirituality that his life on earth embodies.

Yet beyond this, the statements and messages and other verbal content came to birth through a certain authorial process and textual genealogy. Meher Baba was not a conventional author. Maintaining complete oral silence from July 10, 1925, during the period of his Western tours he communicated by pointing to letters on an alphabet board, which a disciple would read out and, when the occasion called for it, transcribe. When authoring messages or books, Meher Baba did not typically dictate word for word. Rather, his usual method was to convey essential points, the gist of a message, to disciples, who wrote this content up, read it back to him, and incorporated corrections. As best we can gather, the primary texts of this book were produced by Baba through such a process. Yet in certain cases the literary content published in Europe in the 1930s has a prehistory that takes us back to India and Baba's work there during the preceding decade. Such relevant background information as we have been able to glean, then, both historical and textual, is set forth in the sections below.

Over the course of his life and Avataric mission Meher Baba traveled to the West thirteen times—ten times between 1931 and 1937 and thrice in the 1950s. Of most immediate relevance to the content here are the second through the eighth tours, which spanned the period from March 1932 through February 1935. But we will begin our survey in the previous decade, when Baba was still working in (what was from the world's standpoint) comparative obscurity, in Bombay, Meherabad, and Nasik, India. It was during this time that Meher Baba laid some of the foundations on which his work in the West in the early 1930s was built.

Discourses and Publications in India in the 1920s

While Meher Baba attained to the Realization of God in 1913 as a young man of nineteen, the intensive training of his Indian disciples did not begin in real earnest until almost ten years later, during what is known as the Manzil-e-Meem phase in Bombay (now called Mumbai), from June 1922 through April 1923.[2] Literally "House of the Master," the Manzil-e-Meem was a sizable bungalow in the Dadar district where Baba's men lived with him under a regimen of strict discipline. Among the varied activities which Baba had them carry out, one involved seeing to the composition, editing, and publication of a book, *Sakorina Sadguru,* which was the biography of Baba's own Master, Upasni Maharaj. Baba himself had inaugurated this effort in January 1922 when he dictated points of information to his disciple Baily, who wrote them up over the following months. But during his stay in the

---

[2] Most of the following information about Baba's publication activities in the Manzil-e-Meem has been taken from *Lord Meher;* see *LM* (Mownavani), vol. 1, pp. 271–357 and *LM* (Manifestation), vol. 2, pp. 380–503.

Manzil-e-Meem, Baba arranged to have Baily's Gujarati text edited, translated into Urdu and Marathi, and published in all three languages.[3] For this purpose, in November 1922 Baba's disciple Rustom established a publishing firm, Circle & Company, with an office in the Manzil itself. Leaflets were printed, and over the next year several of Baba's mandali had the assignment of hawking the book, sometimes under most embarrassing circumstances. In October 1923, after successfully selling off the stock of 1,000 copies of the Marathi translation, Baba had Circle & Company formally dissolved.

During the next few years Baba seemed to take no direct interest in publishing as such. Yet the early Meherabad period, especially from 1925 to 1928, gave birth to a mass of literature which remained, for the most part, in manuscript form for the rest of Meher Baba's lifetime. Clearly the most significant act of authorship by Baba himself was his composition of what is known as "The Book," which he wrote in his own hand. During the subsequent decades of his ministry Baba kept "The Book" unread, under lock and key; and today no one knows its whereabouts. Yet at the very same time Baba was pouring out a wealth of material through "oral" (that is, live dictated) discourses to his disciples. The manuscript recently edited and published under the title *Infinite Intelligence*[4] probably originated in Baba's dictations to his mandali in 1926; during that year and the next Baba gave to his disciples a series of talks that Framroze Dadachanji (known as Chanji) took down, edited, and wrote up again in the manuscript bearing the title "Tiffin Lectures."[5] In fact, Chanji's diaries record a considerable mass of additional material from this period; and over the four-year span 1924–28 a group of Baba's disciples (including Chanji) were keeping a detailed daily history of Baba's activities in a document known as "The Combined Diary." It has not yet

[3] Baba even gave instructions for an English version, which could be sold in the West; but such a volume never eventuated.

[4] Meher Baba, *Infinite Intelligence* (North Myrtle Beach, South Carolina: Sheriar Foundation, 2005).

[5] These lectures are currently being edited for publication under the auspices of the Avatar Meher Baba Trust, Ahmednagar, India.

been possible to study in detail all the manuscripts and other papers from this early Meherabad phase; much still remains unknown. Yet we know that at least some of this content was used by later writers and editors; and a certain amount seems to have found its way into some of the early Western publications that are the subject of this book.

Though the first great Meherabad phase came to an end in May 1928 when Baba moved the ashram to Toka, the next year witnessed the launching of the first major periodical explicitly dedicated to Meher Baba and, in much of its content, written by his disciples. The *Meher Message* issued on a monthly basis from its editorial office in Nasik (where Baba was headquartered during much of this time) from January 1929 through the last quarter of 1931. Its editor, Kaikhushru Jamshed Dastur, numbered among Baba's disciples, though in the second half of 1931 he was becoming seriously disaffected from his Master; and by the next year he had embarked on a campaign of his public denunciation. The first twenty-five-odd issues of the *Meher Message,* however, give no hint of this coming breach of relations; and much of their content holds great interest for students of Meher Baba's life and message. The *Message* aspired to be a magazine of note and quality, and to some degree it succeeded in this.

Of special significance were the literary materials that the *Meher Message* published under Baba's own name. Every issue from January 1929 through April 1931 opened with five "Sayings" from the Master; as we will see, these same sayings were collected and republished by Baba's early Western disciples in London in 1933. In addition, the *Meher Message* carried several serials. "Fragments from Spiritual Speeches of His Divine Majesty Sadguru Meher Baba" (1929–31) brought to print certain of Baba's "talks," of which at least some we know to have been recorded by Chanji. While the "Fragments" treat various and largely unrelated topics, three other series of articles examine major spiritual subjects in a more systematic way. Nine articles on "God, Creator and Creation" (1929) explore metaphysical matters; the six articles in the series "On God-Realization (The Practical Side of Self-Realization)"

(1930–31) review the major yogas and paths to God; the ten-part treatise "On Inner Life (The Mystical Side of Self-Realization)" (1930–31) outlines the architecture of the spiritual path in its major stages and spheres. Most and perhaps all of this content from the *Meher Message*, in one form or another, was made available to certain of Meher Baba's early Western disciples in the 1930s and informed their efforts as they embarked on their own literary services in their Master's cause.

Though Dastur himself (as we have noted) turned apostate to Baba during the second half of 1931 and thereafter led the attack as one of his fiercest public critics, some of the material attributed to Baba that Dastur had edited and published in the *Meher Message* was subsequently reworked by another of Meher Baba's Indian disciples, A. K. (Ramjoo) Abdulla, and incorporated into his book *Shri Meher Baba: His Philosophy and Teachings.*[6] In fact, Ramjoo himself was probably the one who took the original dictations from Baba and carried out the first draft write-ups on which some of the *Meher Message* articles were based. For in his introduction to *Philosophy and Teachings,* Ramjoo, writing in 1933, says that his book is a compilation from Baba's own dictations over the last five or six years. Many pages and passages in *Philosophy and Teachings* are demonstrably rewrites of *Meher Message* articles; and this suggests that those articles too were at least in part Ramjoo's handiwork. Herbert Davy and others among Baba's early Western disciples were aware of Ramjoo's literary undertakings and conceived his book as an important exposition of Baba's philosophy. In other words, the labors of Meher Baba's Indian disciples and of Baba himself in the "literary" arena over the decade of the 1920s and early 30s were very much in the awareness of Baba's early Western disciples and constituted a background to their own efforts.

---

[6] Nasik, India: Rustom K. Sarosh Irani, 1933.

Six Messages and the 1932 Western Tour

Meher Baba's first visit to the West was a low-key affair.[7] Indeed, he managed to effect his late-August 1931 departure from India in almost complete secrecy, so that few of his followers and even close disciples got wind of it until he was well out of the country.[8] Though Baba kept to his cabin and out of public view, during the last few days of the sea voyage on the S. S. Rajputana from Bombay to Marseilles Baba had a series of meetings with Mahatma Gandhi, who happened to be traveling on the same boat; and thus was inaugurated a relationship that continued until Gandhi's assassination seventeen years later. Yet during the three weeks from September 12 to October 3 that Baba spent in London and Devonshire, and during the month from November 6 to December 5 that he passed in New York, Meher Baba generally avoided publicity in the form of large meetings and interviews with the press.[9] No major messages to the general public issued from this tour. Rather, Baba seems to have concerned himself with personal interviews and the establishment of links with individuals. Many of the persons who subsequently proved to be his closest Western disciples met him for the first time during this Western visit—Herbert and Kitty Davy, Margaret

---

7 Most of the information in the following account of Meher Baba's early tours to the West between 1931 and early 1935 has been taken from *Lord Meher;* see *LM* (Mownavani), vols. 2–3, esp. pp. 1008–1415; *LM* (Manifestation), vols. 4–6, esp. pp. 1378–1950.

8 Baba brought with him on this trip only his disciples Chanji and Rustom and, interestingly enough, Agha Ali, still a teenager, who, as a student in the Prem Ashram in Meherabad in 1927–28, had been the central figure in some of the great dramas there, as Ramjoo Abdulla recounted in detail in his book *Sobs and Throbs* (Meherabad, Ahmednagar, India: N. N. Satha, 1929).

9 The one major press presentation of Meher Baba during his first Western tour was the article that Charles Purdom published in the September 24, 1931 issue of *Everyman,* reprinted here on pp. 28–32. I have not been able to locate other articles about Baba from this period. During his stay in London Baba met with Harry J. Strutton, editor of the *Occult Review,* but Strutton appears to have published no account of his interview (though he later served as an adviser for the Circle Editorial Committee). Baba also met with Christmas Humphreys, founder of the Buddhist Society; Humphreys's recollections of that meeting, reprinted here on p. 56, were not written up and published until ten years later. Among the rare instances of public exposure, one occurred aboard the steamboat S. S. Bremen from New York to London, when Baba allowed newspaper reporters to take some photographs and a reel of film; but this material seems to have been lost. (The surviving footage of Baba on board the S. S. Bremen in New York harbor was shot the next year.) Traveling on the Narkunda from Marseilles to Bombay, Baba was reluctantly persuaded to address several of his fellow passengers; although an audience of six or seven had been expected, 300 turned up. This was the first and last occasion on this 1931 tour on which Baba "spoke" at a public gathering.

Craske, Charles Purdom, Kim Tolhurst, Mabel Ryan, Quentin Tod, Delia DeLeon, Enid Corfe, Malcolm Schloss, Jean Adriel, Norina Matchabelli, Anita de Caro (later Vieillard), Elizabeth Patterson, Nadine Tolstoy, and others. Though of course one cannot presume to fathom the real significance of the Avatar's activities, from the best that we can tell much of his attention in his first visit to England and America seems to have been devoted to laying the foundations for later work through the gathering of his close Western followers and circle members.[10]

Returning to India via Europe, where he met again briefly with some of his newly won British disciples, Baba's inaugural Western tour came to an end when his ship docked in Bombay on January 1, 1932. While as we have seen Baba had succeeded in passing "beneath the radar" in this his first foray into Europe and America, the world tour that followed it three months later—Baba's first complete round-the-globe expedition—could not have been more different.[11] Attracting widespread public interest and media fanfare from the very outset, this time Baba was pursued by a press corps, whose representatives broadcasted his remarks to national and even

---

[10] This brief history cannot, of course, do justice to the extraordinary impression that Meher Baba made on his first visit to the West in 1931; but some sense of it can be gleaned by the accounts his disciples later gave of their first meetings with him. *Lord Meher* provides a rich selection of these. For those who would like to delve into this topic more deeply, the bibliography (sections B and C) gives many references; see especially the citations under the names Jean Adriel (including numerous accounts of other disciples), William Backett ("Impressions"), Margaret Craske, Framroze Dadachanji (especially parts three and four in the four-part series in the *Glow International*), Kitty Davy *(Love Alone Prevails)*, Delia DeLeon, Rom Landau (who quotes at length from an interview with Norina Matchabelli), Elizabeth Patterson, Ann Powell, Charles Purdom (especially his articles in *Everyman*), Josephine Grabau Ross, Malcolm Schloss (especially "When the Master is Ready," part 1), Quentin Tod (in "When I Saw Him" and Jean Adriel's *Avatar*), and Nadine Tolstoy (especially part two in the serial "Meher Baba and My Spiritual Path"). Ruano Bogislav and Rano Gayley recount comparable stories of their first meetings with Meher Baba in 1933.

[11] For a full account of this world tour of Meher Baba's (from March 24 through July 15, 1932), see *LM* (Mownavani), vol. 2, pp. 1120–23, vol. 3, pp. 1141–1235; *LM* (Manifestation), vol. 5, pp. 1542–1681. Kitty Davy provides a detailed narrative, with numerous quotations and extracts from the diaries of others among Baba's disciples, in her three-part article, "Baba's First World Tour, 1932," part 1, *Awakener,* vol. 12, no. 1, pp. 1–34; part 2, *Awakener,* vol. 13, no. 3 (Summer 1968), pp. 1-21; and part 3, *Awakener,* vol. 14, no. 1 (1971), pp. 19-36. For a first-hand account of the American leg of this tour, see Quentin Tod, "Meher Baba in America, 1932," *Glow,* November 1972 (vol. 7, no. 4), pp. 3–8.

international audiences. The trip was further distinguished by the size of Baba's entourage: twelve of his Indian disciples took part, six traveling with him to England and America and six more sent to meet up with him in China.[12] Over the next few years Baba visited the West many more times. But of all his world expeditions, this the second of them, during March–July 1932, stands out as the occasion on which Baba most openly exposed himself before the eyes of a general lay public through its media and most directly introduced himself to the world in its own language.

The cause of the publicity probably traces to a twenty-five minute interview that Baba gave to James A. Mills, a reporter from the Associated Press on March 20, four days before he embarked on the steamship Conto Rosso from Bombay. The story that resulted, "Indian Seer Starts for American Tour," was carried by major newspapers throughout America and the West.[13] By the time he arrived in Italy and England ten days later, Baba was already being courted, pursued, and hounded by major film and news agencies—Fox, Hearst, and Paramount. During his stay in London and Devonshire in April, a spate of articles flooded the English newspapers; and Paramount captured a short interview on film. Baba's subsequent brief sojourn in New York in late May produced feature articles in *Time* magazine, *Liberty* magazine, and the *New York Times.* Crossing the American continent by train, Baba's appearance precipitated news reports in the *Kansas City Evening Star* and, upon his arrival in Los Angeles, media outlets there. During his week-long stay in Hollywood from May 29 to June 4, Baba was feted by many of the leading celebrities of film world and taken on tours of Paramount, Universal, and Goldwyn Mayer Film Studios. Douglas Fairbanks and Mary Pickford threw a gala reception for him in their Pickfair mansion,

---

[12] As *Lord Meher* (in progress) relates: "The six going to China were Gustadji, Jalbhai, Pendu, Raosaheb, Rustom and Vishnu. In his own party, Baba was taking his two other brothers Adi Jr. and Beheram, Adi Sr., Chanji, Ghani and Kaka [Baria]."

[13] For a few examples, see appendix 1, p. 279. Section D of the bibliography lists seventeen articles based on Mills's story.

and many of the leading stars from what we now look back to as the golden age of Hollywood sought his interview. Indeed, it would be no exaggeration to say that, for this brief historical moment, Meher Baba, Avatar of the Age, had become a media sensation.

All this hullabaloo was brought to an end in a surprising way. During his three-week passage across the American continent Baba had been promising that, after completing his projected visit to China, he would return to California and break his seven-year silence in the Hollywood Bowl. Indeed, plans were well under way to broadcast Baba's silence breaking over the radio! But while his ship was at dock for four days in Honolulu in the middle of his trans-Pacific cruise, Baba sent back one of his disciples, Quentin Tod, with the message that he was canceling the event. This seemingly erratic behavior on Baba's part—a lifelong habit of his and part of his way of working—disappointed many who had been drawn to him largely through the limelight glamour of his American visit and subjected his newly won Western followers to the humiliating ordeal of having to explain their continuing allegiance to Baba to critical friends and family members.[14] But from that time on, media interest subsided; and on his subsequent trips to the West Baba was able to carry on with his work and activities without constantly being besieged by the press.

It was during this highly publicized tour of England and America from early April to early June 1932, while he was still the darling of media attention, that Baba issued the six major statements that collectively stand as a significant part of the Avatar's first public self-presentation to the Western world. These messages do indeed cohere as a group, and evidently they were understood that way by his disciples. For one indication of this, in *Messages of Meher Baba Delivered in the East and West,*[15] a collection compiled and

[14] Jean Adriel writes powerfully about this experience in *Avatar: The Life Story of Meher Baba* (1947; rpt. Berkeley: John F. Kennedy Univ. Press, 1971), pp. 144–46.

[15] Ahmednagar, India: Adi K. Irani for the Publication Committee, Meher Baba Universal Spiritual Centre, 1945, pp. 81–101.

published in 1945 by Baba's secretary Adi K. Irani, the entire second section, "Messages of Meher Baba Delivered in the West," is comprised exclusively of these six items. Further, among Kitty Davy's papers at the Meher Spiritual Center are corrected typed versions, perhaps early copies of manuscript drafts made for a permanent record; and they are headed by a title page listing the six messages by the occasion, audience, and date of their delivery.[16] Naturally these six public addresses are related to each other by the fact that they all arose in the same brief period of time and are all tailored to the demands of an audience with significant press corps representation. Yet in addition, they exhibit a stylistic consistency and revolve around a common group of themes—personal, spiritual, socio-economic—that Baba keeps returning to and slowly begins to develop as the messages progress. As a group these communications indeed hold their own special place in the body of literature that Meher Baba composed. There is nothing else quite like them.

The first of these messages Baba gave out in response to the dogged determination of Paramount Film Company, which had tried unsuccessfully to capture in film his arrival at the docks in Venice in early April and later at Victoria train station in London. Acceding at last to their insistence, on April 8 Baba allowed a filming in the garden outside the home of the Davy family at 32 Russell Road, Kensington (in West London), owned by the parents of Kitty and Herbert, both of these siblings at the time Baba's disciples. The Paramount Newsreel that resulted has often been displayed over recent decades at meetings of Meher Baba's followers around the world. In this film, Baba dictates on his alphabet board a statement that is read out by Charles Purdom, a noted scholar and editor of the magazine *Everyman,* who had met Baba the year before and by this time numbered among his close followers. Undoubtedly the actual text was composed by Baba prior to the filmed scene of dictation, since the message exhibits signs of careful literary composition; it is unlikely,

---

[16] Henceforth this manuscript is called "A" (see p. 269 below). Special thanks to the Meher Spiritual Center, Inc., Myrtle Beach, South Carolina, for providing access to this material.

moreover, that Charles Purdom after so brief an association with Baba would have been able to read out his dictation on the alphabet board so fluently.[17] The full message that Baba gave out is much longer than the edited film version, which selects just a few short lines.

The other five messages Meher Baba issued on the American leg of his trip. During this phase of his expedition Baba had in his entourage a number of disciples with literary aptitudes who might have taken part one way or another in the composition and publication process.[18] Chanji, Baba's secretary, maintained a copious diary and over the years wrote a stream of articles about Baba for various publications. Dr. Abdul Ghani, witty and brilliant, always played a role in the literary life of Baba's various ashrams and, as resident provocateur among the mandali, created the occasion for many of Baba's discourses, formal and informal. Among the Westerners who accompanied Baba on the ship from London to the United States, Meredith Starr, who at this time was presenting himself to the press as Baba's chief disciple, was an accomplished poet. Arriving in New York, Baba was joined for the duration of the American expedition by Malcolm Schloss, another poet and lifelong writer. Any of these men might have been yoked by Baba into literary service. At the very least, someone must have transcribed Baba's dictation; for in addition to maintaining complete verbal silence, Baba had abstained from writing with his own hand from the beginning of 1927.

We may, in fact, be able to take the speculation a step farther. One of the new Western disciples who accompanied Baba from New York to Los Angeles at the end of May 1932 was Jean Adriel, at that time Malcolm

[17] One of Baba's disciples who witnessed this filming was Adi K. Irani, who wrote the following in his diary under the date April 8, 1932: "The invitation of *Paramount* to film Baba is granted. They come at 5 p.m. Baba's dictated message is read out by Mr. Purdom as per Baba's wishes. It takes about an hour." See Adi K. Irani, "Diary of a Disciple," *Glow International*, February 1993, p. 6. Though the wording of this diary entry is not altogether unambiguous, it perhaps implies that Baba's message had been dictated ("Baba's dictated message") before it was read out.

[18] We do not include Adi K. Irani in the following inventory since he did not accompany Baba to America: on May 12 Baba sent him from England directly back to India ("Diary of a Disciple," p. 9).

Schloss's wife. Recollecting that period in her biography *Avatar,* Adriel describes a rivalry that was emerging between her husband and Meredith Starr. During the cross-continental train trip,

> Both would be asked to put into literary form Baba's message to Hollywood. Then Baba would accept Malcolm's version, praising it highly, while the other man, who prided himself on his writing ability and priority of place in Baba's group, would writhe and squirm.[19]

Now while we cannot know for sure which of Baba's three Hollywood messages this passage refers to, most probably it is the first, "Message to Reporters in Hollywood," given immediately upon his arrival on May 29 —though quite possibly Baba continued to favor Malcolm Schloss over his English fellow disciple and literary competitor in the composition of the two other messages that Baba had delivered during the next three days. Extrapolating backwards, one might reasonably speculate that it was Meredith Starr who wrote up the two messages that Baba had given in New York; indeed, Baba had Starr present his message at the Stokes residence on May 22. Starr might even have written up Baba's original "Message to the West" delivered in London on April 8. (Of course we cannot discount the possibility that Charles Purdom, who read this message out before the Paramount cameras, drafted what he read; but this supposition does not concord especially well with the rather drastic editorial pruning that Purdom himself subjected this message to before publishing it in the April 24 issue of *Everyman.*[20])

In any case, it was during the ocean voyage aboard the S. S. Bremen from London to New York that Baba dictated his first message to America. Indeed, he had copies printed on the ship's press. At the time none of his disciples understood why he took this step; but the reason emerged when the boat docked in New York on May 19 and reporters swarmed on board,

---

[19] *Avatar,* p. 142.

[20] For more on this, see p. 268. The text of Purdom's version is reproduced in facsimile on p. 278, the four indented paragraphs in the far right-hand column.

soliciting interviews and photo ops. Baba declined to meet with them personally, though he did eventually permit a brief filming that resulted in a 45-second "Universal Newspaper Newsreel"; but in the meantime he had his disciples give out printed copies of his prepared statement.

A few days later Baba gave another address, this time at the home of J. Graham Phelps Stokes and his wife Lettice at 88 Grove Street in Greenwich Village, New York. Scion of a wealthy family, Stokes had, in addition to a long history of involvement in socialist causes, deep interests in both Christian and Indian spirituality. Meeting Baba the first time during his visit to New York on November 9 of the previous year, Stokes had invited him to stay in his Manhattan residence, an opportunity of which Baba had availed himself a few weeks later during that 1931 trip. And now, upon Baba's return to New York in 1932, the Stokeses hosted a dinner reception in his honor on May 22. About 300 people attended, and Meredith Starr read out to them some remarks on Baba's behalf.

The last three messages were issued by Baba during his week in Hollywood. Immediately upon his arrival there on May 29, Baba delivered (that is to say, had read out) a major statement to reporters at a press conference. Interestingly, Baba's final paragraph, on the spiritual unimportance of miracles, is a verbatim repeat from the message that he had given to reporters ten days earlier upon his arrival in New York. On May 31, at a reception at the Knickerbocker Hotel attended by almost 1,000 people, Baba gave an address that started from the theme of self-interest—the source, as Baba explained, of the world's social problems. Finally, during the reception held for him at Pickfair—the personal residence of Mary Pickford and Douglas Fairbanks—on June 1, Baba discoursed on the subject of "moving pictures" and the responsibility which those involved in the film industry bore regarding the spiritual upliftment of humanity.[21]

[21] Meher Baba gave another message on this topic a quarter-century later, "On the Spiritual Potential of the Film-World," Awakener, vol. 6, no. 1 (Winter–Spring 1959), pp. 3–5; rpt. as "The Spiritual Potential of the Film World," in Meher Baba, *The Path of Love* (North Myrtle Beach, South Carolina: Sheriar Foundation, 2000), pp. 124–27.

When one surveys these six messages in overview, one notes that, while the specific topics and lines of exposition vary, certain emphases repeat. During this period in the early 1930s, the Western world was suffering from a severe economic depression; the resulting confusion and social turbulence had been aggravated in America by the legal prohibition of alcohol and its unintended consequences. Alluding to these disturbances, one of Baba's recurring points was that social, economic, and political problems ultimately trace back to a spiritual cause. World disharmonies and human suffering, he said, are made inevitable by the soul's identification with the false ego. Baba went on to set the problem of egoism in significant cosmological contexts as he discussed the evolution of consciousness, sanskaras, the three bodies, the spiritual path, and the role of Perfect Ones. Repeatedly Baba emphasized that dry creeds and ritualism cannot satisfy the needs of the human spirit; Baba himself had not come to create a new religion or cult. Though he did not directly assert his Avatarhood, in several of the messages Baba spoke of himself as possessing "Christ Consciousness," and he made it clear that his mission entailed the spiritual transformation of all humanity.

Articles in the Mainstream Press

Much of the publicity which attended Meher Baba's second world tour came in the form of newspaper and magazine articles, a hefty selection of which has been reproduced in appendix 1.[22] A few of these pieces to one degree or another tried to maintain an objective perspective and to present reasonably accurate information. Others were sarcastically toned and played to the bias in European and American culture at that time against Eastern religion generally

[22] See pp. 276–308. This material has been assembled with the outstanding help and contributions of several persons around the world who have gone to great lengths to research newspaper and periodical archival collections. Special thanks is due to Jamie and Zo Newell and Dru Swinson, who were able to locate many key articles from the United States; Keith Miles, who has assembled an extensive collection of magazine and newspaper materials from Great Britain; and another anonymous researcher, who has supplied materials of many kinds. Among the many others who have helped with this work, Peter Ravazza greatly enriched the book with his suggestions and guidance.

and Indian mysticism in particular. Some purveyed obvious misinformation —that Meher Baba was a Hindu, for example—and tried to sensationalize the subject. While one can hardly fault those who approached Meher Baba and his claims with strong doubts, as a body of literature these articles do not always present the journalistic profession in an especially creditable light.

Out of this mass of written matter a handful of articles emerges as exceptionally powerful or insightful or offering some unusual angle of vision. Perhaps the first significant piece to appear in the Western press was published while Baba's first Western tour was still in progress. A day after his arrival in London on September 12, 1931, Baba set out on the 230-mile drive to East Challacombe, the ashram that Meredith Starr had founded near the village of Combe Martin in Devonshire, where Baba stayed for ten days. By chance one of the small group of Britishers awaiting him there was Charles Purdom, at that time editor of the weekly magazine *Everyman.* A man of wide intellectual interests and considerable literary accomplishment, Purdom became, over the half-century of his active career until his death on July 8, 1965, the author of some twenty books on such diverse topics as Welwyn Garden City and town planning, economics, dramatic productions and festivals, William Shakespeare, George Bernard Shaw, and Harley Granville Barker.

Yet his meeting with Meher Baba in East Challacombe in 1931 proved to be the defining moment of his life. Indeed, as a close follower and disciple, Purdom played the role, more than any other man, of introducing the Avatar of the Age in an informed and thoughtful manner to the educated, literate British public. After a series of noteworthy articles in *Everyman* in 1931 and 1932 that followed from his stay in Combe Martin,[23] Purdom commenced research on a biography of Meher Baba, which was published in

[23] These three articles are: "A Perfect Master," *Everyman,* 24 September 1931, pp. 272, 274; "The Need of a Teacher," *Everyman,* February 11, 1932, pp. 80, 82; and "More About a Perfect Master," *Everyman,* April 21, 1932, pp. 400, 402. They were republished in *Meher Baba,* by His Eastern and Western Disciples (Bangalore: Publication Committee for Meher Baba Universal Spiritual Centre, 1939), pp. 1–5, 5–9, and 9–13. The second of these articles, "The Need of a Teacher," does not refer to Meher Baba by name, yet clearly Purdom's description of the true teacher is based on his own experience.

1937 by Williams and Norgate under the title *The Perfect Master.* In 1955 Victor Gollancz published Purdom's one-volume edition of Meher Baba's discourses under the title *God to Man and Man to God;* and in 1964, shortly before his death, Allen and Unwin published his great biography, *The God-Man.* All of this work was ground-breaking. Combining carefully researched scholarship, a critical and discriminative perspective, and the deeply insightful appreciation of a genuine seeker, Purdom's body of writings about Meher Baba has earned an enduring place in the Avataric legacy.

This literary work in Meher Baba's association began with Purdom's first article in *Everyman,* published in the September 24 issue (while Baba was still in London) and based on his East Challacombe experience. In fact, as he recounted many years later, Purdom had not especially cared for the extreme emotionalism exhibited by some of the new Western followers that he saw around Baba during these early meetings. He was deeply struck with Baba himself, however; and his editorial entitled "A Perfect Master" in the "Literature and Life" section of the magazine was essentially a testimony to the first impression that Baba had made upon him. Characteristically, Purdom relates little of a personal nature; he does not describe in any detail his own conversations with Baba or the anecdotes circulating around Baba at that time. He maintains his focus rather on a philosophical plane; that is, he speaks to his *Everyman* audience as a man seriously grappling with fundamental questions relating to the meaning of life and the transformative role of a Perfect Master in such a search. Taken in its proper mode and genre and historical moment, Purdom's article is an eloquent statement of the impact of Meher Baba's presence and the greater significance which Purdom found in him.

Since Baba assiduously avoided the press in his first Western tour, no other in-depth articles appeared at that time. But his second tour six months later precipitated a veritable avalanche of publicity. One of the earliest and at the same time most distinguished contributors to this spate of journalistic effervescence was James Douglas, a friend of Charles Purdom and a leading writer on religious subjects for the London *Daily Express*.[24] Approaching the much heralded "New Messiah" with an understandable skepticism, Douglas took the precaution of consulting first with Sir Denison Ross, an eminent scholar in Persian and Arabic studies, and with his help compiling a list of questions "designed to trap the teacher," as Douglas himself frankly acknowledged. Further, he paid his visit unannounced, to catch Baba off guard and unprepared. (A guest at the Davy residence in Kensington, Baba had just arrived in London on April 7 and had dictated his "Message to the West" before a Parmount film crew the next day.) But to his surprise Douglas found himself much affected by the power of Meher Baba's presence, and Baba answered his carefully prepared questions with a sublime simplicity. "[H]e smilingly threaded his way through [the questionnaire] without stumbling," Douglas wrote. "His mastery of dialect[ic] is consummate. It was quite Socratic in its ease." The interview that resulted stretched to a full hour and engaged substantial topics both in the domain of "philosophy" and concerning Baba himself and his mission. It still stands as one of the most interesting and wide-ranging presentations of Meher Baba to have appeared in the mainstream press.

Douglas's interview was published the next day on the front page of the April 10 *Sunday Express,* under the provocative title, "A Talk with the Strange Messiah."[25] During the 1930s the *Daily Express* (of which the *Sunday Express* was a weekly feature) ranked as one of the world's most successful newspapers with a huge circulation. Founded in 1906, it led the British newspapers of its time in diversifying its coverage into areas such as sports, gossip, and women's interests. The *Express* also carried articles on religious subjects, which accounts for the newspaper's interest in Meher Baba. Published so prominently in such a major venue, Douglas's article, in the words of *Lord*

---

[24] Much of the information that follows is taken from *Lord Meher;* see *LM* (Mownavani), vol. 3, pp. 1145–51; *LM* (Manifestation), vol. 5, pp. 1557–64.

[25] *Sunday Express* (London), April 10, 1932, p. 1. Facsimiles of the original article appear on pp. 23 and 292 of this book. Portions of Douglas's interview were reprinted in Ramjoo Abdullah's *Shri Meher Baba: His Philosophy and Teachings,* pp. 79–80.

Meher, "had a great impact on many readers and numerous people found out about Meher Baba from it."[26]

One of the disciples accompanying Baba on this tour was Chanji, Baba's secretary and frequently Baba's interpreter who read out from the alphabet board. Eleven years later, in a Gujarati biography of his Master, Chanji presented out his own full account of the interview between Baba and Douglas. This was translated into English by Naosherwan Anzar and published in a February 1980 issue of the *Glow International;*[27] and we have reproduced Chanji's translated reminiscence, along with Douglas's original *Express* article, in part two of this book. Much of the interest in Chanji's version lies in the fact that it contains more of the actual interview than appeared in the *Express.* Yet in addition, Chanji describes vividly the extraordinary impression that Baba appears to have made on the distinguished English writer—an aspect of their meeting that Douglas, as a reputed professional journalist, could hardly have been expected to discuss in his own published narrative. Baba, for his part, seems to have taken a special liking to his well-known interlocutor and extended himself to an unusual degree. Indeed, looking back on the episode a decade later as the veteran of almost all of Baba's early Western tours, Chanji writes, "Meher Baba had never entered into such a long conversation with any visitor. . . . It is for this reason that I have considered the lengthy interview of an hour with Mr. James Douglas important and have narrated it in detail." Juxtaposed with each other, the two versions of this interview, Douglas's and Chanji's, make for a fascinating pair of reflecting mirrors, with Meher Baba as their common subject.

The articles we have reviewed so far have all presented Meher Baba in

---

[26] *LM* (Mownavani), vol. 3, p. 1151; *LM* (Manifestation), vol. 5, p. 1564.

[27] Framroze [Hormusji] Dadachanji, "Meher Baba, Part IV: The West Bows Down," translated by Naosherwan Anzar, *Glow International,* February 1980, pp. 3-29; the account of the Douglas interview appears on pp. 13-17. Naosherwan Anzar's translation abridges and extracts key sections from pp. 301–28 of Chanji's original Gujarati text, *Meher Baba, Emnu Jivan-Charitra: Shikshan-Updesh, Sandesh. Bustak Pahelun ["Biography of Meher Baba: His Teachings, Discourses, and Messages. Book One"],* by "Manzil" (Ahmednagar, India: Adi K. Irani for the Publication Committee, Meher Baba Universal Spiritual Centre, 1943).

a favorable light; but it was during this, the European leg of Baba's 1932 world tour, that his critics delivered the first major broadside. In its May 7, 1932 issue *John Bull* magazine, a publication specializing in scandalous revelations and the debunking of frauds, carried a full two-page spread with photos under the title "All Britain Duped by Sham Messiah."[28] (The article is reproduced in facsimile on pp. 280–81). Purporting to provide inside information, the exposé, when one reads it closely, proves to be thin on fact but rich in insinuation. The "New Messiah," we learn, accepted exaggerated titles ("The Blessed Lord," "The Indian Avatar," "His Divine Majesty") and the homage of "beautiful young white girls"; his doctrines suffered from vagueness; claims as to the size of his following had been overblown; former disciples complained that he had not kept his promises. Now in themselves, these charges do little more than register vague negative representations and subjective impressions; they convey little content. The manner of writing, however, implies that a world of scandal lies behind them. In the absence of a fuller investigation with clear charges enunciated and substantiated with evidence, the *John Bull* article is nothing more than a smear piece. Yet it is representative of a major current of opposition and negative publicity that continued throughout the phase of Meher Baba's early Western tours and indeed, throughout his entire life.

When asked by his new Western disciples who the source of the *John Bull* attack was—for the article had been published anonymously—Meher Baba explained that the instigator was K. J. Dastur and the actual writer Raphael Hurst.[29] Dastur we have already encountered: for three years until his disaffection in late 1931 he had been the editor of the *Meher Message* —and in that capacity had more than anyone else cultivated the use of those very flowery titles ("His Divine Majesty," etc.) that the *John Bull* article derided. Indeed, it was Dastur himself who first introduced the Western

---

[28] *John Bull,* May 7, 1932, pp. 8–9.

[29] See *LM* (Mownavani), vol. 3, pp. 118–82; *LM* (Manifestation), vol. 5, pp. 1609–10. See also Adi K. Irani's remarks in "Diary of a Disciple," p. 9.

reading public to the silent Master through his article "His Holiness Sadguru Meher Baba" published in the August 1929 issue of the *Occult Review.*[30]

Raphael Hurst, for his part, had his own interesting prior connection with both Baba and Dastur. Born Raphael Hirsch and later publishing under the *nom de plume* of Paul Brunton, Hurst had originally been attracted to Baba through his correspondence with Dastur, possibly in connection with Dastur's 1929 article, since Hurst himself was a regular contributor to the *Occult Review* during the 1920s and 30s. For a time Hurst became one of Baba's ardent enthusiasts, and he filled several pages of the *Meher Message* with encomiums. Traveling to India late in 1930, he actually met with Baba and stayed for a few days at Meherabad in November 1930; and at the end of his Indian tour he visited Baba again in Nasik the following February. Yet over these four months Hurst seems to have turned against the one he at first took to be his Master; and the account that he penned in his influential book published in 1934, *A Search in Secret India,* is highly critical.[31] It is little to be wondered at, then, if Hurst and Dastur, both of them former acolytes, became, after their alienation, cohorts in Meher Baba's denunciation during the *John Bull* period, when Baba was bursting upon the Western scene.

Interesting though they are, we do not reproduce here Brunton's interviews with Baba in *A Search in Secret India,* since they derive from the Meherabad and Nasik phases and not the period of Baba's early Western tours. Yet Brunton's attack on Baba had an enduring influence—*A Search in Secret India* is still in print; it stands at the fountainhead of one of the major streams of adverse commentary during Meher Baba's lifetime.

These two opposed currents in the journalistic coverage of the time,

---

[30] Vol. 50, pp. 175–78. For facsimile reproductions, see p. 277.

[31] See Paul Brunton, *A Search in Secret India,* third edition (London: Random House, 1983), esp. chapter 4, "I Meet a Messiah," pp. 46–65, and chapter 14, "At the Parsee Messiah's Headquarters," pp. 253–62. Brunton's book was favorably reviewed in the *New York Times;* see "The Wonders of Eastern Mysticism," *New York Times,* September 15, 1935 (see p. 305 below). Though no devotee of Meher Baba and a sharp critic of Meher Baba's followers, Kevin Shepherd turns a critical eye on Brunton's account, in *Meher Baba, an Iranian Liberal* (Cambridge, England: Anthropographia Publications, 1986), pp. 146–76.

the laudatory as represented by Douglas and the denunciatory as represented by Brunton, met in the account of another writer of the period with interests in world spirituality and mysticism. Published in 1935, Rom Landau's *God Is My Adventure,* a wide-ranging, 400-page excursus with sections on such well known figures as Rudolf Steiner, Krishnamurti, Ouspensky, and Gurdjieff, includes a chapter on Meher Baba that features an interview with Baba during this same London visit in 1932.[32] As Landau himself explains, he was motivated to seek Baba out largely because of Douglas's piece in the *Sunday Express* several weeks earlier. Yet by contrast with Douglas's interview, Landau's own seems to have been rather flat. Baba, Landau says, declined to answer most of his questions on the grounds that long explanations would be required: he would write to Landau further in a day or two. In consequence Landau relates nothing substantive from the meeting itself; and the tone and perspective of his reportage is ironic and sometimes almost snide, though he does make some honest efforts to maintain balance.[33] (Later in the chapter it emerges that Landau had been influenced by Brunton, whose book was published the year before his own and whom he quotes at length.) Yet what gives Landau's account interest, and the reason that we include selections from it here, is because of the material which Baba had his attending disciple send to him in the subsequent letter. Landau quotes about a page from this; and while he does not pretend to be doing other than reproducing selected extracts, the passages seem authentic, in some cases they match what has been published elsewhere, and several of them are rather striking and new.

The journalism that we have been reviewing until this point all emanated

---

[32] See "Portrait of a 'Perfect Master,' Shri Meher Baba," pp.130-48 in *God is My Adventure: A Book on Modern Mystics, Masters, and Teachers* (London: Ivor Nicholson and Watson, 1935). The book was published in its American edition the next year (New York: Alfred A. Knopf, 1936); for the chapter on Meher Baba see pp. 126-43. For a review of Landau's assessment of Meher Baba, see Kevin Shepherd, *Meher Baba, an Iranian Liberal,* pp. 176–82.

[33] Later in the chapter Landau quotes in some length from one of Charles Purdom's articles in *Everyman;* yet Landau seems to have been most impressed by the beautiful and effervescent Norina Matchabelli, whom he interviewed in her flat in New York. His reportage of that interview makes for most interesting reading.

from England. But when Meher Baba crossed the Atlantic in May 1932, the American press corps was awaiting him there, and articles appeared in such major publications as the *New York Times, Chicago Daily Tribune, Los Angeles Times,* and *Time* magazine. Most of these were news stories rather than editorials or interviews; and while some of them presented their factual information accurately, few of them tried to delve into their subject in any depth.

One exceptional story did appear, however. Its author, Frederick L. Collins,[34] was a forty-year-old New-York-based journalist who over the quarter-century from the 1920s through the 1940s published about a dozen books on topics of general interest. As he relates in the article itself, Collins was reluctantly persuaded to meet the "Sadguru," just arrived in New York, by a nagging friend; like Douglas, he approached Meher Baba with profound skepticism. But to his own surprise, in Baba's presence he was thoroughly charmed on a human level:

> Well, here he was, this perfect master, in his doubtful chinchilla jacket, on Mrs. Phelps Stokes' square-backed sofa. And here was I, the unbeliever, sitting joyously beside him.
>
> He just looked at me and smiled. I think I smiled, too. We sat that way a long time. I know you will laugh, but we *did!* Baba believes in meditation; and when you are with him you believe as Baba does. I can hardly believe it now, but I distinctly remember I was having a good time.

As to the substance of his interview, Collins's questions were oriented less towards the religious and spiritual domain than Douglas's had been and more towards topics of current social interest—prohibition, the depression, divorce. Like Douglas, however, Collins was impressed with the directness and simplicity of Baba's answers.

Conducted during Meher Baba's brief three-day stay in New York in

---

[34] Frederick Collins, "I Can Hardly Believe It," *Liberty,* August 27, 1932, pp. 26–27. The article is reproduced in facsimile on pp. 290-91.

May 1932, Collins's interview was published in the August 27, 1932 issue of *Liberty* magazine. At that time *Liberty* was widely regarded as one of the leading weeklies in America, second only to the *Saturday Evening Post* in circulation. Once again, an in-depth presentation of Meher Baba, both in his personality and in his "philosophy," had been made available to the Western world through one of its leading mainstream publications.

Part two of this book concludes with the opening and closing paragraphs of a short article by Christmas Humphreys. Born in 1901, Humphreys became, over the course of a long and distinguished career, probably the best-known British convert to Buddhism during the century. In 1926 he founded the Buddhist Society, which provided the main channel and framework for the flourishing of Buddhism in England over the following decades. Meanwhile, he gained fame and distinction in the British legal process as a leading barrister; at the time of his retirement in 1976 he was a judge in the Old Bailey. Over this entire period he wrote prolifically, authoring, co-authoring, or editing almost forty books, most of them on the subject of Mahayana Buddhism.

Humphreys met Baba during his first visit to London in September of 1931.[35] Ten years later he wrote about this experience in "The Man of Love," an article published in *Buddhism in England,* vol. 16, no. 4 (November–December 1941), p. 77. (*Buddhism in England* was the official organ of the Buddhist Society.) Much of Humphreys's article reviews and comments on Charles Purdom's *The Perfect Master* (1937) and Meher Baba's discourse on "The New Humanity" (published in the November 1940 issue of *Meher Baba Journal*). Though Humpheys offers valuable insights, Purdom's biography and Baba's discourse postdate the period of the early 1930s that is the focus of this book. But Humphreys's reminiscences in the first and final paragraphs, which we republish here, bear on Meher Baba's very first visit to

[35] For a more detailed account of this interview, see *LM* (Mownavani), vol. 2, pp. 1043–45; *LM* (Manifestation), vol. 4, pp. 1431–33.

the West—the visit that elicited Purdom's first article in *Everyman.* Writing during one of the darker periods of World War II, Humphreys powerfully evokes what he characterizes as Meher Baba's "irradiation" of love. While Humpheys' own spiritual path lay through Buddhism, his article testifies eloquently to Meher Baba's extraordinary impact when he first came to the West.

In reading the written material published about Meher Baba in the mainstream media contemporaneously with his early Western tours, one needs to bear in mind that Baba rarely if ever tried to correct misinformation or inaccurate quotes attributed to him. His own words are best ascertained through the books and messages to which he appended his own name. Nonetheless, taken as a kind of mosaic, the journalistic coverage provides a remarkable testimonial to the impression that he made. While occasional newspaper or magazine articles appeared in later years, never again did the Avatar of the Age open himself to the plain view and commentary of the world press as he did in the months of April to early June in 1932.

Questions and Answers

As we have noted, the messages and articles republished here in parts one and two come from a unique phase in Meher Baba's life, when he was actively presenting himself and his mission to the general public. In the 1950s in India once again Baba held numerous open public gatherings at which he gave substantial messages. Yet during this latter period Meher Baba as the Avatar of the Age was giving darshan to his lovers and followers. By contrast, in Baba's 1932 world tour he spoke to the secular world on its own terms.

That tour, and that phase in his work, came to an end when the S. S. Kaiser-i-Hind, on which Baba had embarked in Shanghai after six days in China, reached port and docked in Bombay on July 15, 1932. But three days later Baba departed from India on another ship for Europe; and by the end of 1933 he had traveled to Europe four more times.[36] Avoiding publicity, much of Baba's attention during these visits centered on the deepening of his connections with his Western disciples and the beginning of their spiritual training. He met with them in London and other cities in Europe, cultivating intimacy and an easy familiarity of relations; he held interviews with newcomers; with parties of disciples he resided in villas at Santa Margherita and Portofino in Italy, taking walks on the beach and through the hills, eating at restaurants, assigning roles and duties in the life of the household, making plans for future work; he traveled with them through Spain; he carried out spiritual work at Assisi and other sacred sites and made contact with his spiritual agents. He even invited a group of them to India in April 1933, where for the first time the Western women met Mehera and Baba's Indian women mandali, and subsequently traveled with him through north India and Kashmir. Through all this whirlwind of activity Baba was using different means to cultivate his disciples' love-connection, while at the same time training them in obedience and preparing them for the work in the decades ahead.

One of the major lines of work that Baba got under way and began to engage the efforts of some of his new followers in was the literary. As it turned out, a number of Meher Baba's close Western followers had literary aptitudes; and much of what Baba initiated during this early period came to a fuller flowering several years later with the publication of the monthly magazine, the *Meher Baba Journal,* between 1938 and 1942. But the first fruit of this work in the literary sphere was a short booklet published in the autumn of 1933 entitled *Shri Meher Baba, the Perfect Master: Questions and Answers.*

In later years other books with "questions and answers" about Meher

[36] For full accounts of Baba's activities during his world tours of 1932-33, see *LM* (Mownavani), vol. 3, esp. pp. 1141–1343; *LM* (Manifestation), vol. 5, pp. 1542–1841.

Baba came into print;[37] but this 1933 publication stands apart from them in many ways. Its fifty-eight questions, and Meher Baba's responses to them, register the sensibility of the Western world in that era, which approached Baba largely from a Christian background and orientation. The editors organized the questions under seven major headings—about Christ, the spiritual path, the Messiah or Avatar, spiritual masters, Meher Baba's mission, Baba personally, and other miscellaneous topics. Questions and their responses are interrelated through a detailed system of cross-referencing, and occasional footnotes give further clarifying information. An oddity of the book is that the "answers" refer to Meher Baba himself in the third person and do not, apparently, purport to present his own words in his own voice. Some of the very same content, however, appears elsewhere in published messages where Baba does indeed speak these same words in the first person.[38] But a few responses in the book contain material that Meher Baba would have been unlikely to have said for his own part.[39] In such cases one presumes that the editors were amplifying on points that Baba had given with clarifying content

---

[37] See, for example, *Who is Meher Baba? Questions and Answers on Meher Baba* (Ahmednagar, India: Adi K. Irani, Meher Publications, 1967); *61 Questions and Answers on Meher Baba,* compiled by A. C. S. Chari (Calcutta : Society in West Bengal for Meher Baba [1968]), whose enlarged second edition, entitled *84 Questions and Answers on Avatar Meher Baba,* was published in New Delhi : A. C. S. Chari for Avatar Meher Baba Centre [1969]; and *Questions Meher Baba Answered* (Poona : K. K. Ramakrishnan, Meher Era Publications, [1975]). Records of 43 personal interviews with Meher Baba during his early Western visits were published by Charles B. Purdom in the earliest Western biography of Meher Baba, *The Perfect Master: The Early Life of Meher Baba,* orig. published 1937; 2nd edition (North Myrtle Beach, South Carolina: Sheriar Press, 1976), pp. 237–59. The content of the 1933 *Questions and Answers* is altogether distinct from that in these later publications.

[38] The endnotes to *Questions and Answers* identify many passages that have been taken from other sources. Answers 5, 10, 12(a), 21, 26(b), 31, 32, 35, 49, 51, 52, and 55, for example, draw on material from the six messages that Baba gave on his 1932 tour. On close comparison, sometimes one finds that the editors of *Questions and Answers* have selected their quotations in such fashion that Baba's first-person pronouns have been avoided; in other cases, pronouns in the first person have been replaced by the third person ("he").

[39] The first answer, for example, quotes from the New Testament. Though it is not unlikely that one of Meher Baba's disciples read him this passage in the course of soliciting his responses, Meher Baba himself rarely quoted from any of the sacred scriptures of the world's great religions. The nineteenth answer, consisting of a lengthy quotation from Rabindranath Tagore's translation of Kabir, was, according to the prefatory material (p. 66 in this book), introduced at the suggestion of "an English writer"—probably Charles Purdom, who had quoted another passage from Kabir in the article he wrote for *Everyman* in 1931. As these examples illustrate, Meher Baba's Western disciples appear to have played an active role in the compilation of at least some of the answers.

of their own. The answers can nonetheless be taken as directly representing what Baba wanted to convey to the world, since he was intimately involved with the editorial process throughout, almost certainly reviewed the text before it was sent to press, and sanctioned its publication. The book is his.

Where did this material come from, and how was it assembled together into a single published collection? On the basis of currently available evidence, it appears that questions and their responses were being collected from as early as December 1931, during Baba's first Western tour.[40] The job was taken up in earnest, however, during June–July 1933, when Baba and a large group of his Western disciples were staying at the Villa Altachiara, a large house overlooking the Mediterranean in Portofino, Italy. While other disciples may have made their contribution, the leading part in the editorial preparation of *Questions and Answers* seems to have been played by Herbert Davy, at this time a young man of thirty-four who during the previous year, on sponsorship by the League of Nations, had served as a Professor of English at National Central University at Nanking. The careful editorial style and meticulous organization evident in both *Questions and Answers* and *The Sayings of Shri Meher Baba* probably represent Herbert's handiwork.[41] At the same time, an editorial committee for Baba's work was being constituted, and under its auspices, plans were afoot for the translation of *Questions and Answers* into many languages—German, French, Italian, Romanian, Russian, Spanish, and

---

[40] Fliers with some of the material that appeared later in the booklet were prepared, evidently by Malcolm Schloss, in December 1931 and February 1932; for details see endnote 35 on p. 404. These fliers were found among the papers of J. Graham Phelps Stokes, now housed in the Columbia University Rare Book and Manuscript Library. These and other materials from the Stokes collection were procured by David Fenster, who has graciously made them available for the preparation of this edition. All references hereafter to correspondence between Herbert Davy, Graham Stokes, and Norina Matchabelli are based on this collection of source material.

I am also grateful to David Fenster for his many suggestions and astute guidance, based on years of research into the life of Meher Baba, in many matters of historical and biographical detail.

[41] David Fenster procured from the Stokes collection of Columbia University Rare Book and Manuscript Library (see note 40) a semi-final typed draft of "Questions and Answers" with revisions and corrections in Herbert Davy's hand. (A page of this manuscript, with handwritten notes added, is reproduced in facsimile on p. 7 of "Answers: The True Messiah" *Glow International*, Spring 2009, pp. 3–15.) Almost all of these handwritten changes were incorporated into the 1933 booklet.

perhaps others.[42] Indeed, after his return to India in September, Baba arranged to have the book translated into Marathi, Gujarati, and Persian.[43] From the fact that a number of the questions and answers appear in Ramjoo Abdulla's *Philosophy and Teachings* (whose introduction was dated September 21, 1933), it seems probable that a draft of this material found its way into Ramjoo's hands during this same period.[44]

In all these various aspects and lines of activity, then, the book remained a major focus of attention during the stay in Italy and for the months following. While it might be open to discussion whether Baba was actually initiating these literary and publishing endeavors or whether he was primarily supporting and feeding the enthusiasm of his new Western disciples, in any event, the fact of his own direct involvement, from first to last, is beyond dispute.

The Circle Editorial Committee, which not only oversaw the literary preparation of *Questions and Answers* but actually served as its publisher, emerged out of a significant background in the context of Baba's life and mission. Over the decades of the 1920s and 30s Baba had applied the term "circle"—a reference to the spiritual circle of a God-realized Master whose

---

[42] Copies of the French and German translations still survive; neither bears the name of its translator. The French edition is entitled *Shri Meher Baba, le Maître Parfait: Questions et Réponses* (Paris: Éditions de la Revue Mondiale, 1934); and the German translation, *Shri Meher Baba, der Vollkommene Meister: Fragen und Antworten* (Erlenbach, Switzerland: Rotapfel-Verlag [1934]. Both of these translations are listed in *Avatar Meher Baba Bibliography,* compiled by Bal Natu, and edited and prepared for publication by J. Flagg Kris (New Delhi: J. Flagg Kris, 1978), an invaluable resource that has been used regularly in the preparation of this present edition.

[43] According to *Lord Meher* (in progress), Baba had *Questions and Answers* translated "into Marathi by Kalemama, K. K. Manekar and Kelkar of Dhulia, into Gujarati by Soma Desai (with Chanji's help), and into Persian by Raosaheb, who daily read out his version to Baba." This quotation from David Fenster's January 2009 draft updates and corrects *LM* (Mownavani), vol. 3, p. 1317; and *LM* (Manifestation), vol. 5, p. 1805.

[44] Compare Ramjoo's Philosophy and Teachings, pp. 84–99, with *Questions and Answers,* nos. 2, 10, 12(a), 13–15, 20–25, 27–28, 35–37, 42, and 49. Since Ramjoo's book and *Questions and Answers* were published almost concurrently, there is little likelihood that Ramjoo could have used the Circle Editorial Committee's booklet as his source. In fact, Ramjoo's text matches almost exactly that of the typed manuscript in the Stokes collection (see note 41); the handwritten notes on the Stokes manuscript, which were incorporated into *Questions and Answers,* were not entered into the text of *Philosophy and Teachings.* (Ramjoo has, however, incorporated certain small edits of his own.) In short, Ramjoo must have had access to a copy of the Stokes manuscript—without Herbert Davy's handwritten emendations—which he must have used as his source.

structure Baba later explained in two of his discourses[45]—to various groupings and activities among his close disciples. As noted earlier, between 1922 and 1923 Baba and his disciples operated a publishing house, "Circle & Company," with an office in the Manzil-e-Meem in Bombay. In December 1925 a "Circle Committee" was constituted to manage the Meherabad estate and its affairs. The "Circle Cinema" in Nasik, property of Baba's disciple Rustom Irani, was inaugurated in February 1931, and it became a hub of Baba's activities over the next few years. When the focus of Baba's work shifted to Europe and America, as we have seen, the newly constituted Circle Editorial Committee involved in its activities a number of Baba's Western followers and concerned itself with a variety of literary projects during the years 1933–34.[46] And in June 1934, Baba's disciples founded Circle Productions, Inc., a corporation with Baba himself as its president, dedicated to the financing and production of a film on a spiritual theme whose outlines Baba had dictated. The frequent use of the word "circle" in connection with all these entities is probably related to the fact that during these years Baba was drawing into his fold new followers and disciples who naturally took interest in the idea of a spiritual Master's circle as it might relate to their personal association with Baba himself. As time passed and Baba's disciples matured, groups with "circle" in their title slowly disappeared.

In any event, the formation of a Circle Editorial Committee seems to have been undertaken during the Portofino stay in the summer of 1933. On August 10 (two weeks after the Portofino sojourn ended) Norina Matchabelli wrote a letter to Graham Stokes in New York, conveying to him

---

[45] See "The Circle" and "The Circles of the Avatar," pp. 288–92 and 293–97 in Meher Baba, *Discourses*, seventh edition, edited by Eruch Jessawala, Bal Natu, and J. Flagg Kris (1987; rpt. North Myrtle Beach, South Carolina: Sheriar Foundation, 1995).

[46] While the Circle Editorial Committee concerned itself with literary matters, during 1933 Baba seems to have envisioned a "Circle Committee" that could fulfill more pragmatic functions as well. For among Kitty Davy's papers at the Meher Spiritual Center is a letter from Meher Baba to Herbert Davy, dated December 8, 1933, in which Baba discusses the terms of a prospective deed of a "Circle Committee" which could own properties, presumably in the service of Baba's work. Baba even says, "all that I receive in future—including even wills (even if it is given to me privately) will be turned over to the Circle Committee." (For the full letter, see pp. 329–30.) This planning seems to have been one step on the road that culminated in the creation of the Avatar Meher Baba Trust in 1959.

Baba's invitation to become a member of this group along with herself, Herbert and Kitty Davy, and Charles Purdom. Stokes declined, however; for as he made clear in a subsequent correspondence with Herbert, he could not accept what he took to be the exaggerated spiritual claims being made on Baba's behalf by Baba's disciples. A committee was formed nonetheless, maintaining an office at 50, Charing Cross, London; and a letter to the general public dated October 1933 lists its members as Herbert Davy, director, in London; Walter Mertens, in Zurich; le Marquis Illan de Casa Fuerte, in Paris; Malcolm Schloss, in New York; Rustom Irani, in Ahmednagar; Sampath Aiyanger, in Madras; and Behram Faridun Irani, in Yezd, Persia.[47] This membership did not represent the real editorial body of the committee; rather, it was meant to function as Baba's representatives in different parts of the world, for sales of publications and further information about Baba. The actual core of individuals engaged in serious work for Baba in the Western literary sphere included Herbert and Norina, Charles Purdom, Will Backett, and perhaps one or two others.[48] Purdom by this time had already begun research for what later emerged as the first Western biography of Meher Baba, *The Perfect Master,* released in 1937. Norina, a charismatic princess and talented actress, could fill many roles, especially as a public figure in high society, an arena where few could move as freely as she. But the actual head of the committee was Herbert; and it was he who managed most of the transactions connected with *Questions and Answers* and its successor booklet, *The Sayings of Shri Meher*

---

[47] A copy of this letter, made available for this edition by David Fenster from his personal papers, has been reproduced in appendix 3. For reminiscences connected with the committee's office in Charing Cross, see William Backett, "Incidents from the Master's Work at 50, Charing Cross, London (1933–37) and Elsewhere in London," *Meher Baba Journal,* 3, no. 1 (November 1940), pp. 31–40. As Backett recalls Baba once commenting, "You have no idea of the work I am doing at the office" (p. 33).

[48] An article entitled "Answers: The True Messiah," *Glow International,* Spring 2009, pp. 3–15, contains, as display insets on pp. 9–13 and 15, facsimile reproductions of the minutes to the original meeting of Circle Editorial Committee on October 18, 1933, attended by Meher Baba, Norina Matchabelli, Herbert Davy, Kitty Davy, and Will Backett. These five handwritten pages outline many of the Committee's policies, procedures, and personnel.

Baba, during the second half of 1933 and on into the next year.[49]

Questions and Answers was published probably in September 1933. Unwin Brothers Limited in London, a printer associated with the distinguished publisher George Allan and Unwin, printed 5,000 copies. Responding to Baba's request, Circle Editorial Committee sold the booklet at a low price, sixpence per copy in England and fifteen cents in America. Since Stokes declined to use his good offices for the distribution of the book in the United States, the American distribution effort probably drew on names and contacts that Malcolm Schloss had cultivated during the years up through 1931 when he had run an occult book shop, "The North Node," in Manhattan. Elizabeth Patterson helped and participated in various ways. In a letter to Herbert and the Circle Editorial Committee dated December 5, 1933,[50] she reported that she had sent out 7,500 notices by post and that the book was selling briskly, at about ten copies a day. At the same time batches were being dispatched to Baba in India through Sarosh Motor Works in Nasik; and Baba himself said that he would arrange for their distribution as necessary to Persia. Clearly Baba's disciples—with Baba's own direct encouragement—put a serious effort behind the book. Most of its first edition seems to have been sold off by the end of the year.

With the book successfully released to the public, during the late autumn of 1933, under Baba's direction Herbert was preparing a second edition. Though no copy of this second edition has surfaced, in print or manuscript form, a body of correspondence between Herbert Davy and Graham Stokes does indicate the general character of the editorial changes that were to go into it. Most importantly, it was to incorporate five new

49 Earlier editions of *Lord Meher* state incorrectly that Norina had been put in charge of the Circle Editorial Committee's work. The current draft of *LM* (in progress), however, indicates that, in meeting of the Circle Editorial Committee on October 27, 1933, "Herbert was appointed the director, and Norina took an active role, and also the Backetts." Herbert Davy is identified as the Committee's "Director" in the first page of the "Minutes" to the October 18, 1933 meetings (see previous note).

50 See appendix 4, pp. 325–27.

questions and their answers from Baba, which Baba dictated personally ("almost word by word," as he put it) and sent to Herbert from Port Said in Egypt in a letter dated November 6.[51] Further, in a letter dated December 7, 1933, Herbert related to Stokes that he had personally cleared up with Baba confusions that he found in the original edition "between Mind and Intellect, partly because we used 'mental body' as the adjective form for Mind Body."[52] Presumably Herbert made (or planned to make) the corresponding terminological adjustments in the second edition. Finally, Stokes himself had suggested numerous revisions—undoubtedly many of them substantial—in the copy of the first edition that Herbert had sent to him.

Evidently Herbert relayed Stokes's suggestions on to Baba, conveying at the same time that that the second edition was ready to go to press, because in a letter to Herbert dated December 8, 1933, Baba replied, "You may accept his [Stokes's] minor suggestions and corrections as you think best, without altering, as far as possible, the sense of the Answers. But I cannot see how you can do it if (as I understand from your letter) the second edition has already gone, or will soon go, to the press. Or do you mean for the third edition? However, use your discretion and act, I repeat, as you think best. What more can I say?"[53] Two months later, however, it appears that the book still had not been published. For in a letter to Baba dated February 3, 1934, Herbert suggested that the five additional questions and answers previously slated for the second edition of *Questions and Answers* be incorporated into "Philosophical Fragments," the new project that he was working on at the time; and in his reply dated March 13, Baba approved this idea.[54] Since Herbert's connection with Baba dissolved soon after this, one doubts that the second edition of *Questions and Answers* was ever printed, if indeed Herbert completed the drafting of it.

---

[51] See appendix 4, p. 324. The letter is reproduced in facsimile on p. 58.

[52] See appendix 4, p. 328.

[53] See appendix 4, p. 330.

[54] See appendix 4, pp. 334–35, 337–38.

Clearly the five new questions and answers would have comprised the heart and core of the "value added" in this second edition. Yet though Baba's dictated text cannot now be located, by a curious chance we have been able to recover its essential content. For as described earlier, when the Circle Editorial Committee was established in the summer of 1933, it took upon itself the task of translating *Questions and Answers* into a number of languages. One of these, the French translation published in 1934, has been found, and it contains, in addition to the original fifty-eight questions and answers, five new ones, nos. 59–63.[55] Moreover, Kitty Davy's papers in the Meher Spiritual Center include four typed pages with "Questions and Answers," numbered 59 through 63, that are "[t]ranslated from the French edition of 'Questions & Answers' by S. M. B." This exact same English translation was published in two parts in successive issues of the *Meher Baba Journal.*[56] From these materials we have been able to compile an English version that has been included in this present book as a supplement to *Questions and Answers* in part three. Amusingly enough, the text that you will find there represents a translation into English from the French edition,[57] which was itself a translation into French from a (now lost) English original that Baba had dictated probably while cruising on the Viceroy of India back to India in November of 1933 in the aftermath of his trip to Spain. By such circuitous routes do these particular words of Meher Baba's descend to us today.

---

[55] *Shri Meher Baba, le Maître Parfait: Questions et Réponses,* pp. 53-58. A copy of the German translation has just been located; and it too contains the five additional questions and answers.

[56] See the two identically titled articles, "Question Baba Answers," the first, in *Meher Baba Journal,* vol. 2, no. 6 (April 1940), pp. 353–55 (containing questions nos. 59–61), and the second, in vol. 2, no. 7 (May 1940), pp. 415–16 (containing questions nos. 62–63). Detailed textual evidence points to a direct genetic relationship between these to *Journal* articles and the typed manuscript among Kitty Davy's papers; see, for example, p. 272 and footnote 87.

[57] This English translation closely follows the text of the translation in the *Meher Baba Journal* (see previous note), with certain corrections and revisions by Françoise and Daniel Lemetais as well as this present editor. The French text that was the source for this English translation has been reproduced in appendix 6.

The Sayings

The release of *Questions and Answers* was followed in short order by another booklet, *The Sayings of Shri Meher Baba,* also published by the Circle Editorial Committee in London. *The Sayings* consists of 136 maxims varying in length from a sentence to a short paragraph. Like *Questions and Answers, The Sayings* has been divided into seven sections, each with its own topic: divine love; religion or shariat; the spiritual path; intellect, mind, and Maya; the spiritual planes and inner spheres; the Perfect Master; and God. Again like *Questions and Answers,* the new book begins with a preface that gives biographical details about Meher Baba and certain information about the manner of his authorship and dictation through the medium of the alphabet board. The text of *The Sayings* is somewhat more fully annotated than *Questions and Answers* was, however, and it concludes with a glossary that defines thirty-two key terms both from English and the Indic languages. Meticulous and thorough in its preparation, *The Sayings,* like *Questions and Answers,* stands as a first-rate piece of work, indeed a credit to those who carried it out.

As we gather from the Herbert Davy-Graham Stokes correspondence, the booklet was published and available for sale in December of 1933.[58] Herbert wrote to Stokes on February 12, 1934 that "5,000 copies have been sent to India and Persia; 5,000 are for Western distribution." The success of *Questions and Answers* must have emboldened the Circle Editorial Committee in venturing on so large a press run.

The correspondence between Herbert Davy and Graham Stokes supplies other interesting pieces of information about the new book. In a

---

[58] The correspondence quoted from below is reproduced in full in appendix 4, pp. 327–36. None of the correspondence or other biographical sources now available refer to the matter of translating *The Sayings*—which, as we have seen, was such a major undertaking in connection with *Questions and Answers.* However, *Avatar Meher Baba Bibliography* (p. 42) cites a 44-page "German translation of Baba's sayings," *Shri Meher Baba, der Vollkommene Meister: Ausspruche* (Erlenbache, Switzerland: Rotapfel-Verlag [1934]). Since the bibliographer (Bal Natu) reports that this book was "unavailable for review," we cannot speak with assurance about its contents. But since its publisher in that same year published a German translation of *Questions and Answers,* it seems not unlikely that *Ausspruche* is a German translation of *The Sayings.*

December 7 letter, written at the very time that *The Sayings* was being published, Herbert Davy, responding to Stokes's criticisms of *Questions and Answers,* introduced him to the new release as "less controversial" than its predecessor and "more interesting for the general public." The sayings are "literally his [Baba's] own words, subject of course to the same limitations, mentioned above, that are imposed by the use of the [alphabet] board." In a subsequent cover letter (dated December 18) with which he enclosed a complimentary copy of *The Sayings,* Herbert said more. He acknowledged that the style and English of the sayings are

> very imperfect I know, but they're really Baba's own words, given through the medium of the alphabet board, he did not wish to correct or put them into a more literary form.
>
> They are best regarded as channels by which his power may reach a wide public; the only test for Shri Meher Baba's claims is their capacity to awaken the spiritual life in an ever increasing number of mankind. This must not be judged by literary taste & purely intellectual canons.

Stokes received the copy of *The Sayings,* and in a letter to Herbert Davy dated January 18, 1934 he praised it as an "admirable little booklet." At the same time, he criticized the Circle Editorial Committee for the way in which it presented Baba's material, particularly in the annotations. In his reply dated February 12, Herbert corrected Stokes's criticisms on one point:

> . . . the notes were not written by the [Committee], though we are responsible for the juxtaposition of the sayings and the notes. In this we may have erred. But the notes themselves are taken from Baba's own works. Some of those to which you refer, concerning the nature of Paramatma, were taken from "Philosophical Fragments". . . .
>
> I am personally often conscious of having made mistakes, and I am very grateful to you for your criticisms and suggestions. I expect Baba will answer you directly. Philosophical Fragments

> is the next book to be published. Perhaps we shall be able to have the benefit of your criticism and judgement before publishing? I hope we shall.

One gathers from this correspondence that Herbert Davy believed the primary content of *The Sayings* consisted of Baba's own words, raw and unedited. The fact is, however, that all of the 136 sayings had been published before. For as we noted earlier, the *Meher Message,* published out of Nasik on a monthly basis between 1929 and 1931 under the editorship of K. J. Dastur, began each of its issues, from January 1929 through April-May-June 1931, with five "Sayings of His Divine Majesty Sadguru Meher Baba." Thus a total of 140 sayings were released first in the *Meher Message,* all but four of which were reissued in the Circle Editorial Committee's booklet.[59]

Despite this, we cannot be sure that Herbert Davy, though he seems to have known about the *Meher Message,* ever actually saw copies of the magazine or realized the sayings had already been published there. After all, an obscure Indian periodical on spiritual subjects would not quickly have found its way into the hands of Britishers many thousands of miles distant, especially in this colonial era when literary prestige gravitated towards London as the capital of the empire and not towards colonial outposts like Nasik, India. Of course, the Indian disciples accompanying Meher Baba on his Western tours knew the magazine intimately; but since its editor had turned apostate to Baba in 1931 and was by the time of Baba's early Western tours publishing articles against him, doubtless they would have preferred to bring Baba's writings before the eyes of his new Western followers through some other channel and not to have promoted a deceased periodical and a controversial episode that could raise questions in their minds.

Where the "sayings" are concerned, an Indian disciple such as Chanji could well have provided the Circle Editorial Committee with this same content in typed form without necessarily drawing attention to its publication in

---

59 The four sayings not incorporated into the booklet are reproduced in appendix 7.

the magazine. And in fact, a document answering to this very description has surfaced among the J. Graham Phelps Stokes papers at Columbia University Rare Book and Manuscript Library (see footnotes 40 and 41 above). The twelve-page typed manuscript in question, headed by the title "Sayings of Shri Sadguru Meher Baba," could, in various copies, have supplied both Dastur and Herbert Davy with their source material. For it contains the same 140 sayings that appeared in the *Meher Message* during its three-year run. The date "January 1929," which appears directly below the manuscript's title, corresponds to the very month of the *Meher Message's* inaugural issue. The document was probably prepared, in other words, to provide Dastur with sufficient matter for a feature column in the magazine over an extended period. Yet we can say more, for the Stokes manuscript gives us another interesting piece of evidence, in the circled handwritten letters "C.E.C." in the top left corner of the first page. This abbreviation doubtless stands for "Circle Editorial Committee." One can reasonably hypothesize that Herbert Davy, the head of this committee, had a copy of this document himself, perhaps given to him by Baba's secretary Chanji. The probability is, then, that K. J. Dastur and Herbert Davy were each individually using their own copies of this same document. By this supposition they acted independently; the magazine and the booklet, in other words, probably derived separately from the same source in one or another typed version or carbon copy.

Where did this typed manuscript itself come from, and does it indeed contain "Baba's own words," raw and unedited, as Herbert Davy supposed? At this stage in the research into Meher Baba's life and message, we do not know. A few of the sayings have been taken from talks Baba gave to the mandali in the mid-20s as recorded in "Tiffin Lectures." But the full researching of sources has not yet been carried out; and in any event there remains a large quantity of relevant archival material that is not yet available for study. But in the absence of this information, it would not be unreasonable to suppose that whoever took down and later collected these 140 sayings to some degree edited them as a part of the job. Indeed, Meher Baba seems to have expected no less of those who prepared his words for publication. As already noted, to the best of our knowledge the process of Meher Baba's authorship almost always entailed the literary services of disciples. The seal of his authorship consists not in some preconceived notion of authorial "purity" but in his having lent his name to the final, published result.

The text of the 140 maxims in the Stokes manuscript was reproduced by Dastur in the *Meher Message* in the exact same sequence and with only a scattering of alterations of a typographic and mechanical sort. Did the Circle Editorial Committee do likewise in *The Sayings?* As we have seen, the editor thoroughly reordered the 136 sayings under seven major rubrics. As to the text, detailed comparison shows that Baba's words underwent some minor editing in their passage from the typed manuscript (if this was indeed the Committee's source) into the booklet. The overwhelming majority of these edits pertains to the mechanics of writing—punctuation, italics, and so forth. Others extend to minor rewordings. There are a few sayings, however, that undergo major revision. An example appears below.

Though we do not know for certain that the hand that produced this

Stokes manuscript, "Sayings of Shri Sadguru Meher Baba," no. 1, corresponding to *Meher Message*, vol. 1, no. 1 (January 1929), saying no. 1	*The Sayings of Shri Meher Baba,* p. 131 in this book.
Sannyas does not necessarily consist in the putting on of an ochre robe and gadding about with a staff in one hand and a begging bowl in another. The true sannyasin is he who has renounced his lower self and all worldly desires.	Wearing the yellow robe, begging for bread, visiting the holy places, do not necessarily prove Sanyas or Renunciation. The true sanyasin is he who has renounced his lower self and all worldly desires.

particular change was Herbert Davy's, to my eye at least, the literary sensibility that governs it exhibits a British sobriety. We do know from the correspondence that Baba authorized Herbert in his editor's role. Taking the book as a whole, the overall scope of the editing was so slight (unlike the exceptional extreme example highlighted above) as to warrant Herbert's expressed view that the text we find in *The Sayings* represents essentially Baba's own words, authentic and untampered with.

So much for the primary text in *The Sayings;* now what of the annotations, which (as we have seen) provided the subject for some slight verbal sparring between Herbert Davy and Stokes? The main annotations in *The Sayings* occur on pp. 133, 135, 138, and 151; evidently the most problematic of these, from Stokes's point of view, was the last. Herbert Davy asserted that the source material for at least some of these annotations was Baba's own words in the forthcoming book entitled "Philosophical Fragments." As it happens, the final page of *The Sayings* lists as a work "in preparation" the title "The Philosophical Fragments of Shri Meher Baba," by A. K. Abdulla, known to Baba's followers as Ramjoo.

Now though no volume entitled "Philosophical Fragments" survives among the existing published literature, late in 1933, as we have seen, Ramjoo published *Shri Meher Baba: His Philosophy and Teachings,* which he describes in his introduction as having been "compiled from [Meher Baba's] own dictations." One of the annotations in *The Sayings* (see p. 151) borrows exact phrases from its first chapter (*Philosophy and Teachings,* pp. 2–7). None of the other notes in *The Sayings* derives directly from this book, although some of the subjects and usages of terms in the two works are generally reminiscent of each other. Yet letters between Herbert and Baba in the months February through May 1934[60] show that Herbert was reworking Ramjoo's text with a view to publishing it as a Western edition. "Philosophical

[60] See especially the letters dated February 3, February 28, March 13, May 6, and May 25, 1934, in appendix 4, pp. 334–35, 336–37, 337–38, 340–41, and 341–42.

Fragments" was his working title; and he seems to have applied this title retrospectively to Ramjoo's book, no doubt under the presumption that this older version would be superceded when the Western edition came into print. In his letter to Baba dated February 3, 1934, Herbert proposes incorporating into the new text of "Philosophical Fragments" material which Baba had given him in Portofino the previous July, which consisted of select articles from the *Meher Message.* In short, we know that Herbert was working closely with all of this material—Ramjoo's *Philosophy and Teachings* as well as certain articles from the *Meher Message*—during the early months of 1934; it seems probable that he used it while editing and annotating *The Sayings* in the late months of the previous year.

In fact, we can gather a more precise inventory of some of the texts available to Herbert Davy, once again, through the Graham Stokes papers in the Columbia University Rare Book and Manuscript Library. Two typed compilations from the Stokes collection, the first entitled "Fragments from Spiritual Speeches by Shri Sadguru Meher Baba," and the second, "Articles by Shri Meher Baba," represent themselves (accurately) as being "from" the *Meher Message.* Moreover, several of the title pages feature the circled handwritten inscription "C.E.C." Again, this probably abbreviates "Circle Editorial Committee," and it suggests that the manuscripts were sent to Stokes by Herbert Davy. Several of the annotations in *The Sayings,* including some of the small notes, clearly derive from passages in the "Fragments from Spiritual Speeches"; and it is likely, at least at one point, that Herbert Davy drew from the "Articles" as well. In all of these cases Herbert's use of his source manuscripts was intelligent and discriminating; he did not copy passages in bulk but selected phrases and sentences that would illuminate specific unfamiliar ideas in *The Sayings.* A number of his notes in the book, however, including some of the substantial ones, do not point to any source in either the Stokes papers or *Philosophy and Teachings.* One presumes, then, that Herbert Davy must have had other manuscripts at his disposal besides those that we know about.

In summation, one can assert with confidence that a body of

"philosophical" writings attributed to Meher Baba was in circulation at this time, that Herbert Davy saw it, that he drew on some selection from it in his work on *The Sayings,* and that the Circle Editorial Committee envisioned its future publication in some form as a part of its work of presenting Meher Baba to the Western world. In the actual event, none of this philosophical material got published in the 1930s, apart from Ramjoo Abdulla's *Philosophy and Teachings,* the distribution of which was largely confined to India. But the foundation had been laid for future efforts in the literary arena. Between 1938 and 1942 the *Meher Baba Journal* brought before the world a magnificent exposition of Meher Baba's "philosophy and teachings" in the form of his discourses, subsequently compiled and published in book form.[61] The *Journal* published many other significant items in the philosophic vein, particularly by Baba's disciples Ghani, Deshmukh, and Ramjoo. This line arrived at its culmination a decade later in *God Speaks,* Meher Baba's supreme statement in the domain of theosophy and cosmology that will doubtless provide the major foundation in the understanding for philosophically minded seekers for the next 700 years.

Ironically enough, during this very period in 1933–34 when Herbert Davy was playing the leading part in the publication of the first two books of Meher Baba's words ever to appear in the Western world, Herbert himself was passing through a crisis of faith regarding his own connection with Baba. A series of poignant letters between him and Baba exhibit, as Baba himself put it, a clash between Herbert's head and his heart. By the middle of 1934, Herbert had broken off his connection with Baba; and while his sister Kitty remained Baba's close disciple for the rest of her life, Herbert never renewed that link. Born on January 18, 1899, he died at the age of eighty-three on December 29, 1982; and his obituary makes no mention of the three-year phase of his close association with the Avatar of the Age whom he had been one of the first in the Western world to meet and recognize. But throughout the term of that association, his

[61] These discourses appeared as the first article in each issue; for detailed information, see Meher Baba, *Discourses,* revised sixth edition (North Myrtle Beach, South Carolina: Sheriar Foundation, 2007), vol. 4, pp. 116–39.

conduct indeed upheld the ideal of the British gentleman in the best sense. He performed outstanding literary work for his Master, as he took him to be at the time; and his memory should be held in honor.

Two Religious Conferences

We take a moment to digress briefly from our principal narrative to recall a curious interlude that played itself out in mid-1933, just as the work with *Questions and Answers* was getting seriously under way, involving *religious conferences*. On June 3–5, 1933, a week before Baba set out for Italy on his fifth Western tour, an All Faiths Conference took place in Nasik, with Circle Cinema, whose proprietor, of course, was Baba's disciple Rustom K. Irani, as its venue. Representatives of various religions attended under the auspices of the All Faiths League, and the proceedings, published later that year out of Bombay, comprised a book of 165 pages with the summaries of more than twenty papers. Though Baba was invited to attend, he did not, but sent a short message that was read to the gathering by Ramjoo Abdulla; and it appeared on page 17 of the book. The text of this message is reproduced in appendix 2.

Soon after that, while Baba was sojourning at Portofino with his Western disciples, Graham Stokes passed along to him an invitation to participate at the World Fellowship of Faiths conference being held at Chicago, with its "culminating convention period" from August 27 to September 17. Billing itself as a convention in the tradition and lineage of the celebrated 1893 Parliament of Religions in Chicago at which Swami Vivekananda was first introduced to the Western World, the World Fellowship Conference of 1933 was to be a stellar event with sponsors and attendees of international renown. Another formal invitation from the executive director of the conference reached Baba upon his return to Nasik. Baba agreed to come and began preparations for another visit to America. But in subsequent correspondence the conference organizers found themselves unable to pay any of Baba's travel or hotel accommodation costs. Baba cancelled his plans; and during the months September–October he traveled with his Western disciples through Spain instead.

Meher Baba was never an enthusiast of religious conferences; rarely did he associate with them in any way. These two conferences in 1933, one in India and one in America, represent, as it were, the perigee in this Avataric advent: they were as close as he ever came to participating in events of this kind.

How It All Happened and Baba's Work in Film

We come last to Meher Baba's work in the domain of film. As we have seen, in his early tours to the West, Baba seems to have progressed through the various media of communication, from the most personal (individual interviews) to the most sophisticated and technological (motion pictures). Nonetheless, though it did not become Baba's main focus until this early Western phase was nearing its end in 1934–35, he sowed the seed for this film work at the beginning, during his first trip to America in 1931.

The story runs thus. Arriving in New York on November 6 of that year, Baba's activities in the month that followed centered in a house thirty miles up the Hudson River from New York City in the town of Harmon. Though Malcolm and Jean Schloss, two of Baba's first American disciples, were occupying the house at the time and running it as what they called the "Meherashram," its owner, Margaret Mayo, a wealthy and successful playwright, made it available for Baba's use during his end-of-the-year visit. It was during this stay, a week before his departure for India, that Baba gave out the main piece of narrative material around which his subsequent activities in the arena of motion pictures revolved. We quote at length from *Lord Meher.*[62]

> At Harmon, the topic of making a film on spirituality was brought up for the first time. It would be a topic that would occupy much of Baba's attention over the next few years. The theme of the film was to be according to Baba's explanations on the purpose of creation, the outcome of the universe and the spiritual journey. Margaret Mayo had close connections with the American film industry: Several of her Broadway plays had been adapted for the silent

[62] *LM* (in progress).

> screen, and her play *Polly of the Circus* became the first film produced by Goldwyn Company in 1917, of which she was a founding member along with her former husband, Edgar Selwyn, a Broadway producer.
>
> On Thursday, December 3, 1931, Margaret Mayo spoke to Jean and Malcolm about her friend Harry E. Aitken, a movie producer who had worked with the famous director D. W. Griffith. She suggested that he would be a suitable person to organize everything connected with the film, as he was interested in spirituality. She then explained to Baba that she could write a detailed scenario if points were give to her. Baba immediately accepted her offer and began dictating points to her. In about an hour Baba finished dictating the whole plot—the beginning of creation, the developing stages of evolution, reincarnation and the stories of three characters through five lifetimes to Realization. After reading it to the group, all said that it was splendid and it was typed out.
>
> Later that evening, Harry Aitken, 54, was invited over. Baba's story was read out. Impressed, Aitken said it was a grand idea. "Can it be properly worked out [into a movie]?" Baba asked him. "Certainly," Aitken assured him, and the film was discussed further. (Aitken suggested the film be shot in India, and that its opening be there also, with Baba in attendance!) Its suggested title was *A Touch of Maya.*

The scenario which Baba dictated and Margaret Mayo wrote up still survives in manuscript form; slightly expanded through the incorporation of new material about the planes that Baba added in 1934, it provides the main basis for the text of "A Touch of Maya" republished in part five. The story in its 1931 draft opens with a creation sequence, whose cinematic expression would have depended on special effects. The bulk of the narrative, however, is devoted to the phases of reincarnation and the ascent to God, as we follow the careers of three souls, X, Y, and Z, through five lifetimes. In the first lifetime they enter the human life stage as cannibals, fighting and killing for the sake of food and sexual prerogatives. In each successive lifetime they find themselves thrown together in situations determined by their connections from the past; but gradually their responses become more enlightened. In the fourth and fifth lifetimes one of the characters, X, progresses through the seven planes of consciousness: and Baba plainly intended that the vision and experiences of these planes should be depicted cinematically. In the end, X becomes a Perfect Master and Y and Z his disciples. In notes dictated in 1934 Baba indicated that these five incarnations were not to be understood as the *only* lifetimes that these three souls pass through, though the fourth and fifth lifetimes do follow in immediate sequence. The succession of lifetimes, each with its own particular theme and dramatic nexus, illustrates magnificently not only the working out of reincarnation and karma but the process of spiritual transformation: by repeatedly presenting itself in new scenes and human configurations, the past provides the medium for the soul to transcend its limitations and fulfill its latent potentialities. Tracing the entire human arc from its beginnings in animalistic degradation to the heights of spiritual splendor, the story is truly an inspiring one.

This narrative of X, Y, and Z remained as the abiding center and core of the project, subsequently re-titled *How It All Happened,*[63] to which Baba devoted the main thrust of his efforts in the following years. Other film concepts came into the picture as the film work progressed, it is true; yet the "Touch of Maya" story, along with the body of philosophical-cosmological material that Baba dictated in 1934 (to be described shortly), seemed to represent the theme and content that he wanted to bring into expression.

Though the dictation to Margaret Mayo in December 1931 was not immediately followed up on, either by Baba or his followers, over the next two or three years film and filmmaking came increasingly into the picture in a variety of ways. As we have already recounted, during his American tour of

---

[63] Chapter five in Ramjoo Abdulla's *Philosophy and Teachings,* pp. 53–75, bears this same title and conveys its own version of the Divine Theme. Ramjoo's chapter does not relate in any direct way, however, to the material Baba prepared in the course of his film work.

May–June 1932 Baba was feted by some of the leading luminaries of the Hollywood film industry in its golden age, and one of his major messages in the Los Angeles area specifically addressed the topic of motion pictures. Meanwhile, an interest in filmmaking was flourishing among certain of Meher Baba's mandali in India. In 1931 Baba's disciple Rustom K. Irani had established Circle Cinema in Nasik; and for a time in 1933, the mandali, with Baba's approval, planned to undertake the creation of original films. In a meeting between Baba and his mandali in Nasik in August 1933, it was decided that, while Baba was away on his upcoming Western tour, his disciples Pendu and Beheram would learn to operate a motion picture camera, and Baba's brother Jal would study acting.[64] In a discussion with several of his disciples in December of that year, Baba even suggested having a film studio constructed at Meherabad and the film sent to Bombay for processing![65] In short, work in the domain of film was moving ahead among Baba's disciples concurrently in India and the West, just as was happening during this same period in the literary arena.

But in relation to his work with the West, film did not become Baba's predominant focus until after his return from Spain in November 1933. At that juncture, for the next fifteen months or so, Baba's film undertakings moved to the front burner and seemed to absorb most of his energy. During the early part of 1934, as the new film projects were starting to take shape, Baba corresponded extensively with his disciple Norina Matchabelli and her former husband Karl Vollmoeller, a playwright and screenwriter with Hollywood connections. Largely as a result of these communications, Baba planned another trip to Europe in the summer of 1934, where the relationships could be firmed up and the projects made definite. In fact, Baba's seventh and

---

[64] *LM* (Mownavani), vol. 3, p. 1316; *LM* (Manifestation), vol. 5, 1804–5. In a personal note David Fenster writes: "Rustom intended to set up a film company to make commercial films with spiritual themes —independent of Baba's film projects. Rustom actually made one movie, *Nigah-e-Kamil,* circa 1937–38." Apparently Rustom himself played the lead role, and Baba himself watched it in a Bombay theater. Unfortunately the film did not succeed with the public, either in Nasik (where it premiered in Rustom's own theater) or in Bombay, where it ran for only a week.

[65] *LM* (Mownavani), vol. 3, p. 1349; *LM* (Manifestation), vol. 5, 1853.

eighth tours to the West, during the months June-July-August 1934 and November-December-January 1934–35, were specifically dedicated to this effort. While the projects inaugurated then had a lingering afterlife that continued into 1936 and 1937, this period from early 1934 to the beginning of 1935 was the nub and the crux, the historical moment when the Avatar was most exclusively concentrated on the film medium.

In preparation for his trip to Europe scheduled for the next month, at the end of May 1934 Baba took time out from his other activities to create new material that would supplement and flesh out the original film idea. As *Lord Meher* describes it, Baba

> began dictating for the first time the Theme of Creation in the room on the back veranda of the Mess Quarters at lower Meherabad. Baba would dictate on the alphabet board, which Chanji would read. Feram Workingboxwala would take it down in shorthand and later type it out. Adi Sr. and Minoo Pohowala were allowed to be present and listen.[66]

The Archives of the Avatar Meher Baba Trust contain a body of content that seems to have resulted from this work of Baba's in May 1934.[67] Some of it has already been published in *Lord Meher;*[68] but much of it has not. Part five presents a compilation of the main core and substance from this miscellany of documents. Since the originals take the form of rough dictations, notes extracted from reference sources, figures clipped out from a book, and charts and illustrations drawn by Baba's mandali, the text in part five has been edited, largely for fluency and readability. That is to say, though the prose has to a certain extent been rewritten, nothing of substance has been added or deleted, except certain passages of densely scientific discourse

---

66 *LM* (Mownavani), vol. 3, p. 1361; *LM* (Manifestation), vol. 5, p. 1871.

67 The Archives team made a special effort to locate, rehouse, and digitally scan this material in order to make it available for presentation in this book. Special thanks are due to Janet Judson, Meg DeLoe, Patrick Finley, William Ward, Meredith Klein, Martin and Christine Cook, Frank Bloise, and Meherwan Jessawala, without whom this presentation of Meher Baba's film work would not have been possible.

68 *LM* (Mownavani), vol. 3, pp. 1361–65; *LM* (Manifestation), vol. 5, pp. 1870–75.

whose content has been summarized editorially (and reproduced in its entirety in appendix 8). Also, since the original materials as we have them today are fragmentary, part five reassembles them in what was clearly their original intended order. (The first page of the document entitled "Scenario," reproduced on pp. 191–92, spells out the film plan and how the elements of content ought to be arranged.) In short, part five, and especially the section entitled *How It All Happened,* has been assembled in its present form for publication in this book. But *all* of its content comes from the original notes in the Trust Archives. The substance is entirely Baba's.

Seen in overview, the material that we have in the form of original documents cannot be said to constitute a book, or even the makings of a book, despite the fact that it evidently incorporates some of Baba's own dictations. It is better understood as preparatory notes for a film; or even more exactly, as notes for presentation to business executives and artistic talents in the Hollywood film world. But what stands at its center, unmistakably, is what Baba later called the "Divine Theme."[69] The film was indeed to relate *How It All Happened*—the original creation of the universe, the evolution of form and consciousness culminating in the soul's achievement of man- and womanhood, reincarnation in human form, spiritual advancement through the planes of consciousness, and the final Realization of the "I am God" state. Baba had covered some of this ground in *Infinite Intelligence,* dictated at Meherabad in 1926. In later years Baba returned to this subject—in some of the *Discourses,* in the *Divine Theme,* and most importantly, in *God Speaks.* In terms of their philosophic content, then, these 1934 dictations take their place in this line of development in Meher Baba's "teachings." One is struck by the fact that, in this first great exposition of his message that the Avatar intended for the film medium, the content that he wanted to communicate was philosophical and

[69] See Meher Baba, *Divine Theme: Evolution, Reincarnation, Realisation* (Meherabad, Ahmednagar, India: Published by Adi K. Irani for the Publication Committee, Meher Baba Universal Spiritual Centre, 1943).

cosmological. In view of the predominant emphasis over his lifetime that Baba gave to the theme of *love,* one might have expected him, in his entry into the world of film, to concentrate on the more personal and devotional aspects of spirituality. Yet the story that he chose to relate was a metaphysical one, that is, the narrative of the soul's journey from its original unconsciousness to its consummation in union with God.

The most extensive and developed document in the 1934 material, a manuscript that we are entitling "Creation and Evolution," is comprised of an introduction (in three parts) and four chapters. (This document stands as the textual source for the introduction and first movement in *How It All Happened,* 161–79.) After establishing in the introduction an overall framework for the soul's journey, which consists of a Descending Track (creation and evolution), a Transverse Track (reincarnation), and an Ascending Track (spiritual advancement through the planes), the four chapters cover the entire process of the evolution of form and consciousness as far as the emergence of the earliest human. Chapters 1 and 2 give information about the interrelations of Space and Energy (elsewhere called *Pran* and *Akash*) and the emergence of 276 subtle gases, information that significantly adds to the account of creation in *God Speaks.* Chapters 3 and 4 discuss the evolution of life forms from the vegetable through the animal. Some elements of this content—such as the description of the three-headed fish-reptile, the bat-bird, and the "missing link"—must have been given directly by Baba. Much of the material, however, derives from a reference source in evolutionary biology; indeed, the original text of chapter 4 refers to page and figure numbers, and some of these figures and text, clipped out of the original book, have been preserved in the Trust Archives files.

Quite obviously, then, the original text in "Creation and Evolution" is heterogeneous, mixing Baba's own dictation with extracts from contemporary scientific discourse. Evidently Baba intended, in this segment of the film, to integrate his own cosmological scheme with the discoveries of contemporary science. It is hard to think of another instance during his lifetime when the Avatar engaged science in this way. One would misconstrue in supposing that Baba meant to confirm the pronouncements of evolutionary science at that particular moment in history in the 1930s; indeed, this scientific material in "Creation and Evolution" was undoubtedly compiled by his mandali and intended for use in representations in Hollywood. Yet perhaps Baba did mean to suggest how such projects should be pursued in the future, and that artists and scientists should collaborate in the formulation of a unified cosmological vision.

The second great movement in *How It All Happened* is related through the narrative "A Touch of Maya" that Baba originally dictated to Margaret Mayo, as described earlier. Though the core narrative of the three souls through five lifetimes went unaltered from the time of its original dictation, Baba appears in 1934 to have given supplementary information about the experience of the planes of consciousness. To date we cannot locate in the Trust Archives any single document that contains "A Touch of Maya" in its full, expanded version; yet all of its pieces can be found in one place or another. The version of "A Touch of Maya" that we reproduce in part five was published by Filis Frederick in the *Awakener,* vol. 22, no. 1 (1986), pp. 1–4. We find in that *Awakener* text some slight editing, perhaps performed by Filis herself. Yet whoever it was, the editor has followed the primary sources closely, introducing only small stylistic changes that improve the text's readability. Through this narrative account of the five lifetimes, Baba was fleshing out an understanding of the "Transverse" and "Ascending Tracks," that is, the processes of reincarnation and spiritual advancement. The first half of the film, as outlined in "Creation and Evolution," was to relate how the soul got separated from God; and the second half, in "A Touch of Maya," tells how it achieves its reunion.

The Trust Archives contains various other items and documents that convey further sense of the nature of the work in the film medium that Baba was engaged in; and part five continues with a selection of these. A seventeen-page typed manuscript, plainly compiled by one of Meher Baba's mandali, assembles a mass of information about the different geological eras and stages and species in the evolution of the life forms down to the human. Another seven-page typed document, "Introduction to Planes and Reincarnation," reproduces verbatim material from Ramjoo Abdulla's *Philosophy and Teachings,* pp. 19–25 on the process of human rebirth and spiritual advancement, though the order of the paragraphs has been somewhat rearranged. Another four-page document, "Introduction to Planes," constitutes a first draft of the description of character X's passage through the planes of consciousness that in a revised and improved form appears in "A Touch of Maya."

But particularly noteworthy is the spectacular, five- by seven-and-a-half-foot chart that Adi Sr. drew under Baba's instructions. The "Film Master Chart," reproduced on p. 194 and as a 17" x 22" insert inside the back cover, is a highly developed, early illustration of the Divine Theme. That is, it depicts the movement from God Unconscious to God Conscious, a movement that traces its course from the creation of the universe through the "Projection Point" on through evolution, reincarnation, and spiritual advancement, and that achieves its goal and terminus in the Realization of God. Many of the points of information in the chart link explicitly to the text of *How It All Happened.* Other visual material that Baba had prepared at this time includes the two drawings of exotic creatures—the fifteen-foot bat-bird and the 175-foot three-headed fish-reptile. The chart and drawings were obviously intended give *How it All Happened* a visual outline and a few vivid images.

At present we do not have any way of knowing with exactitude who assembled all this material, how much of it was dictated by or read out to Baba in May of 1934, and what selection Baba took with him and used during his Western visits. Yet the overall picture is clear. Baba and his mandali were assembling notes, drawings, narrative sketches, cosmological explanations, and other materials in preparation for meetings with representatives of the film world. These documents cannot rightly be understood as literary or artistic exposition in their own right: they were not originated in that intent. They are rather a collection of rough notes, the records of brainstorming sessions, of cues and suggestions, of vistas and envisionings, to be further developed and fulfilled by creative artists in the medium of the motion picture.

Such was the creative work that Baba and his mandali appear to have accomplished in the first half of 1934, culminating in the week at Meherabad from May 23 to June 1. Part five of this book compiles the essential core from this content.

Armed with this new assemblage of philosophical, scientific, artistic, and narrative materials, Baba traveled to Paris, London, and Zurich in June–July 1934 with the evident purpose of forging external frameworks and personal links through which this film work could be advanced. Many of the crucial contacts during this year were established by Norina Matchabelli, a princess of wide acquaintance among the cultural elites in Europe and America. Two decades earlier Norina had starred in the London stage production of the sensationally successful pantomime play *The Miracle*, which ran for thousands of performances. The play's author was Karl Vollmoeller, at the time her husband. As we have seen, Vollmoeller corresponded with Baba extensively in the early months of 1934; and for a year after that he assumed a central role in Baba's film projects, participating in key planning meetings and writing some of the screenplays. Another important figure whom Norina drew into the work was Gabriel Pascal, a celebrated Hungarian film director and producer who was the first to successfully create film versions of the plays of George Bernard Shaw.[70] (Though in the end no film resulted from the association, Pascal kept up a warm personal link with Baba until he died in 1954.) Baba met with these two men during his visit to Europe in July and established working relations with them. They took their place in the creative nucleus of Baba's film team; it was through them, over the next six months, that several other talents got drawn into Baba's association.

Another important piece of the puzzle that was put into place during this visit to Europe was the legal incorporation of Circle Productions

[70] According to *Lord Meher* (in progress), Shaw himself said, "Pascal is doing for films what Diaghilev did for dance . . . the man is a genius."

on June 28, 1934, with Meher Baba himself as its president and Norina Matchabelli, Elizabeth Patterson, Elsie Henry Domville, and Gabriel Pascal as vice-presidents. Circle Productions was established with the purpose of raising funds (at the time a million rupees were envisioned) for the financing of Baba's film, whose aim he described thus:

> The film will actually demonstrate the purpose of creation, evolution, reincarnation, illumination, Realization—the whole process of inner and outer progression up to the point of the fulfillment of all life, which is the union with God. The facts so far as real experience, no human being has any real conception of, but a God-conscious Perfect Master sees and experiences it all every moment.
>
> The entire process will be portrayed and depicted as vividly as possible, and the film will be personally supervised by me. The role of reincarnation and the seven planes will be shown by means of charts, animation and special effects photography. A perfect understanding of what death is will be given to man, and once he realizes it, he will never fear the inevitable death that all have to undergo.
>
> The film will aid in the upliftment of all humanity by illustrating the real purpose of life—union with God. It will portray man's transformation of consciousness in fulfilling this purpose. The film will show to people what life truly is, its goal, the mechanics of the universe, the nature of God, and lastly, how the inherent spiritual life ascends the divine ladder towards its source.[71]

During 1934 and over the next several years Baba seems to have gone to considerable lengths to find a screenwriter who could draft a film treatment expressing these ideas. As early as April 12, 1934, in a letter to the "Gopis" (including Norina and Elizabeth), Baba wrote, "It is quite possible [Gabriel] Pascal might get the scenario written out and induce some party in America to take up this work in all earnest, impressed as he is with the story

---

[71] *LM* (Mownavani), vol. 3, pp. 1368–69; *LM* (Manifestation), vol. 6, pp. 1879–80.

as mentioned in your cables. . . . Meanwhile, the best thing for you to do is to get the scenario written out by Karl [Vollmoeller] of course, but if he refuses or sticks to his rigid attitude on any grounds, by any other great scenario-writer of repute through Pascal or anyone else whom you know of and who could do it and is worth the confidence you place in him."[72] Apparently Vollmoeller accepted this commission, because according to *Lord Meher,* he presented Baba with a completed script when they met in Paris at the end of June. Baba then proceeded to discourse "for three hours about creation, transmigration, reincarnation and God-realization, and showed him the chart which he had brought. Vollmoeller was impressed and Baba instructed him to write a new story based on the explanations and chart that he had given."[73]

The Elizabeth C. Patterson Archives in Myrtle Beach, South Carolina contains a 44-page booklet by Karl Vollmoeller that probably brings to print the text of the scenario that Vollmoeller wrote in the spring of 1934 prior to his meeting with Baba. Published by Circle Productions in 1935, Vollmoeller's *How It All Happened* is essentially an anti-war tract reflecting the political mood of much of the European intelligentsia in the early 1930s. Its story pits a powerful multinational conglomerate of munitions industrialists, representing the forces of evil, against a pacifistic disarmament movement led by the charismatic John King, who turns out to be a spiritual Master. Apart from a brief flashback to a previous lifetime of several of the leading characters, Vollmoeller's story contains no trace whatsoever of the cosmological and narrative material that Baba had in mind for the film. Whatever its other merits, Vollmoeller's script was obviously unsuited to Baba's purposes; one presumes that it played no further role in Baba's discussions and negotiations on the film front after this meeting with Vollmoeller in Paris. (Interested readers will find further discussion in appendix 9.)

So far we have been attending exclusively to *How It All Happened,* which

---

[72] See appendix 4, pp. 338–39.

[73] *LM* (Mownavani), vol. 3, p. 1368; *LM* (Manifestation), vol. 6, p. 1878.

undoubtedly was Baba's main thrust. But during the summer of 1934 two other projects were introduced as candidates for inclusion in Baba's portfolio of planned moving picture ventures. The story entitled *This Man David,* first drafted and probably conceived by Vollmoeller, tells of a Christ-like stranger who mysteriously arrives in an ordinary American town, through his example transforms the lives of many of the townsfolk there, arouses the hostility of some of the entrenched elites, and eventually gets lynched from a neighborhood maple tree. *Hell—Earth—Heaven,* another brainchild of Vollmoeller's, is essentially a melodrama that opens on a plane flight from California to New York and reaches its climax in a Park Avenue dress shop. While there is no reason to believe that Baba had anything more than a passing association with the latter story, *This Man David,* held its place in the "active projects" file of Baba's film team for two or three years. During this time Baba evidently directed several of his followers to devote their effort and talent to it; and to this day it is widely regarded as one of Baba's main film projects.

Frankly, many unanswered questions linger concerning the history of Baba's film work and particularly the nature and extent of his connection with the Vollmoeller material. Because of the complexity of this topic, a fuller discussion has been reserved for appendix 9. There readers will find plot summaries of the three Vollmoeller stories, a survey of the manuscripts, and some literary analysis. Despite the present paucity of evidence, our overall assessment is that Baba should not be regarded as the author or originator of *This Man David,* though from Vollmoeller's point of view he clearly inspired it, and for a time he took it on as a film that could express something of his message to the world. And as we have already noted, Vollmoeller's *How It All Happened* in its content bears almost no relation to Baba's concept of this project.

In any event, all this preparation during the first three quarters of 1934 reached its culmination in Meher Baba's eighth tour to the West—and second round-the-world trip—that began on November 15 and concluded with Baba's return to Bombay on February 16 of the next year. The plan was to concretize arrangements for the two films *How It All Happened* and *This Man David*

(*Hell—Earth—Heaven* having been dropped by this time). For that purpose Baba had meetings in New York and stayed in the Hollywood area for more than three weeks, from December 18 until January 7. Though his visit was conducted in secrecy and contacts with the press were avoided, Baba met with many motion picture executives, once again visited the leading film studios, and made contact with some of the prominent Hollywood stars and screenwriters. One of these, Hy Kraft, an accomplished screenwriter and noted figure in this epoch in cinematic history, was for a time drawn into Baba's contact and with Vollmoeller actually coauthored a treatment of *This Man David.* At the end of December Baba met Mercedes de Acosta, a screenwriter and close friend of Greta Garbo; Mercedes kept up her association with Baba for a number of years. In January she introduced Baba to another friend, Garrett Fort, a successful Hollywood screenwriter involved with the screenplays for the Frankenstein and Dracula films. Fort became devoted to Baba, even to the extent of traveling to India to take part in the ashram Baba established for the Westerners in Nasik in late 1936 and the first half of 1937.

Yet Baba channeled his main efforts in this tour through the daily meetings that he held "with Norina, Elizabeth, Vollmoeller and his assistant named Drake, Pascal and his friend Hy (John) S. Kraft to discuss films. Baba explained to them in detail the theme of creation, reincarnation, the planes and God-realization. Baba's ideas were quite novel revelations for these men and they found it difficult to portray everything in the way Baba wished." The same difficulty seems to have arisen in Baba's meetings with the executives, directors, producers and managers from the motion pictures: "It was found difficult to blend the material aspect of production with the spiritual theme in an instructive and interesting presentation that the public would find appealing."[74] In the end, these meetings and plans proved inconclusive, and in January Baba announced his intention to continue on with his journey back to India. His new associates were shocked by this—they had assumed Baba would

[74] *LM* (Mownavani), vol. 3, p. 1407–08; *LM* (Manifestation), vol. 6, p. 1937.

stay on in California for many months, since without him it was hard to envision how these films would ever see the light of day. But as Baba explained, he had other work and priorities, especially in India, and could not spare more of his time. He urged them to continue nonetheless with "the making of the film as instructed, adhering mainly to the points and spiritual themes I have dictated. And wherever I am, I will always guide and help you internally."[75]

In retrospect we can say that Baba's departure from Los Angeles on January 7, 1935 marks the beginning of the end of his work in the film medium. He did not say this at the time, however, but to the contrary, gave his disciples and close followers working in this field the impression that a film was still in the offing. Norina and Elizabeth, principals in Circle Productions, continued to seek out talent, particularly among screenwriters, and Baba still met with contacts from the film world from time to time. Evidently Mercedes de Acosta was asked to write a synopsis of *This Man David,* and it is possible that Garrett Fort composed the 102-page treatment of that story that still survives in the Avatar Meher Baba Trust Archives. As *Lord Meher* relates, Baba's on-going search for gifted screenwriters resulted in his meeting Alexander Markey in London in November 1936, whom Baba, again, set to the task of writing an adaption of *This Man David.* Film projects were still on the agenda during the Westerners' residency at the Nasik ashram in 1937; and even during Baba's visit to Cannes later that year, he held further meetings on the subject with Alexander Markey and Gabriel Pascal.

Also during this period Baba directed energy and effort towards the film's choreography. Margaret Craske, one of his close Western disciples who had been a member of Sergei Diaghilev's celebrated Ballets Russes and later the world's leading teacher in the Cecchetti technique of ballet instruction, along with Quentin Tod, a professional London entertainer in song and dance, was asked to choreograph dance numbers, particularly in connection with the "spirits dance" that the character X witnesses during his journey

[75] *LM* (Mownavani), vol. 3, p. 1412; *LM* (Manifestation), vol. 6, p. 1944.

through the planes of consciousness (during his fourth lifetime). Margaret writes amusingly of this assignment as it played itself out during her stay at the Nasik ashram in 1937.

> One day Baba called me and said that I must set to work and arrange a large dance for this movie. There were to be 120 dancers in the ballet, all moving together to express some kind of spiritual awakening, and since there were no dancers at Nasik, I was to work out the patterns on Rano (representing 60 dancers) and Delia (representing 60 other dancers)![76]

Though he followed their efforts with great interest, "after about two weeks Baba said that nothing more need to be done to the ballet until the actual time for the filming should arrive. Which it never did." Eventually the film projects died a quiet death, and the focus of Meher Baba's work turned elsewhere.

Through all this swirl of activity, the failure of *How It All Happened* to eventuate as a film could be traced to a number of causes. But the piece of the puzzle that seems to have been missing more than any other was the suitable writer. Margaret Craske commented on this; and so did Baba's disciple and close friend Dr. Ghani, writing five years later, who observed that, despite the readiness of a "Hollywood syndicate" to produce the film, "the Master ultimately postponed the project as no one from the West could evolve a story satisfactory to him."[77] And indeed, when one studies the material on creation, evolution, reincarnation, and Realization in part five, and sets it against the kinds of stories summarized in appendix 9, this explanation rings true. Hollywood in the 1930s had not yet reached a level of maturity in spiritual understanding where it could adequately render the Divine Theme in story form.

---

[76] *The Dance of Love: My Life with Meher Baba* (North Myrtle Beach, South Carolina: Sheriar Press, 1980), pp. 59–60.

[77] Dr. Abdul Ghani Munsiff, *The Spiritual Hoax of Lt.-Col. M. S. Irani* (Bangalore: Bangalore Press, [1940]), p. 22. According to Margaret Craske, *The Dance of Love*, p. 59, "Many well-known writers had presented scripts, none of which, up to the Nasik period, was found acceptable by Baba." See also Jean Adriel's comments in *Avatar*, pp. 218–19.

In overview, if one looks back on Baba's varied undertakings in the arenas of public communications during this period of world tours during the early to middle 1930s, from a worldly standpoint one might conclude that an enormous quantity of *sturm und drang* came to almost nothing. After a sensational series of self-presentations before the world press in 1932, Baba promptly "discredited himself," so to speak, through the Hollywood Bowl episode and largely disappeared thereafter from the world scene as it was covered by the mainstream media. After the promising publication of two booklets in 1933 that sold reasonably briskly and augured well for further ventures in this line, Baba disinvolved himself from literary composition and declined to take on the mantle of mystic philosopher and teacher to a Western public, after the model, say, of a Krishnamurti or Vivekananda. After having engaged the active services of several major talents in the American film world, instead of staying on in California and pressing his projects home to completion—as he could perfectly well have done at the time—Meher Baba returned to India, devoted himself to seclusion work and the small affairs of his ashrams there, and allowed the accumulated energies of the film work gradually to dissipate.

In all of these cases, promising beginnings apparently came to naught as a result of Meher Baba's arbitrariness in shifting the focus of his work before his efforts, and those of his disciples, could come to their natural fruition. Yet as students of Meher Baba's life know all too well, these are not isolated instances. Baba's entire career, from first to last, is marked by what outsiders might perceive as sudden bursts and enthusiasms followed by seemingly erratic ruptures and discontinuations and abandonments of projects in midstream. To the eyes of the worldly minded, to whom the ways of the Avatar will forever remain an enigma, this seems like madness. Yet the effect that the Avatar intends to achieve is nothing less than the transformation of the consciousness of all humanity. For this purpose he utilizes inner means beyond the sight and understanding of the ordinary human intellect. Doubtless much of what Meher Baba did in his early Western tours was archetypal; and the passage that he accomplished in miniature (as it were) through the various media of communication (interviews, public talks, books, films) will yield its visible harvest in the civilization of the New Humanity that will arise in the aftermath of his advent during the centuries to come.

Interestingly, the one line of work that Meher Baba did not break off and discontinue was that which he undertook to establish first, the forging of the links with his disciples. Most of those whom he drew into his circle in 1931 remained in his close contact for the rest of their lives. The Avatar himself is the embodiment of Love Divine; and these links of love belong to the essential tissue of his body and manifestation in this world of illusion.

Editorial Practices and Textual Sources

In making the literary materials in this book easily available again to the general public after most of them having been long out of print, part of our job has been to try to establish the most authoritative texts. This task entails, first of all, identifying the most authentic editions or versions. It also involves the formulation and application of editorial principles, especially in the area of textual emendation. Since the primary texts in question are nothing less than the words of the Avatar of the Age, we wish to be completely transparent as to the policies and practices that have been employed.

In his "Last Will and Testament," executed on June 17, 1967, Meher Baba bequeathed to the Avatar Meher Baba Trust the copyrights in all his literary works except those which he had specifically assigned to Sufism Reoriented a decade earlier. It has been the Trust's responsibility, accordingly, to formulate editorial policy regarding the books and messages of Meher Baba's that are under its custody.

In the last four or five years the Trust or its representatives have published several statements and explanations on this subject, whose bulk forbids their full restatement here.[78] But to summarize, the Trust permits the editorial re-composition of literary works originating in Meher Baba's dictation if they were not published during his physical lifetime. This editorial reworking, however, has to be faithful to the guideline laid down by Meher Baba himself when he said, "My explanations may be re-composed in forceful and stylish language, but the spirit and meaning must remain unchanged."[79] The Trust also requires that the original unedited manuscripts, which stand undisplaceably as the authoritative texts, should be permanently made available, at least in facsimile, to the general public.[80]

This portion of Trust editorial policy pertains to the materials on film on part five of this book. *How It All Happened* (pp. 161–85) is a composite based on several source documents. Those sources, housed in the Archives of the Avatar Meher Baba Trust, will be made available in facsimile on the Avatar Meher Baba Trust website.

On the other hand, literary works that were published under Meher Baba's name during his physical lifetime with his evident knowledge and approval must be republished in their original form, essentially unaltered. "Essentially" in this case means that the Trust does permit minor emendations in the mechanics of writing—such as the correction of misspellings, changes in punctuation and capitalization, correction of problems of grammatical agreement, etc. For a full listing of the areas in which changes are admissible, see pp. 432–33. Yet even where emendations are allowable in theory, in practice Trust editorship is intensely conservative and tries to preserve the form

---

[78] For major statements of Trust editorial policy and practice, see two articles in the Avatar Meher Baba Trust's newsletter, "Trust Embraces Editorial Policy" and "The *Discourses,* Copyright, and the Preservation of Meher Baba's Words," *In His Service,* July 2006, pp. 2 and 3; *Discourses,* revised sixth edition, vol. 4, pp. 72–78; and *Infinite Intelligence,* pp. 531–47.

[79] The comment of Baba is recorded in "The Combined Diary," vol. 2, folio 355, under the date August 7, 1927. The full statement is reproduced in *Infinite Intelligence,* p. 604. The rationale for the re-composition of the raw manuscript material in the "Intelligence Notebooks" in the edited text of *Infinite Intelligence* is set forth, with examples, in the supplement to that book on pp. 531–36.

[80] In the case of *Infinite Intelligence,* the manuscript (consisting of the two volumes of the "Intelligence Notebooks") has been published in facsimile on the Avatar Meher Baba Trust's web site.

and flavor and style of the original sources. Many of the changes are introduced in the interests of consistency: that is, when a book or message is erratic in the application of its own evident editorial principles, we have standardized. Sometimes (as in the case of British versus American quotation practices), we have emended to create a uniformity within the book in which the original messages are being republished, thus pursuing consistency in this sense.

In certain sections of the present volume, however, another principle comes into play. Some messages were published in Baba's life and with Baba's approval in versions that differ from each other. Moreover, in a few instances we have been able to locate early manuscripts that have evidentiary value. All these variant versions have been carefully collated and compared; and the texts that we publish here contain what this process has found as most authentic. Lest readers should fear otherwise, let us emphasize that most of the variations under discussion here are extremely minor. In only a few cases has the primary source been found deficient in some significant respect. All substantive textual problems and cruxes are examined fully in the endnotes.

In keeping with Trust policy, we have compiled a "Register of Editorial Alterations" and published it in pp. 432–43 of this book.[81] For purposes of the register, for each text published here one previously published version has been selected as the source text, and emendations are identified as against this source.[82] The register also identifies the category of editorial change. When sources other than the primary source provide some of the rationale for an emendation, these sources have been listed.

Before turning in detail to the textual sources, published and unpublished, used in the preparation of our primary texts, a few general comments on style and editorship are in order. As regards quotation styles, all the primary texts in this book have been normalized in favor of American

---

[81] This practice was first implemented in the revised sixth edition of Meher Baba *Discourses;* see vol. 4, pp. 230–41.

[82] The one exception is "Five Additional Questions and Answers," for which we take there to be two sources of equal authority. For further explanation, see pp. 235–36 and 272–73.

usage—double instead of single quotation marks, and commas and periods inside these marks rather than outside. American spellings have been preferred to the British everywhere except in parts three and four. In fact, the original books reproduced in these two sections—*Questions and Answers* and *The Sayings*—exhibit a high quality of editorship, and for this reason, whenever possible, we have refrained from tampering with the original editorial decisions, even in matters of spelling. The items in part two, which were originally published in mainstream magazines or newspapers, have needed virtually no editorial emendation at all. The greatest need for the exercise of editorial discretion arises with respect to the material in part one, the "Five Additional Questions and Answers" in part three, and appendix 2. These more than any of the other primary texts in this book have been brought into conformity with contemporary stylistic usage.

A final comment needs to be made regarding the distinction between footnotes and endnotes. All footnotes that you will find in the primary texts of this book (a category that does not include, of course, this essay) have been reproduced from their original publications. None has been added. The endnotes, however, are the product of this book's editorship. Some of them explain emendations and the textual cruxes or variations that called for them. Others supply helpful information, particularly concerning relevant secondary sources. We have also noted and sometimes offered explanations when details in these primary texts diverge from or even contradict what Meher Baba said in the latter, classic books of the late 1930s through 1960s.

We conclude with a review and discussion of sources for those parts of this book that contain primary texts of Baba's own words—that is, parts one through five, and appendix 2. (Appendix 9 provides its own full review of source documents, which in any case were not composed by Meher Baba.)

PART ONE. SIX MESSAGES. The six messages to the press and general public that Meher Baba delivered in London, New York, and Los Angeles during his 1932 tour have been republished many times in many places.

In its original 1933 edition, *Questions and Answers* (p. 8) makes reference to *Messages to London, New York, Hollywood, and India.* If indeed such a compilation ever existed, it probably took the form of typed manuscripts. In any event, no trace of it turns up in any of the bibliographies or library collections researched or among any of the persons consulted in the preparation of this book. If these messages were published in the early 1930s in the form of a booklet, evidently it has been lost.

In the absence of a reliable collection from the early 1930s, a collection published in the next decade by Adi K. Irani, *Messages of Meher Baba Delivered in the East and West* (Ahmednagar, India: Adi K. Irani for the Publication Committee, Meher Baba Universal Spiritual Centre, 1945), pp. 83–101, has been taken as the primary source. Though this short book, prepared for print and released by Meher Baba's own secretary under the auspices of an organization that Baba himself founded in 1939, is unique in bringing all six of these messages together at an early date, the texts as they appear there cannot always be trusted. Accordingly, certain other sources have been drawn upon for correcting and emending the text of *Messages* when it seemed to be defective or inferior. There are seven of these.

1. *MEHER GAZETTE,* vol. 2 no. 1 (April 1933), pp. 1–3, which reproduces (under the title "The Master's Message") Baba's "Message to Reporters in Hollywood," given by him on May 29, 1932; and the subsequent serial publication of Baba's "Message to Reporters and Press representatives," May 19, 1932, under (once again) the title "The Master's Message," in vol. 2, no. 2 (May–June 1933), pp. 1–2, vol. 2,no. 3 (July–August1933), pp. 1–2, and vol. 2, no. 4 (September–October 1933), pp. 1–2. It is probable that Sampath Aiyangar, the editor of the *Gazette,* received copies of these messages directly from Baba's own disciples. For this reason these early published versions carry weight.

2. CHARLES PURDOM IN *THE PERFECT MASTER,* first published in 1937, which provides the text of the messages that Baba gave on May 19, May 22,

May 29, and May 31, 1932.[83] As a distinguished magazine editor and author trained in the methods of scholarly exactitude, Purdom provides a weighty witness; his versions are usually free from typographic errors and erratic editing practices. Yet sometimes Purdom assumed the prerogative to introduce his own edits—including edits of substance; and for this reason he is not always the most reliable guide to the original form of Baba's messages.

3. Charles Purdom's article "More About the Perfect Master," *Everyman,* April 21, 1932, pp. 400, 402, which incorporates (on p. 402) the text of Meher Baba's "Message to the West."[84] Purdom had a special connection with this message: not only is his the earliest published version, but in addition, it was he who read it out before the cameras when it was filmed by Paramount News on April 8, 1932. With these credentials one might expect Purdom's text to represent the most authoritative of those available to us. It turns out, however, that Purdom edited the original so severely as to make his version ineligible as the primary source. It has been used nonetheless for reference in points of detail.

4. Kitty Davy's *Love Alone Prevails: A Story of Life with Meher Baba* (North Myrtle Beach, South Carolina: Sheriar Press, 1981), which on p. 42 incorporates the text of Baba's "Message to the West." Though we do not know what Kitty used as her source—her text may indeed be a derivative one—we should not forget that she was present at the original reading out of the message, which took place at her parents' house. Her text does omit an important clause.

---

[83] See pp. 165-68, 169–70, 172–74, and 174–76 in the 1976 republication of *The Perfect Master* by Sheriar Press. Some of this material is republished in Purdom's subsequent biography *The God-Man;* but the versions in the earlier book are more complete.

[84] Purdom's article was reprinted in *Meher Baba,* by His Eastern and Western Disciples, pp. 12–13. The *Everyman* article has been reproduced in facsimile (with Baba's "Message to the West" visible in the four indented paragraphs in the far right-hand column) on p. 278.

5. A THIRTEEN-PAGE TYPED MANUSCRIPT—hereafter called "A"—among Kitty Davy's papers at the Meher Spiritual Center in Myrtle Beach, that contains the full text of all six messages and is prefaced by a title page listing the original date and occasion of each. Since it lacks any message to India, this collection could not be the one referred to in *Questions and Answers*, p. 66 earlier. The sheets and type convey the appearance of age, however, and may represent an early draft or copy.

6. A ONE-PAGE TYPESET AND FULLY JUSTIFIED TWO-COLUMN SHEET—hereafter called "B"—among Kitty Davy's papers at the Meher Spiritual Center in Myrtle Beach, that contains the text of the message Baba gave to the reporters in Hollywood on May 29, 1932. Conceivably this may be a broadsheet that Baba had printed up for circulation among the Hollywood reporters, after the pattern of Baba's arrival on the S. S. Bremen in New York ten days earlier, when he distributed his message to reporters there in printed form. *Lord Meher* gives no indication that Baba did this in California, however.

7. A TWO-PAGE TYPED MANUSCRIPT—hereafter called "C"—in the Archives of the Avatar Meher Baba Trust, that contains the text of Baba's "Message to Reporters and Press Representatives" given when the S. S. Bremen arrived in the port of New York on May 19, 1932. Bearing the title "Shri Meher Baba's Message" and preserved in an original file entitled "Important Diaries & Letters and Notes & Circulars Ramjoo-Chanji-Norina, 1928-1934-1945" that was among Eruch's papers when he passed away in 2001, this old document represents, at the least, an early copy, and perhaps even the original typed source for this message.

In addition to these sources from the 1930s and 40s, one more recent republication deserves mention. In an issue of the *Awakener* devoted to Baba's visits to Hollywood, Filis Frederick reprinted four of the messages Baba gave on his 1932 tour.[85] Filis appears to have used *Messages* as her source, however, as indicated by the fact she reproduces the titles from *Messages* verbatim. As a later textual branching in the genealogical tree for these messages, then, the *Awakener* republication has little independent evidentiary value.

Most of the variations among these different sources are minor; the more significant of them are discussed in the endnotes. The one major editorial crux concerns the paragraph on miracles that appears at the end of two separate messages, the one Baba gave aboard the S. S. Bremen in the port of New York on May 19 and the message Baba gave to reporters in Hollywood on May 29. While this paragraph has been variously assigned to one message or the other in various republications, as best we can determine it was originally included in both.

There is no indication that in their original form the six messages had been given titles. The headings in *Messages* and in the title page of the typed manuscript in the Meher Spiritual Center archives are not true titles but descriptive information. In this book we have recast this descriptive information into a form where the top line of each can serve as a quotable title.

Part Two. Selected Articles in the Mainstream Press. The six items in part two were previously published, most of them in the 1930s or 40s, in newspapers, magazines, or books. The references are as follows.

Charles B. Purdom. "A Perfect Master." In *Everyman,* September 24, 1931, pp. 272, 274.

James Douglas. "A Talk with the Strange Messiah." *Sunday Express* (London), April 10, 1932, p. 1.

Framroze Dadachanji. Extracts from his 1945 Gujarati book, *Meher Baba, Emnu Jivan-Charitra: Shikshan-Updesh,*

[85] *Awakener,* vol. 18, no. 1 (1978), pp. 26–31 contains Baba's messages delivered on the May 22, May 29, May 31, and June 1, 1932.

Sandesh, translated by Naosherwan Anzar.
Glow International, February 1980, pp. 13-17.

Rom Landau. *God is My Adventure: A Book on Modern Mystics, Masters, and Teachers.* London: Ivor Nicholson and Watson, 1935, pp. 131–34. Rpt. New York: Alfred A. Knopf, 1936, pp. 127–30.

Frederick Collins. "I Can Hardly Believe It, Myself." *Liberty,* August 27, 1932, pp. 26–27.

Christmas Humphreys. "The Man of Love." *Buddhism in England,* vol. 16, no. 4 (November–December 1941), p. 77.

In a few cases the original publications contained small errors of a typographic order. Elsewhere the original style (as in the use of quotation marks) diverges from the conventions employed in this book. These corrections and adjustments have been made silently here.

PART THREE. QUESTIONS AND ANSWERS. The primary source is the original publication by Circle Editorial Committee (Charing Cross, London) in 1933, probably September of that year. As discussed earlier, the text appears to follow that of the typed manuscript in the Stokes collection, with Herbert Davy's handwritten notes incorporated. A number of the questions and answers were republished in Ramjoo Abdulla's *Philosophy and Teachings* (for details see footnote 44 earlier). Since neither the manuscript nor Ramjoo's book nor any of the other sources cited in the endnotes gives evidence of any defect or corruption in Herbert Davy's final published text, this present republication follows the original edition faithfully, with only a few minor emendations. The "errata" listed in the original 1933 booklet (p. 8, reprinted in this book on p. 244) have been inserted in their proper places. Other emendations are described in the endnotes.

The original booklet has certain other information—a citation of printer, a list of forthcoming publications, and price—that, since this information is now dated, we have deleted from the primary text in part three. For the use of historians and textual scholars, however, all of this deleted content (including the errata list) has been reproduced in appendix 5.

As discussed earlier, by December 1933 Herbert Davy seems to have intended to prepare a second edition that would have incorporated five additional questions and answers that Baba had dictated probably in November, 1933. While the original text of these has not been found, the French translation, *Shri Meher Baba, le Maître Parfait: Questions et Réponses* (Paris: Éditions de la Revue Mondiale, 1934), pp. 53–58, contains five questions and answers (nos. 59–63) that do not appear in the English edition. We take this to be a French translation from Baba's dictated text in Herbert's edition of it, which the French translator must have had available in some form. That French text is republished in appendix 6, pp. 347–51.

A four-page typed manuscript ("D") found among Kitty Davy's papers at the Meher Spiritual Center in Myrtle Beach has these same five questions and answers in English, which are characterized as "translated from the French edition of 'Questions and Answers' by S. M. B." This same exact translation is reproduced in two articles in the *Meher Baba Journal,* vol. 2, no. 6 (April 1940), pp. 353–55, and vol. 2, no. 7 (May 1940), pp. 415–16, both of them entitled "Questions Baba Answers," both of them with the byline "By a Westerner,"[86] and both represented as translations from the French through the following footnote (repeated in each of the two articles): "These questions and answers have appeared in the French edition of 'Questions and Answers' (Paris)." The fact that D has handwritten corrections that were incorporated into the text of the *Journal* articles suggests that this manuscript in some copy served as the very source for the Journal articles.[87]

Close study has revealed that both the French translation (of the lost

---

[86] That "Westerner" was almost surely Herbert Davy, who was primarily responsible for the compilation of the second edition of *Questions and Answers* into which these five additional questions and answers were to be incorporated; see pp. 234–36.

[87] For example: D uses the spelling "towards" in every case except one, where it unaccountably modulates to the variant spelling "toward." The *Journal* follows suit exactly. It is hard to explain this correspondence except on grounds that D provided the explicit source for the *Journal* text.

English original) in *Shri Meher Baba, le Maître Parfait: Questions et Réponses* and the English translation (of that French translation) in the two *Meher Baba Journal* articles have their respective strengths and weaknesses. For this reason, in the preparation of the text in part three, Françoise Lemetais, Daniel Lemetais, and this writer have treated the English and French versions equally as our source text. That is, after detailed comparison and analysis, we have introduced a few corrections and changes into the translation from French to English, all of them fully explained in the endnotes. To keep the "Register of Editorial Alterations" from becoming too complex and bulky, we list there only those emendations that deviate from the English text of the *Meher Baba Journal.*

PART FOUR. *THE SAYINGS OF SHRI MEHER BABA.* The original text of this book, first published by Circle Editorial Committee (Charing Cross, London) in December 1933, has been reproduced in this book with only minor emendations.

As described earlier, all of the sayings in the booklet had previously been published, five per issue, in the *Meher Message* between 1929 and 1931. The J. Graham Phelps Stokes papers in Columbia University Rare Book and Manuscript Library contain a typed manuscript entitled "Sayings of Shri Sadguru Meher Baba" and dated January 1929 with exactly the same sayings in the same order as were published in the periodical. Evidently the Circle Editorial Committee had a copy of this manuscript: the probability is that both the *Meher Message* and *The Sayings* were based on this same source. In any case, the close comparison of the booklet, the magazine, and the manuscript has led to no emendation in the text that we republish here.

The list of forthcoming publications that appeared on p. 49 in the original booklet has been deleted from the republication in part 4, since that information is now outdated. Yet since it may carry significance for historians and textual scholars, we have reproduced it in appendix 5, p. 346.

PART FIVE. *HOW IT ALL HAPPENED* AND BABA'S WORK IN FILM. While the first four sections of this book reproduce texts that were published in the 1930s with Meher Baba's oversight, part five presents materials that during Meher Baba's lifetime went unpublished and that descend to us as typed documents, drawings, and other items that have been preserved in the Archives of the Avatar Meher Baba Trust.

The main item in part five, *How It All Happened,* is a composite that we have assembled from several sources. Its plan, however, has been clearly spelled out on the first page of the document entitled "Scenario" (pp. 191–92); and all of its pieces can be found in one place or another. Since the original texts in the Trust Archives do not pretend to be more than rough drafts, for presentation here their prose has been revised in the interests of clarity and readability. Certain passages in the originals that do no more than recapitulate scientific information obviously gleaned from standard reference sources have been deleted and replaced by editorial summaries.

The editing that produced what we are calling the "First Movement" of *How It All Happened* was done by this writer. The "Second Movement" is based on the text that Filis Frederick published under the title "'A Touch of Maya': A Scenario by Meher Baba" in the *Awakener,* vol. 22, no. 1 (1986), pp. 1–4. Though Filis's own sources cannot now be located among her papers, from other archival sources described below we can say that she (or whoever did this editorial work) has combined the text that Baba dictated to Margaret Mayo on December 3, 1931, up through the conclusion of the narrative section of the fourth lifetime, with the fuller description of character X's passage through the planes that survives in the Trust Archives and that Baba probably dictated in 1934. All of this has been edited minimally yet skillfully.

The essential documentary sources, then, are these:

1. AN UNTITLED EIGHTEEN-PAGE TYPED MANUSCRIPT to which we give the title "Creation and Evolution." It consists of an "Introduction," formally divided into three parts, and four chapters. The introduction

and first chapter together contain a total of five diagrams, two of which are the same chart drawn twice. The eighteen pages of this document serve as the source for the "Introduction" and "First Movement" in *How It All Happened,* 161–79.

2. "POINTS FOR SHRI MEHER BABA'S FILM." This four-page typed document, which is preserved in what appears to be an original copy dated "Dec. 3 1931," represents Margaret Mayo's write-up of what Baba dictated to her on that day. (For a full account of this episode, pp. 246–47.) "A Touch of Maya" in its "scenario" sections for the first four lifetimes and in the entirety of its fifth lifetime draws directly from this original dictation of Baba's. "Points" has its own version of the creation sequence, and a less developed description of the experience of the planes than what finally emerged in "A Touch of Maya." But since this earlier version carries its own interest, these two portions of "Points" have been reproduced on pp. 186–88.

3. A FRAGMENTARY FIVE-PAGE DOCUMENT bearing the title "Scenario." The first page has been separated from the succeeding four, and we do not know with complete certainty that they comprise a single continuous manuscript; but since pages 3 through 5 have the running header "scenario" (scribbled out by pencil), we presume that all five pages belong together. While page 1 of this document is reproduced here on pp. 191–92, pages 2–5 constitute the source draft on basis of which the description of the experiences of the first five planes of consciousness in "A Touch of Maya" has been composed.

4. "INTRODUCTION TO THE PLANES," a four-page typed manuscript that served as a rough draft for the description of the experiences of the planes in pages 2–5 of "Scenario." Since the opening and concluding portions have not been incorporated into *How It All Happened* elsewhere, we reproduce them on pp. 189–90.

The Trust Archives contains other notes, compilations, textual extracts, drawings, and figures relevant to Meher Baba's film work in 1934; probably this material was assembled by Baba and his mandali in May of that year. For further discussion, see pp. 250–55.

Appendix 2. Four Messages to India, 1932–34. A major source for these four texts is *Messages of Meher Baba Delivered in the East and West,* pp. 5–7. Yet in several cases other sources are both earlier and perhaps more reliable; when it seemed appropriate they have served as the primary sources for this edition.

The first item, "Meher Baba's Message to India on His Fourth Voyage to Europe, 1932–33," is based exclusively on the text of *Messages.* But Baba's "Message to All Faiths Conference in Nasik, June, 1933" was first published in the proceedings of that conference, *All Faiths Conference: Proceedings of First Conference Held at Nasik*—June 1933 (Bombay: R. P. Mansani, Honourary Secretary, All Faiths Conference, Bombay, 1933), p. 17; and this has served the primary source here. This text was sent to Sampath Aiyangar by the president of the All Faiths Conference, and Aiyangar republished it, with slight variations, in *Meher Gazette,* vol. 2, no. 5 (November–December 1935), pp. 1–2.

Baba's fortieth birthday message was delivered at the home of Sampath Aiyangar, who published it in the *Meher Gazette,* Fortieth Birthday Supplement Issue (1934), p. 1. (An early typed manuscript, found in a folder entitled "Important Diaries & Letters and Notes & Circulars Ramjoo-Chanji-Norina, 1928–1934–1945" in the Archives of the Avatar Meher Baba Trust, matches the text of the *Meher Gazette* version almost exactly.) Baba's message on the eve of his eighth voyage to the West was sent specifically to the *Meher Gazette* where it was published in vol. 3 no. 5 (Nov–Dec 1934), p. 97. Naturally, the *Meher Gazette* has been selected as the primary source for these two messages.

Appendix 1
Newspaper and Magazine Articles

Meher Baba's 1932 Western tour precipitated a tsunami of publicity. The following newspaper and magazine articles, reproduced in facsimile, are selected from over 165 known to have been published in the mainstream press from the early- to mid-1930s.

HIS HOLINESS SADGURU MEHER BÀBÀ
By KAIKHUSHRU JAMSHEDJI DASTUR, M.A., L.L.B.

IN *The Everlasting Man*, Mr. G. K. Chesterton asserts that no religion has declared the Avatarhood of God in terms as clear as those of Christianity, and that the Bible is the only book in which we find " the loud assertion that this mysterious Maker has visited His world in person." . Mr. Chesterton is admittedly a man of talent and brilliant wit, but he displays a fossilised mentality when he takes on himself to deal with religious or spiritual subjects. He may have studied carefully the religions of the world, but in the very nature of things he cannot do justice to them. Anything pertaining to religion that he may see will be distorted by the false medium of his mental prejudices.

In reply to Mr. Chesterton 's *ipse dixit*, it should be remembered that though some God-realised souls have preferred to hide their light under a bushel, others, like Jesus, because of the nature of their work, plainly avowed the fact of their union with God, or of Avatarhood. The Hindu child prays daily to God : " As the different streams rising from different sources all flow into the sea, so, O Lord, Thou art the one goal for the different paths of religion that human mind takes through different inclinations."

Christians should disabuse their minds of the idea that Jesus was the only incarnation of God and that there can be none like Him. Jesus Himself said, " Be ye, therefore, perfect, even as your Father who is in heaven is perfect." Yet, despite this clear declaration, the average Christian persists in believing that Jesus alone was perfect ; that the world has never seen another Christ ; and that every man is essentially a sinner.

Jesus was certainly God-realised, although He was only one of many incarnations of the Divine. The world has seen many such ; and of all the countries in the world India has produced a larger number than all the others combined. Even at the present time there are a few God-realised personages, of whom the most renowned is my beloved Master, His Holiness Meher Bàbà. Before I write anything about him, Who is the crown of all my joy, and in Whom I have found my ideal, let me explain that by God-realisation, I mean complete union with the Divine. Such union is accomplished only by spanning the first six planes and going into the heart of the seventh. But let it be borne in mind that no one in his gross body can reach the seventh plane without

176

Written by K. J. Dastur, Meher Baba's disciple and editor of *Meher Message*, this four-page article, published in August 1929, may have been the first major presentation of the Avatar of the Age to the Western reading public. At this time the *Occult Review* was a leading periodical in the domain of the occult, parapsychology, and mysticism.

EVERYMAN April 21 1932

Literature and Life By THE EDITOR

More About the Perfect Master

DURING the past few days the newspapers have been publishing sensational accounts of an Indian "Messiah" who has lately come to this country. The subject of those accounts is the Perfect Master about whom I wrote in these pages a little more than six months ago. I promised then to write more about him, and many readers have reminded me of that promise. If in fulfilling it I tell a rather different story from that which has appeared in the newspapers, the reader can be sure that I have verified my facts.

It will be as well if I start by giving a brief outline of his history. Shri Sadguru Meher Bábá is a Persian, born in Poona, South India, on February 25, 1895. His father, Irani Sheriar, was a spiritually-minded man, who from boyhood until he was a grown man spent his life wandering in the jungle in search of spiritual experience. At the age of thirty-five he was told that he should resume a normal existence. This he did; he married and had six children. Meher Bábá was the second son.

His father is a Zoroastrian, and Meher Bábá was brought up in that religion. He went to school and college in Poona. When he was seventeen he was met by Shri Hazrat Babajan, an ancient woman, as a result of which Meher Bábá entered a super-consciousness state in which he remained for nine months entirely oblivious of earthly life. It took seven years before he regained normal human consciousness. During the whole of that time he had to be taken care of. His return to normal consciousness was brought about by meeting Shri Sadguru Upasni Maharaj in 1921.

He spent the first two years after that experience in writing an account of what happened to him. This book has not been seen by anyone. He was never married; nor did he ever engage in any trade or occupation, for he was still at college when the experience I have mentioned came to him.

His time has been spent during the past eleven years in travelling throughout India, alternating with periods of complete retirement. He visited the West for the first time last September, when he spent about three weeks in England, and afterwards went to America for a few weeks. He returned to England from India a fortnight ago, and at the beginning of next month intends to go back to America for an extended period. His reason for visiting America is, he says, that America being most deeply engrossed in material things, and suffering most in consequence, is the soil in which a new spiritual re-birth will first take place. He declares that America requires only the guiding hand of a Perfect Master to redirect its material powers to the heights of spirituality.

On his first visit to this country he saw a few people who came to him in London. He also saw Mr. Gandhi. On the present occasion, however, the news of his coming was spread from India, and he was met on arrival with the full blast of British newspaper publicity.

It would be easy to write a sensational story upon this remarkable being, though he is himself the least sensational of men. It would not be difficult to make the most exaggerated claims for him. I should like the reader to get a picture of him as he is, a quiet, simple, happy man. He does not shrink from contact with others, though he seeks to withdraw himself as much as he can. In appearance he is under middle height, delicately built, with a light brown skin, gentle brown eyes, long brown hair, strong features, and a serene expression. Perception silently emanates from his presence. He wears Eastern dress in the house, but in the street usually wears ordinary European clothes. He is not an ascetic, and does not advocate asceticism. He lives, of course, in utter simplicity. He has not spoken for more than seven years, and communicates with others by signs, and by pointing to roman letters painted on a small board. This silence is not the result of a vow, but is undertaken for spiritual reasons. He says that he will break it soon in America.

He understands English perfectly, and long conversations can be held with him, either with the aid of one of his attendants reading from the board or by following oneself his spelling of words on the board. The latter is not as difficult as it may seem.

What Meher Bábá is people must discover for themselves. His authority must convince without argument. He must be recognized by the heart. His mere appearance convinces seekers of his spiritual integrity. One recognizes in him a spiritual Master—or one does not. I see in him the Teacher about whom I wrote in EVERYMAN on February 11. He differs from other teachers I have met because he has power. This power is not magnetism or personality, much less is it any sort of hypnotism. It is a feeling of confidence that he has achieved complete self-mastery and can help the rest of us to do the same. He teaches what he is. "The wise man is a Divine mercy to created beings," said a mediæval Persian poet. That is what I find in Meher Bábá.

He has no doctrine; he is a living truth. Therefore it is not what he says that matters. That is why the fact that he does not speak seems of such small consequence. Always it is the power of the realized truth that convinces, not the mere utterance of the truth. I have never before met a man of whom I could say that with such certainty. In his presence I feel that I know the answers to the questions that have hitherto perplexed me. Indeed, since I first met him six months ago, I have realized that the difficulty is not to get questions answered, but to act upon what one knows.

A Perfect Master does not merely answer questions but he gives the ability to do what is required, because he has arrived where we want to go. He is a guide who can point out the way and help to bring us there. This is important, for it is not mere advice that we want. There are plenty of people who can tell us what to do: we need something more than that. We need something more, too, than momentary inspiration. We look for permanent realization of the ultimate reality,

Continued on column 3 page 402

April 21 19[illegible]

More About the Perfect Master

Continued from page 400

We have those who write poetry; we want one who lives it.

If it is dangerous to ascend a difficult mountain without a guide, it is even more dangerous to attempt to disintegrate and reintegrate our personality without the help of a skilled teacher. The many failures of psycho-analysis have made this abundantly clear. A Perfect Master helps to break down our personality, because he helps us to get rid of the ego; but he also enables us to build it up again. I find Meher Bábá to be above all practical. He is concerned with everyday life. He does not invite people to leave the world but to make use of it, to raise it to spiritual values. We should live in the world, he says, and yet be not of it, attend to all worldly duties and yet be completely detached from their results.

He does not seek to convert men to anything; certainly he does not attempt to change their religion. All religions are revelations of God. What he does say is that whatever religion one has should become experience. It should transform life. Until it does that it is a dead religion. If a man has no religion, believing that all religions are outworn, he does not argue with him, but tells him to act on his own highest ideals. What matters is character. Opinions do not matter. It is what you are that counts.

Meher Bábá dictated the following statement when he arrived in England in view of the many questions that had been asked of him, which I print here for the first time:

> My coming to the West is not with the object of establishing a new creed or spiritual society or organization, but is intended to make people understand religion in its true sense. True religion consists of developing that attitude of mind which ultimately results in seeing one Infinite Existence prevailing throughout the Universe, thus finding the same Divinity in Art and Science and experiencing the Highest Consciousness and Indivisible Bliss in everyday life.
>
> The West is inclined towards the material side of things, which has from untold ages brought in its wake wars, pestilences and financial crises. It should not be understood that I discard and hate materialism. I mean that materialism should not be considered an end in itself but a means to the end.
>
> Organized efforts such as the League of Nations are being made to solve world problems and to bring about the Millennium. In some parts of the West, particularly in America, intellectual understanding of Truth and Reality is attempted but without the true Spirit of Religion. This is like groping in the dark.
>
> I intend to bring together all religions and cults like beads on one string and revitalize them for individual and collective needs. This is my mission to the West.

He does not bring Eastern ideas for us to act upon, but intends to help us to act upon what we already know. He revivifies unused knowledge. He does more than that, of course, for he shows us the necessity for a change of heart and enables us to gain real knowledge through experience. Above all he unites the mind and heart so that we need no longer be divided personalities, but can live as entire men.

Charles Purdom's second article about Meher Baba was printed in the April 21, 1932 issue of *Everyman*, a weekly magazine that Purdom edited. The four indented paragraphs in the far right column contain Purdom's version of Baba's "Message to the West" (see p. 5). Appearing when English press coverage of Baba's tour was at its zenith, this may represent the first publication of Meher Baba's own words in the Western print media.

BABA COMING TO UNITED STATES

Indian Spiritual Leader Proposes to Break Down All Religious Barriers

By JAMES A. MILLS

BOMBAY, India, March 25—(AP)—Meher Baba, the Indian spiritual leader whose disciples call him "the Messiah" and "the God-man" left here today for a new crusade in America.

He intends, he said, to break down all religious barriers, destroy America's materialism and amalgamate all creeds into a common element of love.

For eight years Meher Baba has been observing a vow of silence, which he said he would break upon his arrival at Harmon, N. Y. where he plans to establish a spiritual retreat similar to Mahatma Gandhi's in India.

Giving his first interview to an Associated Press correspondent by means of a blackboard, Meher Baba, who in the eyes of his followers has performed many miracles, said Gandhi had promised to come with him to the United States as soon as his political work has been finished a year hence.

Many Indians regard Meher Baba as Gandhi's duru, or spiritual adviser.

Meher Baba is a parsee (priest) of the Zoroastrian faith, and say he is god and man. He explained that he attained a super-consciou state in which he merged into Go and returned again to the uni- cerse to carry out his mission of redeeming the world.

Discussing on his blackboard th miracles which he allegedly h performed, Meher Baba wrote:

"A person who becomes one wi Truth can accomplish anythin It is weakness, however, to perform a miracle only to show others one's spiritual powers. Christ, who made the blind see and the deaf hear and raised the dead to life did nothing to save himself from suffering the agony of the world."

Meher Baba said he expected to convert thousands of Americans from sin, and by faith to heal the sick.

"The only miracle for the perfect man to perform is to make others perfect, too," he said. "I want to make Americans realize the infinite state which I myself enjoy."

INDIAN SEER STARTS FOR AMERICAN TOUR

Meher Baba Hopes to Elevate People Here to "Infinite State" He Enjoys.

TO BREAK VOW OF SILENCE

He Will Establish Spiritual Retreat at Harmon, N. Y., and Seek to Break Religious Barriers.

BOMBAY, March 25 (AP).—Meher Baba, the parsee seer whose followers call him the "god-man," left today for the United States to make the Americans realize the "infinite state" which he has enjoyed since he first saw the divine light many years ago.

He discussed his crusade with The Associated Press correspondent, but he did not speak a word, for he took a vow of silence eight years ago. Instead, he answered questions by writing on a blackboard. He will break his vow, he wrote, when he gets to Harmon, N. Y., to establish a spiritual retreat something like that which the Mahatma Gandhi maintains in India.

There he intends to break down all religious barriers, destroy American materialism and amalgamate all creeds into a common element of love.

"Any one who becomes one with truth can accomplish anything," he told the correspondent, spelling out the words with his piece of chalk, "but it is weakness to perform a miracle simply to show one's spiritual powers."

This was in answer to a question about the numerous miracles which this man's followers say he has performed.

"Christ, who made the blind to see and the deaf to hear, who restored the dead to life, did nothing to save Himself from suffering the agony of the world," the Baba wrote. "The only miracle for the perfect man to perform is to make others perfect, too. I want to make the Americans realize the infinite state which I myself enjoy."

Meher Baba is of the faith of Zoroaster. He realized his mission on earth, he wrote, many years ago when he met Baba Jan, an Indian saint who died at Poona not long ago at the reputed age of 130 years.

For nine months after that meeting, said the Baba, he lay in a state of coma, neither sleeping nor eating. At the end of that time he saw the divine light. He had attained a superconscious state in which he merged into God, then returned to the universe to carry out his mission of redeeming the world.

The Zoroastrian doctrines which the Baba follows teach that at the beginning of things there were two spirits, good and evil. The history of their conflict is the history of man, and the soul of man is the object of their war.

INDIAN PRIEST COMING TO U. S.

Expects To Make Convert Healing of Ill Through Faith

By JAMES A. MILLS (Associated Press Staff Correspondent)

BOMBAY, India, March 26.—(AP)—Meher Baba, the Indian spiritual leader whose disciples call him "the Messiah" and "the God-man," left here today for a new crusade in America.

He intends, he said, to break down all religious barriers, destroy America's materialism and amalgamate all creed into a common element of love.

For eight years Meher Baba has been observing a vow of silence, which he said he would break upon his arrival at Harmon, N. Y., where he plans to establish a spiritual retreat similar to Mahatma Gandhi's in India.

Giving his first interview to an Associated Press correspondent by means of a blackboard, Meher Baba, who in the eyes of his followers has performed many miracles, said Gandhi had promised to come with him to the United States as soon as his political works has been finished a year hence.

Many Indians regard Meher Baba as Gandhi's duru, or spiritual adviser.

Meher Baba is a parsee (priest) of the Zoroastrian faith, and says he is god and man. He explained that he attained a superconscious state in which he merged into God and returned again to the universe to carry out dis mission of redeeming the world.

Meher Baba said he expected to convert thousands of Americans from sin, and by faith to heal the sick.

"The only miracle for the perfect man to perform is to make others perfect, too," he said. "I want to make Americans realize the infinite state which I myself enjoy."

Versions of Associated Press reporter James A. Mills's interview with Meher Baba that precipitated the frenzy of publicity attending his 1932 Western tour. *(LEFT)* Article from the *Centralia Daily Chronicle* (Centralia, Washington), March 25, 1932. *(MIDDLE)* Article from the *New York Times*, March 26, 1932. *(RIGHT)* Article from the *Ogden Standard-Examiner* (Utah), March 26, 1932.

JOHN BULL — MAY 7, 1932

Sensational "John Bull" Exposure

ALL BRITAIN Duped by

The "New Messiah" with some of his followers in their retreat in Devonshire. On the right is Mr. Meredith Starr, his principal disciple

AN unusual flood of publicity has greeted the recent arrival in this country of an Indian mystic of seemingly miraculous prowess, known as Shri Meher Baba, and heralded as the New Messiah.

Nearly every important newspaper in the country has devoted columns of space to glowing descriptions of his appearance, doctrines and future aims.

The British public is being told in one report or another that he is a spiritual superman; a healer with majestic personality and divine power; that the day will come when he will deliver a wondrous message to the world.

Publicity, which is really just the sort of thing that Meher Baba and his most devoted followers desire, was, we can say, chiefly inspired through the tireless efforts of a gentleman named Meredith Starr.

Starr is to be found at a seventeenth century farmhouse known as "East Challacombe," in North Devon, and is the "Messiah's" principal agent for Europe and America.

A charlatan

The truth is that the British public has been duped. Letters are arriving at "East Challacombe" from people in all parts anxious to join the cult.

Whatever the exalted rank bestowed upon Meher Baba, however great the stupendous claims attributed to him, we can here reveal him in a much less complimentary light.

Having completed a thorough investigation into his operations of recent years we assert that only one name can be aptly applied to him—that of charlatan.

Among other impressive titles, Shri Meher Baba has been known as:—

"The New Messiah."
"The Blessed Lord."
"The Indian Avatar."
"His Divine Majesty."
"The Master." "The Holy Garu."
"The Indian Christ." "The Saint."

When he arrived in England from India he made a brief stay in London to the delight of his followers, who included several beautiful young white girls and numerous coloured men of all ages.

Then, after extraordinary homage had been paid to him, in a manner rarely practised in the West, he departed in state to his principal disciple's farm in Devon.

Shri Meher Baba, according to Mr. Starr and other devotees, is famous throughout India for his spiritual teachings and is worshipped there by millions of followers as the Greatest Master of all time.

It is claimed that, following his great work in the East, he has suddenly been "called" to the West to exercise his power for good, prior to the happening of a great catastrophe and spiritual upheaval that is shortly to engulf this part of the world.

Colonies, one is led to believe, are firmly established under his saintly leadership in Persia and India, where lepers have been cured and many other sufferers relieved by miracles performed through his "high state of consciousness."

If all now goes according to plan, Shri Meher Baba will demonstrate his miraculous powers in due season. He will heal the sick, make the blind see, and, among other superhuman achievements, walk upon the surface of running water!

The colony, conducted at East Challacombe by his devoted agent, Meredith Starr, seems strangely remote and inaccessible as the Western headquarters for so vast a movement.

It is peopled, apart from Meher Baba and Mr. and Mrs. Starr, by men and women, young and old, white and coloured, who agree to give themselves up completely to "The Master's" teachings in order to strive towards what is termed "the Greater Realisation."

At the moment this mixed community numbers about a score. All are living in this "modernised" farmhouse, which has barely half a dozen bedrooms, practising a "religion" that is both unorthodox and weird in the company of grunting black pigs, bleating sheep, lowing cattle and miscellaneous farmyard livestock!

So acute has the problem of accommodation become that some of the cowsheds have been converted into bedrooms!

Must be humble

It is impossible to gather any accurate idea of the real character of Meher Baba's doctrines from such printed matter as is available at the colony.

"Here one may rest," one is told, "and become acquainted with those forces which, when liberated, will enable the student to realise greater possibilities in accordance with the Inner Laws of Nature and Life.

"Many people have reached a higher level of consciousness here—tone and rhythm have been imparted to body and mind, the spiritual horizon has expanded, repressions have vanished, and the energies set free have resulted in a new, affirmative and enthusiastic orientation to life. . . . It is only possible to teach what has been lived. . . ."

Self-willed people, however, are not acceptable at the colony.

Admission is strictly limited to those who are "humble and sincere." They must break down their pride and follow faithfully the teachings selected for them, which differ according to their individual requirements.

Fees, it should be noted, can be as low as two and a half guineas a week, though devotees are urged to give all they can to Meher Baba's "great cause."

A JOHN BULL representative, who has just visited the colony, learned that some of the visitors possess troublesome complexes and go there to be "cured" by spiritual influence.

Sunbathing, violent physical exercises in the open air, the study of psychological books on burning problems, and the process of leading a simple life under Meher Baba's saintly banner are al[l] prescribed.

Bagpipes greeting

So it would seem that the colony is a sort of combined monastic retreat and physical culture academy.

It was to this isolated farmhouse, with its cowshed bedrooms, that the "New Messiah" retired, then, to hold court among his strange disciples.

This retreat is three miles from the little village of Combe Martin and only accessible on foot to those who brave a tedious uphill journey through narrow, muddy lanes and across endless fields.

His Highness Shri Meher Baba, in his flowing robes and primitive sandals, must have found the going hard indeed.

An eye-witness of his arrival with his strange retinue declares that the spectacle "almost beggared description."

But, assisted by Mr. and Mrs. Starr, the "Master" eventually reached his chosen retreat, where he was greeted by the strains of bagpipes.

Long silence

Gesticulating Indians and other devotees clustered round him, kissing his hands and basking in the favour of his magnanimous smiles.

Since he arrived at the farm Shri Meher Baba has adopted a pose of rigid silence. Starr and his other disciples say that he is pledged not to speak a word for seven years, when he will come fully into his own—whatever that may be.

As in London, he expresses himself by dumb pantomime on an alphabet board, which he fingers like a typewriter, while

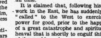

Surely they realise the hollowness of his claims?—Baba in the centre of his devoted band

After a month of sensational press coverage, this two-page article in *John Bull*, a weekly magazine specializing in exposés, purported to unmask Meher Baba as a fraud being

MAY 7, 1932 JOHN BULL

SHAM MESSIAH

Shri Meher Baba, the ' New Messiah"—silent mystic who shortly leaves England to open "Colonies" in America

follower stands by to interpret his eaning.

But he has not objected to being freely otographed, sometimes with admiring omen lying at his feet, or assuming an ipressive stance in a white and scarlet be.

While several fascinated followers ive even considered it a privilege to ss his bare feet, most people will agree at the whole thing reeks of sham.

They will be more than ever convinced this respect when we say that, though feher Baba is wily enough to avoid expressing himself to the Press, he takes particular care to read every reference to his activities that appears in print.

So far he has been deeply gratified that so much notice has been taken of him and that his various claims have been set forth in complimentary terms.

But we doubt whether he will find equal pleasure in adding this present article to his growing collection of Press cuttings.

His real name is Shri Sadgaru Meya Baba, and he was born in Poona, India, in 1894. Until a few years ago he earned a livelihood peddling a native liquor in the byways of Nasik.

How, then, has he risen to his present self-exalted heights?

As a matter of fact, he blossomed forth as a Messiah only in recent years, and far from being acclaimed throughout India or worshipped by millions of followers, as some of his publicity suggests, he is practically unknown.

His following in and around Nasik numbers a few thousand at the most.

No miracles

One man who was led to believe in him and who now realises that he has been grossly deceived is a Mr. K. J. Dastur, M.A., LL.B., a young Parsee lawyer of varied accomplishments.

Until recently he was a leading disciple of "The Messiah" and acted as his chief propagandist in India.

Having thrown up his career in order to follow the great man, he was rewarded by a gradual revelation of the hollowness of Meher Baba's claims. In vain he waited for his Master to perform miracles, but he was put off with various excuses until he broke away in disgust.

Since then he has publicly expressed his regret for the years wasted in following an impudent impostor.

Here is one of his many denunciations to which, for obvious reasons, Meher Baba has not deigned to reply:

"All the promises which Baba gave me he has not kept. This, coupled with the non-fulfilment of his various prophecies, his queer conduct on occasions, and the violation of his own principles, have made me reverse my opinion of him."

Mr. Dastur admits that while he was under the fascination of Meher Baba's personality he was blind to many things; but he now sees him as a charlatan.

Glib excuses

But he gave him every chance to prove himself. Months before he broke away he warned his Master that he would go unless long-promised proof of his power was forthcoming.

When our representative raised this point with Mr. Meredith Starr, the latter suggested that the New Messiah had failed to keep his promises to Mr. Dastur because of something in the young lawyer's innermost soul which prevented miracles from happening!

But if Meher Baba has lost one follower, he has gained others, many of whom are wealthy people—a point worth noting, since it is said that he has "nothing but what his followers give."

The fact is that Meher Baba, who always works through a leading disciple, has raised and expended huge sums of money on various schemes that have come to nothing.

One was a big kinema he ordered to be built in the sacred city of Nasik, but which was never completed because creditors could not get paid. A strange sideline, surely, for a Messiah.

Then there was a school he opened in Ahmadnagar for boys of various castes, creeds and races.

Pupils were to be spiritually trained to become future "ambassadors," or minor Messiahs, in all parts of the world. One feature of the queer training they received consisted of urging them to love and worship Meher Baba in person and to think of him constantly throughout the day.

The effect of such doctrines upon impressionable boys may be imagined, and the school closed down after a scandal had been disclosed regarding one particular boy who had become mentally unbalanced.

Questioned on this point, Mr. Starr made some frank and startling remarks. The youth, he declared, was moved by Sadistic impulses and, rushing up to the New Messiah in perverted adoration, was finally so carried away by hysteria that he bit the Master violently!

Yard steps in

Then there is an incident which happened much nearer home, which Mr. Starr did not seem too happy to discuss.

On one occasion, when Meher Baba wanted European boys for this school he sent an emissary to England to find likely material.

Several English lads were actually sought out and the parents favoured with glowing stories of the learned Messiah's desire to train world ambassadors.

The parents of three boys ultimately gave permission for their children to go to the distant college for high education, the arrangements being concluded by Mr. Meredith Starr himself on behalf of the emissary, whom he had met casually in London.

Fortunately, Scotland Yard detectives got word of what was afoot and called upon Mr. Starr and plied him with questions at the instance of the India Office, which effectively scotched the deal and stopped the boys from sailing.

Blind man's plight

It was as a result of the wonderful things this particular disciple told Mr. Starr that the latter decided to go to India and interview the great Master, which led to his appointment as "Representative of Meher Baba to the White Races."

Apart from the financial aspect of this cult—and money has been freely collected from misguided followers for years—the menace to the minds of simple people cannot be exaggerated.

A man who has been blind for forty-seven years recently heard of the New Messiah's arrival and travelled all the way from Bradford to the isolated headquarters in Devon.

He beseeched Meher Baba to restore his sight at any cost to himself, but there was not even house room for him at the colony and he had to tramp back to the village.

For days he made a desperate pilgrimage through muddy lanes and fields until finally received by the New Messiah, who intimated, *viâ* his alphabet board and his interpreter, that the man's sight would be restored in November next!

Back to obscurity!

So the poor fellow is cherishing this hope, buoyed up by the assurance that the day will come when he will regain his sight and be privileged to look upon the New Messiah's features, vaguely at first, but gradually more distinctly until full vision is restored!

Meher Baba even professes the power of being able to raise the dead, but he has yet to produce evidence of a single cure.

Meanwhile, his own father is a semi-invalid, compelled to lie on his couch for hours every day in his residence in Poona, a victim of a painful malady.

Miracles, like charity, should surely begin at home?

But—Shri Meher Baba is no miracle worker, has no right to the various majestic titles he assumes, and has only one real duty to mankind.

That is to retire into the obscurity from which he originally sprang, with all possible speed.

perpetrated on the English public. Though published anonymously, it was written by Paul Brunton with the help of K. J. Dastur (see pp. 221–22).

SHRI MEYER BABA, the " New Messiah," photographed on arrival at the Retreat of his followers at East Challacombe, Combe Martin, North Devon. (Photo: Topical)

Meher Baba's visit to East Challacombe in Devonshire during April 1932 was extensively covered by the local newspapers. Photo in the *Western Independent* (western England), April 24, 1932.

Shri Meher Babi, the "new Messiah," who has sworn himself to silence for seven years, is " in retreat in North Devon, and has chosen East Challacombe, Combe Martin. He is here seen with followers of his cult, whilst below is a specially posed photograph. See news columns.

Photos by Knight (Barnstaple).

Photo in the *Western Times* (Devon), April 22, 1932. Two articles from the same edition appear on the facing page.

(BELOW) Article from the *Western Morning News and Daily Gazette* (Devon and Cornwall), April 16, 1932, published the day before Baba's arrival at the East Challacombe retreat.

INDIAN MYSTIC AND DEVON

ARRIVAL EXPECTED AT WEEK-END

MAY SPEND SOME DAYS AT COMBE MARTIN

Shri Mehar Baba, the Indian mystic who has been claimed as a new Messiah, and who arrived early this month in London, was expected at Combe Martin yesterday, where it had been announced he would be staying with Mr. Meredith Starr at the retreat founded by the latter at East Challacombe, Combe Martin. Shri Mehear Baba has now, however, postponed his visit to North Devon for a few days, and is expected to arrive to-morrow or Monday.

Mr. Starr, seen by a "Western Morning News and Daily Gazette" representative, said he did not think Shri Mehar Baba would remain longer than eight to nine days, and that he would not speak whilst he was here. He would be accompanied by his party, and he (Mr. Starr) was proceeding to London to meet him.

BEDROOM AT THE RETREAT.

Mr. Starr referred to reports appearing in certain newspapers regarding the bedroom which the visitor would occupy, and which one paper described bedstead. He then showed "The Western bedstead. He then showed the "Western Morning News and Daily Gazette" representative the room, which is tastefully furnished, with a 3ft. 6in. iron bedstead with spring mattress, and a brilliant quilt. By the bedside was a mahogany table, covered with a Zapense cloth, and there were also a white washstand and cupboard, and a mahogany stool. A huge window gave the room plenty of light. In the corner was the attendant's bed.

MAY SEE PRESSMEN.

Asked if Shri Mehar Baba would see the Press representatives on Sunday, Mr. Starr said it was possible. He might see them all together.

Mr. Meredith Starr met Shri Mehar Baba in India, and stayed with him at his retreat there for six months in 1928. It was on his return that he founded the retreat at Combe Martin, which has been prepared "for those who are earnestly striving towards a greater realization."

Since its foundation the retreat has had a large number of visitors, to whom "individual help and instruction in meditation and practical psychology are given by the founder."

THE WESTERN TIMES, FRIDAY, APRIL 22, 1932.

The New Messiah in Devon

Meher Baba's Message to England

GREETED BY INDIANS

Sightseers Avoided at Combe Martin

SWIRLING gusts of sea mist swept across Combe Martin Sunday afternoon, when Shri Meher Baba, the Indian new Messiah, who has established a retreat at East Challacombe, arrived. The Meher Baba reached Combe Martin from London by car at 3.30, and he escaped the attention of the Combe Martin sightseers, who had anticipated his arrival at a later hour.

A SPECIAL PATH.

Walking with his secretary and a small party from the retreat Meher Baba proceeded through the muddy lanes and gazed admiringly at the wild flowers that were in bloom on the hedges. Reaching the stiles the Baba was assisted over them by members of the retreat. From West Challacombe a special path had been made which diverted from the ordinary route, and was ankle deep in mud.

Mr. and Mrs. Starr met the Baba near the retreat and walked one each side of him. The Baba greeted them heartily. As he reached the retreat Mr. Kenneth Ross, brother-in-law of Mr. Starr, played Scottish bagpipes to the farm. At the summit of the hill the party halted and were photographed, the Shri Meher Baba's long black hair streaming in the wind as he was posing for the camera man. A thick Ulster coat protected him from the bitter north-easterly wind.

Nearing the retreat a group of seven Indians dashed across the cobbles to greet him, and he shook them warmly by the hand.

A galaxy of gorgeous blooms made the plain interior of the farmhouse look beautiful, and the devotees of the cult waited in hushed expectancy for their leader to arrive.

THE BABA'S MESSAGE.

Permission was immediately solicited by our representative to interview the Baba on his arrival, but he was informed that he would not see any Press representatives that day. Asked to give a message to England from the retreat, Shri Meher Baba declared through his interpreter who worked on an alphabet that "coming to this retreat is like coming home. Here, spirituality is made practical. I find the atmosphere and training here result in ideals being reached. Head and heart must go together. Physical, mental and spiritual equilibrium must be achieved to ensure permanent results. For the present crisis to pass away and matters become normal again, the West must understand the importance of spiritual development, and must realise divinity in every phase of life, in art, science, nature, and the daily routine. Infinite consciousness must be experienced. Then only can there be peace in the real sense of the word. But if, as at present, only the material aspect continues to be stressed, then there will be still greater discord which will cause untold suffering."

Photos on Page 5.

The New "Messiah's" Retreat in North Devon

(From Our Own Correspondent.)

Barnstaple, Saturday.

MY visit yesterday to the "Retreat" at East Challacombe, Combe Martin, to enquire of the arrival of Shri Meher Baba, the new "Messiah," was a disappointment to me.

I was expecting to find all sorts of weird things. I had read that the Meher's bed was of wooden construction on a cement floor; and I was under the impression that the members of "The Retreat" were weird people.

I was frankly disappointed, for on my arrival a messenger of exceptional culture announced my arrival to Mr. Starr, and later a lady of superior class conveyed me to the Bungalow in a most courteous manner as if I was a guest.

I found at the Bungalow interior many basket chairs and books of various writers. But what caught my attention were the wooden forms and beds. They were strongly constructed and capable of resting any weight. Everything was simplicity.

I had not been there long before Mr. Starr arrived, and I made my introduction. He was the essence of intellectualism, and his piercing eyes upon me caused me to wonder whether I should be well received or not.

But Mr. Starr talked with ease. He told me that if I was seeking sensational journalism I should not find it at the "Retreat."

Mr. Starr went on to explain about a report that had been published with regard to the Baba's bedroom, stating that a free lance reporter must have seen the wooden-made bedstead on the cement floor in the Bungalow, and had come to the conclusion that it was the place for the Baba.

FIRST TO SEE BEDROOM.

No Press representative, he said, had yet seen the Baba's bedroom, "and if I take you, you will be the first Press representative to see it in the country."

It was not long before I proceeded with him to the Baba's bedroom, and I was astonished to find that it was an ordinary pale-distempered room, with a single size bed on one side, and an attendant's bed on the other. The Baba's bed had a mattress and overlay covered with a beautiful quilt —made by Mr. Starr's relative.

The room was neatly furnished and overlooked the hills around the moor. One member of the household had made a stool out of a piece of African mahogany gathered from the sea shore. It was just like an ordinary room, with plenty of light and ventilation.

Mr. Starr told me he did not expect that the Baba would speak whilst he was at the "Retreat" but would do so in America.

Asked if he would see Press representatives on Sunday, he said that he could not say. The Baba would see them all together. They were going to be photographed.

The Baba would remain at the "Retreat" for about eight or nine days, and then would leave for America. No special arrangements were being made for his arrival as they were so quiet living people.

I came away from the "Retreat" feeling somewhat disappointed. My only thought was for the members of the household, for they had selected a lovely part of the moor for their retreat. The morning was bright and the sun was shining across the hills which gave an added pleasure to the visit.

(ABOVE) Both articles appeared in the *Western Times*, April 22, 1932. The paragraph on the bottom left, entitled "The Baba's Message," contains a significant statement anticipating some of the themes of Baba's messages and addresses in America during the next month (see also pp. 284 and 285).

Describing Meher Baba's arrival at the East Challacombe ashram in the village of Combe Martin, this vivid and colorful article appeared in *Ilfracombe Chronicle and North Devon News*, a local newspaper, April 22, 1932. Baba's message in the last two paragraphs was also published in the *Western Times and North Devon Herald* (see pp. 283 and 285).

BIBLICAL SCENE

Indian Mystic Arrives at Combe Martin

MEHER BABA'S MESSAGE

Residents of Combe Martin were shaken out of the usual stoic calm of a typical Sunday afternoon by the arrival in the village of Shri Meher Baba, the Indian, acclaimed by all his devotees as the new Indian Messiah.

A Chronicle representative was privileged to be invited to East Challacombe farm to witness the arrival of Shri Meher Baba, and the spectacle as the procession neared the farm almost beggared description, being more reminiscent of a biblical scene than of the surroundings of a sleepy Devon farm.

The grey of the old house contrasted strangely with the colour in the procession, and, as the latter neared the entrance, it was seen that Shri Meher Baba was accompanied by his personal servant and secretary, an Indian, and that Mr. and Mrs. Meredith Starr, the leaders of the Combe Martin colony, were holding his arms as he walked through muddy lanes and over wet fields.

As Shri Meher Baba came close to the house Mr. Kenneth Ross, a Scotsman, and brother-in-law of Mr. Meredith Starr, rushed to the terrace fronting the house and set up a wild skirling of the bagpipes.

Never in all the long centuries of its history had East Challacombe farm seen such a strange company enter its portals, but the strangest scene came when seven Indians rushed across the yard, gesticulating wildly and talking in their own language, and greeted Shri Meher Baba.

After being photographed on the terrace the whole party went indoors, many devotees of the sect rushing to Baba and holding his hands. He was obviously delighted at the magnanimity of the welcome accorded him, for he smiled and clasped all by the hand.

His long black tresses (reaching his shoulders) streamed in the north-easterly wind. He has a most impressive, kindly, and cultured visage. His looks would command in anyone, except the ignorant, more than a little respect.

One thing that struck our representative was the obvious sincerity and kindliness of all the people staying in the Retreat.

Immediately the party had entered, Mr. Meredith Starr was approached and asked if Shri Meher Baba would see the Pressmen. They were told that he would not that day see them, and Mr. Starr was thereupon asked to see the Baba and elicit from him a message to England—the first ever given to the public from the Retreat.

By means of an interpreter working an alphabet almost as fast as speech, the following message was transmitted from Shri Meher Baba to the Press through Mr. Meredith Starr:

Coming to this retreat is like coming home. Here spirituality is made practical. I find the atmosphere and training here result in ideals being realised. Head and heart must go together. Physical, mental and spiritual equilibrium must be achieved to ensure permanent results.

For the present crisis to pass away and matters to become normal again, the West must understand the importance of spiritual development, and must realise divinity in every phase of life—in art, science, nature, and the daily routine. That Infinite Consciousness must be experienced. Then only can there be peace in the real sense of the word. But if, as at present, only the material aspect continues to be stressed, then there will be still greater discord which will cause untold suffering.

SHRI M.B.

Published in *North Devon Herald*, April 21, 1932, this article describes Meher Baba's arrival at the East Challacombe retreat. Baba's message to the press appears in the final paragraph (see also pp. 283 and 284).

SHRI MEHER BABA.

Pressman's Visit to East Challacombe.

When visiting the retreat, East Challacombe, Combe Martin, on Friday to enquire concerning Shri Meher Baba's arrival, I was somewhat disappointed, for I expected to find weird people, living in a place of weird things. Instead I found everything of the simple and ordinary kind. There were no unusual and awe-inspiring furnishings in the residence, but such articles as forms, tables, and several basket chairs. On the side of the bungalow were beds of wooden construction and attractive design. Mr. Starr cordially received me, and gave evidence of possessing a keen intellect.

A point on which the public and the Press had been curious was the Baba's bedroom, and Mr. Starr, in showing it t me, said I was the first Press representative to be permitted to view it. The room contained a single-size bedstead of iron with mattress and overlay covered with a hand-made quilt. By the side of the bed was a small mahogany table covered with a Japanese cloth, and adjoining was a white wood washstand. At the other end was a hand-made cupboard, and near it a wooden stool made by a member of the colony from African mahogany picked up on the seashore. A huge window faced the bedroom. The room had plenty of light and ventilation. Mr. Starr told me that the Baba would probably remain at the retreat eight or nine days, and then proceed to America.

Like Mr. Starr, the other members of the retreat were obviously cultured persons. Mr. Starr said he resented very much the attention of journalists who were looking for sensational matter, but he would gladly welcome anyone who sought the truth. He slightly smiled as I mentioned the recent "hold up" of journalists in the vicinity by a supposed Indian, and characterised it as a village prank.

Whilst passing West Challacombe on my return from the retreat I was hailed by a village farm hand, who said "You bain't running away to-day, then?"

Shri Meher Baba arrived at East Challacombe, Combe Martin, about 3.30 on Sunday afternoon—earlier than anticipated. By so doing he escaped the attention of many

doing he escaped the attention of many sightseers. He made the journey from London by car, and then proceeded through the muddy lanes to East Challacombe in company with his secretary, gazing admiringly at the wild flowers in the hedgerows. He was protected from the cold north-easterly wind by an ulster coat.

Members of the Retreat, including Mr. and Mrs. Starr, met the Baba just below West Challacombe Farm, and he greeted them heartily. They walked on each side of him and proceeded through a newly-made lane to the Retreat. On his arrival at the Retreat a party of seven Indians rushed to him, followed by other members of the colony, and he greeted them warmly. Mr. Kenneth Ross, brother-in-law of Mr. Starr, then skirled a welcome on the Highland pipes, parading up and down the terrace fronting the farm. At the summit of the hill the party halted and were photographed.

A hushed silence, in keeping with the Baba's observance, came over the farm as he walked solemnly along with his black hair streaming in the wind.

The interior of the farm was tastefully decorated with choice flowers for the reception.

Permission was sought by our representative to interview the new Messiah, but he was informed that no interview could be granted that day. Through Mr. Starr Shri Meher Baba sent the message:—"Coming to this retreat is like coming home. Here spirituality is made practical. I find the atmosphere and training here result in the realisation of ideals. Head and heart must go together. Physical, mental, and spiritual equilibrium must be achieved to ensure permanent results. For the present crisis to pass away and matters to become normal again the West much understand the importance of spiritual development, and must realise divinity in every phase of life in art, science, nature, and the daily routine. That infinite consciousness must be experienced. Then only can there be peace in the real sense of the word. But if, as at present, only the material aspect continues to be stressed, then there will be still greater discord, causing unto'd suffering."

S. R. C., Ilfracombe.

Leader of Indian Cult Leaves Ship in England

Dover, England, April 7 (A.P.) — Meher Baba, proclaimed by his followers as the "god man" and "new Messiah," arrived here tonight from Bombay and had considerable difficulty with port officials on account of his eight-year vow of silence.

Other members of the party of the Parsee and mystic, who has said he was going to the United States to convert them to his faith, did the necessary talking for him, and he was permitted to proceed. The Parsee left by automobile, presumably for the college of his followers at East Challacombe, in Devon.

(LEFT) Announcement of Baba's arrival in London, published in the *Washington Post*, April 8, 1932.

THE DAILY MIRROR, Saturday, April 9, 1932.

FAMOUS AIRMAN DIES IN 'PLANE

Daily Mirror

THE DAILY PICTURE NEWSPAPER WITH THE LARGEST NET SALE

No. 8,854 ... One Penny

INDIAN "MESSIAH": EXCLUSIVE INTERVIEW—Page 3

Wireless on Page 16

MELLON'S ARRIVAL

Mr. Andrew Mellon, one of the richest men in the world, on arrival in London yesterday to take up his duties as American Ambassador. He was received by British and foreign State officials.

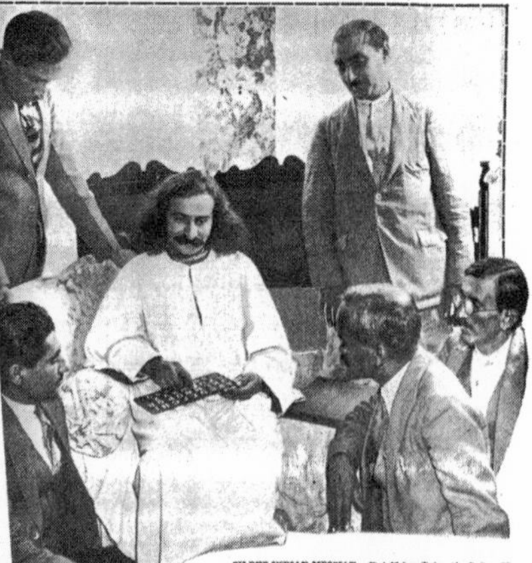

SILENT INDIAN MESSIAH.—Shri Meher Baba, the Indian Messiah, discussing his philosophy with disciples by means of his alphabet board in London yesterday. He is shortly going to Devon, where he may break his self-imposed seven years of silence.

Saturday, April 9, 1932 THE DAILY MIRROR *Late London Edition* Page 3

"MIRACLE MAN" TALKS TO "DAILY MIRROR"

Indian Mystic's Finger Signals to Preserve Seven Years' Silence

HIS MESSAGE TO THE WORLD

Waiting for Spirit to Move Him to Revelation —Miracles Performed "If Necessary"

Shri Meher Baba, the Indian mystic, who has been claimed as a new Messiah capable of performing miracles, talked on his alphabet-board with the *Daily Mirror* in London yesterday during an exclusive interview.

He has come to England to join a little community of devotees at Combe Martin in Devonshire, and during the interview preserved his seven years' silence by a system of finger signals.

"I can perform miracles if necessary," was one of his communications, but he added that miracles were unimportant and "child's play to anyone who has reached my state of consciousness."

Baba is expected to give a message to the world when he goes to America. "He is waiting for the spirit to move him to a revelation," said one of his disciples.

TO LEAD WESTERN WORLD

Shri Meher Baba on His Plans During Visit to England

BY A SPECIAL CORRESPONDENT

"The statement that I am a 'Messiah' is not to be taken in a literal sense," Shri Meher Baba, the new Indian religious teacher, told me yesterday.

Shri Meher Baba was seated in his apartment in West London, surrounded by five faithful disciples who are travelling with him. His slight figure was wrapped in a simple white robe, emphasising his mane of dark hair and heavy eyebrows and moustache.

He has a gentle, affectionate manner and welcomed me with a graceful inclination. His large, lustrous, black eyes very observant, lit up with a pleasant expression as his thin brown finger moved swiftly across an alphabet board on his knee.

The interview had started. Meher Baba, who has been claimed as a new Messiah, was trying to speak to me through the veil of his self-imposed silence of seven years.

One of his disciples turned to me and said: "Baba says that you are good. . He is pleased to meet you."

NO CHURCH NOR CREED

What was his message for the English people? I wanted to know. And very swiftly the finger moved again. He was spelling in English, but with short cuts and abbreviations that only the swift and practised eyes of his disciples could follow.

The Western world, Baba thought, tended to concentrate too much upon materialism. Materialism was not an altogether bad feature of Western life. It was, indeed, valuable in the development of our lives.

BABA'S REVELATION

But he wished to lead the West towards spiritual truths, without Churches or creeds, to a realisation of the possibilities of the spirit that might become a part of our everyday life.

Asked when he would be able to give his message publicly to the world, Baba told me that he would be going within a month to America, where it was possible that within two or three months' time he might break his silence.

I was told by a disciple that Baba did not make any vow to keep silent for seven years. "He just entered into the silence, and when the time comes, sooner or later, he will speak." He is waiting for the spirit to move him to his revelation.

Meanwhile, he is giving counsel to those who seek it. He will go within a week to Devon, where he will be welcomed at the Ashram, near Combe Martin.

"What do you teach your inquirers?" I asked.

"According to their individual needs. But when I speak to the whole world, then my teaching will be universal."

Asked if it were true that he would perform miracles, Meher Baba replied, "If necessary." But he did not think that he would perform miracles in England perhaps in America it might happen.

NO MIRACLES "TO ORDER"

One of the disciples explained that Baba did not perform miracles "to order."

Baba made further signals, describing how he had performed miracles in India. He had bathed lepers and they had been cured; he had cured people of contagious diseases.

"Can you raise the dead?" I asked.

"If necessary," replied Baba. But he did not know why I was so insistent on miracles. Miracles, he explained, were really unimportant. One who had passed into his high spiritual sphere had travelled beyond the earthly manifestations that one associated with miracles.

"To anybody who has attained the state of consciousness that I have reached miracles are child's play."

He conveyed that the attainment of a spiritual unity with the non-material world was something far greater than any outward sign that he might make.

The beginning of Meher Baba's religious experience is traced to his meeting with an Indian saint, Baba Jan. I asked if she had taught him all he is teaching now.

THE DOOR UNLOCKED

"No, she did not teach me exactly," replied Baba. "She unlocked the door. I knew that I had powers within me, but it was she who showed me what they meant. It was not something to be taught, but to be lived and experienced."

I asked if he imposed any discipline or rule of life on his followers. Did he encourage fasting, or vegetarianism?

"Only according to their individual needs. One of my disciples in India has lived for four years on water and a little milk."

He said that he had no interest in the political affairs of India, and asked me to correct the statement that he was the spiritual adviser of Gandhi.

(Continued on page 6)

FOR GERMAN TENNIS

Miss Helen Jacobs, the American Wightman Cup lawn tennis player, has announced her intention of participating in the German championships next month.

'MIRACLE MAN'S' PLANS

(Continued from page 3)

"Gandhi met me on the liner Rajputana and we talked of spiritual experiences. Gandhi was interested, and said that he would like to meet me in America. I said that he could come to me after he had finished with his political work," was Baba's explanation.

"You mean that you do not think politics and the spiritual life have much to do with each other?"

"Not directly," replied Baba. "But eventually, of course, the spiritual experience becomes universal and includes the political affairs of the world."

He wanted all the nations to be brought together, he did not wish to work for India alone.

A disciple informed me that Baba has "many thousands of followers in India. It is impossible to say how many. They are chiefly round about Bombay and many are in the Madras Presidency."

"MIRACULOUS CURE"

Meher Baba thought it was unlikely that he would hold any public meeting in England, but it would depend upon circumstances. He had addressed a large gathering (by means of his alphabet-board) during the voyage on the liner.

He showed me correspondence from America, indicating that his visit to the United States is being preceded by a wave of publicity.

A disciple showed me a copy of a letter from a woman devotee to the Countess Tolstoy, in which it was stated that Meher Baba had miraculously cured her of a tumour. I was told that such miracles are a matter of faith.

"From which religious teacher do you derive your philosophy?" I asked. "From Christ? ... or Buddha?"

"From no one teacher in particular," Baba replied. "Christ, Buddha, Krishna . . . these are names for states of consciousness. . . ."

"And you have studied them all?"

Shri Meher Baba nodded and smiled.

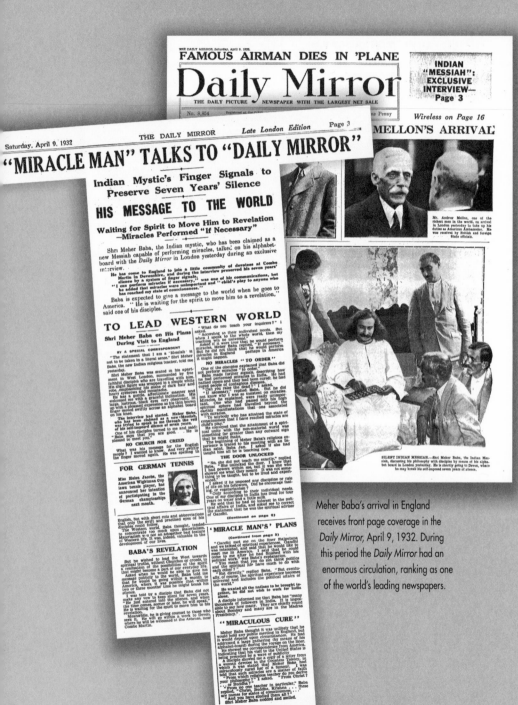

Meher Baba's arrival in England receives front page coverage in the *Daily Mirror,* April 9, 1932. During this period the *Daily Mirror* had an enormous circulation, ranking as one of the world's leading newspapers.

THE DAILY MIRROR, Friday, April 8, 1932.

INDIAN MESSIAH ARRIVES—P. 2

Daily Mirror

THE DAILY PICTURE NEWSPAPER WITH THE LARGEST NET SALE

No. 8,853 Registered at the G.P.O. as a Newspaper. FRIDAY, APRIL 8, 1932

FOUR PAGE LONDON FILM REVIEW

Page 2 THE DAILY MIRROR Friday, April 8, 1932

INDIAN "MIRACLE MAN" ARRIVES IN ENGLAND

WELCOME BY DEVOTEES

Devon Colony Awaits "The New Messiah"

7 YEARS' SILENCE

FROM OUR SPECIAL CORRESPONDENT

COMBE MARTIN (Devon), Thursday.

Shri Meher Baba, who claims to be another Messiah and capable of performing miracles, is expected here a week to-morrow.

He reached Dover from India to-day, accompanied by eight Indian devotees, who act as secretaries and servants.

Fatigued by his long journey from Meherabad, he will rest with friends in London a few days, and then motor to his English Ashram, the seventeenth century farmhouse lying in the shadow of Hangman Hill.

Here to-day I found a little community of devotees of Baba, led by Mr. Meredith Starr, living in excited anticipation but making no material preparation for the "Master."

Baba takes things as he finds them, with humility and without question, so that the tortuous path winding its muddy and rocky way through the heights of Ashram cannot upset him.

His sandalled feet may slip many times before he has negotiated his 700ft. climb, but adoring followers will be always at hand.

MESSAGE TO THE WORLD

Little is known in this country as yet about Baba. Mr. Starr declares that soon the whole world will ring with his name and his message.

Baba imposed silence on himself for seven years. That period is almost ended, and when it is Baba will address the world.

It may be from the Ashram here in Devon, or it may be from America.

I asked Mr. Starr whether Baba would proclaim himself Messiah, and he said that was a question only Baba could answer.

"May I say this?" said Mr. Starr. "He is regarded by thousands as having the same consciousness as the Messiah, and I share this view. I do not consider it important whether he is a reincarnation or whether he is another perfect 'Master,' as all perfect masters are essentially one."

Baba, Mr. Starr informed me, was born in Poona of Parsee parents thirty-eight years ago.

He was the only Indian boy in the European school that he attended, and as a boy showed remarkable powers of leadership.

TRANCE OF NINE MONTHS

"When he was about eighteen he met a great Indian saint named Baba Jan. She was a perfect 'Master,' and when she died last year she was not less than 130 years old."

"Exactly how old she was nobody knew, but she was fully 130 when I met her in India in 1928.

"As a result of his meeting with her, Baba went into this high state of consciousness instantly. He was unconscious of his body for nine months, and only regained full consciousness of the physical world seven years later, through the help of another 'Master.'

"For another six years he continued his spiritual work in the school he founded, and then decided not to speak for seven years.

(Continued on page 4)

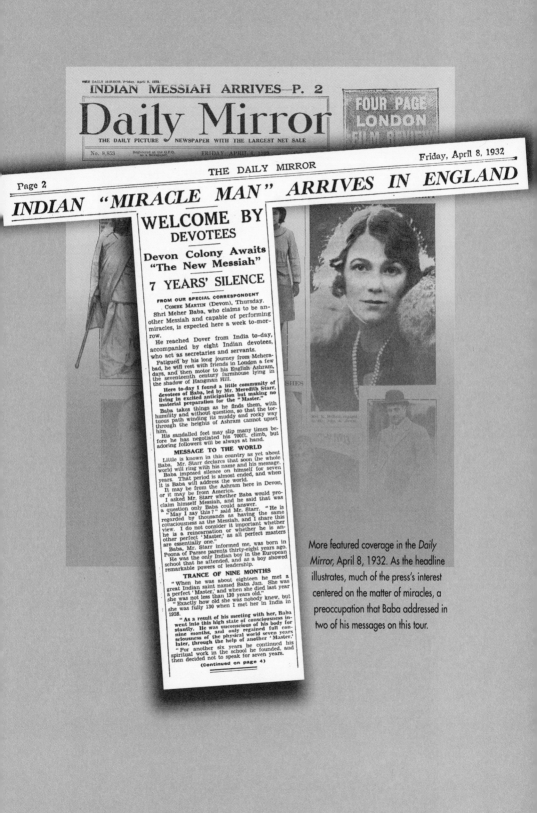

More featured coverage in the *Daily Mirror,* April 8, 1932. As the headline illustrates, much of the press's interest centered on the matter of miracles, a preoccupation that Baba addressed in two of his messages on this tour.

DAILY SKETCH, MONDAY, APRIL 11, 1932

'THE BLACK FALCON INN,' JUNE BOLAND'S SERIAL: Page 14

DAILY SKETCH

No. 7,167. [Registered as a Newspaper.] MONDAY, APRIL 11, 1932. ONE PENNY.

Foreign WIRELESS —SEE PAGE 12

WAITING FOR NEW "MESSIAH"

Evening meditation in the lonely retreat near Combe Martin, Devon, where a devoted community are awaiting the arrival of Shri Baba, the Indian mystic who claims to be the Messiah. A photograph of Baba, who is now in England, is on the mantelpiece.—(*Daily Sketch* photograph.)

KILLED IN HEAD-ON COLLISION

HINDENBURG ELECTED

EVE OF POLL SCENES

DAILY SKETCH, TUESDAY, APRIL 12, 1932

IS THIS A PAGAN AGE? Read Candidus on Page 7

DAILY SKETCH

No. 7,168. [Registered as a Newspaper.] TUESDAY, APRIL 12, 1932. ONE PENNY.

START OUR NEW SERIAL TO-DAY

PROPHET TELLS OF "DIVINE" KISS

ondon's strangest visitor, Shri Meher Baba, from India, who claims to be the Messiah and has a community of aithful followers in Devonshire. He has dark, flashing eyes and a mass of black hair, and is here seen in European dress. He claims to have received divine inspiration from a woman "saint," Hazrat Babajan (left), whom he met under a tree in Poona and whose kiss transformed him. She was said to be 130 years old when she died last year.

CABINET MINISTER'S SON MARRIED IN PARIS

BROKEN ROPE

In Climbing Tragedy

Front page coverage in the *Daily Sketch*, another leading English newspaper, April 11 and April 12, 1932.

(TOP) Baba's followers at the East Challacombe retreat, Devonshire.

(BOTTOM) Photos of Meher Baba and Hazrat Babajan.

THE DAILY MIRROR, Thursday, April 7, 1932.

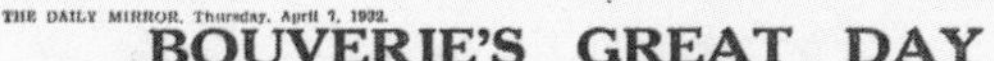

BOUVERIE'S GREAT DAY

Daily Mirror

THE DAILY PICTURE NEWSPAPER WITH THE LARGEST NET SALE

No. 8,852 — Registered at the G.P.O. as a Newspaper. — THURSDAY, APRIL 7, 1932 — One Penny

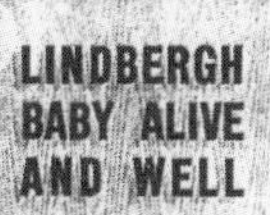

Wireless on Page 16

INDIAN "MESSIAH" VISITING ENGLAND

TO "RAISE THE DEAD" IF NECESSARY

Shri Meher Baba, who has been acclaimed as the "new Indian Messiah" and is arriving in England to-day or to-morrow. He is worshipped by thousands of Indians and has declared that, if necessary, he will "raise the dead, heal the sick and make the blind see" during his stay in this country. Gandhi has visited him for spiritual guidance. It is stated, however, that Meher Baba intimated that he could only give him the full help he required after Gandhi had given up politics. The "new Messiah" has not spoken a word for seven years, and expresses himself by means of an alphabet board. The picture above shows him in his retreat at Ahmednagar, India. There is a small colony of English followers in a secluded part of Exmoor. Below are some of its members with their leader, Mr. Meredith Starr (seated, centre).

Meher Baba in the Western clothes he is to wear in England. He is about thirty-eight years old and was a seller of toddy—a drink extracted from palm—until 1922, when what he considered a revelation came to him. He preaches the necessity of uniting mankind spiritually.

The entrance of the "Messiah's" cave for meditation, Panchgani, India.

The main building of the Exmoor colony, near Combe Martin.

Front-page coverage in the *Daily Mirror,* April 7, 1932, the day of Meher Baba's arrival in England. Photographs of Meher Baba and the East Challacombe retreat in Devonshire.

I Can Hardly Belie

A Portrait of a Happy Man, Silent Seven Years, Who Is Seeking to Right the World Through Love

(Reading time: 9 minutes 55 seconds.)

"I WANT you to come to tea," said my friend, "with Shri Sadguru Meher Baba."

"With what?"

My friend smiled in her most superior manner.

"With the new perfect master from India."

I am not much on perfect masters, myself. Or on tea. But my friend was insistent. So off we went to visit her globe-trotting Parsee. But in the taxicab my reluctance grew into a sort of terror.

"What language does this friend of yours speak?" I asked.

"He doesn't speak at all," was the reply. "He hasn't spoken for seven years."

The interview was looking sourer and sourer to me.

"What did you say his name was?" I asked in desperation.

My companion was very patient. "Shri," she said, "which means Sir. Sadguru, which means perfect master. Meher, which means compassionate. And Baba, which means father."

Sir Perfect Master Compassionate Father! That was a large order. But I must say that Shri Sadguru Meher Baba, in spite of the fact that he had dressed up for tea in an imitation-chinchilla coat and light-gray flannel pants, looked every inch the part. Not very many inches, to be sure; for Baba—that's what I decided to call him—was small, in the Oriental fashion; yet somehow strangely impressive.

How, in such a get-up, he managed to be anything but funny was more than I could see. Certainly it was not the sartorial or tonsorial effect of Shri Sadguru Meher Baba, as he sat draped over the soft red upholstery of Mrs. Phelps Stokes' best square-backed couch, that kept me from laughing out loud. It must have been—although I was loath to admit it—the man himself.

A stunning yellow-headed, ruddy Englishwoman was pouring Baba's tea—on her knees by a small tabouret in front of the Sadguru. Baba is not married. At thirty-seven, he even flirts tentatively with the doctrine of celibacy as a sort of world sedative. But his disciples made it clear that he did not prescribe celibacy for his followers.

"Sex for me," he said, "does not exist."

Of course, he did not *say* it; but he communicated it to me by a method I'll explain in a minute.

"Modern marriage is too much of a business affair," he continued. "No wonder it so often results in divorce. Husband and wife should put each other first. It is essential for a happy family life that selfless love should predominate over lust."

I ventured to suggest that we who live in America had a good many problems right now besides sex problems. Baba smiled sympathetically, humorously. His smile was like an open fire in a cold house.

"Things *have* been messed up a good deal here," he said, "by lack of understanding."

The fact that this Parsee messiah was discussing our American problems in American language as naturally as if he had lived here all his life didn't seem so strange as you might think.

And the fact that he was discussing them, not with his perfectly good voice but by means of letters which he pointed to on a small blackboard which he held on his lap, did not seem strange, either.

Seven-year silences, it seems, are not uncommon events among the holy men of India. The uncommon thing about Baba's was that he made you forget it so soon and so completely. He could "talk" in seven different languages on his little board, and could spell out his words in any of the seven faster than human eye could follow. He was articulate in many other ways, this odd little man who had come out of the East to save the world. He talked with his eyes, which I mu say are the largest and softest and shiningest and smilingest ever saw; and with jolly little grunts; and with affectiona pats of approval and agreement. Then there was his smil

"What are you going to do," I asked, "for this 'messed-up country of ours?"

"It is my country, too," he said simply.

Apparently he feels that way about every country. Whe Gandhi came to him and asked him to help him, Baba replie

"Not until you abandon politics. I have no politics."

Baba is not an Indian in the sense that Gandhi is. He is Persian, born in Poona, South India, on February 25, 189 He was by birth a racial internationalist. And by profession religious one. He tolerated, he said, all cults and all faith His aim was to make those who professed faith worthy of th faith they professed. It happened that he himself was born the religion of Zoroaster, but he was apparently no proselytize for any creed or dogma.

"I intend to bring together all religions and cults like bea on one string and revitalize them," he said, "for individual an collective needs. This is my misson to the West."

His special reason for visiting *us* for the purpose of breakin his seven-year silence was, he said, that America, being mos deeply engrossed in material things, and suffering most i consequence, was the soil in which a new spiritual rebirt would first take place.

"When you break your silence," I asked, "how will you d it? By radio?"

"Surely not by radio!" exclaimed one of his London disci ples in his most horrified British manner.

"Why not?" spelled out Baba on his board.

FREDERICK L. COLLINS

is the author of such sprightly books as This King Business, and has been a magazine editor and publisher. During the World War he served in the War, Treasury, and Interior Departments.

Skeptic that I was, I could not doubt his sincerity Or his courage. When I asked him to particulariz about the kinds of messing up to which we in Americ had been subjected, he might easily have sough refuge behind one of the general vague assertions c principle with which all Eastern writings are filled.

"AMERICA has great energy," he said, "but great deal of it is misdirected; and misdirecte energy produces destructive complexes, and these turn produce fear, greed, lust, and anger, whic result in moral and spiritual decay."

"Those are strong words," I protested.

He smiled reassuringly. He certainly could d wonders with that smile!

"Is your aim to help us with our spiritual problem or our practical problems?" I asked.

"Our spiritual problems *are* our practical ones."

"And just how do you intend to help?"

"The help I will give will produce a change c heart in thousands, and then right thinking and li ing will result automatically."

"Will that solve the depression problem?"

"It will solve *every* problem."

"Prohibition?"

"Yes—and the problem behind prohibition," he said. " do not believe in drink, and none of my followers drink. But know that prohibition should never have been put in effect th way it was."

"All at once?"

"Yes. Spirits should have been barred, but not beer an wine. Then we might have had a law that could be enforce As it is, we have a law which makes money for dishonest officia and increases all vices everywhere."

You may not agree with this opinion. But, at least, it *is* a opinion. I had to admit that, for all his seven-year silenc

26

Two-page feature story on Meher Baba by Frederick Collins, *Liberty* magazine, August 27, 1932. At this time *Liberty* was the second best-selling weekly magazine in America.

It, Myself

By
FREDERICK L. COLLINS

Acme photo

Shri Sadguru Meher Baba, Parsee messiah, with the board on which, while silent, he spells out his message.

er Baba had said more in few spelled-out sen- s than many a senator rty platform maker had thed in seven-hour hes.

believe in self-control." ontinued, "not in coer- Coercion is based on ession, and results in and hatred. Self-control ires courage, and may be ced by love. We will do things for those whom ove which we would not narily do—which we d not ordinarily have the igth of mind and power . How many habits have been able to break, igh love, which we would r have had the strength eak without love? And when the love is universal love, abits which are detrimental, either to the individual or to social order, will be dissolved in its light.

It is the same way with this economic situation you were ng me about," he added. "There is a very close connection een a man's character and his circumstances, between his rnal environment of thoughts and desires and his external ronment. 'As within, so without,' is the law.

If we are dissatisfied with our environment, it is usually use we do not know how to adjust ourselves properly to the ronment. Instead of thinking, 'How can I get out of this?' becoming discouraged or depressed, we should think, at is the lesson I should learn from this experience?'

Poverty, if cheerfully endured, provided one does one's to find work, develops humility and patience, and can tly assist spiritual progress. It is a test of character. I v it is difficult to be cheerful when starving, but all the th-while things are difficult.

Even millionaires are unhappy unless they have learned ink and live rightly."

asked him if he thought a general acceptance of his doctrine ve would bring about a more equable distribution of what and I need every day—money.

It must," he replied. "Suppose we all loved each other eeply as we now love the one whom we love best. The most ral desire of love is to share what one has with the beloved. desire to share with everyone would produce a condition er which it would be a disgrace rather than an honor for one to possess more than anyone else."

ex. Prohibition. Poverty. All were to be banished by !

"Do you expect to do this all at once?" I asked.

"No. But sooner than you think. People will respond."

"Why?"

"They will have to."

He did not explain. But he didn't need to: I knew he would say that the compelling force would be love.

"What are you going to do first?" I asked.

"Go to China. But I shall come right back. I am only staying there a day."

I knew he had recently come sixteen thousand miles from his native India by way of Port Said, Marseilles, Southampton, and Greenwich Village. And now he was planning to go to China just for a day. To China, by way of Hollywood and Honolulu!

"I want to lay a complete cable," he said, "between the East and the West."

I did not laugh. I might have, half an hour before. I am sure I would have three years before, when the gospel of acquisitiveness was saving, or enslaving, the world. But now, God knows, we need a cable layer, a Sadguru, a perfect master—someone to lead us out of the slough of materialistic despond—and if he comes in the guise of a mustachioed Parsee in an imitation-fur pyjama jacket and gray flannel pants, who cares?

AND, after all, why shouldn't he? In his *ashram* in India—an *ashram* is a sort of retreat—Baba is treated almost as a god. Listen to the words of a disciple:

"The devotion inspired by Shri Meher Baba has to be seen to be believed. Practically everyone in the *ashram* would have laid down his life for the master. A glance or a touch from him was more esteemed than a handful of jewels. *Even at a slight reproof men have been known to sob for days.*"

"Oh, that's all right for India," you say; "but this—"

Well, here he was, this "perfect master," in his doubtful chinchilla jacket, on Mrs. Phelps Stokes' square-backed sofa. And here was I, the unbeliever, sitting joyously beside him.

He just looked at me and smiled. I think I smiled, too. We sat that way a long time. I know you will laugh, but we *did!* Baba believes in meditation; and when you are with him you believe as Baba does. I can hardly believe it now, but I distinctly remember I was having a good time.

Everybody does have a good time with Baba; for he is that rare being, a happy man!

THE END

The article is based on an interview at the Stokes residence in New York in late May. (For a full transcript, see pp. 50–55.)

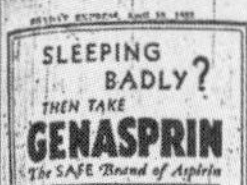

Sunday Express

Founded by LORD BEAVERBROOK.

LATE FINAL

NO. 603. LONDON, APRIL 10, 1932. TWOPENCE.

A TALK WITH THE STRANGE MESSIAH.

What He Told JAMES DOUGLAS In A Kensington Bedroom.

"MY MISSION WILL LAST FOR 33 YEARS."

THREE HOURS' SLEEP A DAY.

SILENT INTERVIEW WITH AN ALPHABET.

By JAMES DOUGLAS.

SHRI SADGURU MEHER BABA received me yesterday afternoon in his bedroom in a Kensington house.

He has been described as the Indian Christ or Messiah. He arrived in England on Friday.

His mission, his disciples declare, is to save mankind, East as well as West.

He is a saint and a mystic, a Mahatma or spiritual superman. It is said that he can perform miracles.

When I arrived a procession of his disciples filed out. First a bevy of beautiful young white girls passed me, then several young Indians departed.

Meher Baba was sitting on a sofa. He wore a dressing-gown, and a soft blue silken scarf round his neck.

What He Is Like.

He is a slender man of thirty-eight, but he looks ten years younger. He wears his dark brown hair very long. It flows down to his shoulders. He reminded me of the young Paderewski.

He has a brown moustache. His face is ascetic. The chin is rather pointed and not powerful. His forehead is lined.

His eyes are large and radiant. They [illegible] with happiness and serene joy. His smile is charming. It is gay and boyish and childlike.

I am told that he is a brilliant cricketer. He is obviously healthy and natural in his manner. His hands are eloquently artistic. They are the hands of a virtuoso. They talk. They are hypnotic.

He has immense magnetism. As I entered the room I felt a rush of personal fascination and force. It seemed to fill the chamber with its warmth.

As he grasped my hand I felt a strange thrill. He bade me sit close to him on the sofa, and during our talk he perpetually caressed me, laying his hand on mine, or touching me on the back. A very magnetic personality.

He Does Not Speak.

As a rule I shrink from the human touch, so I guarded myself against physical hypnotism. I armoured myself with scepticism, but I melted under his enchantment in spite of my caution.

Meher Baba does not speak. He says he has not spoken for seven years. Our talk was conducted through a young Indian, who rapidly interpreted the Master's signs.

On his knee rested a small board with the letters of the Roman alphabet painted on it. His slim fingers flashed from letter to letter. He does not spell words. His telegraphy is too rapid for that.

His interpreter reads the alphabet upside down. I do not know how he does it, for the pace is as swift as speech.

I had prepared a questionnaire with the help of Sir Denison Ross, the Oriental scholar. It was designed to trap the teacher, but he smilingly threaded his way through it without stumbling. His mastery of dialect is consummate. It was quite Socratic in its ease.

He frequently put questions to me which startled me by their penetration. But he never evaded a direct question. His simplicity is very subtle.

"I am a Persian," he said. "I was born in Poona, but my father and mother were Persians."

He is above races and religions. He is universal. He is one with God, and God is everywhere in every one.

"*Do you know Gandhi?*" I asked.

"Yes. I met him in the steamship Rajputana. He is not as far advanced as I am. He asked me to help him, but I will not help him until he abandons politics. I have no politics."

"*Are you a Mahatma?*" I asked. He smiled.

"What is a Mahatma?" he replied. "I know the truth. You live in London. You know it, I know."

"*Are you divine?*" He smiled.

"I am one with God. I live in Him, like Buddha, like Christ, like Krishna. They know Him as I know Him. All men can know Him."

"There Is No Evil."

"*Have you solved the problem of evil?*"

"There is no evil," he said. "There are only degrees of good."

"*The world is perplexed with disaster. Is there any way out of the world crisis?*"

"Yes."

"*How long will it last?*"

"Only another year. Then there will be recovery and deliverance."

"*Christ's mission was accomplished in three years. How long will your mission last?*"

"Thirty-three years," he replied.

"*What is your secret?*" I asked.

"The elimination of the ego," he replied.

Then I put my questionnaire.

"*Have you a Scripture, a Bible, a Koran, an inspired book?*"

"No, I teach. I am a teacher."

"*Do you believe in Buddha and the Eight-Fold Path?*"

"Yes. All religion is ascent by stages to perfect union with God."

"*What God do you believe in?*"

"There is only one God for all men."

"*What religion is nearest to yours?*"

"All religions are revelations of God."

"*Is there a future life?*"

SHRI MEHER BABA, the new Indian Messiah.

LINDBERGH DRAMA IN BRITAIN.

POLICE FIND CODE SENT TO UNKNOWN AGENT.

"DEPART AT ONCE!"

KIDNAP ENVOY TO MEET DETECTIVE.

A SURPRISING turn to the Lindbergh drama which took place in Britain last night suggests that the events which will lead to the restoration of the kidnapped baby will take place in this country.

[illegible]

LUCKIEST WOMAN.

Fell On Line, But The Engine Saved Her.

[illegible]

Girl Of 18 Shows The Tennis Stars How.

This is the story of a slim, quiet girl, who has just showed four Wightman Cup trial players how to play tennis—but has not herself been chosen for the trials.

[illegible]

MISS STAMMERS.

THE LAST "DOUBLE."

SHOT DEAD IN BARRACKS.

LINDBERGH ROBBED OF $10,000.

[illegible]

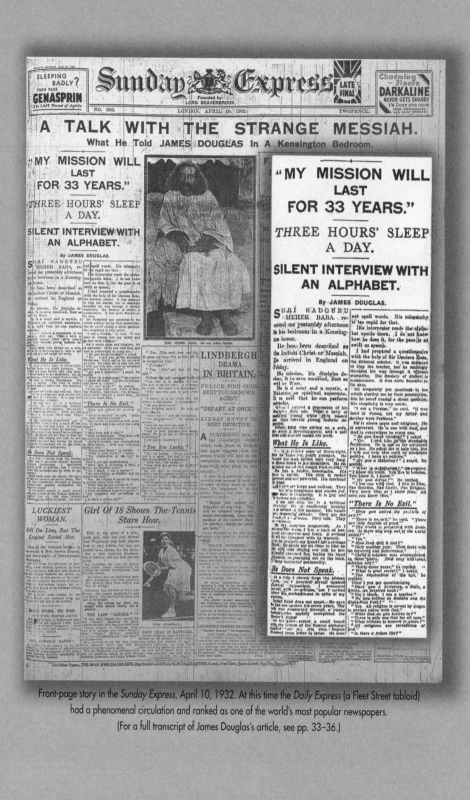

Front-page story in the *Sunday Express*, April 10, 1932. At this time the *Daily Express* (a Fleet Street tabloid) had a phenomenal circulation and ranked as one of the world's most popular newspapers. (For a full transcript of James Douglas's article, see pp. 33–36.)

A PERSIAN MYSTIC.

Meher Baba Passing Through Colony.

MESSAGE FOR THE WORLD.

A most interesting personality is visiting Hongkong at present, in the person of Meher Baba, a Persian mystic, who has come from America. He arrived by the Empress of Japan at Shanghai, later visiting Nanking, and is leaving by the Kaiser-i-Hind for France and Italy, afterwards continuing his wanderings. Meher Baba took a vow of silence seven years ago, and communicates to people his ideas, and replies to questions, by means of an interpreter, who is able to read what the mystic desires to convey with great facility, although the communication is spelt out rapidly with the fingers on a board marked with an alphabet and numbers.

Some call Meher Baba a seer, and he claims to have a message for the world which will be disclosed within a year, when the time comes for him to break his silence. The name Meher means, in Persian, "light," and the mystic is believed by some to represent the new light which is needed by mankind: certainly, although a Zoroastrian, he claims no special part of mankind for his message, but has intimated that the words he has to utter will be for every race and creed to hearken to.

A man of striking personality, Meher Baba, who is about 38 years of age, with piercing eyes, a thick moustache, and long, flowing hair, has made a great impression everywhere. In Hollywood he was the guest of honour at a reception where over 1,000 prominent people gathered, including practically all the film stars. He has Ashrams, or retreats, in India, England (at Coombe Martin, Devonshire), and in New York, and his appeal, made through his interpreter, is for a change of heart for the whole of humanity. His view of the future is an optimistic one.

Meher Baba spends many hours in contemplation, sleeping only two or three hours out of the twenty-four. He is a vegetarian, drinking water and occasionally a little buttermilk. He adopts the dress of whatever country he may visit, and in Hongkong yesterday was in a summer lounge suit, with an open-neck shirt.

The July 3, 1932 issue of *South China Morning Post,* a daily newspaper in Hong Kong, reports on Baba's visit to the British colony on July 1. Baba spent a week in China on the final leg of his 1932 world tour.

A SILENT SEER COMES TO AROUSE AMERICANS

Shri Meher Baba, Who Has Lived Seven Years Plunged In Thought, Teaches Disciples by Means of Signs

By HENRY JAMES FORMAN.

SPIRITUAL guides, teachers, swamis and so-called yogis from India are not unusual phenomena in America, but seldom does the cable announce their coming in advance. Yet a recent dispatch told of the sailing from Bombay of Shri Meher Baba, a spiritual leader whom his many disciples and devotees style by such transcendent appellations as "the Messiah," "the Avatar," "Sadguru" and "the Perfect Master." Together with some of his disciples he is on his way to the United States with the avowed purpose of "breaking down America's materialism," of quickening and harmonizing all creeds, of awakening the country to a new spiritual life.

Expected to arrive in New York the last week in April, he will go directly to an ashram, or retreat, already prepared for him at Harmon-on-the-Hudson, and there commence his self-appointed mission.

Tenets Explained.

"Roughly," in the words of a disciple explaining his master's tenets, "every 2,200 years the sun enters another sign of the zodiac. We are now entering a new solar epoch. The critical condition of the world is due to this fact. An old age is dying: a new age is being born. The world is convulsed by the birth-pangs of a new civilization. Now, as always, when the need of mankind is most pressing, a great spiritual push will be given to the world. But first a great darkness will fall on the world. This darkness, however, is only the shadow cast by a great light.

"This is both a wonderful and a terrible time. It depends on how you look at it. Everywhere old forms, mental as well as physical, are breaking up. The wise see in these changes the bursting asunder of the chrysalis that frees the golden butterfly.

"During the last 2,000 years the lower human mind has developed to its zenith. Now the divine or universal mind is stirring from its age-long slumber, and the new era which we are about to enter will mark the unfoldment of the divine mind. This implies an immense outpouring of spiritual energy, a quickening of the life impulse on a universal scale; the manifestation of a new type of consciousness—a higher synthesis of heart and mind.

"Shri Meher Baba is regarded as a perfect master, or Sadguru, all over India. He visited a retreat established by one of his disciples in England, and during his stay of eleven days every one there was transformed, permanently transformed, radiant and at peace with himself and the world."

A Disciple's Experience.

The disciple here quoted is Meredith Starr, a poet, who established the retreat in North Devonshire after a visit to Shri Meher Baba in India.

Mr. Starr's meeting with "the master" he recounts in some detail.

"Baba's age," he says, "seemed to be about 35. His skin was fair as any European's; his hair and mustache were dark brown, making a vivid contrast to his face, and he had large, luminous eyes. Serenity and strength radiated from his presence, and his face seemed lit up as if by an inner light.

"He told us not to worry about anything, but just to trust him and follow his instructions, and that if we did so we could not fail to progress. * * * In a few days we felt completely at home. There were some 300 people in his ashram, including about seventy boys. * * * On the fourth or fifth day Shri Meher Baba asked me to keep silence and to spend practically all my time in meditation. I remained silent for six months, only resuming speech on the day I left for Bombay. The Master had been silent for nearly seven years. He communicates by means of signs and an alphabet board.

Results of Meditation.

"After a few weeks I became unconscious of space or time. The outward world ceased to exist for me and I experienced immense inrushes of cosmic consciousness.

"A love so immense flooded my being that for three months tears continually streamed from my eyes—yet I am by no means a sentimental man. The deepest springs of life in my heart had been awakened. My life had been kindled by the flame of Divine Love which radiates continually from the Master. The springtide of creation was born anew in my soul. The old consciousness dissolved like a mist before the rising sun and was replaced by a new heaven and a new earth. My life was one continual symphony of inspiration. I could have written poetry all day and all night for months on end."

Pilgrims from all parts of India came daily "to take the dust of the Master's feet," often fifty or more pilgrims at a time, bringing gifts of sweetmeats, fruit and flowers. Sometimes whole processions came singing and dancing, accompanied by shell-music drums, cymbals and flutes. Every one there, declares Mr. Starr, "would have laid down his life for the Teacher." After six months Mr. Starr returned to England and founded his retreat in North Devon.

Last Autumn, when Gandhi sailed from India for the London Round-Table Conference, Shri Meher Baba was a silent fellow-traveler of the man the Occident calls the Mahatma. Gandhi is said to have asked to be allowed to come for a sojourn at Shri Meher Baba's ashram in India. The answer was that he would be welcome after he had done with and laid aside political activity.

After a stay of a few days in England Baba suddenly decided in November to come to America. He wished his visit to be unheralded, and unheralded it remained even to his departure in December. He visited New York and Boston, visited theatres and cinemas, the crowded streets of Broadway and Fifth Avenue, wherever American life in this region was at its busiest. The greater part of his brief stay, however, he spent in a little stone house at Harmon, lent by its owner for his use.

His communion with people who met him here was entirely silent. The few words that passed were indicated by his index finger pointing to the letters of the alphabet on a small wooden board he carried with him.

Arrangements for Return.

His devotees and disciples believe Shri Meher Baba to be a Messianic being, intent upon rendering great service to mankind in its present spiritual doldrums. He receives no money for his ministrations, but some of the friends he made during his visit to America are facilitating his return. Besides the retreat at Harmon other such ashrams are being prepared in New England and in California. People from some of the Southern States who have heard of him have written to Harmon offering their homes for visits and sojourns of Meher Baba.

He has no desire, his disciples assert, to found any cult, creed or society; people from all creeds, castes and races come to him and receive the help they need. His help consists, we are told, not in words or explanations, but results from "the grace and spiritual love and power that perpetually stream through him."

Hazarat Qibla Meher Baba was born at Poona, not far from Bombay, on Feb. 17, 1894, of Parsee parents, which means in the Zoroastrian faith. He was a carefree boy, from native accounts, a good student, a poet, a lover of nature and an excellent cricketer. In 1914 a Parsee woman "saint," Hazarat Babajan, of Poona, who died a year ago at an age said to have been more than 130 years, saw the young student and, so it is related, by a single glance conferred upon him "super-consciousness."

From that day he dedicated himself to the mystical life until, by the help of another saint, Shri Sadguru Upasni, the "Perfect Sight" came to him. Disciples and devotees began to gather about him, coming at times in hundreds, it is reported, to his ashram in Ahmednagar District, in the Deccan, intent, after the Indian manner, upon "God-realization." Last year 30,000 people gathered to celebrate his birthday.

Five years ago, in May, he opened a free school, perhaps unique in the present-day world, to teach young boys the spiritual life. Secular education was not neglected, and in general the boys were taught English, mathematics and literature as in other native schools of a certain grade. The Hazarat Babajan High School, however, differs in this: Spiritual instruction of a non-sectarian character is an important feature of the curriculum.

HOLY MAN FROM INDIA

Associated Press Photo.

Shri Meher Baba.

MYSTIC 'REDEEMER' AWAITED AT CROTON

Meher Baba, Who Has Kept Vow of Silence for 7 Years, Expected at Retreat About May 15.

PLANS TO END SPELL HERE

Aides Prepare a House of Margaret Mayo, Playwright, for Use as "Peaceful Meherashram."

Special to THE NEW YORK TIMES.

CROTON-ON-HUDSON, N. Y., May 7.—Meher Baba, the Eastern mystic, will arrive here about May 15 to begin his redemption of America, according to Jean and Malcolm Schloss, who maintain his retreat here in a house belonging to Miss Margaret Mayo, playwright.

The retreat is on the original Albany Post Road, which is still of dirt and gravel and over which, in olden days, coaches carried Colonial visitors to the Van Cortlandt Manor House.

The fieldstone house with red window frames, set high on the river's bank, overlooks the Croton River and the not far distant Hudson. There are no houses near by on the same side of the river, but on the western bank, opposite the Meher Baba retreat, a roadhouse stands in contrast to the spiritual purpose of "The Peaceful Meherashram," as the mystic's headquarters is to be called.

The Schlosses were won to Meher Baba several years ago, and when they heard he was coming to this country they appealed to Miss Mayo to let them entertain him in one of her houses in this locality.

Miss Mayo agreed that they should have the stone house on the old post road, and on last Nov. 6 Meher Baba came here to make his first American visit. He was to stay here only a week, but he stayed a month, more than 200 persons coming from all over the country to see him.

Miss Mayo, impressed with Meher Baba and his work, agreed to let him have the house for one year, according to the Schlosses, who have stayed here since his departure from America last December to carry on his work in this country and to make ready for his return.

Associated with the Schlosses in their work at the retreat are Mary Antin, author of "The Promised Land," and her daughter.

A feature of Meher Baba's visit to America will be the breaking of his seven-year silence. All of his utterances during the period of silence have been in writing or by means of an alphabet board which he carries with him.

Indian Mystic's Silence Vow Delays His Entry at Dover

By The Associated Press.

DOVER, England, April 7.—Meher Baba, proclaimed by his followers as the "God Man" and "New Messiah," arrived here tonight from Bombay and had considerable difficulty with port officials on account of his eight-year vow of silence.

Other members of the party of the Parsee and mystic, who has said he was going to the United States to convert them to his faith, did the necessary talking for him. The Parsee left by automobile, presumably for the college of his followers at East Challacombe in Devon.

The mystic is expected to return home and embark for America soon on a campaign to break down all religious barriers, destroy American materialism and amalgamate all creeds in a common element of love.

He said he would break his vow of silence on his arrival at Harmon, N. Y. He is of the Zoroastrian faith and claims to have been made both divine and human after attaining a super-conscious state.

Three articles in the *New York Times*, which gave extensive coverage to Meher Baba's 1932 world tour.

(TOP LEFT) The April 24, 1932 issue featured this in-depth introduction to Meher Baba, his teachings, and his following, by Henry James Forman, a noted journalist and writer of *Times* book reviews.

(TOP RIGHT) On May 8, 1932, the *Times* reported on Baba's anticipated arrival at Margaret Mayo's residence in Crofton, which was then being managed as Meherashram by Malcolm and Jean Schloss.

(BOTTOM RIGHT) On April 8, 1932, the *Times* reports on Baba's arrival in England.

(RIGHT) Los Angeles Times, May 29, 1932, at the beginning of Meher Baba's weeklong, high-profile visit to Hollywood.

(BELOW) Los Angeles Times, May 26, 1932, during Baba's cross-country train journey from New York.

SILENT MYSTIC OF INDIA TO ARRIVE HERE TODAY

Materialistic Hollywood today will come under the scrutiny of Shri Meher Baba, Indian mystic, whose belief it is that Europe and America pay too little attention to things spiritual and therefore are passing through an era of depression.

Hollywood has been selected by Baba as the place where next month he will break a seven-year silence begun in Bombay when he took a vow of silence to give an example of self-discipline. The breaking of the lenthy silence will be done in a typically American way, according to Baba's plans, with a national radio hook-up carrying his first words.

Arriving at Alhambra at 10 a.m. he will be taken by automobile to the home of M. E. Jones, author-philosopher, at 2400 North Gower street, where he and several of his nine disciples are to be guests for five days. Baba and his disciples will go to San Francisco at the end of five days to embark for Shanghai and will return to Hollywood for the ending of the seven-year period of speechlessness.

Unlike Krishnamurti, Hindu philosopher known throughout the world for his teachings, Baba believes that only through modern means can a message concerning spiritual matters be properly carried to the world's masses, and for that reason will begin a campaign with the breaking of his silence, which will find radio and the press carrying his messages, according to Jones.

The Hollywood writer's residence has been selected to house the mystic during his visits because of Jones's friendship with Mr. and Mrs. Malcolm Schloss of Harmon, N. Y., Baba's chief disciples in America, where he has hundreds of followers, Jones said. The Harmon couple will be in the party accompanying Baba to Hollywood. Others in the group will be Mr. and Mrs. Meredith Starr,

(Continued on Page 2, Column 5)

Indian Mystic Arrives Soon

HARMON (N. Y.) May 25. (AP)—Shri Meher Baba, Indian mystic, will leave tomorrow for California to visit Hollywood and other cities. He will be accompanied by nine disciples.

Baba, called Messiah by his followers, will stay in Hollywood for five days and will go to San Francisco, whence he will sail for Shanghai. He plans to return to California July 12 and break his seven-year silence the following day.

SILENT MYSTIC ARRIVES TODAY

(Continued from First Page)

the former an English poet and mystic, Quentin Tod, also a Britain. Baba's two brothers, Adi and Byram and Indian followers.

Baba's title means Mr. Enlightened Father, Jones explained yesterday. His proper name is Meherban Sheriar Irani. His followers refer to him as "the Messiah." His belief, similar to Krishnamurti's, is that the world's spiritual life is composed of two forces, good and evil, and that the latter has too great a grip on the consciousness of folk of Europe and America, according to Jones.

Baba, when interviewed, uses an alphabet board, pointing to letters on the board and spelling out words in answering questions. He claims to have told Gandhi to "get out of politics first," when the Mahatma asked to be permitted to study the Baba philosophy. Baba has been the guest of the Harmon couple since arriving in America on the 19th inst.

ON WAY TO U. S.

Meher Baba, the "God Man," a priest of the Zoroastrian faith of India, who is on his way to the United States with the announced purpose of breaking down all religious barriers, destroying this country's materialism and uniting all creeds in a common element of love.

[Associated Press Photo.]

(ABOVE) From the *Chicago Daily Tribune*, March 30, 1932

Indian "Messiah" to Lead America from Materialism

* * * * * *

Mystic, Who Denied Counsel to Mahatma Gandhi, Convinced We Need Him. To Break Seven-Year Silence at Los Angeles Next Month.

SHRI BABA "CONVERSING" WITH A FRIEND — JEDDU KRISHNAMURTI.

Convinced that America needs saving from the jungle of materialism in which it is wandering about, Shri Meher Baba, Hindu mystic and new "Messiah," has come to the United States to lead the country to spiritual understanding. The Baba, who has not spoken for seven years, having taken a vow of silence to keep himself more in tune with the Infinite, will begin his campaign of salvation at Los Angeles next month, when he will break silence. Although the Baba is a mystic, he is an athlete, cricket and ping-pong being his favorite sports. He is also fond of music and the movies. During his visit to Los Angeles he hopes to meet some of the famous movie stars he has seen on the screen. He will also meet in the film capital a contemporary "Messiah," Jeddu Krishnamurti, who, it will be recalled, was a protege of the late Anne Besant, apostle of the Theosophists. Krishnamurti has not been active as an evangelist for some time, but he is still regarded as the "Messiah." Though the Baba refuses to speak, he is not averse to conversation by means of the alphabet board which he carries for the purpose. He also employs a secretary who transacts any business with which the "God Man" does not want to be annoyed. Shri Baba is the guest of one of his American disciples, Malcolm Schloss, of Harmon, N. Y.

New York—Convinced that the world is in dire need of a pilot with the ability to lead it out of the jungle of materialism into which it has strayed in the last few hundred years, Shri Sadguru Meher Baba, Indian "God-Man," has dedicated himself to the long felt want and for that purpose has chosen the United States as the starting point of his operations.

The Baba arrived in New York recently in a silence that could be heard for blocks. Not even the well known blarney of ship news reporters could extract as much as a grunt from the mystic who has not spoken for seven years. But the "Messiah's dapper little secretary. Quentin Tod, made up for the Coolidge-like attitude of his master with a long statement setting out the aims of the world's latest uplifter.

According to his amanuensis, the Baba decided that America needed saving after he made a trip here last Fall, incognito. His present visit to these hospitable shores is for the purpose of beginning that salvation. Of course, the business of making America heaven-minded is not the Baba's sole aim. He also plans to perform a few miracles, "should the necessity arise," and he may go into the movies—as a convenient medium for bringing his message to the world's millions.

The new "Messiah," through his secretarial mouthpiece, intimated that his work will permeate every phase of life. The spiritual campaign he has planned will sweep the world, automatically adjusting such vexatious problems as economics, sex and politics.

Although the Baba claims he has been in tune with the Infinite since taking his vow of silence seven years ago, he keeps in touch with the march of progress and current events. In fact, he professes a frank fondness for the movies and one of his ambitions, apart from making Americans potential harpists, is to meet some of his favorite movie stars, amongst whom he numbers Anna May Wong, Marlen Dietrich, Ronald Coleman and Victor McLaglen. This ambition the Babe hopes to have realized when he goes to Los Angeles to break his long silence and start his campaign.

In the film capital, the "God-Man" will also meet Krishnamurti, a contemporary "Messiah" of the Theosophists, who, it will be recalled, was a protege of the late Anne Besant. Krishnamurti has apparently decided that the world is not so bad after all, as he seems to have given up the attempt to lead it from the primrose path back to the rugged road to Paradise.

The Baba, who dose all his personal conversing by means of an alphabet board, desires it to be known that he is not in the United States under the auspices of any sect or organization. He was born a Parsee near Bombay, In[illegible]dia, but has "gone above religion" and has taught Brahmins and "untouchables" to sit at the same table just like one big happy family.

The "Messiah" is a striking looking man with long flowing locks and a silky mustache. He is a vegetarian and his build bespeaks the athlete rather than the dreamer and, as a matter of fact, he is a mixture of both, for he is devoted to music and athletics, cricket and ping-pong being his favorite [illegible]

(LEFT) The *Daily Independent* (Monessen, Pennsylvania), May 25, 1932. The two weeks of the American leg of Baba's 1932 world tour triggered an avalanche of coverage not only in the major metropolitan areas but in small local newspapers as well.

MATERIALISM IS TARGET

INDIAN LEADER, CONFIDANT OF GANDHI, DISCLOSES PLANS FOR TRIP TO U. S.

BOMBAY, March 25, — Meher Baba, Indian spiritual leader, called the "Messiah," left on a crusade to America.

He intends to break religious barriers, destroy American materialism and amalgamate all creeds in the common element of love.

Eight years he has observed silence insofar as possible which will be broken on his arrival at New York, where he plans a spiritual retreat similar to Gandhi's here.

He said Gandhi has promised to join him in the United States as soon as his political work here is finished a year hence.

Many Indians regard Baba as Gandhi's spiritual adviser.

Article from the *Fairbanks Daily News* (Alaska), May 25, 1932. Newspaper coverage of Baba's tour extended even to the fringes of the Arctic.

(RIGHT) Article from the *Daily Gleaner* (Kingston, Jamaica), March 29, 1932.

(BELOW) Article from the *Fitchburg Sentinel* (Massachusetts), May 20, 1932.

(BELOW RIGHT) Article from the *Chicago Daily Tribune*, May 20, 1932.

Meher Baba Plans Crusade In U. S.

Spiritual Leader Leaves India For America To Establish Retreat at Harmon.

(By Air Mail to the Gleaner).

BOMBAY, March 25.—Meher Baba, the Indian spiritual leader, whose disciples call him "The God-Man," left here to-day for a new crusade in America. He intends, he said, to break down all religious barriers, destroy America's materalism and amalgamate all creeds into a common element of love.

For eight years Meher Baba has been observing a vow of silence, which he said he would break upon his arrival at Harmon, N.Y., where he plans to establish a spiritual retreat similar to Mahatma Gandhi's in India.

Giving his first interview to an Associated Press correspondent by means of a blackboard, Meher Baba, who in the eyes of his followers has performed many miracles, said Gandhi had promised to come with him to the United States as soon as his political works has been finished a year hence.

Many Indians regard Meher Baba as Gandhi's Duru, or spiritual adviser.

WOULD REDEEM WORLD.

Meher Baba is a parsee (priest) of the Zoroastrian faith, and says he is both divine and human. He explained that he attained a superconscious state from which he returned to carry out his mission of redeeming the world.

Discussing on his blackboard the miracles which he allegedly has performed, Meher Baba wrote:

A person who becomes one
truth can accomplish any-
g."
eher Baba said he expected to
ert thousands of Americans
sin and by faith to heal the
and help the halt.
The only miracle for the per-
man to perform is to make
s perfect too." he said. "I
to make Americans realize
nfinite state which I myself
."

MET INDIAN SAINT.

parsee said he first realized
ission on earth many years
by coming in contact with
Jan, the Indian saint who
ecently in Poona at the age
years.
nine months after meeting
Jan, Meher Baba said he lay
tate of coma, neither sleep-
r eating, and drinking only
asional drop of water. It
ter this, he said, he saw
ine light and realized his
to the world. He said he
eived overwhelming offers
ey and land from Ameri-
o believe in his teachings.

loctrine of Zoroaster holds
the beginning of things
isted two spirits, good and
he history of their conflict
istory of man, and in the
man is the object of the

rsees in and around Bom-
taken Zoroaster, a Per-
phet of ancient times, as
n, and have adopted the
religious usages of his
their doctrine is a pure
sm.

Indian Mystic Arrives to Break 7-Year Silence

NEW YORK, May 20 (AP)—Shri Meher Baba, Indian mystic, has come to the land of talkies and loud speakers to break his seven years' silence.

He maintained his vow as he arrived on the steamer Bremen from England yesterday by chanting a number of questions onto his English secretary, Quentin Tod. For such personal communication as he saw fit to make he was armed with a small blackboard, on which were painted letters of the alphabet and numerals.

With him he brought a 1000-word written statement. His secretary explained it was his message to America. In it Meher Baba proclaimed himself "one with the infinite source of everything."

"When I speak," the statement said, "my original message will be delivered to the world and it will have to be accepted."

Whether he will break his silence while at a retreat maintained by his followers at Harmon, N. Y., or wait until he reaches California, his ultimate destination in this country, was not made plain.

He had no comment to make on the Indo-British situation and it was explained for him that when Mahatma Gandhi sought his teachings, he told Gandhi to quit politics.

His followers explained that "superconsciousness" was bestowed upon Meher Baba when he was a youth by the kiss of a Parsee woman saint, Hazarat Babjan. After seven years another saint, Shri Sadgur Upasni, conferred "perfect sight" upon him and disciples began to flock to him.

This is not Meher Baba's first visit to America. He was here last October.

Messiah, Hollywood Bound, Keeps His 7 Year Silence

New York, May 19.—(AP).—Shri Meher Baba, whose disciples call him the Messiah, came from far away India today to kindle "American materialism" with the fires of Zoroastrianism. He was in the midst of a seven year silence and could not explain his campaign, but his secretary said he would first go to Hollywood and might enter the movies if that proved to be the best avenue of approach to the American mind. Surrounded by a retinue of followers in Hindu dress, he stood on the deck of the incoming Bremen and looked profound while his aides spoke for him.

INDIAN WHO HAS BEEN SILENT 7 YEARS HERE.

Times Wide World Photo.

Shri Meher Baba is shown holding a placard showing the alphabet on which he spelled out his statements. He came on the Bremen with nine of his disciples.

INDIAN MYSTIC COMES WITH MESSAGE FOR US

Shri Meher Baba Will Break His Seven-Year Silence on Visit to Harmon, N. Y.

Shri Meher Baba, the Indian mystic who has not spoken for seven years, arrived yesterday on the North German Lloyd liner Bremen to break his lenghty silence in a message to America. This message will be given to a group of disciples at Harmon, N. Y., where the mystic visited last October.

The Indian, whose name means Holy Compassionate Father, sent out his English secretary, Quentin Tod, to talk with reporters, distribute a printed statement containing many of his views on life, and to answer questions as to his life and the purpose of his visit.

The statement said that Shri Meher Baba did not come here to establish any cult, society or organization, and that his religion taught the knowledge "of the one behind the many." His religion, he said, had no ritual save to "teach humanity to discriminate, express and live rather than utter it."

(LEFT) An article from the *New York Times*, May 20, 1932. The "printed statement" alluded to in the final two paragraphs is Meher Baba's "Message to Reporters and Press Representatives" (see pp. 6–8).

Silent Hindu Defers Radio Talk.

LOS ANGELES, July 13 (AP).—Shri Meher Baba, who came here recently heralded as the East Indian "holy man," and who supposedly has not uttered a word for seven years, will not deliver his "message to the world" tomorrow over a national broadcast from Hollywood. Quention Tod, the mystic's secretary, telegraphed from Santa Barbara that Baba had decided to postpone the word-fast breaking until next February—because "conditions are not yet ripe."

(ABOVE) Article from the *New York Times*, July 14, 1932, announcing the cancellation of Meher Baba's silence-breaking. Baba's previous plans to break his silence over he radio at the Hollywood Bowl on July 13 had been widely publicized.

22 TIME May 2, 1932

RELIGION

Keystone

SHRI SADGURU MEHER BABA
. . . *bringing an infinite state to Harmon.*

At Harmon, N. Y. where New York Central trains change from electric to steam engines, not far from Briarcliff, stands ready a retreat called Meherashram (Home of Compassion) where the pious of any & all sects may soon meet with a long-haired, silky-mustached seer who calls himself Shri (Mr.) Sadguru (Perfect Master) Meher (Compassion) Baba (Father). To his Indian co-religionists the Parsees, Meher Baba, 38, is the "God Man" or the "Messiah." To many another follower he is simply the "Perfect Master." His U. S. sponsors, Malcolm and Jean Schloss who await him at Harmon, think and write of him in upper-case: He, Him, His, Himself. Next week the God Man is to sail from England, will arrive at Meherashram May 16.

At 19 Meher Baba met a holy woman named Baba Jan (Angel of the Father) who died lately at Poona at the reputed age of 130. Meher Baba soon had a vision of his divine nature. For nine months he lay in a coma, came out of it "merged into God." It is explained that many people are in such a super-conscious state but few can remain in touch with the world, like Meher Baba, and help others to attain divinity.

For almost seven years Meher Baba has uttered no word. When he arrives at his U. S. retreat his lips will be unsealed with much ceremony. Meanwhile he carries a small board with letters and figures to which he points when he has something to say. He intends to found retreats in New Hampshire and California. Meher Baba is supposed to have performed many miracles but now he wishes only to make "Americans realize the infinite state which I myself enjoy." His method of accomplishing this is cryptic yet reassuring. "Let God flood the soul. What I am, you are."

Two articles from *Time*, a leading American weekly magazine.

(ABOVE) An article from the May 2, 1932 issue, in anticipation of Baba's arrival at Harmon. (Some of the original column design has been altered to fit the article on this page; the text itself is unchanged.)

(RIGHT) A follow-up article in the July 25, 1932 issue, ten days after the cancellation of Meher Baba's silence-breaking.

God Man Still Silent

With an alphabet board under his arm and adroit publicity before him, Shri Sadguru Meher Baba, Parsee "God Man," arrived in the U. S. last May (TIME, May 2). Though long-haired, silky-mustached Meher Baba indicated he had spoken no word for nearly seven years, he was willing to be interviewed by pointing to his little board, and to be photographed while doing it. Not every one was aware that this was not the God Man's first arrival in the U. S. Last December he quietly terminated an unpublicized stay in Harmon, N. Y., returned unostentatiously to India while his sponsor, a retired bookseller named Malcolm Schloss, began making plans for a triumphal re-entry. Meher Baba, said Sponsor Schloss, would bring to the U. S. an "infinite state." In July he would break his silence with an internationally broadcast talk. What Meher Baba did was eat, play ping pong and cricket with his followers, many of them socialites, at Harmon. Still keeping mum, the God Man visited San Francisco, suddenly went to Shanghai where he stayed one day, "for spiritual reasons." Last week Meher Baba was to have spoken. But he changed his mind, announced through his secretary that "conditions are not yet ripe." He indicated they would be ripe next February.

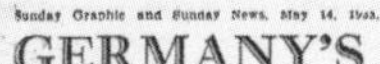

Sunday Graphic and Sunday News, May 14, 1933.

GERMANY'S CASE, By DR. ROSENBERG

Wireless Page 19

SUNDAY GRAPHIC

and SUNDAY NEWS

No. 945. [Registered as a newspaper.] SUNDAY, MAY 14, 1933. TWOPENCE.

AFTER MIDNIGHT — GREAT NEW SERIES

HITLER DISTURBS POLAND

Hitler's latest coup has created a tense situation in Poland. Machine-guns were out in Danzig yesterday, and a general strike followed the German dictator's seizure of trade union headquarters. Polish patrols are seen guarding the frontier.

"THE NEW MESSIAH"

These first pictures—wired from Marseilles to Paris and thence by aeroplane last night—show (left to right) the Misses Delia and Araminta de Leon, the actress sisters of Mr. Jack de Leon, the theatrical producer, and Miss Catherine Davy, of West Kensington. Disciples of Shri Meher Baba, the Indian mystic and the "New Messiah," they are on their way here with him. After seven years' silence he will deliver his "message to the world" in London instead of America, as originally planned.

CHURCH IN "QUARANTINE"

CHARGED at Marylebone in connection with the painting red of the Tussaud effigy of Hitler, Mrs. Bradley was given the "benefit of the doubt" and discharged

The Rev. A. R. Tremearne, vicar of Redbourne, Lincolnshire, hoisting a yellow flag of quarantine on his fourteenth-century church. His action follows a dispute with his congregation concerning the cutting of grass in the churchyard and the erection of tombstones.

Sunday Graphic, May 14, 1933. When Meher Baba's Western disciples returned to their homelands after an unexpectedly brief stay in India, the press took interest, perhaps in expectation of a story of spiritual fraudulence and exploited gullibility. *(BOTTOM LEFT)* Photos of Delia DeLeon, Minta DeLeon, and Kitty Davy (the group's spokeswoman).

(BELOW) Photograph from the *Daily Herald* (England), May 23, 1933, of Baba's English disciples recently returned from India.

MEHER BABA'S DISCIPLES.—The arrival in London last night of three of the London girls—disciples of Shri Sadguru Meher Baba, who have preceded the Indian holy man to prepare the way for his visit.

Three disciples of Shri Meher Baba, the Indian Christian Mystic—Miss Catherine Davy, Miss Delia, and Miss Araminta de Leon—on arrival yesterday at Marseilles.

HIS SEVEN-YEAR SILENCE

MYSTIC WANTS TO TALK AGAIN

From Our Own Correspondent

MARSEILLES, Saturday.

"WHEN Shri Sadguru Mehmer Baba, the Indian mystic, breaks his seven-years silence in London soon he will reveal who he is and what he is doing for the salvation of the world."

So said Miss Catherine Davy, one of the English girls who have become his disciples, when she landed here to-day.

Asked why she and the other four English girls who went to India with Baba had suddenly decided to return to England instead of carrying out the original programme to go to Hollywood she replied there was no other reason than that the mystic was to break his silence in London, where his disciples would prepare his European tour.

"I can state that he is most anxious to speak," said Miss Davy.

(ABOVE) Article from the *Sunday Dispatch*, May 14, 1933. The disciples in the two photographs are (left to right) Kitty Davy, Delia DeLeon, and Minta DeLeon.

SILENT MYSTIC'S DISCIPLE SPEAKS

FROM OUR OWN CORRESPONDENT

Marseilles, Saturday.

MISS CATHERINE DAVY, the Kensington girl who is one of the followers of Shri Meher Baba, the Indian "Messiah," was the only person authorised to make a statement to-day when the mystic's band of disciples arrived at Marseilles on the liner Britannia on their way to England.

SHRI MEHER BABA

It was at the moment the party was embarking in India, Miss Davy said, that the mystic announced through his alphabet board that he had given up his idea of breaking his self-imposed seven years' silence at Hollywood, and had decided instead to speak for the first time in London.

It will probably be in July or August, though the exact date has not yet been decided.

The reason why the Messiah abandoned his idea of breaking his silence at Hollywood was that it had "lost its importance."

The disciples are preceding their leader to London to make the necessary preparations for him to deliver his message.

Baba, who is Parsee-born and nearly forty years old, has multitudes of disciples in India, many drawn from the Orthodox creeds.

He underwent a long ecstatic experience after being kissed by an old woman saint at Poona, and then, after seven years' study, began his mission of the regeneration of humanity through love and service, making a vow of seven years' silence.

He established a colony at Combe Martin, Devon, where his English disciples shared his own simple existence.

Baba is a vegetarian and does not smoke or drink.

Article from *The People*, May 14, 1933.

The "Messiah" of India Coming

Meher Baba, Holy Man of the Hindu Yogis, Who Hasn't Spoken a Word in Eight Years and Claims He Can Perform Miracles, Will Try to Start a Colony of Mystics in America

Meher Baba, the Indian "Messiah," Discussing His Religion With Disciples by Means of His Alphabet Board, for He Has Taken a Vow Never to Speak a Word.

THE United States is promised a visit from Meher Baba, the famous "holy man" from India, known as the "Messiah," and said to be the inspirer of Mahatma Gandhi.

In India a holy man's fame depends largely on how long he can go without eating, or whether he has lived for years without having spoken any words, or can hold himself upside down on a pole, or remain for many days buried in the ground with only his head showing.

Meher Baba can do many of these tricks, and in addition is supposed to be able to perform miracles. The ignorant and simple-minded natives of India are greatly impressed by "holy men" and it is expected that the credulous-minded in America will also take Meher Baba seriously and chip in liberally when those who are promoting the holy man pass around the hat. But when it comes to performing miracles, men of science or real intelligence will want to be shown.

Meher Baba is credited with many supernatural achievements in his native India. It is seriously stated that when he was crossing the Ghat Mountains in an automobile with a few friends they reached a dangerous corner. Here the mountain road was bordered on the left side by a towering mass of solid rock, and on the right side it was completely unprotected. Below yawned a terrifying precipice with a drop of several thousand feet.

Suddenly the automobile stopped, owing to the stalling of the engine, as they climbed up the steep road. Then it began to slide backwards, to the great alarm of its occupants. The driver applied the brakes, but they failed to act. The auto quickly approached the edge of the cliff and death seemed to be inevitable for all in the car. At this psychological moment Meher Baba touched the side of the auto and lightly snapped his fingers. At once the auto was brought to a standstill by a "miracle," the report goes.

On another occasion, it is related, when Meher Baba had made his headquarters in the little town of Tokar in Western India, it so happened that a great scarcity of rain prevailed in the region. According to local customs the people indulged in various ceremonies, including a tom-tom procession, in order to propitiate the goddess of rain. But their efforts were of no avail. Famine and starvation threatened the whole district.

The headman of the town went to Meher Baba and humbly begged him to use his miraculous powers to bring about some good showers of rain. The holy man said, "It will soon begin to rain now."

Within less than an hour of this, dark clouds began to gather over Tokar and in a few minutes it rained. Thereafter tremendous showers fell for nearly a whole week, to the relief of the population. At last the rain became excessive and threatened a flooding of the town and destruction of the crops. The headman came once more to Meher Baba and begged him to stop the rain. Almost immediately, it is said, the showers came to an end.

Meher Baba was born in 1894 in Poona, India, and was the son of a respectable Parsee family, which means that he is of Persian descent. He is learned in the philosophy of the famous philosopher Zoroaster, but experts in the higher lines of mysticism in all Oriental countries belong to the same union. While he was a student at the University of Bombay, an old Mohammedan woman fakir became his spiritual guide.

One day, as she sat under the "nimb-tree," where she was a familiar figure to the people of Poona, she called to him. He obeyed her and thereupon, he says, she embraced him and immediately he felt "a psychic and spiritual thrill."

He abandoned his college course and devoted himself to the study of mysticism and acquiring "Yoga." He traveled all over India visiting the mysterious cave temples of the Himalaya Mountains, the sacred shrines of Benares, and out-of-the-way centers of mysticism in the south. During his wanderings he came into contact with "Yogis," "Rishies" and magicians. Eight years ago he took a vow of silence and has not spoken since, while once he fasted for five-and-a-half months. He communicates with English speaking people by means of a cardboard on which is printed the English alphabet, pointing with his forefinger to the different letters and thus composing words.

He has long, silky hair which falls to his shoulders and gives him a very "holy" look. His eyes beam with a light that is supposed to have a magical effect.

The "Messiah" is now in England and expects eventually to reach the United States. It is said he plans to establish a colony at Harmon, New York, something like that which the Mahatma Ghandi maintains in India. He announced his intention to break down all religious barriers, destroy American materialism, and amalgamate all creeds into a common element of love.

He admitted that he could perform all sorts of miracles because, as he said, anyone who becomes "one with truth" can accomplish anything. But he was reticent as to the particular miracles he would perform. If Meher Baba undertakes miracles in the United States, he will be watched very carefully. He has been advised that not all Americans are easily fooled.

The word "Baba," applied to this holy man and others, is a title of respect in many oriental countries and has a meaning something like "Father" or "Reverend." His full name is Shri Sadguru Meher. He belongs to the class of advanced mystics known as Yogis, which means that they have reached a certain degree of proficiency in the philosophy of Yoga. To do this they must go through a long course of stunts and exercises which impress people very much and are supposed to give them control over matter and enable them to do supernatural things. The Hindu word "Yoga" means union and is defined by the Encyclopedia Britannica as "diversion of the senses from the external world and concentration of thought within."

A famous Indian Yogi named Narasingha Swami, noted for his ability to eat poison, recently came to a tragic end. The Yogi died in a British hospital in Rangoon, Burma, as a result of eating at a public exhibition a handful of crushed glass, a teaspoonful of nitric acid, several times a fatal dose of strychnine, a similar dose of potassium cyanide, and finally, by way of dessert, a spoonful of sulphuric acid.

It was the strychnine, hospital doctors report, that ended the Yogi's career. According to the report, he survived all the other poisons, but for some reason the strychnine acted more strongly than usual. The Yogi, it was said, had been accustomed for several years to make his living by eating in public these same poisons in equal or greater amounts. The real secret of how he did the trick was not revealed.

The reason why the last assortment proved fatal is said by the Yogi's manager to have been the accidental omission on the fatal day of the mental and physical exercises prescribed for experts in Yoga, and which the Yogi was accustomed to carry out before all of his poison-eating feats.

Most statements that Yogis and other Hindu ascetics can perform genuine miracles, such as raising the dead, are found to rest on popular report and not on the evidence of scientific Western witnesses. The superstition of the people is unlimited. Lowell Thomas mentions a remarkable Hindu fakir named Saddho Binodianaan Dhan whom he visited at Puri, and who was widely credited with having the power of raising the dead. A native government official told the American visitor that he saw the fakir bring to life two birds which had been thoroughly strangled and dead four hours.

When Mr. Thomas visited the fakir, he says he saw him take a piece of clean cotton and by focusing the sunlight on it cause it to smell successively of violets, attar of roses and a native scent. Mr. Thomas did not see the fakir raise the dead.

Swallowing fire is reported to be a common accomplishment of the ascetics, but the magician Houdini has shown that this can be done sufficiently well to impress ordinary people by soaking the mouth thoroughly with spirits of sulphur.

Enduring snake bites and swallowing scorpions are other reported Yogi stunts. There is a lack of satisfactory proof that the reptiles had their venom, but in any case magicians have proved that there are several effective ways of protecting the body against snake-bite.

There are 84 principal postures called "asanas," which the Yogi practices in order to obtain complete control of the body and impress the public. They are said to unite the Yogi with the powers controlling the universe and help him to perform miracles. The asanas look difficult and require a special diet. There is an old Hindu saying that it is easier to stand on the sharpened edges of razors than to follow the Yogi discipline.

One of them, known as "sirshasana," consists of reposing head downward as long as possible under the shade of a tree. This is only one of the simpler asanas. It is said to be excellent for the circulation of the veins. Another exercise called nauli consists of moving the muscles of abdomen and stomach independently and overcomes intestinal stasis. There seems to be no doubt that the asanas are first-class stretching exercises.

A posture called veda-purana consists in lying stretched out on the left side with the right leg curled around the back of the neck in a position which few Americans could assume. One ascetic assumes this position in the middle of a narrow Calcutta street, thus requiring a detour by taxis and other wheeled vehicles that wish to pass.

In one posture the ascetic supports himself entirely on his hands with his legs curled up off the ground. Some Yogis curl their legs behind their backs in such intricate knots that it is hard to tell where they begin and end. Such postures cannot be attained by an ordinary grown person, but it is stated that an American contortionist could accomplish them if he began young.

Resting upon the head and hands with the legs held up in the air calls for an advanced degree of skill. Among the 84 postures, 34 have been credited with much more merit than the rest. The excellence of some of the 34 postures is due to the mental powers they are supposed to give. Others are alleged to cure certain physical ills or to check undesirable tendencies through control of nerves and organs.

In India, Yogis have an unwritten right to live and sleep in any spot in the open air which they choose. They are never prosecuted for vagrancy. Meher Baba usually occupies a cave with a wide entrance so that everybody can see him.

The perfect Yogi is said to be able to make himself invisible, to fly through the air, and to possess other unusual accomplishments. It is predicted that this "Messiah" will not try any of these "miracles" in front of the sharp eyes of American scientists.

Meher Baba has no sympathy with modern civilization—he believes man should spend his life in contemplation and spiritual development. The Yogis perform no useful, practical service to mankind. If, down through the ages, everybody had been a Yogi sitting in contemplation of spiritual matters there would have been very little practical progress of mankind; things would be somewhat as they were in cave-man days. Disease, famine and misery would still sweep the world as it did in earlier ages and as, indeed, it does now in India, which is known as the most backward and unenlightened country in the world.

This Holy Man Is Attaining Bodily Purity by Going Without Food—the Less He Eats the More Spiritual He Becomes.

The Head Downward Position Said to Be Very Effective in Purifying the Blood and Checking Worldly Desires.

One of the More Difficult "Asanas" by Which the Yogis Assert They Attain the Power to Perform Miracles.

In This Contortion the Mystic Is Trying to Acquire Control Over Matter.

An Indian Yogi of the Baba's School Practicing a Holy Posture—Stretched Out With His Right Leg Curled Around His Neck, Oftentimes in the Middle of the Street. This, He Thinks, Purifies His Soul.

Article from the *San Antonio Light* (Texas), May 8, 1932. Concentrating on supernatural powers and characterizing Meher Baba as the "Holy Man of the Hindu Yogis," this article illustrates the confused misrepresentation and stereotyping that afflicted some of the press coverage of this time.

The Troubles of a Modern "Messiah"

One Widely-Acclaimed Holy Man Refuses to Play the Part Any Longer and Another, Who Hasn't Spoken a Word in Eight Years, Still Declines to Give the World His Promised Message

Encampment of a Thousand Disciples of the Young Indian "Messiah," Krishnamurti, in the Hills Near Los Angeles During a Congress of His Followers.

MORE than eight years ago Shri Meher Baba, a holy man of India, announced that he had an inspired message that would straighten out all the world's troubles.

Crowds dropped work and hurried to hear the good news. But the Baba would not tell them and never has to this day. For fear a crumb of wisdom might fall from his lips he has only communicated with his adoring followers by sign language and occasionally, when this was not sufficient, spelling out a sentence by pointing to an alphabet board.

Naturally there was disappointment when the crowd had to go home to its unsolved troubles no wiser than it left. A few irreverent persons called the holy man a practical joker, comparing his promising a message of salvation and then shutting up, to a person who threatens to sneeze but doesn't do it. A sneeze or a message that had been suppressed nearly nine years would have to be pretty good when it did explode, in order to justify such awful suspense.

But that shows how little they know about the traps and problems that beset the path of one of these modern messiahs, such as Jeddu Krishnamurti and Mahatma Gandhi. By simply keeping his mouth shut, the Baba has avoided all these troubles and built up a large following all over the world, including the wealthy Princess Norma Matchabelli, who has given up her worldly life to spend her fortune and time waiting on the silent messiah by inches, in the pious hope that she will be there to take down the message when the "enlightened one" finally decides to let go of it.

Recently Meher Baba toured the United States, visiting, among other places, Chicago and drawing greater crowds than the most learned lecturer, all in the hope that he might be moved to reveal the secret that all the human race is waiting to hear. But the moment was still not quite propitious and he went back to England, with the secret hidden in his swarthy chest.

This messageless messiah who has contributed in return for his keep and worship not a single bit of material, labor or expressed thought, merely sits and thinks. He is an unusually impressive sitter and thinker because he happens to resemble Prof. Einstein, who also sits and thinks. But Prof. Einstein, in order to become a celebrity, had to say something.

The Baba is much better off today than the other messiah, Krishnamurti, who also comes from India, like most messiahs of the present. Why these message bearers, yogis, mahatmas, babas (enlightened ones) should come from the most unenlightened, backward, hungry, poverty-stricken, sickly and generally unhappy large country of the globe is one of those occult things that have not yet been revealed.

Probably no messiah, since the idea first started in Egypt, nearly 4,500 years ago, ever had such a good start as that of Krishnamurti, who was discovered and vouched for by the late Annie Besant, International President of the Theosophical Society, as the true successor not only of Buddha and other celebrated messiahs but even of the Christian Saviour Himself. He was the son of a native Indian magistrate, young, good-looking, educated, intelligent and of flawless moral behavior. Also he seems to have been perfectly sincere, with no notions that he was a messiah until that famous woman so informed him. Mrs. Besant felt that a messiah was overdue, and, looking around, her occult senses told her that this attractive, modest boy was the vehicle through which the divine message was to come.

When the news was flashed to all countries it created a sensation, but though there was some discussion at first among the millions of Theosophists, the tremendous influence of their leader caused the great majority to accept the youth at her own valuation. A great international organization, "The Order of the Star," was formed, with Krishnamurti as its head, to receive and spread the new gospel. The sincerity of the members is proved by the way funds poured in. These allowed the boy to travel around the world in state like a prince, though old-style messiahs had to go it mostly barefoot and begging their way.

In Australia, a huge concrete stadium was built especially to hear and see him. They showered wealth on him in the form of real estate in various parts of the world including the Castle Eerde, in Ommen, Holland. In Paris he attracted a larger and more imposing gathering of wealthy society women than probably would have turned out for any other foreigner except Lindbergh. Col. Lindbergh had to risk his life to become known, but Krishnamurti merely had to travel around in luxury, and while waiting for the message to come, make a few very simple addresses to his followers. It seemed about as easy and successful a career as could be imagined but those addresses were finally his undoing.

They were harmless platitudes at first and certainly not inspired. Also he was carefully protected from newspaper interviewers who sometimes have a shameless habit of asking embarrassing questions. But his own followers asked for help in their own simple problems. It seemed to them and to him that this consecrated vessel of wisdom ought to have some ideas of his own.

Being a conscientious young man, Krishnamurti tried to make good, studying the sages of the past and repeating their messages in modern terms. But to his dismay, the criticism was:

"Old stuff! That's no message."

Even such time-honored advice as to make long fasts to aid clear thinking brought criticism. Scientists had experimented with fasts and found that far from aiding clear thought they made it almost impossible. Actual tests have proved that long fasts tend to cause hallucinations, weakening and upsetting the brain as much as the muscles and organs.

Fasting thoughts are half-crazy thoughts. The way to think straight is to have a good night's sleep, a light breakfast and a good cup of coffee. Then if a person has any brains he can use them to advantage. Press and letters told him that it was not only an old idea but a poor idea. One day he had an inspiration, at least the idea was his very own and not copied from any previous messiah. He said:

"Live splendidly!"

That is the way ninety-nine out of every hundred people would like to live if they had the money to manage it. But virtually all previous messiahs, in good standing, had preached just the opposite. They exhorted everyone to live as slovenly, shabbily and hungrily as possible, some even considering dirt a positive virtue. So there was another indignant storm of protest. Even those who were frank to admit sympathy with the idea said the advice was no good because he did not tell them how to get the money on which to live splendidly. Had he been able to tell them that he might have been a very popular and successful messiah.

Some were unkind enough to point out that Jeddu was living splendidly on the gifts of others. Being a sincere young man, anxious to be a good sort of messiah, he promptly handed back all his wealth but still persisted in wearing well-cut European clothes, playing tennis and attending afternoon teas. Tea and tennis are not exactly sinful nor is admitting a keen interest in baseball, but somehow they did not seem fitting in a messiah.

His was a thorny path. Though Krishnamurti had been pursued by many of the world's most successful vamps, eager for the notoriety of an affair with the eminent young saint, there had never been a breath of scandal about him. However, even the best young man is expected to fall in love with some nice girl and want to marry her. This happened to the messiah, who fell in love with Miss Helen F. Knothe of Ridgewood, New Jersey. The love was reciprocated but the match was broken off by the indomitable will of Dr. Besant who convinced Krishnamurti that marriages and messages are incompatible.

Devoting himself to strictly spiritual matters again, Krishnamurti strove to increase the membership of his organization in Europe. Among other things he ordered his followers to make the sign of the cross. This was an excellent idea in getting members where Christianity predominates and was approved by his Christian following. But in India the Hindu members opposed it vehemently.

In disgust the messiah disbanded the organization saying that his message was for the whole human race and no society or creed. He was now free from his society, his worldly possessions and soon broke away from his sponsor and discoverer. In 1931 he turned up at Los Angeles, unannounced, and when discovered by the press, stated that his interviews would no longer be "staged." He said that Dr. Besant had dramatized him and theosophy though probably unconsciously.

Whether consciously or not, it should be said in Dr. Besant's defense that no messiah could be put over with the public unless staged, dramatized and given plenty of "atmosphere and scenery." For instance Mahatma Gandhi, though preaching the simple and inconspicuous life, dramatized himself in the most startling manner possible the last time he went to London. Had he really wished to be simple and inconspicuous he would have worn conventional clothing, instead of that breech clout which made him more conspicuous than would ten brass bands and a troop of cavalry.

Krishnamurti, free to be himself, rapidly destroyed all the glamour that had surrounded him. He said:

"I am no actor. I have refused to wear the robes of a messiah.

"They called me the Christ. But Christ is potential in all of us."

By these plain, honest statements, Krishnamurti stepped down from the divine pedestal on which Dr. Besant had placed him, to the ranks of ordinary people, where he was just a nice, sincere boy, who had traveled a lot. Since the depression, people were less interested in spiritual values than in cash values, less in future enjoyment than in present employment. This boy seemed to have no message on those questions. Men lost interest and now that he had given up both his worldly property and his divinity, so did the women. Mrs. Besant died but before that he had dropped out of sight.

The other day the ex-messiah turned up as the guest of Lady Lutyens in her English country home where he had once before visited, at the height of his splendor, but now he was frankly down and out financially.

"I am just living," he said. "I'm a beggar now. I roam from country to country, living first with one old friend and then another. I have no home, no property nor money in the bank.

"I could have been a rich man. For years people showered money offers on me. Besides a magnificent castle in Holland, with 500 acres of gardens, I was offered $10,000 a week by Hollywood film interests and they were eager to build a beautiful temple for me. I was maturing then and did not know quite what to think of those things. But when I found women actually worshiping my picture, I knew that it was all wrong."

While shouting evangelists have made themselves rich, this young man has pauperized himself because his conscience would not permit him to accept wealth and worship. Meanwhile Shri Meher Baba, whom the irreverent call "the dumb Einstein," is not so dumb practically. He still sits silently thinking, but he "sits pretty." He has never enjoyed the dizzy heights to which his brother messiah reached, but he has never fallen from them. Nobody bothers him because he won't talk and nobody criticizes his message because nobody knows what it is. He has everything he wants, without work, including the perpetual service and adoration of a wealthy Princess who is herself a remarkable psychological phenomenon.

This beautiful woman was leading a gorgeous, worldly life as the wife of Prince Georges Matchabelli from the same Georgia whence came the Mdivanis. The Princess Matchabelli, who had been the Italian actress Maria Carmina, was delighted with her title until she returned to the stage to play the Madonna in Reinhardt's "The Miracle," and "got religion." She never got over it and became a follower of Messiah Meher Baba.

She was divorced from the Prince not long ago, and he was quoted as saying:

"When the Princess thought she would enter into this religion of Baba we decided she should go her way and I should go mine. But we are are still good friends."

To some people the Princess's choice seems a wretched and humiliating life. But if by chance the Baba really has an important message and does not procrastinate delivering it until death silences him permanently, the Princess will be forever famous and holy in sacred history, long after the last Georgian princeling is forgotten.

The Princess Matchabelli, Who Gave Up Home and Career to Become a Devoted Follower of Meher Baba.

Jeddu Krishnamurti, a "Messiah" Appointed by the Late Annie Besant, the Head of the Theosophists of the World.

The Late Dr. Annie Besant, Who Picked Out Young Krishnamurti and Started Him on His Career as a "Messiah," Which He Has Now Abandoned.

Shri Meher Baba, a Holy Man of India, Who Says He Can Work Miracles and Has a "Message" for Mankind. He Has Not Spoken a Word for Eight Years and Now and Then Answers a Question by Spelling It Out With His Fingers on an Alphabet Board.

8

Another article from the *San Antonio Light* (Texas), December 17, 1933. At this time Meher Baba was often associated in the Western public mind with his contemporary Jiddu Krishnamurti (1895–1986). During the previous two decades the Theosophical Society had proclaimed Krishnamurti as the long-expected World Teacher, a role that Krishnamurti himself had repudiated in 1929.

World Fellowship

To the Editor of San Antonio Express: August 27th is the fifth anniversary of the signing of the Briand-Kellogg Pact of Peace. It is also the opening day of the culminating period of the convention of the World Fellowship of Faiths, which has held intermittent sessions in Chicago since June. During the three weeks of daily sessions, August 27th to September 17th, the convention will be addressed by over 300 of the world's most famous religious, social-service, cultural and political leaders.

Among the noted people scheduled to address the congress during the culminating period are Jane Addams, Justice Florence E. Allen, His Holiness Shri Meher Baba of India, Sir Albion Banerji of India, M. Henri Barbusse of France, Sufi Mutiur Rahman Bengalee of India, Senator Smith W. Brookhart, Rev. S. Parkes Cadman, Bainbridge Colby, Senator Royal S. ...

Charles Frederick Weller, internationally famous social worker of Chicago.

The avowed purpose of this—the greatest congress of religions the world has seen—is to unite the inspirations and essential aspirations of all faiths and creeds in a tremendous moral effort to solve the great problems hindering the progress of humanity today, perhaps specially those on war and peace; to promote interreligious, interracial and international tolerance, cooperation and fellowship—"To unite the best inspiration from all Faiths upon Spiritual Solutions for man's Present Problems," as expressed in the circular distributed from the Chicago headquarters.

History has entered a new era. Mankind is again at the crossroads—at the parting of the ways—and nationalistic aggrandizement has completely defeated the Disarmament and Economic Conferences. The politicians and economists have failed to secure that internationalism which would prevent war and attain prosperity. Tariffs, trade wars and armaments are increasing; tension is at the breaking-point. Will the world explode again as it did in 1914—or will the spiritual leaders of the race succeed where our diplomats and economists have failed? If they, too, fail to stem the rising tide of nationalism, fascism and imperialism, the future holds no dawn, no star, nothing but fear and hate, rattling sabers, want and war. Again the Rachels of the world will weep for their sons as they are herded by the warlords, through gaudy, flag-draped streets, and down to the hideous fields of slaughter!

Science has reduced the globe to a neighborhood; but it has also armed the neighbors with a thousand poisonous gases and other instruments of murder. Therefore, if man is to be saved from his own foolhardiness, religion and rationalism must weld the world into a brotherhood. To maintain armies and navies, to insist upon absolute national sovereignty, to proclaim the *superiority of one faith over another*, is to renounce our heirship to [t]he spiritual life of the ages, and to [i]mpeach as liars the great Masters who [h]ave crowned our inglorious world with [p]erfumed flowers of perfect speech.

Internationalism or world fellowship [is] not the antithesis to nationhood and [di]versity of culture, but a synthesis of [na]tions and cultures. No nation, no [re]ligion can ever consider itself free or [vic]torious if it seeks freedom and vic[tor]y for itself alone. Nations and re[lig]ions are many—but the world is one [an]d we are all brothers—the leaves of [a] tree.

RALPH J. WESTLAKE.

[S]outh Charleston, Ohio.

Charles Frederick Weller, internationally famous social worker of Chicago.

The avowed purpose of this—the greatest congress of religions the world has seen—is to unite the inspirations and essential aspirations of all faiths and creeds in a tremendous moral effort to solve the great problems hindering the progress of humanity today, perhaps specially those on war and peace; to promote interreligious, interracial and international tolerance, cooperation and fellowship—"To unite the best inspiration from all Faiths upon Spiritual Solutions for man's Present Problems," as expressed in the circular distributed from the Chicago headquarters.

History has entered a new era. Mankind is again at the crossroads—at the parting of the ways—and nationalistic aggrandizement has completely defeated the Disarmament and Economic Conferences. The politicians and economists have failed to secure that internationalism which would prevent war and attain prosperity. Tariffs, trade wars and armaments are increasing; tension is at the breaking-point. Will the world explode again as it did in 1914—or will the spiritual leaders of the race succeed where our diplomats and economists have failed? If they, too, fail to stem the rising tide of nationalism, fascism and imperialism, the future holds no dawn, no star, nothing but fear and hate, rattling sabers, want and war. Again the Rachels of the world will weep for their sons as they are herded by the warlords, through gaudy, flag-draped streets, and down to the hideous fields of slaughter!

Science has reduced the globe to a

Article from the *San Antonio Express* (Texas), August 10, 1933, reviewing the World Fellowship of Faiths conference taking place in Chicago. Characterizing it as "the greatest congress of religions the world has seen," the article attests to the scale and perceived importance of this event. Meher Baba had originally accepted an invitation to participate, but in the end the plans fell through (see pp. 245–46). Meher Baba's name appears in the fifth line of the second paragraph.

The Wonders of Eastern Mysticism

A SEARCH IN SECRET INDIA. By Paul Brunton. With a Foreword by Sir Francis Younghusband. Illustrated from photographs. 312 pp. New York: E. P. Dutton & Co. $3.50.

BELIEVE it or doubt it, there are some amazing things to be learned from the Yogi of India. We have Mr. Paul Brunton's word for it, backed up by the testimony of Sir Francis Younghusband, who writes a foreword to this record of a search for the secret of India's spirituality.

The more interesting approach to a book setting forth the wonders of Eastern mysticism is via belief, even when one is naturally inclined to be skeptical. On the whole, Mr. Brunton's method can be profitably adopted by his readers: "I keep my mind open, uncritical, and offer no mental resistance."

Covering the greater part of India in his search, he made pilgrimages to the abodes of several of the best accredited Yogis, and spent days or weeks in interviewing them. There was Meher Baba, the Parsee Messiah who held forth half a day's journey from Bombay. Since 1925 this holy man had not uttered a word, and he communicated his thoughts by spelling out words on an alphabet board. His younger brother told Mr. Brunton that when the new messiah breaks into speech, his message will startle the world. Still maintaining his silence, he later made a theatrical journey to Hollywood, where, the author says, he was entertained by Mary Pickford and a thousand leading people were presented to him at the film colony's leading hotel. After considerable study of this self-styled messiah, the author concluded that

Covering the greater part of India in his search, he made pilgrimages to the abodes of several of the best accredited Yogis, and spent days or weeks in interviewing them. There was Meher Baba, the Parsee Messiah who held forth half a day's journey from Bombay. Since 1925 this holy man had not uttered a word, and he communicated his thoughts by spelling out words on an alphabet board. His younger brother told Mr. Brunton that when the new messiah breaks into speech, his message will startle the world. Still maintaining his silence, he later made a theatrical journey to Hollywood, where, the author says, he was entertained by Mary Pickford and a thousand leading people were presented to him at the film colony's leading hotel. After considerable study of this self-styled messiah, the author concluded that "Meher Baba, though a good man and one living an ascetic life, is unfortunately suffering from colossal delusions about his own greatness."

strangles a sparrow, leaves it for an hour, and then brings it back to life, apparently unharmed, for

part of what he reads and still find it of great interpretative value.

EDWARD FRANK ALLEN.

Edward Frank Allen reviews Paul Brunton's *A Search in Secret India* (1934) in the *New York Times*, September 15, 1935. The inset highlights comments on Meher Baba. Brunton's unfavorable assessment of Baba influenced Rom Landau and many others.

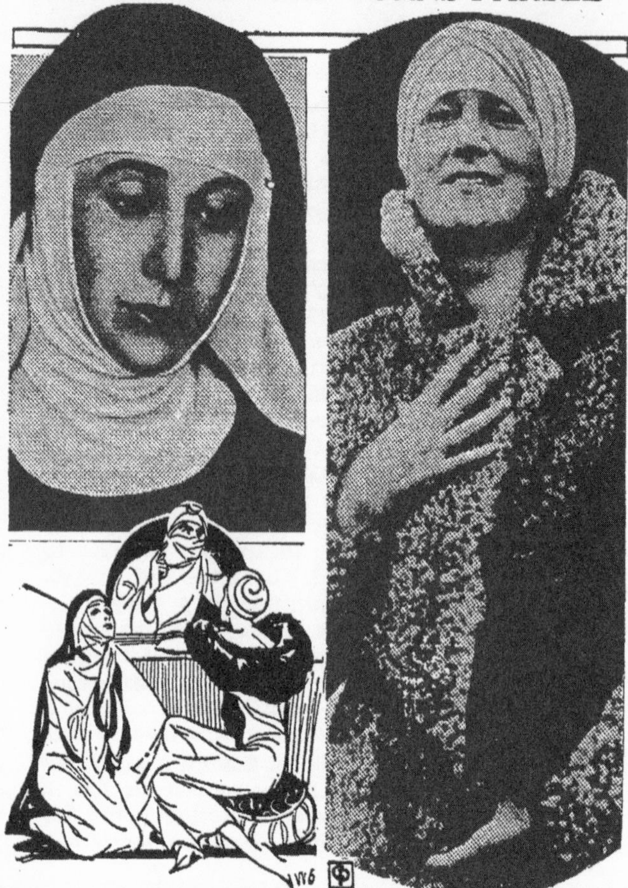

NUN IN 'MIRACLE' TURNS PARSEE

Maria Carmina—Princess Matchabelli—as the nun in "The Miracle". and as she looked when returning from Europe.

Maria Carmina, the beautiful Italian actress who is known in private life as Princess Matchabelli, and who alternated with Lady Diana Manners in the role of the nun in "The Miracle", has embraced the Parsee religion, and is a devotee of Shri Sadgura Meher Baba, who has not spoken for nine years. The princess claimed that she was cured of tuberculosis by impersonating the Madonna in the pageant. Her husband, Prince Matchabelli, a Georgian, is said to be contemplating a divorce on account of the princess' religion.

Article from the *Evening Gazette* (Xenia, Ohio), November 22, 1933. Two decades earlier Princess Norina Matchabelli, under the stage name Norina Carmai, had starred in the role of the Madonna in *The Miracle,* a sensationally successful play written by Karl Vollmoeller, her husband at the time. In 1933, with the announcement of her impending divorce from her second husband Prince Matchabelli, several newspapers carried articles on her career and newly formed connection with Meher Baba.

8 THE SALT LAKE TRIBUNE, SUNDAY MORNING, MARCH 7, 1937.

Had to Flee His Frankensteins!

Garrett Fort's Dramatic Escape from the Appalling Effects of Monsters He Created for the Movies

By Marjorie Driscoll

True! nervous—very, very dreadfully nervous I had been . . . I heard all things in the heaven and in the earth. I heard many things in hell. —EDGAR ALLAN POE, in "The Telltale Heart."

GARRETT FORT, 37, chief "horror expert" of Hollywood writers, was nervous: *dreadfully so.*

An outstanding member of the West Coast's movie colony, for several years Fort had devoted all his working time to devising and adapting stories of mystery and terror for the screen.

He had attained the peak of his profession. But at a wrenching cost. In troubled sleep his eerie brain children still pursued him. The wraith of Dracula invaded his dreams. Frankenstein's monster tormentingly mastered his reveries.

Fort felt he was on the verge of some appalling, if nameless, calamity. Psychic? Or physical? He wasn't sure. But frankly he was afraid.

In like plight, most men would have done one of two things: consulted a nerve specialist and retired for six months to a sanitarium, or tried to face the frightful music, with collapse inevitable.

Fort did neither. Instead, he left Los Angeles quickly and quietly, his destination a secret to even close friends. Now, after a lapse of appreciable time, comes the startling and gratifying news that the troubled scenarist has reached surcease from the hideous apprehensions that were hounding him. In his own phrase: "*I have found peace—with a God-man.*"

Garrett Fort, whose film "treatments" of "Dracula's Daughter," "Frankenstein," "The Suicide Club" and "The Invisible Man" raised universal hair and curdled the blood of all beholders, is, today, in India.

In a stainlessly white temple, set high in the hills at Nasik, the ex-sophisticate and California hotspot-haunter sits tranquilly at the feet of a famed Hindu mystic. To join the little known but integrally powerful colony of mystical Shri Meher Baba, Fort fled from a Western world where wealth and merriment dance frantically together.

He is content—as content as other members of the Baba's group. The identities of most of these men and women are rigidly withheld from the public; exploitation, the mere thought of the slightest notoriety, would shock and revolt the Baba and his followers.

It would strike at the very keystone of their philosophy: Thought can accomplish anything, *everything*, be it good or bad; speech is a superfluity.

In proof of this credo, the Baba fairly recently began to practise definitely and impressively what he always has preached. Three years ago, Shri Meher paid a casual visit to Hollywood. He had made this "pilgrimage" because, he said, he had heard from authentic sources that life in the cinema citadel was compounded of many diverse elements, some practical, others of deep psychic import and occult significance.

It so happened that at the time of his California hegira, the Baba was immersed in a great silence. He had taken the solemnest of vows—to himself—that he would not open his lips in human speech for eight years.

And it was at this time that he and Fort met at the home of a common friend, Rolf Passer, who, like Fort, was a concoctor of fantasies for the films.

Passer and his lustrously lovely wife, Marina, had been converted to the esoteric beliefs of the Baba for some time. They were proud and glad to be the means by which the troubled soul of their colleague and pal could seek peace in the Baba's society.

But they didn't imagine then that Fort would instantly listen to the call of the East; at once forsake his old, time-honored haunts on the West Coast for the spiritual joys awaiting him in India.

They, like all Garrett's friends, were puzzled when he suddenly disappeared from their midst. Various rumors began to form and float about.

It was said that the writer had (1) sought seclusion to devote his whole time to research on some new occult photoplay idea; (2) that he had returned to New York to write a book dealing with vampires, demonology and the celebration of the Witches' Sabbath, as chronicled in the Brocken scene of Goethe's "Faust," or (3) had retired from the world of sham and tinsel to give his remaining years to holy meditation.

The last-named surmise proved to be correct. But the fact was not fully established till Fort wrote the Passers a letter, explaining his actions and outlining his future plans.

"I became deeply engrossed in the great mystic's power-of-thought philosophy from the moment I met him at your home," wrote Fort. He went on to emphasize the hours he had spent speaking to the Oriental mystic with the bushy hair and the weirdly compelling eyes.

Shri Meher took no actual vocal part in these "conversations," Garrett told his friends. Instead, since his "reign of silence" was still operative, the Baba "replied" to questions by spelling out his answers in chalk on a portable blackboard.

These answers gave the dream-wracked scenarist plenty to ponder. And aside from the imagery presented by the Baba's undoubted intellect, there was the question of his standing in the different communities he had visited.

Everywhere, simply as a human being, he had made the most affecting and durable friendships. People of all ranks "took to" the taciturn Hindu instantly, and their liking for him lasted.

Among his intimates and associates, for a long time now, has been Maria Carmi, the world-celebrated Nun in Max Reinhardt's spectacular stage pageant, "The Miracle," known in private life as the Princess Matchabelli.

But it wasn't only the famous and socially important who formed a fondness for the Baba. Quite simple souls—laborers in ordinary jobs—were irresistibly drawn toward him.

Shri Meher had already taken his oath of silence when he left the land of his birth in 1934. On his world tour no word escaped those ascetic lips. When officials at various ports peppered him with personal questions, he stayed speechless. When would-be interviewers sought him out to establish his reactions to this or that event, his impressions were locked in his inscrutable breast. Always the Baba's smile was serene with an other-worldly quality that both amazed and soothed. Always he gestured his devoted secretary to give out such information as might be thought necessary for public and press.

Naturally such a personality was bound to leave its imprint on Hollywood. But no one could have foreseen that, among the California converts to Shri Meher's placid faith would be—Garrett Fort!

For Fort was, or seemed, at the other end of the psychic and esoteric scale from the Baba. Fort, like his new master, had thought deeply on many matters. But they were dark, dire things, lit up by the red glare from the imagination's most sinister gulfs.

In his work as screen adapter for such powerful fictionists as Poe, Robert Louis Stevenson, Bram Stoker and other practitioners of the macabre and lethal literary arts, Fort had experienced all the soul tremors of such authors' heroes.

He had undergone the grinding torments of Dr. Jekyll as he turned into the hideous Mr. Hyde. He had writhed in the frantic self-reproaches of the anguished Roderick Usher. He had known how the Monster of Mary Shelley's fancy felt when first he tasted great power, and had drunk the blood of Count Dracula's victims—figuratively.

These acute agonies of creation in piling shock upon shock and thrill upon thrill which the master-scenarist underwent were, of course, imperceptible to spectators of his horror-movies. From their viewpoint, naturally, the more gruesome the spectacles he evolved, the keener their interest in the theater.

Nothing delights the thrill-addict more than a good rousing feast of suffering, cruelty, revenge and remorse. That was why "Frankenstein," with its piled-up woes, was such a resonant smash at box-offices.

When the inventor (Colin Clive) concocted his monstrous effigy (Boris Karloff) and the latter terrorized the countryside and committed a peculiarly fiendish murder, the Frankenstein fans were thrilled and charmed.

When Count Dracula's daughter (Gloria Holden) saved the soul of her dead, weird father by fair and foul means, there was applause. When the wicked president of the Suicide Club (Reginald Owen) menaced the lives and love of Rosalind Russell and Robert Montgomery, they were appalled—and entertained.

And when Claude Rains as the Invisible Man wrought havoc in an English village and finally died, visibly, in the snow, the actor's reputation was securely established.

But after he had tossed manuscript after brilliant manuscript at the Hollywood producers and all had been directed and released to salvos of appreciation, Garrett Fort began to pay the price.

Nightmares pursued him like infernal hounds from the bottomless pit. Even his daylit hours were stricken through with dreadful dreams.

Now, happily, those dismal days and nights are past. Garrett Fort sits in his white temple high on the Nasik hills, deditating, dreaming, speculating, *thinking* the higher thoughts.

One of hundreds of similar pilgrims to the shrine of Shri Meher Baba, in India, Fort has found his haven from the world. He has achieved peace with the silent help of his "God-man."

DISCIPLES

Above: Followers of Shri Meher Baba Gathered Around Him. Left: Marion Passer, of Hollywood, Who, with Her Husband, Was Responsible for Converting Fort to the Cult.

SILENT

Shri Meher Baba Vowed He Wouldn't Say a Word While He Was Visiting the United States, When This Photo Was Taken, and Followers Said He Did Not.

Article from the *Salt Lake Tribune*, March 7, 1937; the same article and layout was printed in several other newspapers at this time. Garrett Fort, a successful Hollywood screenwriter, composed the screen plays for such celebrated horror films as *Frankenstein* and *Dracula*. Meeting Meher Baba in Hollywood in January 1935, Fort traveled to India to join in the life of Baba's Nasik ashram in 1937.

190 THE LONDON FORUM

had all my life, for example; of doing some action in certain surroundings and suddenly perceiving that I had done that identical thing in the same place and way before—was it in a dream or actually had I experienced these circumstances before? There were other experiences, too, when I had thought of some-one at a distance and had pictured them in need, or mental distress, although I had no reason to believe that they were otherwise than well and happy; and always if I responded by solicitous word or financial assistance, I was just in time—although it took the period of the letter to reach there. What were these feelings and intuitions? Why could not one "turn ... instead of coming as they did in a flash as if by "chance"? ... become more permanent?

A MODERN MEETING OF MASTER AND CHELA

By ELIZABETH C. PATTERSON

This frank self-revelation on the part of an American lady of the reactions of her inner life in the presence of Meher Baba, throws an interesting light on a mystifying personality.

I FIRST heard of Shri Meher Baba through a letter from a friend in November 1932, asking me if I would like to meet him, as he was then in the United States on his first visit from India. The name sounded strange to me, and I wondered what kind of spiritual being a Perfect Master was, though I did vaguely consider that I might be interested. However, I put the letter away on my desk and in the rush of New York events I forgot all about it, until one morning early I received a telephone call from the same friend. Would I come to Harmon that very day, thirty miles up the Hudson River? Baba was there and I could see him for a few moments. My mind was crowded with engagements, never had a day seemed so full, and the idea of the country seemed a long way off in the Fall of the year. I opened my mouth to make my conventional excuses and then something happened—I said yes instead. I had just been looking at my calendar covered by appointments, and suddenly it had become blank. Only much later did I perceive the symbol on this white new page. What actually took place was not on the calendar but in my mind as my seemingly urgent affairs passed through swiftly; as a drowning man is purported to review his life. Each one suddenly faded in importance—someone else could do this to-day, or I could put that off until to-morrow. How grateful now I am that it was not the meeting with Baba which I put off, for I have since seen the effect of one day's delay resulting in a long period of time before meeting the Master. I have also noticed how the call seems to come when people are busiest; or is it that we feel the draw of the world's affairs most when the spiritual impulse calls?

Imagine, I had only to be gone a day, yet here I was making such rearrangements. My city life had indeed caged my independent spirit! A friend from California, with whom I had an

186

Article from *Occult Review*, September, 1934. In this principal literary venue for the Western subculture of those interested in the occult, theosophy, and mysticism, Elizabeth Patterson published a detailed and moving account of her first meeting with her spiritual Master.

Appendix 2.
Four Messages to India, 1932–34

During the early 1930s when the main thrust of Meher Baba's work seems to have been turned towards the Western world, he gave several messages to India. Messages of Meher Baba Delivered in the East and West *(pp. 5–7) collects four from this period; and we reproduce them here.*

The first, as Lord Meher *records, Baba issued to the Indian press shortly after the Italian ocean liner Conte Verde embarked from Bombay on November 21, 1932, inaugurating Baba's fourth Western tour. Taken in the context of the many messages Baba had recently given on the needs and conditions of the West, it is a powerful statement on the spiritual greatness and abiding role of India.*

From June 3–5 of the next year, a large congregation of representatives of different religions and faiths convened at the Circle Cinema in Nasik in what was called the "All Faiths Conference." Though Baba did not attend, he dictated a short message which Ramjoo Abdulla read out on the conference's final day. It was subsequently published on page 17 in the proceedings of that conference, a 165-page book that included summaries of more than twenty papers, remarks and reports from officiaries of the All Faiths League, and assorted short messages from various personalities, including "His Holiness Meherbaba."

Meher Baba's fortieth birthday message was delivered by Rustom Irani in Baba's own physical presence at the culmination of a whirlwind two-day visit in which Baba had traveled to Madras all the way from Meherabad. Baba's host was Sampath Aiyangar, a dear lover and disciple, who had helped to inspire and organize the celebrations on a grand scale. In testimony to the quality of what had been offered him, the theme of Baba's address was the power of love.

Love was again the theme of the two-line message that Baba sent to the Meher Gazette, *a publication edited by Sampath Aiyangar, as Baba was setting off from Bombay on his eighth visit to the West.*

The texts that follow are based not only on the texts in Messages *but various other early sources. For details, see pp. 276.*

MEHER BABA'S MESSAGE TO INDIA ON HIS FOURTH VOYAGE TO EUROPE, 1932–33

India is a spiritual country. It possesses the most fortunate and unique position in the world of being the land of saints and spiritual Masters since ages. Therefore the spiritual atmosphere of India must be kept up even at the cost of being in bondage and materially unhappy.*

It does not matter how much India suffers, as long as its spiritual power and value are retained. Moreover, the result of its present suffering will be freedom and happiness.

It is only after experiencing bondage and misery that true value of freedom and happiness is really appreciated.

But to bring this suffering to an earlier end, there must be love for friend and foe, goodwill, patience and forbearance. Also, India should try to remedy its own defects, instead of clamouring at the faults of others. And the hatred between the leading communities, and their petty yet disastrous quarrels and fights, must cease—and the freedom and happiness of India are ensured.

The world will soon realize that neither cults, creeds, dogmas, religious ceremonies, lectures and sermons on the one hand, nor, on the other hand,

* Shri Meher Baba does not deny material well-being or freedom, but if this is to be had at the cost of spiritual freedom, then material freedom [must] be sacrificed and spiritual freedom upheld.

ardent seeking for material welfare or physical pleasures, can ever bring about real happiness—but that only selfless love and universal brotherhood can do it.

Message to All Faiths Conference in Nasik, June, 1933

I very much appreciate this idea of coming together of the representatives of different faiths, which in fact, are based but on one and the same principle—faith itself. The medium, the surroundings and the settings may be different. It may be formed of images or imagination; it may be based on the intellectual conviction or emotional impression, yet the central jewel of a faith is just the same. There are no two kinds of faiths. Faith is the last thing to be labelled. The only question could be of a strong faith or a weak faith. Some hold it to the point of forms and ceremonies only, and some, going beyond this, stick to the kernel eschewing the crust, either believing in one Impersonal Infinite Existence, or believing in one's own Master. So it is only a question of degree. Unless and until there is complete Realization, which is the goal of all faiths, faith is faith after all, call it blind or call it otherwise. Once God is realized, there is no question of faith at all, just as there is no question of faith for a man to believe that he is a man; because one then, having transcended the boundaries of faith, feels oneself identified with the Infinite, and finds the One Self manifested everywhere. Please convey my blessings to all.

Shri Meher Baba's Fortieth Birthday Message to Saidapet Ashram

Madras, February 18, 1934

(Read by Mr. Rustom. K. Sarosh Irani in Shri Meher Baba's presence)

The reason of my coming here all the way from one end of the country to the other to participate personally in your celebrations is your Love that has irresistibly drawn me to you. Love is a mighty force. It not only enables one to put the ideal of selfless service into practice, but would transform one into God. With Love one can follow any of the yogas most suitable to his or her temperament. It will enable an aspirant to follow the rigid principles underlying the spiritual path, and where and when necessary makes him turn his back to the worldly pleasures for the sake of union with the Beloved.

Where there is Love there is Oneness, and there can be no question of any particular religion or caste or system, superiority or inferiority, and touchability or untouchability. That these distinctions are not real has been proved in a way by the recent earthquake tragedy. The earthquake in Bihar was simply a manifestation of one of the laws of nature. And that disaster spared none, rich or poor, high or low, belonging to this religion or that. It was not divine wrath. It is an eye-opener to the fact that where God and His laws are concerned there is no question of caste, creed or country.

But to realize this natural equality permanently one has to submit to the greatest law of God, which is Love. It holds the key to all problems inasmuch as, under this law, the Infinite is realized completely at all times in every walk of life, be it science, art, religion, or beauty. May the world realize this highest aspect of Divinity more and more.

Message to the *Meher Gazette* on the Eve of the Eighth Voyage to the West, November 15, 1934

Those who are united in love know no separation. Wherever I am, wherever you are, I am always with you. My love and blessings to you.

[sd] Meher Baba

Appendix 3.
A Letter from the Circle Editorial Committee, October 1933

The following letter, made available for republication here from the personal papers of David Fenster, was created in late 1933 to serve as a flyer advertising Shri Meher Baba, the Perfect Master: Questions and Answers, *published by Circle Editorial Committee that September. The membership of Circle Editorial Committee as listed in this flyer consisted of prominent persons in different regions who could serve as effective public contacts and representatives in Meher Baba's work. The actual working body of the Committee was made up of an entirely different group of people, though Herbert Davy was the director and head. For further details,* *see pp. 231–34.*

"I have come not to teach but to awaken"

Shri Meher Baba, the silent Persian Mystic has been acclaimed by many as the new prophet and "Perfect Master of the Age." It is said that his spoken word will affect the spiritual consciousness and the destinies of all mankind. He has now been silent for over eight years, but the time is approaching when he will deliver his spoken message. This long silence is a preparation for his world manifestation.

Religious history and contemporary India provide many examples of hermits and saints meditating in remote places and abstaining from all speech and intercourse with the world, but rarely has a teacher led an active life and maintained complete silence. For the last ten years Shri Meher Baba has administered an Ashram or spiritual retreat where many live and thousands visit. During the last two years he has lived and worked in many great cities of Europe, America, China, India and Egypt. He reads and can speak English and four other languages fluently. During his silence he communicates by pointing to the English letters on an alphabet board, and in this way he has answered the many questions put to him by his Western enquirers during his travels. The most important of these "Questions and Answers" (sixty six[115] in all) have been collected in this small book and they are grouped under these headings:—Christ and the Second Coming; The Spiritual Path; Messiah or Avatar; Spiritual Masters; World and Philosophical Problems; Shri Meher Baba's Life and Mission. He was born thirty nine years ago of Persian parents in Poona, (India). He is a Parsee Zoroastrian by birth, and is unmarried. When he was a college student, nineteen years old, he had a unique spiritual experience, and since 1922 he has devoted his whole life to spiritual work.

If you are genuinely interested in his work or know of any friends who would be interested, please write to "The Circle Editorial Committee" as below for further information and for copies of Shri Meher Baba's "Questions and Answers" (the price per copy is sixpence including postage.)

"Questions and Answers," and some of Shri Meher Baba's other works are being translated into the following languages: French, German, Italian, Roumanian, Russian, Spanish, Gujarati, Hindi, Mahratta and Persian, these will be obtained through the respective National Sections of the Circle Editorial Committee. The following are also in course of preparation:—"The Sayings of Shri Meher Baba," (spoken before he commenced his silence); philosophical articles; and the Biography of Shri Meher Baba.

> "His purpose is not to establish a new creed or another organization, it is to revitalize all religions and cults and to bring them together like beads on one string."

CENTRAL OFFICE: Director—H. N. Davy, M.A.

"THE CIRCLE EDITORIAL COMMITTEE"

Phone: Oct. 1933,
Whitehall 3751 50, Charing Cross, London, S.W.1.

Herr Walter Mertens,
1, Jupiter Strasse,
Zurich, Switzerland.

Le Marquis Illan de Casa Fuerte,
Hotel Regina de Passy,
Rue La Tours, Paris.

Malcolm Schloss, Esq.,
6238, Temple Hill Drive,
Hollywood, California.

R. K. S. Irani,
Meherashram, Meherabad,
Ahmednagar, India.

C. V. Sampath Aiyangar,
Meherashram, Saidapet,
Madras, India.

Behram Faridun Irani
Kubarekei, Yezd, Persia.

Appendix 4.
Correspondence Connected with the Work of the Circle Editorial Committee, 1933–34

Conceived and brought to birth during Meher Baba's stay in Portofino during the summer of 1933, the Circle Editorial Committee in its highly active first six months oversaw the compilation and publishing of two booklets, Shri Meher Baba, the Perfect Master: Questions and Answers *(September 1933), and* The Sayings of Shri Meher Baba *(December 1933).*

Though the exact membership of the committee during this period was still fluid, some of the disciples active in its work were, in England, Norina Matchabelli, Kitty Davy, Charles Purdom, and Will Backett, and on the American side, Elizabeth Patterson and Jean and Malcolm Schloss. But the head of the committee was Herbert Davy, and as the following correspondence shows, he played the main part in the various exchanges and dramas that acted themselves out in connection with the two books.

Many of these letters involve J. Graham Phelps Stokes, a New York millionaire with deep interests in Eastern and Western spirituality. Stokes hosted Baba at his Greenwich Village home during several of his early tours. Yet as his letters make clear, Stokes could not accept Meher Baba's spiritual claims—or, as he chose to see them, the claims being made on Baba's behalf, and so declined to involve himself in the Committee's publishing ventures.

During the same time Herbert Davy himself was passing through a crisis of faith, as letters between him and Baba illustrate in poignant detail. By the end of 1934 he had dissociated himself from his former Master, and he never renewed this connection again.

The correspondence published here has been drawn from two collections.

The papers of J. Graham Phelps Stokes are housed in the Columbia University Rare Book and Manuscript Library. Our thanks to the curators of the library who have allowed the publication of this material in this book. And special thanks to David Fenster, who originally procured it from the library and graciously shared it, along with his own invaluable insights and suggestions based on long research into the life of Meher Baba.

The other collection is located at the Meher Spiritual Center in Myrtle Beach, South Carolina. Our thanks to the Center for permission to publish relevant materials from Kitty Davy's papers in this book.

The letters as reproduced below have been corrected for small grammatical and typographic errors; abbreviations have been expanded, and other small stylistic features standardized in keeping with the style of this book. Irrelevant material in the text of the letters has been deleted, and these deletions are marked with ellipses. No note is made, however, of marginal comments and postscripts, usually of a personal character, that have been deleted silently.

UNDATED MEMORANDUM

This typed page, which has perhaps been separated from a larger memorandum or report, appears to record proceedings of a meeting with Baba that mapped out plans for the future dissemination of his message through publications. Though undated, it was probably composed during Baba's stay in Portofino between June 25 and July 24, 1933. Since the page bears Meher Baba's signature, we know that its contents were endorsed by him. (The original appears in facsimile on p. 58.) From Kitty Davy's papers.

These Answers and Questions dictated by Shri Meher Baba have to be translated into German, French, and Italian.[116]

A publication ought to be arranged in book form. Further publications of it can appear in journals, reviews and magazines.

The Editorial Committee retains the copyright.

The book price should not exceed one lira in Italy, threepence in England, one franc in France, and [blank] in Germany.

The Editorial Committee does not claim any profit until the publisher has covered the expenses for printing and distribution. After this has been covered future terms concerning royalties, price, and future editions will be discussed between the Editorial Committee and the publisher.

In Catholic countries we must consider opposition of the Catholic Church (Index of heretical books).

It is advisable to handle this matter in a quiet and tactful way before publication.

Possibly a publisher in London could handle the matter for the whole world.

Editorial Committee: Norina Matchabelli
Graham Phelps Stokes.
Charles Purdom.
Kitty Davy.
Herbert Davy.

[sd.] MS Irani[117]

August 10, 1933
Norina Matchabelli to J. Graham Phelps Stokes

Norina Matchabelli writes from London to convey to Graham Stokes Baba's invitation to become a founding member of the Circle Editorial Committee. From the Stokes papers.

My dear Graham,

A very urgent matter that I wish you would consider and take very much to heart. It is a message from Baba. He wishes to have published in America some sixty questions and answers <u>as soon as possible</u>. After this, his "Life"[118] and other material will also be published.

We had thought to form an editorial committee comprised of the editor and writer C. B. Purdom, Herbert Davy and Kitty Davy and myself. Will you accept Baba's direct invitation to join this committee and act for America? If you can send by cable your consent we would like to include your name as a member of the "Circle Editorial Committee." This title was chosen by Baba himself and it will handle all his world publication in future. Enclosed the "Questions and Answers" and other material which can be used as you think fit, but "Questions and Answers" as Baba wishes have to be published this early part of September—if possible before the seventh of September.

We are now in touch with a London publisher and will let you know immediately the results—we would like your advice as to whether it is better for the London publisher to negotiate direct with the New York publishers or to ask you to consider an independent publisher in America. (Kegan and Paul of London [illegible] philosophical publishers, have a contract with Dutton of New York for American distribution).

We are not at all sure today whether they (Kegan and Paul) will publish such a small pamphlet as "Questions and Answers." Therefore will you please explore possibilities—that is, if you accept Baba's invitation and join this great work that you have so generously supported from the commencement.

We had a glorious time at Portofino—a life full of work and learning. Baba said that he has done very important work there. He left on the 24th and is expected back here on the 12th. The date of his manifestation will be decided by the 5th of September and we will be informed by that time—and no statements about it should be given out till then . . .

Norina

August 20, 1933
Cable from J. Graham Phelps Stokes Norina Matchabelli

Responding to her letter of August 10, Stokes addressed this telegram to "Princess Norina" in London. From the Stokes papers.

EXCEEDINGLY SORRY BUT MATERIAL CONTAINING
MUCH TO WHICH I CANNOT POSSIBLY SUBSCRIBE
THEREFORE CANNOT PARTICIPATE IN ITS PUBLICATION
AM CONFIDENT NO PUBLISHER WOULD ACCEPT
MATERIAL IN PRESENT FORM

GRAHAM

SEPTEMBER 3, 1933
HERBERT N. DAVY TO J. GRAHAM PHELPS STOKES

As the head of the Circle Editorial Committee, Herbert Davy followed up on the preceding exchange of communications between Graham Stokes and Norina Matchabelli. From the Stokes papers.

Dear Mr. Phelps Stokes,

Norina handed me your cable in which you said you were unable to accept "Questions and Answers" or to join the Circle Editorial Committee. I am sorry but appreciate your difficulty in accepting some of the statements and implications without a closer study or clearer proofs.

I have come to an arrangement with George Allen and Unwin's, the London publishers, whereby they will publish "Questions and Answers" when the time comes. (I now have the material for Baba's Biography and they will publish that very soon.) Meanwhile, their sister firm, the printers, are printing 5,000 copies of Questions and Answers; I expect to distribute privately 2 to 3,000 in England to those already interested in Baba.

If I send you 2 or 3,000 copies to U.S.A. could you assist us in distributing them to those people whose names are in the file and who are interested in Baba?

The actual printing cost (not including postage, and commercial percentages) is 2 pennies, so the commercial price might be 4^{d} pence to cover the cost of distribution, or postage etc. We may sell it at 3^{d} when privately distributed and when commercially distributed at 5^{d} or 6^{d}.

If I require it this firm is willing to publish it now. But they want to charge [illegible] for a copy.

Shri Meher Baba particularly instructed us to sell it at the lowest possible figure—therefore 3ᵈ is best.

I will distribute it privately at this figure.

When Baba speaks and the general public demands copies the Publishers (having the type already set up) will have reprints and take the distribution and selling of it for us.

Several publishers have asked for the Biography of Baba—but I shall give it to the same publisher (Allen and Unwin) who can also negotiate with their agents in New York for the American edition.

I hope you will not object to my writing about this matter, and I hope that you will help us to distribute "Questions and Answers" to the friends of Meher Baba in America. This was Baba's wish and instruction—i.e.—that Questions and Answers should be distributed in America, and I hope you will help this work.

Yours Sincerely,

Herbert N. Davy

September 26, 1933
J. Graham Phelps Stokes to Herbert N. Davy

Stokes indicates that the basis for his objections to "Questions and Answers" is certain passages making spiritual claims on Baba's behalf. From the Stokes papers.

Dear Mr. Davy:

I am sorry to have been so delayed in replying to your very kind letter which was itself greatly delayed in reaching me. I have been in the far west for some time, and am just back.

I am sorry—very sorry indeed—to be unable to aid in the manner proposed in the distribution of "Questions and Answers" in their present form. If certain omissions could be made of claims that Baba himself has expressly disapproved, and that I have abundant reason, I believe, to regard as highly prejudicial, I should be more than happy to do what I can to promote the distribution of the remainder. But I cannot disregard the light of my own conscience, or accept anyone's statement as of more compelling authority than That. What the Baba is, will sufficiently appear. I will not join any of my friends in making statements about him, or claims for him, that turn people from him, and deprive him and his great message of the wholly respectful hearing both should have.

I refer of course to the very many passages in Questions and Answers making (whether directly or by obvious implication) claims for the Baba of a sort that he himself has so expressly disapproved. May I refer you especially to his statement on page 17 of Questions and Answers, that claims of the sort referred to have no value until substantiated, and are needless when substantiated.

Claims of that sort have been advanced, in America no less than elsewhere, on behalf of innumerable teachers, small as well as great; but substantiation has in each case, of late, been so notably lacking that continued reiteration of such claims in behalf of the Baba or anyone else, prior to its substantiation, has become not merely "of no value" (as the Baba expresses it), but the cause of needless resentment and prejudice of a sort that I cannot think any true friend of the Baba's could possibly wish to subject him to.

I shall be more than happy to do everything in my power to aid in the accomplishment of the one supreme task of all the great teachers, which as the Baba so clearly expresses it, in referring to his own mission, is "to make mankind realize not merely through the intellect, but by actual experience, the One Infinite Self which is in all"—which in fact is All; but I will not participate, voluntarily, in clouding so great an issue, or in spreading further needless misunderstanding and resentment against wonderful people who devote their lives to this cause.

With very best regards to all, including the very dear friends who differ so greatly from me with respect to this matter, I am,

Very sincerely yours,

J. G. PHELPS STOKES

October 16, 1933
Herbert N. Davy to J. Graham Phelps Stokes

Herbert Davy requests Stokes's detailed criticisms to be utilized in a forthcoming second edition of Questions and Answers. *From the Stokes papers.*

Dear Mr, Phelps Stokes,

Thank you for your letter of 28 [sic] September.

I do appreciate your point of view and quite understand your decision but I should like to know in greater detail the statements to which you take exception. Would you mark them in a copy of the booklet and send to me with any comments which I can show to Baba and for the Editorial Committee.

We have other suggestions also and a new edition will be required before Christmas to embody five new questions and a few alterations elucidating certain points without making extreme corrections. (We have disposed of nearly 4,000 copies already—but some of these are allotted to U.S.A.)

The enclosed leaflet explains the work of the "Circle Editorial Committee"—we need a representative for the East Coast of U.S. America. We have much work in hand—the translations are completed and publishing contracts drawn up but some of these are held up pending further financial aid—the cost of an edition of 3 to 4,000 copies is from £34 to £45.

German and French arrangements are nearly completed. (The German is settled.)

Other books are also to be published this Autumn and Spring of 1934.

Baba's visit to London—two weeks—has been a great success—many new contacts and many interesting people have been drawn to Baba and he has done much work in London.

I hope that later I shall have an opportunity of meeting you—I have heard so much about you from several of Baba's followers.

If you can let me know your suggestions for the new edition—as soon as possible I shall be grateful. But Baba himself will authorise certain minor corrections for the new edition before he leaves for India.

With best wishes,
Yours sincerely,
Herbert N. Davy

November 6, 1933
Meher Baba to Herbert Davy

Writing (through Chanji) from the Viceroy of India during his return to India at the end of his sixth Western tour, Baba conveys instructions concerning the additional material to be incorporated into the second edition of Questions and Answers. (For a facsimile of the original, see p. 58.) From Kitty Davy's papers.

My dearest Herbert,

I am sending the answers to the questions we had discussed about in Madrid. I have dictated them almost word by word. You may make alterations and additions and change the language and phraseology, but retain the sense. You need not send it to me for approval as that would take too much time, but print it, sticking strictly to the original sense. . .

All my love
[sd] MS Irani

November 14, 1933
J. Graham Phelps Stokes to Herbert N. Davy

Along with his annotated copy of Questions and Answers, *Stokes as requested sends criticisms of certain statements in the book. From the Stokes papers.*

Dear Mr. Davy:

I greatly appreciate your exceedingly kind letter of October 16th, and your courtesy in sending me a copy of the little booklet entitled "Questions and Answers," and in inviting me to return the booklet to you with my comments marked upon it.

As I advised Norina some months ago, when this material in typewritten form was first submitted to me, there was much in it to which I could not possibly subscribe. As you will discover, my comments as indicated in the booklet are quite numerous.

Personally, I feel very strongly that the booklet in its present form would be prejudicial to the Baba's cause if circulated in America without material amendment. [sic] It abounds in claims of the precise sort that Baba himself has declared unequivocally to be valueless. Certain statements, as for instance lines that I have struck out in the committee's answer to Question 37, impress me as being actually untruthful.[119] Of course, nothing but truth was intended by the committee, but I am convinced that they inadvertently have stated untruths in this and numerous other instances. I cannot understand how the Baba could permit so many inaccurate statements to be made on his behalf.

Of course, people are differently constituted, and perhaps some would be helped by the booklet in its present form, but I for one regard it as so exceedingly inaccurate and misleading, that I could not possibly have anything to do, voluntarily, with its circulation. I hope the committee will revise it drastically before any more copies are made.

Very sincerely yours,

J. Graham Phelps Stokes

December 5, 1933
Elizabeth Patterson to Herbert Davy and the Circle Editorial Committee

Writing from New York to the Circle Editorial Committee at their office at 50 Charing Cross, London, Elizabeth Patterson reports on the American sales and distribution of Questions and Answers. *From Kitty Davy's papers.*

Dear Herbert and Others,

I want to let you know that there is real response to the booklet of Baba's. Every day about ten copies are sold. Those who come in the shop often stop and talk, saying what Baba has meant to them. I am sorry I have not the time to be there as it would be interesting to see them, but fortunately Mrs. Gorham has met Baba and, although only once, she seems to have a real appreciation. I have been encouraged by the sales to send out notices to Malcolm's out-of-town list,[120] about 2,500 more, making a total of 7,500 notices to be sent out. I feel like the "Bridge of San Luis Rey." There must have been some reason why these people passed through the door of Malcolm's North Node to seemingly just buy a book. In any case they are as good list as any, although the addresses in many instances are obsolete. I find in looking over the response to the notice Stokes sent out last year about Baba's coming, that more out-of-town people replied than those in New York and I am almost sure most of these had not met him. In any case by the time all is finished, I will have a most up-to-date list which can be used for further work, because I have had a special mark put on the envelopes which requests the Post Office to furnish me with forwarding addresses when known. This is a new service of the Post Office here and you pay the same fees as "return postage guaranteed."

On the second 2,500 notices I had a special imprint stating that orders could be taken for the second booklet "Sayings of Shri Baba" which Kitty writes are ready. I have wired you to send 500 copies for I think we can sell them if they arrive before Xmas. I thought first of needing 1,000, but the shipping might be expensive and maybe someone will be coming over later. Also, I do not think we can sell more than that for some time. If I were not so busy with my own business and buying Baba's equipment, then I might go around to other book stores for distribution—it takes personal effort and explanation and I have been swamped so far. Please see that the 500 booklets reach me as soon as possible for they can be shown to the people who come in to buy the "Questions and Answers." In any case all purchasers have their name and address taken so the re-solicitation can be among the interested, and this will save the big expense of future postage—which is quite an item. I think I should have charged more than 15¢ a copy for the booklets, but Baba wanted them sold as cheaply as possible, and the list is valuable to obtain for his whole work, not only for the booklet advertising. The last 2,500 notices will also have the imprint about the "Sayings" so, in other words, only the first 2,500 got out without a special notation, although it is mentioned in the text of the circular.[121]

Enclosed is a letter from the Library of Congress, which please reply in full. I have acknowledged the receipt and said the New York Public Library has the works listed under Meher Baba and that Shri is a spiritual title. But I do not know about the secular names, as there are different mentions in various publications, just as there are various birthdays. Baba however definitely told Norina that his birth date was Feb. 19th so that point is certain. Therefore I leave the reply to you.

Malcolm and Jean are working on this California list but it is not out yet, so I do not know as to the response there. . . .

Please always let me know in advance of publications. . . .

As always,

Elizabeth

December 7, 1933
Herbert N. Davy to J. Graham Phelps Stokes

Herbert acknowledges Stokes's criticisms and corrections marked on his copy of Questions and Answers, *and he invites Stokes' response and comments to the forthcoming book of sayings. From the Stokes papers.*

Dear Mr. Stokes,

Thank you very much for your letter and the corrected copy of "Questions and Answers."

I have written to Baba about your corrections and I will let you know when I get a reply. I think, that Baba will also write to you direct about them.

Many of your corrections would improve the style of the book, and I should be very glad to see them incorporated in a new edition. Personally I much prefer understatement to overstatement and exaggeration.

The use of the board imposes severe limitations and makes it impossible to write or construct long paragraphs. Qualities of style, and well-constructed sentences are sacrificed. The translation of Indian words into direct English equivalents leads to error.

While I was in Spain with Baba, during October, I pointed out to Baba that there is a confusion between Mind and Intellect, partly because we used "mental body" as the adjectival form for The Mind Body. (See Questions, particularly in 24, 25, 35, 58).

So he gave us a definition of Mind and Intellect. And throughout the booklet the substitution of Mind Body for "mental body" clears up the former confusion.

In addition to some other notes and a few corrections, Baba gave us five new Questions and Answers to add, for a second edition. But we had not contemplated publishing this new edition until the old one was sold out. Until Baba speaks there will [not] be a very strong demand for "Questions and Answers," I think. Then the demand for a new edition might be very great. But now we shall have to wait for Baba's comments on your suggestions and corrections, before finally drafting a 2nd edition.

Meanwhile, we have been working on a new publication, less controversial, and far more interesting, I think, for the general public, "The Sayings of Meher Baba," with adequate notes and explanations taken from his own writings. These are literally his own words, subject of course to the same limitations, mentioned above, that are imposed by the use of the board. It is cheaper, and I think far more likely to appeal to the general reader.

May I send you a copy? And perhaps you will not find anything in it to which you cannot subscribe. I do hope you will find yourself in agreement with it, it will come from the printers early next week. The other source of errors, the submitting of answers to Baba for his correction and approval by followers, does not intrude into the "Sayings." The English style is far from perfect, naturally. We have often been asked for Baba's own writings, and his own words. We hope that this will satisfy that demand.

Now I must close, thanking you for your letter, kindness, and the corrections. I hope that before long I shall have the opportunity to meet you, and that we may be privileged to work together in the cause of Truth.

Yours sincerely,
Herbert N. Davy

December 8, 1933
Meher Baba to Herbert Davy

From Kitty Davy's papers.

My dearest Herbert,

. . . I hope your cold has gone completely and I am glad you are working seriously at the new edition of Questions and Answers and the Sayings. Send me a copy each of both immediately they are out of press. Send all the 5,000 copies of the Sayings to India at the Nasik address (c/o Sarosh Motor Works) and I will send as many as required to Persia, from here. I have told Chanji to send you the material for Biography and Quarterly Bulletin, etc., the Meher Message and Sobs and Throbs copies and the information about movements and plans that you ask for. He will do so in a few days. Re: The Circle Committee Deed:

If it is easier and more convenient to leave out "Land," you may do so —I do not mind. But we must be able to convert land which is given to us into cash money or investments, and also to rent land and property.

I do not exactly understand what you mean by trustees. You remember (in Madrid) we appointed an executive committee of three (myself, Adi Sr. and Norina) to control and manage all monetary and other affairs. If by trustees you mean this same Executive Committee, you may include a clause in the deed allowing further trustees to be appointed—we cannot give the names, of course.

You may also include the right of survivorship and the right to add in more members to the Circle Committee—I want a limit of 120, maximum.

I do not intend turning over my existing personal assets and properties—but all that I receive in future—including even wills (even if it is given to me privately) will be turned over to the Circle Committee.

Write to Catherine Gardner to send to the Circle Committee all that may be left over after the sale is completed.

Re: Phelps Stokes: You may accept his minor suggestions and corrections as you think best, without altering, as far as possible, the sense of the Answers. But I cannot see how you can do it if (as I understand from your letter) the second edition has already gone, or will soon go, to the press. Or do you mean for the third edition? However, use your discretion and act, I repeat, as you think best. What more can I say? . . .

I have also told Chanji to get as many dates and other information about past Masters as he can and send it to you as soon as possible.

All My Love,
[sd] MS Irani

December 15, 1933
Elizabeth Patterson to Herbert Davy

Elizabeth discusses the progress of the literary and publishing work and urges Herbert to send to her accounts from his diaries. From Kitty Davy's papers.

Dear Herbert,

Your nice letter came. Yes, please do send me the five new questions and answers; also, your account of the Spanish trip. You never let me see the article you wrote at Baba's direction about your Chinese experiences.

Anything you have as written material, I wish you would "automatically" send me, as I cherish it very much and keep files for all these things. . . .

I have written Jean, at Norina's direction, to hurry along with the material for Purdom's book. I shall certainly be interested to see the "Sayings." The "Questions and Answers" have had a good reception here —but of course not 1,000 are sold yet! If I had time to send it to newspapers for book reviews, and things of this kind, it would be good. . . .

I am only too glad you "made" eight pounds—and that was the understanding—you would repay in dollars (whether they were high or low.) I paid you for my copies of "Questions and Answers"—but not the 1,000 yet. . . .

Affectionately, Elizabeth

December 18, 1933
Herbert N. Davy to J. Graham Phelps Stokes

Writing from the new office of the Circle Editorial Committee in Charing Cross, London, Herbert Davy sends Graham Stokes a copy of the just-published The Sayings of Shri Meher Baba *and invites his comments. From the Stokes papers.*

Dear Mr. Phelps Stokes,

Enclosed is a copy of Shri Meher Baba's "Sayings."

I hope you will think it suitable for distribution in the United States of America. In any case I shall be glad to have your opinion and criticism of the book.

With regard to its style and English, it is very imperfect I know, but they are really Baba's own words, given through the medium of the alphabet board, and he did not wish that we should correct or put them into a more literary form.

They are best regarded as channels by which his power may reach a wide public; the only test for Shri Meher Baba's claims is their capacity to awaken the spiritual life in ever increasing numbers of mankind. They must not be judged by literary taste and purely intellectual canons.

I hope you don't mind my writing to you again.

Yours sincerely,

Herbert N. Davy

January 18, 1934
J. Graham Phelps Stokes to Herbert N. Davy

Responding to Herbert Davy's request for comment and criticism, Stokes praises The Sayings *for its primary text but sharply castigates the Circle Editorial Committee for its notes and editorializing. From the Stokes papers.*

Dear Mr. Davy:

I greatly appreciate your kindness in sending me that admirable little booklet entitled "The Sayings of Shri Meher Baba." I have read it with very great interest. To me it is vastly more interesting and likely to be far more helpful to many than the previous "Questions and Answers." And yet I find it very difficult to resist the wish that the Committee in issuing such little booklets would let the Baba's words stand on their merits, as uttered or written by him, without editorial comment, and without attempt to elucidate or clarify them, editorially, in any way whatever.

It seems to me that the Committee failed to penetrate to the heart or anywhere near to the heart of the Baba's basic teaching; and that in endeavoring to elucidate and clarify they but "step down" his teachings lamentably. To me it would seem ever so much better to present these teachings uncoloured, unlimited in any way, in their own crystal-clear words and phrases.

I think we shall agree that the Baba is a more illumined person than any of the rest of us; and that as such his own formulations of truth are likely to be at least as profound and as clear as ours could possibly be. I feel that in fact his statements are far more profound than those of the Committee. Do consider, for example, the striking contrasts between the Committee's teachings and the Baba's as both are set forth in the present little booklet—the very admirable

"Sayings." May I be permitted to allude in all friendliness to the Committee's concluding observations as they appear on page 45 of the booklet, as contrasted with what I am sure you will feel are the distinctly more exalted teachings of the Baba, with respect to the same matters, on the pages preceding.

The Committee say, for instance, (page 45), "Only three things are of Real Worth." In contrast, the Baba says, "God is one, is everything, and alone is real" (p. 44).

The Committee say, "God, Love and the Perfect Master are almost one." The Baba says, "God is one" (p. 44); "Unity appears as plurality to those who are intoxicated with the wine of egoism" (p. 26). "As long as the Many are seen, the One cannot be seen" (p. 44). "One's own self is the universal Self (p. 16). "Only God is real" (p. 26).

The Committee say, "It is the same One Paramatma . . . who is playing the different parts of The Almighty, The Creator (Ishwar), Shivatman and Jivatman." Why represent Paramatman as though functioning merely from Jivatman up? The Baba presents Him as functioning no less from Jivatman down. "It is the same universal Being," he writes (p. 42), "Who plays the different roles of stone, metal, vegetable, dumb animal and human being," yet Who experiences "His Own Real State" not merely beyond the grosser planes but beyond the "subtle planes" as well.

The Committee say, "The Perfect Master is Love, Lover and the Beloved." So too are you and I. The Baba says (p. 26), "It is Maya that makes you . . . forgetful of your indivisible Divinity."

It seems to me that the Committee constantly err in stressing an alleged actual difference of some sort between the Baba and the rest of "Reality," as though they regarded him as one, and the rest of mankind as "others." This idea of "difference," "duality," something "other," seems to me to introduce an element of basic weakness into almost all of the Committee's statements, and yet the Baba so constantly discourages dualistic thought among adult humans. "You . . . actually are . . . Paramatma"! (p. 43). "To realize the Supreme being as your own Self is to realize Truth" (p. 23).

Of course he who knows the Self knows it is no different in the Baba from what it is in you and me. Surely all who endeavor to speak for the Baba should ever maintain that there is naught else but THAT; that He, We, I, You, They are ONE; that there is naught "else" save illusion, and that the greatest of all illusions is the illusion of the separate self, whether this self be spelt with or without a capital initial.

I certainly reciprocate most heartily your so very kind expression of hope that we may in some way serve "together", or rather as One, in furthering the cause of Truth.

Very sincerely yours,

J. G. Phelps Stokes

P.S. I am taking the liberty of enclosing with this letter a carbon copy, thinking you might possibly wish to send the original to the Baba for his comment, in case he should care to comment upon it.

February 3, 1934
Herbert Davy to Meher Baba

From Kitty Davy's papers.

Dear Baba,

I enclose the proof copy of the photo leaflet we are publishing in reply to the demand for photos. . .

I have been working very hard on Philosophical Fragments. In order that the terminology and definitions should be consistent with the other two books, it has to be carefully compared and arranged.

I do not wish to criticise the devoted work of one so near to you as Ramju, but the English and arrangement of the sentences within paragraphs does need some correction, I think. It could not well be printed in England as it stands in the Indian Edition. You said in Spain that I could include parts of the Meher Articles, Fragments,[122] etc. (those you gave me at Portofino) that

Ramju had left out. I think the part of the 1930 and 1931 articles that deals more fully with the mystic path (pages 34, and the description of the Subtle Sphere pages 39 to 45) might be usefully included in the Western edition.

The biographical notes when dealing with the Western trips are inaccurate. I thought to verify these and to bring it up to date.

As appendices we could include the five additional questions you gave in Spain etc., and a list of the past Sadgurus and their dates. The West finds it difficult to understand that others than Jesus became God-realised.

Lastly, from a Western point of view Ramju's text is overloaded with alternative and foreign words. These can be put in as footnotes, and consistent English translations plus one Sufi or Sanskrit word only in the actual text. . . .

February 12, 1934
Herbert N. Davy to J. Graham Phelps Stokes

From the Stokes papers.

Dear Mr. Phelps Stokes,

Thank you for your letter of the 18 of January, I have forwarded on the copy enclosed to Baba. I am glad that you approve of the Sayings.

I must correct one point, the notes were not written by the Committee, though we are responsible for the juxtaposition of the Sayings and the notes. In this we may have erred. But the notes themselves are taken from Baba's own works. Some of those to which you refer, concerning the nature of the Paramatman, were taken from the "Philosophical Fragments."[123] Sentences torn away from their context may lead to false impressions and interpretations. 5,000 copies have been sent to India and Persia; 5,000 copies are for Western distribution. It seemed necessary therefore while keeping the Indian words to explain them for Western readers.

I am personally often conscious of having made mistakes, and I am very grateful to you for your criticisms and suggestions. I expect Baba will answer your letter directly. "Philosophical Fragments" is the next booklet to be published. Perhaps we shall be able to have the benefit of your criticisms and judgement before printing? I hope we shall.

February 28, 1934
Meher Baba to Herbert Davy

From Kitty Davy's papers.

My dear Sudama,

I received all your letters. I am glad you wrote as you did in your last letter of the 9th inst. It all had to come out, and it is good that it did. I know there is love in you for me—a great love of which you have no idea. Because you were and are "Sudama" but that brain of Herbert always tries to dominate over the warm and loving heart of Sudama, which it cannot do. I know of the inner struggle raging within you, but the heart must always succeed. It did, and will succeed however hard the head may struggle against it. . .

For other work that I instructed you to do, I should like you to continue at least until the expiry of your term of promise, till April. Then, if you decide to stay and obey, I will tell you what to do. If, however, you decide to leave, you may then do whatever you like. I don't mind. I do not want to leave you nor want you to leave me . . . Krishna loved Sudama very much. So do I, my dear boy. In spite of that revolting brain of yours, your heart is always in me, and in my work, which you so splendidly carry out, to my satisfaction. I only wish it had been done without questioning. Its value then would have been unimaginable. But if this experience has showed you your weaknesses and shortcomings, it has done you much good. And I do hope the lesson will be a great help to you in being more loving, obedient, resigned, and less conscious of your academic attainments, so that with my help, you would be able to do much more of the great work for me, which I want you to do. . .

The case of books (Sayings) has arrived in Bombay long since. But the shipping document for the same was received on the 21st. It is sent to the clearing agents and the case is expected to arrive shortly. . .

Tell Mr. Purdom I know all. I want him to do my work which he has undertaken, and not to worry. I love him and am always with him. . .

Re: Mr. Stokes' remarks on the book of Sayings, I will let you know afterwards—after April.

I am going thro' the Deed, and will let you know soon. . .

All my Love,

[sd] MS Irani

March 13, 1934
Meher Baba to Herbert Davy

From Kitty Davy's papers.

My dear Sudama,

This is in a hurry just to reply to your air-mail letter of 2nd inst.

1. Your suggestion re: inserting SUFI and SANSKRIT terms at the bottom of the page to keep consistent English terminology, alright.
2. You can include useful parts from the articles typed in Portofino, about the Subtle planes and the Mystic Path, in the Western edition.
3. Yes, do verify and bring up to date the biographical notes re: the Western trips where you find inaccuracy.
4. Quite right—put in the five extra Questions and Answers as appendixes.
5. Your idea about the list of past Sadgurus and their Masters, is approved, but only when you get correct information as to their names and dates, etc.
6. Yes, I do want to see a proof of the Western edition before it is finally sent to the printers. Never mind the

delay. This should be sent here if I don't come in April. If I do, I will see it there.

7. Only one thousand to be printed for the present, keeping only one hundred for India.

March 20, 1934
Elizabeth Patterson to Herbert Davy

From Kitty Davy's papers.

Dear Herbert,

Just a few lines to say that upon having your Diary retyped . . . I took occasion to amplify your account of the "adventures on the rocks" (from notes in my own diary) and because I took this liberty I thought best to send you a copy. I did not mean to make so many changes—but once one starts changing the others come. . . . However I do not want to become another Stokes with my corrections!

Also, enclosed is a card of registration for the "Sayings." They tell me that no previous copy or fee was received from you, although you mentioned to me about having sent a copy. . . Affectionately,

Elizabeth

April 12, 1934
Meher Baba to the "Gopies"

With preparations afoot for the creation of a film that would convey to the world Meher Baba's cosmology, Baba writes from Meherabad to convey instructions to his "Gopies" (Western women disciples, in this case particularly Norina and Elizabeth). From Kitty Davy's papers.

My darling Gopies,

. . . Norina especially and you all dearest ones have to continue your efforts in this direction as much and as best each can. It is quite possible Pascal might get the scenario written out and induce some party in America to take up this work in all earnest, impressed as he is with the story as mentioned in your cables. . .

Meanwhile, the best thing for you to do is to get the scenario written out by Karl of course, but if he refuses or sticks to his rigid attitude on any grounds, by any other great scenario-writer of repute through Pascal or anyone else whom you know of and who could do it and is worth the confidence you place in him. This work of getting the scenario ready is the first thing you have to do. For, with this in hand, Norina and Pascal could talk to and explain parties interested, and the parties too would naturally ask for this the very first thing. You know that already.

And, if necessary, Norina can go to any place on the Continent or even to America, to arrange this.

To help you all in your work for the film, I am preparing a detailed chart, with illustration, explaining all details about the Creation, Evolution, Re-incarnation, Planes, Illumination, and Realisation, for the film, which will be a guide and of considerable help to those who handle this work of production, even in my absence, giving them ideas to work out other details connected with these. Do not for a moment think I am trying to evade or postpone my coming still further by preparing this chart etc., and instructing you to go on with the production even "in my absence." You scarcely know how eager I am to see you, but it is with a view to let this work of the film to go on, and not let it slip out of your hands in case there are chances or possibilities to arrange it by Pascal or someone else, <u>now</u> or before July, when I can NOT, under any circumstances, come up there, that I have thought of this. This scenario and chart will at least keep those who work at it busy till I come, if arranged and necessary in July. But remember I will come over there only if production is definitely arranged, be it July or later. . .

[sd] MS Irani

MAY 6,[124] 1934
MEHER BABA TO HERBERT DAVY

Baba conveys to Herbert plans for the film work, and describes the film's aim, some of its content, and its significance to the world. From Kitty Davy's papers.

My dear Sudama,

The recent development in the film affairs has necessitated certain changes in my plans, due to my presence now required for proper guidance in the production of the picture. . .

I intend to bring with me about six of the chosen Mandali from here, so that they may also be helpful in some ways in the actual production in some of its Orient aspects, such as genuine Indians. Perhaps, I might bring Rustom with me. Besides, I will take Karl, yourself, Minta, and Tod with me from the West to New York . . .

I am preparing a Chart and will bring it with me.

Tell Karl that I will personally explain and dictate to him certain points for this picture. Meanwhile, just to enable Norina to sign the contract, he should write the best scenario from his own experience and ability out of the materials for five different lives I have already dictated and already in his possession. And also impress on him that this picture will surely create a great hue-and-cry in the whole world, and there will be no limit to the marvelous trick-scenes and photography and film techniques in revealing certain secrets of nature's working, never known or shown up till now on the screen, and quite a surprise for the world too! And in all these, I will personally guide him and take his help in producing this film as a marvel of art, science, religion and spirituality which will certainly revolutionize the whole world. This is his splendid chance of having his name linked with mine through this picture, which will surely earn a unique success and name, as I am personally to guide and instruct every detail of higher spiritual and subtle life according to my own personal experience of the Highest Truth and in accordance also with my own ideas to put them into material expression through the medium of the science of modern picture production, which will be a feature unique in its nature and unparalleled in the history of motion pictures.

Tell Norina to explain Pascal that this picture will not only revolutionize the world, but it will also be a fruitful source of earning money for them (i.e. producing company or group under him), because it will be appealing equally to all the classes and creeds of people—to the Scientist, the materially inclined as also to the spiritually minded—all. I will get the wonderful secrets of Creation and Evolution revealed through trick-scenes, which will impress and appeal [to] scientists all over the world: secondly, the amazing scenes of Higher Planes, Illumination and Revelation and Realization will be depicted through marvelous film techniques, according to my explanations and instructions, which will appeal to all spiritual and religious-minded people throughout the world: while the thrills and sensations that are contained in the five lives re-incarnated and full of thrills of lives of love, hate, romance, revenge, etc., which will appeal to the materially-inclined masses of the world. In short, it will have special features which will have a universal appeal for all. Besides, the picture will have the benefit of the backing of my name—as a Spiritual Teacher—which is so well-known in the East, and also has a good number of admirers in the West, so that there is not the slightest doubt as to the success this picture will have, even commercially, bringing enormous profits for its promoters. . .

[sd] MS Irani

May 25, 1934
Chanji to Herbert Davy

The following selections are taken from the unsigned typed copy of an original letter that discusses various aspects of Baba's work in which Herbert was involved at the time. Particularly noteworthy is Chanji's description of the preparation of film-related materials under way at Meherabad at that time. From Kitty Davy's papers.

My dear Herbert,

. . . Baba has just received your big packet of writings of "Philosophical Fragments"—rough copy—and other diaries too . . .

Baba is very busy with the big Chart for the Creation, Evolution, Revelation, Illumination etc. required for the film. For hours, He explains different details, and a committee of four of the mandali are busy—day and night—assimilating these details into different headings and chapters, drawing numerous figures required, with the aid of scientific books pertaining to the same, to make it all exact in all details, up-to-date and interesting. And when completed, it will be a complete scientific specimen, apart from its requirements for the film production.

The film seems still to be "a problem." Conflicting cables daily cause changes in situation, and to go or not to go is the question . . .

Something will be decided by next week, on receipt of a reply to the last long cable to Elizabeth (send on 22nd). There are probably chances of Baba coming over to the West, at least to Venice, if not to New York to explain to Karl details about the spiritual element, and ending in the picture, to enable him to complete the scenario . . .

Appendix 5. Discarded Material from *Questions and Answers* and *The Sayings*

In their original form, the two booklets published by Circle Editorial Committee in 1933, *Shri Meher Baba, the Perfect Master: Questions and Answers* and *The Sayings of Shri Meher Baba,* contained in their front and back matter items of text that could not appropriately be included in their republications in parts three and four of this book. Some of this information, however, may be of interest to close students of Meher Baba's life and literary works. Accordingly, we reproduce below discarded material that seems to possess historical or textual significance.

Item One. *Questions and Answers,* p. 2, the left-hand page facing the preface (which appears on p. 61 in this edition), provides the following quotation and linguistic footnote.

"I have come not to teach but to awaken."
SHRI MEHER BABA[1]

[1] Shri is an Indian title of respect meaning saintly or holy; Meher means merciful or compassionate—in Persian Meher means light; Baba means father or friend.

(ABOVE) Top of left-hand page facing the preface.
(BELOW) Bottom of left-hand page facing the preface.

Item Two. *Questions and Answers,* page 8 below the note (corresponding to p. 66 in this edition), provides the following errata list.

ERRATA

Page 30, third line from the bottom: *omit* ", like him, to".
" 44, fourth line from the bottom: *for* "either unaware of" *read* "unaware of either".
" 54, line two: *insert* "purpose" *after* "primary".
" 58, *reverse* paragraphs (*c*) and (*d*).

Item Three. *Questions and Answers,* page 61 (corresponding to the recto overleaf following p. 109 in this edition), gives the following bibliographic and address information.

I. A LIFE OF SHRI MEHER BABA is now in course of preparation.

II. ARTICLES AND SPEECHES ON SPIRITUAL SUBJECTS and

"THE SAYINGS" OF SHRI MEHER BABA are available for publication in periodicals.

For information or for further copies write to:—

"THE CIRCLE EDITORIAL COMMITTEE,"
50 CHARING CROSS,
LONDON, S.W.1,
ENGLAND.

or to:—

"THE CIRCLE EDITORIAL COMMITTEE,"
c/o UNWIN BROTHERS LIMITED,
PRINTERS,
10 ST. BRIDE STREET,
LONDON, E.C.4.

Item Four. *Questions and Answers,* page 63 (on an additional folio following the content in item three) reproduces the following quotation.

"I have come not to teach but to awaken."
Shri Meher Baba

Item Five. *Questions and Answers,* page 64 (the overleaf of item four), gives the following printer's notice.

PRINTED IN GREAT BRITAIN
BY UNWIN BROTHERS LIMITED
LONDON AND WOKING

Item Six. *Questions and Answers,* back cover, carries the following price information.

Price SIXPENCE

Item Seven. *The Sayings of Shri Meher Baba,* page 2 (the verso overleaf facing the table of contents, p. 119 in this edition) gives the following quotation.

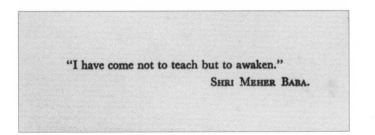

"I have come not to teach but to awaken."
Shri Meher Baba.

Item Eight. *The Sayings of Shri Meher Baba,* page 48 after the last page of the glossary (corresponding to p. 153 in this edition), gives the following bibliographic information and printer's notice.

I. A second edition of "QUESTIONS AND ANSWERS," containing further notes, and five additional Questions and Answers, is in course of preparation. The French and German editions of "QUESTIONS AND ANSWERS" incorporating these notes and additions will be published in December 1933.

II. The following are now in course of preparation:—

"A LIFE OF SHRI MEHER BABA"

and

III. "THE PHILOSOPHICAL FRAGMENTS OF SHRI MEHER BABA," by A. K. Abdulla.

Printed in Great Britain by

UNWIN BROTHERS LIMITED, LONDON AND WOKING

Appendix 6. Five Additional Questions and Answers in the French Edition

The following text has been reproduced, without any correction or emendation, from Shri Meher Baba, le Maître Parfait: Questions et Réponses *(Paris: Éditions de la Revue Mondiale, 1934), pp. 53–58. For further discussion of the peculiar history of this literary work and especially these five additional questions and answers, see the essay on "Historical and Textual Backgrounds," pp. 234–36 and 272–73.*

QUESTION **59**. — *Que doit-on entendre par Destin ou Chance?*

RÉPONSE. — On doit entendre par Destin la Loi divine qui nous guide à travers nos innombrables existences. Chaque âme doit connaître le malheur et le bonheur, le vice et la vertu, depuis le point de départ de son évolution jusqu'au but qui doit être atteint, à savoir la Réalisation de Dieu.

La chance est basée sur le Karma: cette loi des causes et des effets qui gouverne les événements de notre vie présente aussi bien que ceux de nos vies futures. Durant le déroulement de son évolution l'âme reçoit, à travers son esprit, les impressions ou sanskaras. Le processus permettant le jaillissement et, plus tard, l'élimination de ces impressions, peut être dénommé *chance*. La Destinée, ou but que les âmes doivent atteindre, est la Réalisation de Dieu. Mais actuellement la *chance* est différente pour chaque individu. Nous pouvons comparer la Destinée à un fardeau (imaginons-le pesant 700 tonnes, par exemple,) de malheur ou de bonheur, de vice ou de vertu que chaque âme devrait porter au cours de son existence. Une âme porte 700 tonnes de fer, une autre le même poids d'acier, une autre de plomb ou d'or. Le poids est toujours le même. La matière seule change. Les impressions de chacun varient et les "sanskaras" acquises façonnent la structure et les conditions de la vie future de chaque individu.

QUESTION **60.** — *Quelle différence existe-t-il entre le travail intérieur et le travail extérieur d'un Avatar?*

RÉPONSE. — Le travail que fait un Avatar pour le bien de l'Humanité, au moyen de son corps spirituel et de sa volonté divine, sur le plan spirituel et les plans subtils, soit directement, soit par l'intermédiaire de ses agents, constitue son travail intérieur. Le travail qu'il accomplit à travers son corps physique, en prenant personnellement contact avec les individus et en parcourant des pays différents, constitue son travail extérieur. Il incline l'esprit de ces êtres vers la vie spirituelle, les fait progresser vers les plans subtils et de ceux-ci vers les plans spirituels.*

(*Réf. questions* **12, 15, 24, 25, 33, 34, 35.**)

QUESTION **61.** — *Pourquoi certains Avatars étaient-ils mariés et Jésus ne l'était-il pas?*

RÉPONSE. — La façon extérieure de vivre d'un Avatar est réglée d'après les habitudes et les coutumes du moment et il adopte l'attitude le plus apte à servir de modèle à ses contemporains. Mais, en essence, tous les Avatars incarnent un même idéal de vie.

A l'époque où vivait Mahomet, les Arabes étaient très sensuels et il n'était pas considéré mal ou illégal de vivre avec plusieurs femmes. Si, comme Jésus, il ne s'était pas marié, s'il avait conseillé le célibat ou s'il avait imposé aux Arabes l'abstention absolue de tout rapport sexuel, cela eût produit de dangereuses et inévitables réactions. Peu de personnes auraient suivi son enseignement et un plus petit nombre encore se serait senti attiré

* Ce double travail peut être simultané.

par un tel idéal. Mahomet avait eu six femmes mais il n'avait avec elles aucun rapport physique; il était légal d'avoir plusieurs femmes. Aux [sic] temps de Krishna, les Hindous se combattaient entre eux. L'envie et l'avidité prédominaient; la vraie conception de la vie spirituelle et de l'Amour leur était inconnue. Krishna basa son enseignement sur des lois d'amour et sur des amusements purs et innocents. Aussi les êtres étaient-ils dirigés gaiement vers un idéal d'amour désintéressé.

Au temps de Zoroastre, les humains étaient hésitants et manquaient d'équilibre. Ils n'étaient ni complètement matérialistes, ni réellement attirés vers les lumières spirituelles. Il leur apprit à être de bons chefs de famille, à ne se marier qu'une seule fois, à s'abstenir de désirer la femme d'autrui et à adorer Dieu. Sa propre vie reposait sur ce principe: "Bonnes pensées, bonnes paroles, bonnes actions." Zoroastre était marié.

Au temps de Bouddha les êtres étaient en plein matérialisme. Afin de leur montrer que leur conception des valeurs était fausse et qu'ils étaient les victimes de la Déesse Illusion ou Maya, le Bouddha renonça à sa femme, à sa famille, aux richesses du monde pour établir son enseignement sur "samyas" [sic] ou renoncement.

Au temps de Jésus, l'arrogance, le faste, l'orgueil et la cruauté étaient les caractéristiques du peuple. On possédait toutefois une conception légale au sujet des femmes et du mariage et il n'était pas nécessaire, comme en Arabie, de donner un exemple du mariage. Jésus mena une existence faite d'humilité, de simplicité et de pauvreté, et il endura ses souffrances pour diriger les êtres vers le plus pur idéal, vers Dieu. Tous ces prophètes étaient des incarnations de Dieu; ils étaient, par conséquent, au delà de la convoitise et du désir. Ils étaient les manifestations d'un même élément divin.

QUESTION **62.** — *Pourquoi les enseignements des Avatars sont-ils différents les uns des autres?*

RÉPONSE. — Les Avatars, qui sont les manifestations d'un même élément divin, viennent au monde à des moments différents; leur enseignement doit donc s'adapter à la mentalité de leur époque. Tantôt un Avatar base son enseignement sur la recherche d'un Dieu personnel, tantôt il préconise la recherche d'un aspect impersonnel de Dieu. Tantôt il défendra de se nourrir de la viande de porc, de boire du vin, ou de manger du bœuf. C'est un peu comme si les malades se plaignaient dans un hôpital de la soif. Le docteur prescrira du thé ou du café, le matin; dans l'après-midi, de l'eau ou des boissons fraîches; le soir, du petit-lait et, avant de s'endormir, du lait chaud. Dieu, manifesté par un Avatar à différentes périodes, étanche la soif des hommes de différentes manières. Tous les êtres, que ce soit consciemment ou inconsciemment ont une même soif de Vérité.

QUESTION **63**. — *Que pense Shri Meher Baba de la vie après la mort? Quelle est son attitude à l'égard du Spiritisme?*

RÉPONSE. - La sphère semi-subtile est le chaînon qui relie le monde physique matériel au plan subtil. Pendant nos rêves habituels nous nous servons du corps subtil et, d'une façon sous-consciente, [sic] nous percevons des sensations appartenant au monde physique matériel. Dans certaines conditions, il est possible de se servir consciemment des sens physiques de telle sorte que nous prenons contact avec la sphère semi-subtile. Nous pouvons, de ce fait, entrer en communication avec les esprits des morts. Ces communications spirites n'ont rien à voir avec la vie spirituelle, ni avec l'esprit subtil, ni avec les plans spirituels. Il existe une immense différence entre la sphère subtile et la sphère semi-subtile.

Après la mort, les esprits des êtres humains (exception faite pour ceux qui ont assez progressé sur le chemin spirituel pour se trouver au delà [sic] du quatrième plan) parviennent à cette sphère semi-subtile. Selon leurs "sanskaras", ils vont soit au "Ciel", soit à l' "Enfer", et quand leur état a rejoint le point qui devait être atteint, ils peuvent revenir sur terre avec un nouveau corps (se réincarner), ou bien retourner à la sphère semi-subtile pour un certain temps. Ces esprits se trouvent, pourrait-on dire, dans l'antichambre de la sphère semi-subtile et l'on peut entrer en contact avec eux au moyen d'une communication spirite, soit qu'ils aient achevé leur période de joie ou de peine, et attendent une nouvelle naissance, soit qu'ils se trouvent sur le point d'aller au Ciel ou à l'Enfer.

La sphère semi-subtile, le Ciel et l'Enfer avec leurs expériences respectives, tout cela n'a pas de *réalité;* ce ne sont que des joies et des douleurs éprouvées par les organes subtils du corps subtil. Certaines descriptions de la vie après la mort peuvent être exactes, mais il convient de leur attribuer une importance relative.

Des personnes spirituellement évoluées peuvent, bien entendu, communiquer avec des esprits élevés, mais il est préférable de s'en abstenir. Les êtres humains ne peuvent jamais être mis en communication avec les esprits très élevés qui appartiennent aux plans subtil, mental et spirituel, car, même s'ils doivent se réincarner, ils ne séjournent pas dans l'antichambre de la sphère semi-subtile.

La vraie Spiritualité n'a rien de commun avec le Spiritisme et les communications entre les vivants et les morts.*

---

* Les plans sont décrits brièvement dans la note 3, page 21.

Les états appartenant aux rèves [sic] ainsi que le cerveau et les corps subtils sont décrits dans les questions 24, 35 et 56.

Pour ce qui concerne le Ciel et l'Enfer voir la question 54.

Sanskaras ne sont pas synonymes de péché. Voir questions 25, 58, 59.

Cette réponse a été prise aux "Fragments Philosophiques", de Shri Meher Baba.

Appendix 7.
Four Additional Sayings

As described in the essay on "Historical and Textual Backgrounds" (pp. 239–42), the Circle Editorial Committee's 1933 booklet The Sayings of Shri Meher Baba *published 136 of the 140 sayings that had already appeared in the* Meher Message *between 1929 and 1931. It is likely, nonetheless, that the Committee's source was actually a typed manuscript, "Sayings of Shri Sadguru Meher Baba," a copy of which has been located among the J. Graham Phelps Stokes papers in the Columbia University Rare Book and Manuscript Library. The* Meher Message *and the Stokes manuscript contain the same sayings (with only occasional small typographic variations) in the exact same order.*

Since the Meher Message *and the manuscript include four sayings that were omitted from the booklet, we reproduce these below. Drawing on the periodical rather than the manuscript, our sources are:* Meher Message, *vol. 1, no. 11 (November 1929), p. 1; vol. 1, no. 12 (December 1929), p. 1; vol. 2, no. 6 (June 1930), p. 1; and vol. 3, nos. 4–5–6 (April-May-June 1931), p. 1.*

Luck = Fortune = Karma = Dharma = Snarma = Sanskaras, i.e. sanskaras mean Luck = Law = Binding = Dualism = Maya = Kaya — meaning, in short, everything except Paramatman or God.

If it be true that hypocrisy is the homage that vice pays to virtue, then it may safely be said that self-interest is the homage which materiality pays to spirituality.

Those who have become one with the Eternal Light do not attach any importance to visions and consider the circles of light, which many see, with their subtle eye after closing their gross eyes and which is the sixth shadow of the Original and Real Light, as simply trivial.

When one reaches the goal of the Path, one is said to be in the state of Eternal Knowledge, Bliss and Power of the Highest. These three Knowledge, Bliss and Power are different aspects of the Highest.

Appendix 8. Extracts from "Creation and Evolution," Chapters 1 and 4

The introduction and first four chapters of How It All Happened *are based on an eighteen-page typed document in the Archives of the Avatar Meher Baba Trust that we are entitling "Creation and Evolution." Though the manuscript gives no explicit indications of authorship, biographical and archival evidence indicates that this text resulted from work that Meher Baba carried out at Meherabad between May 23 and June 1, 1934. At that time Baba was planning to visit the West in an effort to spark and instigate a film depicting his Divine Theme. "Creation and Evolution" appears to record some of what Meher Baba dictated at that time, together with information from the astronomical, geological, and evolutionary sciences that his mandali extracted from scientific reference sources.*

In the edited text of How It All Happened *presented earlier in this book, the more technical, scientific passages have been omitted. From the standpoint of early twenty-first century scientific knowledge, some of this older science seems rather commonplace, and some of it is dated. Though Meher Baba was the "author" and originator of the Divine Theme as a cosmological explanation for the origin and purpose of the universe, he clearly envisioned drawing into his film information from the science of his day. This scientific exposition and discourse in "Creation and Evolution" comes as part of this effort to integrate science with spirituality; obviously the scientific passages were not authored by Meher Baba himself. We have nonetheless thought it best to remove these portions from the edited text of* How It All Happened *so that readers would not be misled on this point.*

Yet for those who would like to see in its entirety the material that Meher Baba and his mandali compiled, we reproduce below the complete original text of those portions of "Creation and Evolution" deleted from chapters 1 and 4 of How It All Happened *earlier. We have corrected a few gross errors of spelling and grammatical agreement, and replaced underlinings with italics; otherwise the text here is identical to that of its documentary source. While the diagram on p. 356 copies the one that appears on page 4 of "Creation and Evolution," all the other figures in this appendix are copies of illustrations clipped out from some scientific reference source and collected in the old files along with this other material from Meher Baba's film work in the 1930s.*

On the Solar System

From "Creation and Evolution," Chapter 1, pp. 3–4.
This complete original text was summarized editorially in How It All Happened, *pp. 168–69.*

The Solar system includes the sun with those planets, satellites and smaller bodies which revolve around the sun.

The Stellar system includes the Solar system and of the stars and other bodies.

Our Solar system is only a small speck in the great Stellar system.

In the centre of the following diagram, a bright body represents the sun. The circles show the orbits or parts in which the planets revolve. Their sizes are various. The distance is incomprehensible. It is in fact, a small compartment in the infinite world of stars. The distance between the sun and our earth is 93 millions of miles.

There are nine principal planets, viz., Mercury, Venus, Earth, Mars, Jupiter, Saturn, Uranus, Neptune and Pluto, of which the Mercury is the nearest and Pluto the farthest from the sun. The distance from the Pluto to the sun is forty times greater than the distance from the earth to the sun.

The planets of our Solar system are more or less dark bodies, borrowing

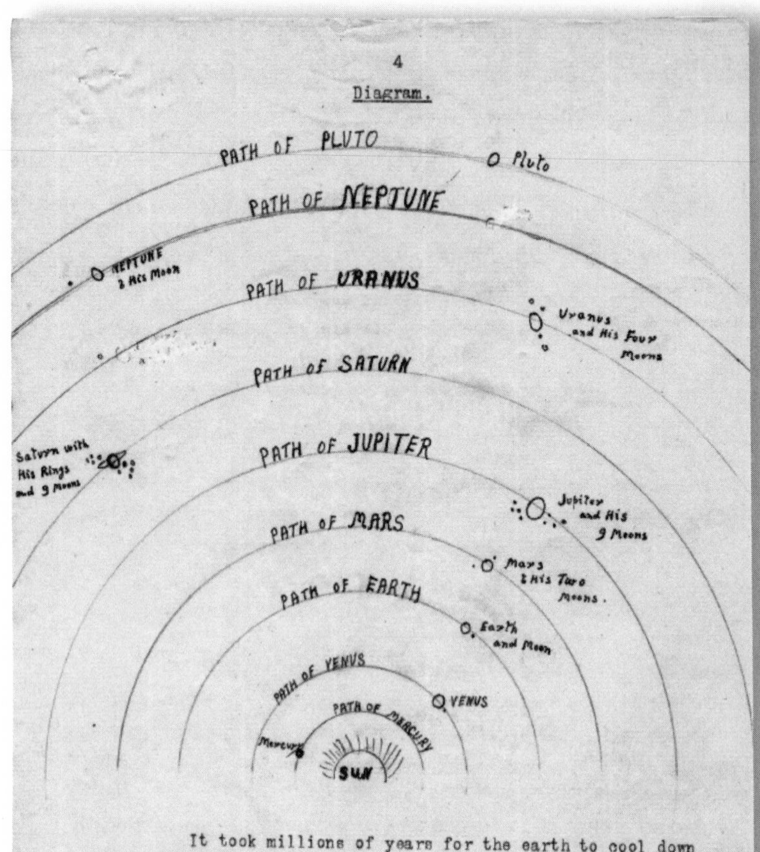

It took millions of years for the earth to cool down gradually. As the gas cooled, it shrank into a solid mass at the edge, thus forming the crust of the earth as shown in the following diagram. Below the crust, the gas began to solidify into huge mountains and rocks, rising and falling in uneven ridges, thus leaving deep gaps between them. The gas in the centre by this time remained a little hot. This little hot gas slowly turned into water which rushed towards the rocks and filled up the deep gaps made by the mountain ridges thus forming oceans. This was the most primal process which caused the oceans to come into existence.

Page 4 of "Creation and Evolution," the primary source document for the presentation of evolution in *How It All Happened.*

their light from the sun. They rotate on their own axis and revolve round the sun, and revolving around them are small bodies called Satellites which also rotate on their own axis.

Jupiter is the giant planet. Its diameter is over eleven times greater than the earth. Its volume is over a thousand times greater, but in density, it is one-fourth that of our planet. Its surface is 122 times that of the earth and the distance from the sun is 483 million miles.

The Saturn is surrounded by a series of rings. Its distance from the sun is 886 million miles, and its greatest distance from the earth is over 1000 million miles.

On the Earlier Forms of Evolution

From "Creation and Evolution," Chapter 4, pp. 9–11.
This complete text was summarized editorially in How It All Happened, *p. 175.*

Invertebrates: out of the Bhanchua evolved a single-cell organism, *Chroococcus* of Monera group (f. 229). *Amoebae* was a distinct advance in cell structure (f.230–231). After the multicellar colony of organism followed the *Acorn Worm* of the Vermalia group (f.239). The *Acorn Worm* (Balanoglossus) exhibits the first signs of *Vertebrae* in the shape of the *Notochord* which burrows its head in the seashore sand, between high and low tide-marks. It is a most primitive member of the very large class of *Vertebrate* animals.

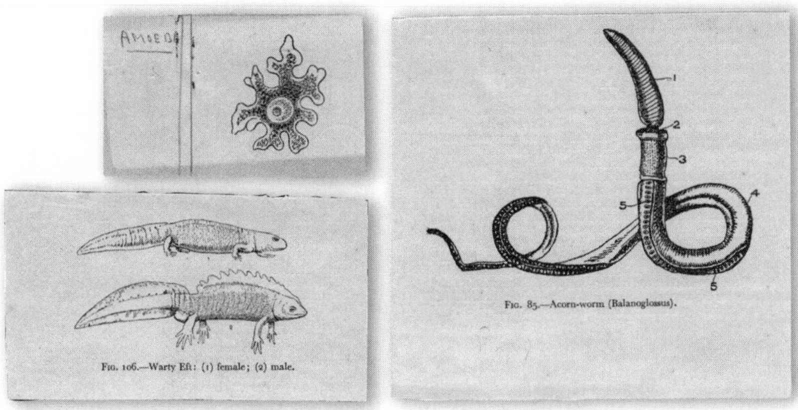

Illustrations of an amoeba *(TOP LEFT)*, two warty efts *(BOTTOM LEFT)*, and an acorn worm *(RIGHT)*.

The *Sea-squirt* or *Ascidian* is a worm that is unable to move about, and lives fixed to some spot at the bottom of the sea (f. 85).

In f. 87 it will be seen how light are the *Larvae* or *Tadpoles* of the Frog and sea-squirt. In each of these Larvae, there exists a Notochord. This is shown in figure 88 as the faint, short line running through the tail below the black nerve-chord that extends throughout the whole length of the body to terminate in front in an enlargement, that is the forerunner of the brain of the *Higher Vertebrates.*

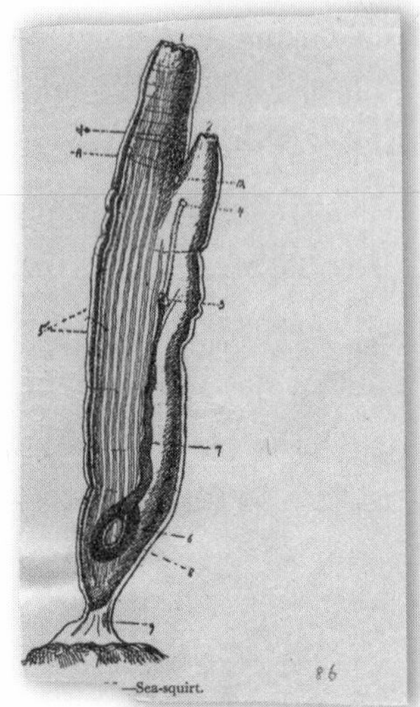

Illustration of sea-squirt

Lancelate (f. 89) is the round-mouthed that marks the division of lower from Higher Fishes. It is the surviving representative of many ancestral forms, from one or the other of which the Fish has arisen.

Vertebrates:

All land Vertebrates including Man have evolved from fish.

Before beginning the Vertebrates, we would point out that from the *Turbellin Worm* group (f. 237), there branch off two lines of worms, the present representatives of which are Snails and Flies.

Lampreys (f. 91–92) belonging to the class of *Cyclostometa* are also the *round-mouthed Fishes.* It is from the low type of fish that a head scarcely marks off from the body. There are low types of *jawless fishes* with a nose that is a mere sack. They are put in a division by themselves to mark them off from higher fishes which possess jaws.

Illustration of Lampreys

Now begin the *Pisces or true fishes.* They have evolved from the class of Lampreys. They are characterised by fins. The paired fins from which have evolved the four limbs of the terrestrial Vertebrates first derived from the splitting up of the two originally dense Lateral Flaps.

In the Pisces can be classified the shark-like primitive fish which commonly share with the Pisces the role of ancestors of all higher fishes. Pisces are divided into three main divisions, viz:

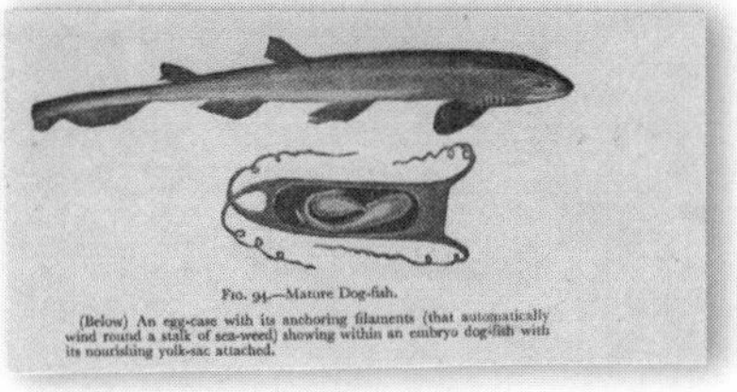

Illustration of a Dog-fish and its egg-case

Elasmobranchii, which comprises of four types of fishes, that is, Dog-fish (f. 94), Skates or Rays (f. 95), Holocephali (f. 96), and Sharks (f. 93).

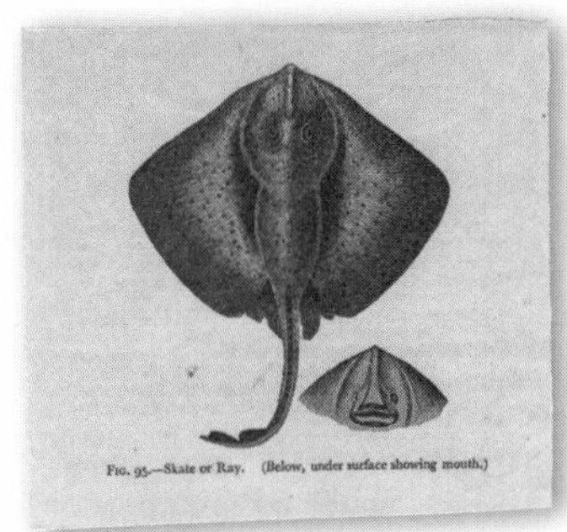

Illustration of a Skate or Ray

Teleostomi, which is sub-divided into two types that have the following fishes:

Ganoids, Taleosat, Salmon (f. 97), Pike, Herring, Solo Perch (f. 102), Sturgeons, Garpipes, Rowfins.

Dipnoid (double-breathers) is the third and most important division of what is called the Lung Fishes (f. 245), which have evolved into *Burnet Salmon* (f. 97), *Mud-fish* (f. 99), and *Lepidosiren* (f. 98). These in turn have evolved into *Bony* and *Lump-sucker* (f. 100), *Sea-horse and Pine-fish* (f. 101), *Climbing Perch of India* (f. 102), *Goggle-eyed Periophtherlmus)* (f. 103) and *Flying Fish* (f.104).

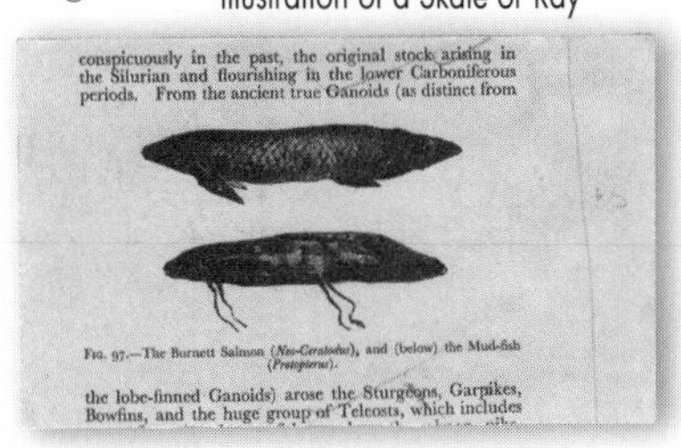

Illustration of a Burnet Salmon and Mud-fish

Blenny & Lumpsucker: Benny brings out her young, and Lumpsucker constructs a nest in which the brood are lodged.

The Climbing Perch of India wanders about on land, climbs on trees and had an accessory breathing organ.

Illustration of a Blenny *(ABOVE)* and Lumpsucker *(BELOW)*

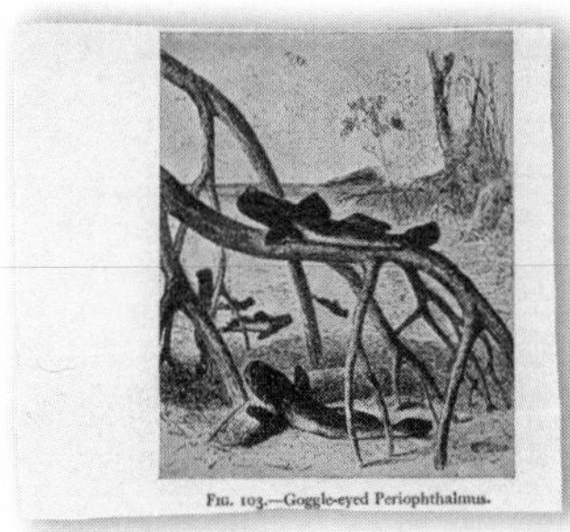

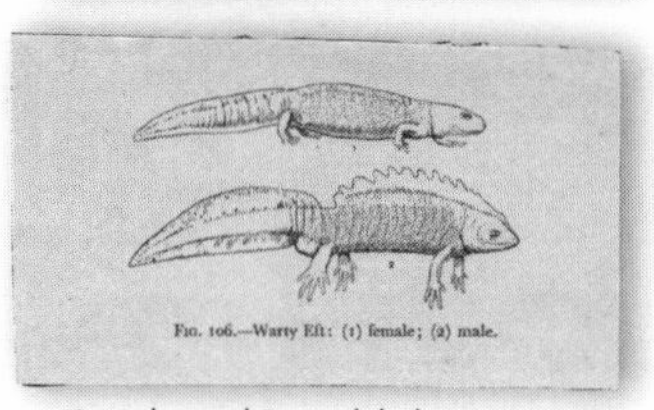

Google-eyed Periophthalmus *(ABOVE)* and Warty Efts *(BELOW)*

The Goggle-eyed Periophthalmus runs about actively over mud flats and climbs up shoots.

The Flying Fish: Its large fins sustain it when it glides through air 200 yards above water.

The Amphibians (Double-livers).

Siren or Mud-eel, Eft or Newt (f. 106) and Frog, these are the Amphibians.

Stagocephala or the roof-headed Amphibian (f. 246) is a very important form from which all the Reptiles have evolved.

On Reptiles and Mammals

From "Creation and Evolution," Chapter 4, pp. 12–13.
This complete original text was summarized editorially in How It All Happened, *p. 177.*

Sphenodon (f. 108) evolved from the pro-reptilian form which, in turn, developed from the *Stegocephala,* which is one of the landmarks in the stages of animal evolution as all the huge reptiles took their birth from this Sphenodon.

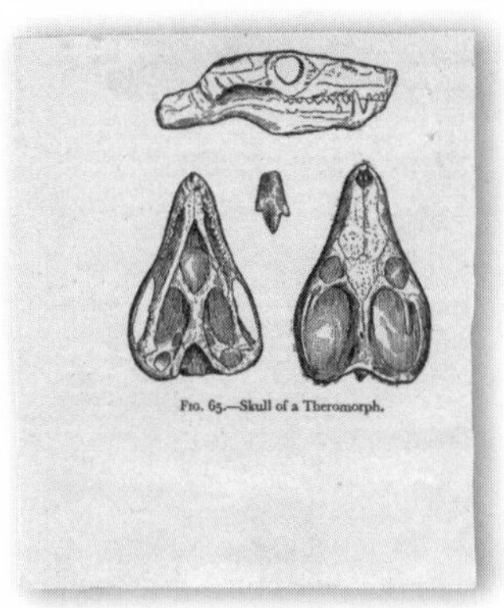

Theromorphan or Prototharia (Primitive Mammals) is the group out of which Primitive Mammals took their rise.

Reptiles.

Among the Reptiles, there are five types, viz., Ichthyasaurs or fish-shaped reptiles (f. 111–112), Dolichosaurs or long reptiles, Pleiosaurs or near reptiles, Theromorphan (origin of Mammals, f. 63–65), Theriodonts (having mammal-like teeth), Diapsid (origin of Birds) and Pterosaurs (winged reptiles).

Reptiles have scaly skins, and most

of them have very short legs. They include Crocodiles, Tortoises, Lizards and Snakes.

Mammals.

Theromorphan or Protothario (Primitive Mammals) is the group out of which Primitive Mammals took their rise.

Duckmole or Platypus (f. 119) is one of the very important of animals forming the connecting link between the lower reptiles and higher mammals.

The Platypus is a connecting link between the lower reptiles and higher mammals.

Echidna and Duckmole evolved from Theromorphan.

From the Echidna family evolved the *Porcupine* and *Ant-eaters.*

Metatheria (modified mammals) are the descendants of the Platypus, Echidna families.

Utheria (perfect mammals) have also descended from Duckmole or Echidna families.

Metatheria mammals are *Marsupials,* having pouches like Kangaroo and Wallaby (f. 120).

The Wallaby is an example of Marsupials

Another branch of the Metatheria mammals is the *Whale* (of the swine family, f. 121).

Utheria or perfect mammals developed into *Insectivora.*

The *Insectivora* group is divided into Shrew (f. 124) Common Mole and Hedge Hog (f. 124). Out of these three Insectivoras five branches have come forth which represent the following classes:

Carnivora, which finally evolved into Tiger, Cat, Dog, Wolf, etc. Some

Insectivoras took to attacking large preys and hence they are called Carnivora. Some became vegetable feeders and are called Hoofed Animals which eventually evolved into Mastodon (p. 50), Machoirodos, Mammoth (p. 50) and elephants as we see today.

FIG. 128.—Black Lemur.

An example of a Lemur

Cows, Eo-hippus, Mio-hippus, Plio-hippus are the three ancestors of the present day horse.

Some took to burrowing, and developed into *Gnawers or Rodents,*—Rabbits, Rats, Mice, Squirrel being the present evolved forms.

The *Weasel-ape* (p. 126) is another branch from Insectivora. It is the connecting link between Bats, Flying Squirrels and Lemurs. Some Insectivoras took to air, the four wings changing into limbs like those of the Bat (f. 123).

On Dinosaurs, Birds, Mammals, and Primates

From "Creation and Evolution," Chapter 4, pp. 13–15.
This complete original text was summarized editorially in How It All Happened, *p. 178.*

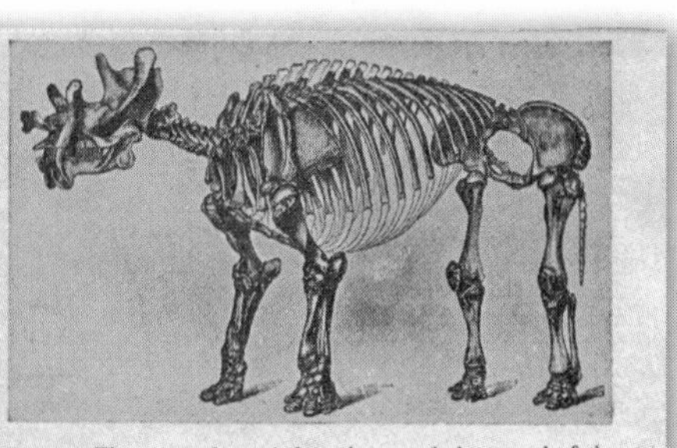
FIG. 74.—Tinoceras, a huge six-horned, two-tusked mammal of the Eocene, the last of its race.
79

An example of the Tinoceras, a six-horned, two-tusked mammal now extinct.

The Primates were the outcome of another branch of Insectivoras including monkey and Man which we shall deal with later on.

Before resuming how the Birds and other Reptiles evolved from the Original Reptiles, we shall first enumerate three forms that evolved from Utheria or perfect mammals. They are *Coryphodon, Hyracotherum* or primitive horse-like animal (f. 72) and *Tinoceras* or six-horned, two-tusked mammal now extinct (f. 74).

Huge Lizards, *Dalichosaurs* and *Plasiorsaurs* developed into Dinosaurs (f. 69).

From Dinosaurs, four branches of Reptiles grew which became extinct in the same period, viz. *Brontosaurus* (f. 66), *Megalosaurus* (f. 67), *Ceteosaurs* and *Allosaurus.*

The Ramphorhycus *(ABOVE)* evolved into Pterodactyl *(BELOW)*

From Diapsis and Pterosaurs there evolved two branches of animals, one being *Dimorphodon* (f. 68) and the other *Ramphorhycus* (f. 113), which in turn, evolved into *Pterodactyl* (f. 114) which again evolved into *Archaopteryx* or Reptilian Bird (f. 115). It is indeed the oldest named bird of the feathered tribe. It was rather smaller than a crow, and united some of the characteristics of reptiles with those of a bird. For instance, it had four developed toes, three of its fingers ended in claws and were free. It had teeth and a reptilian tail in which each Vertebrate carried a pair of quilled feathers. It was, in fact, a link in the evolutionary chain, a creature that was really reptile but was not yet bird.

Despite their many extraordinary resemblances to the birds, the Pterosaurs were true reptiles.

To continue our progress from the Primate group, we have two classes in it, the *Lemuroidea* or Lemur-like Mammals, and *Anthropoidea* or Man-like animals. The Lemur-like animals are divided into ring-tailed Lemurs (f. 127), Black Lemurs (f. 128) and Aye-Aye (f. 129).

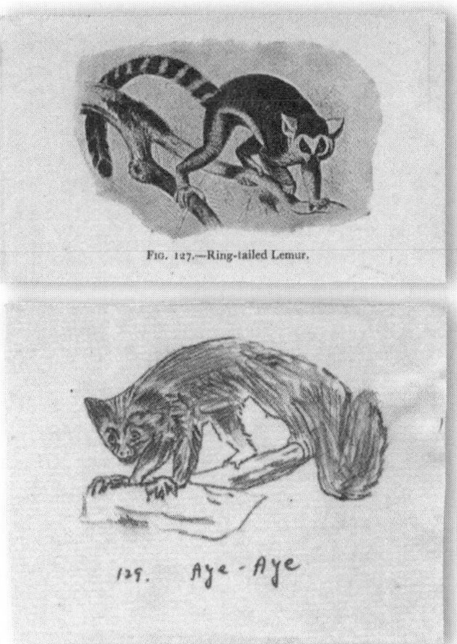

Fig. 127.—Ring-tailed Lemur.
129. Aye-Aye

The Ring-tailed Lemur *(ABOVE)* and the Aye-Aye *(BELOW)* are part of the Primate group.

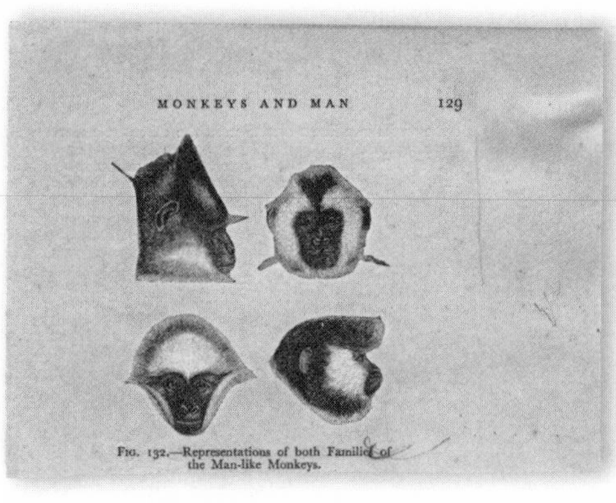

MONKEYS AND MAN 129
FIG. 132.—Representations of both Families of the Man-like Monkeys.

All the Apes and Man himself have evolved from Catarrhines.

Anthropoidea are divided into *Platyrrhines* or flat-nosed American Monkeys like Marmosets (f. 133), Ouakari (f. 134), Saki (f. 134), and *Catarrhines* or narrow-nosed Monkeys (f. 132).

All the Apes and Man himself have evolved from Catarrhines. So we have three divisions, Tail-Apes, Man-like Apes and Man.

The Tail-Apes are sub-divided into *Tcheli* (f. 137 top), *Diana* (f. 137 left) and *Entellus* (f. 137 right).

Man-like Apes are subdivided into *Gibbons* (f. 138), *Orang* (f. 142), *Chimpanzee* (f. 141) and *Gorilla* (f. 139–40).

Three Film Narratives: Introduction and Summaries

As is discussed in detail in the essay on "Historical and Textual Backgrounds" (see esp. pp. 246–63), much of Meher Baba's activity in 1934 was ostensibly aimed at the creation of films that would convey his spiritual message to the general public. At the center of Baba's effort was a film that would relate the story of creation, evolution, reincarnation, spiritual advancement, and the Realization of God. Materials that Baba prepared for this undertaking, to be entitled *How It All Happened,* have been presented in part five.

Even while he was still engaged in formulating the film's theme and dictating some of its contents, from the early months of 1934 Baba began to assemble a creative team with the talents and business connections that would make it possible to translate these ideas into an actual film. A pivotal figure in this process throughout 1934 and on into the next year was Karl Vollmoeller, Norina Matchabelli's former husband, a playwright and screen writer with a long resumé and many links to the artistic world in Europe and America. As was related earlier (see p. 257), Vollmoeller drafted his own version of *How It All Happened,* which he presented to Baba when they met in Paris at the end of June. During that meeting, however, Baba explained to him at length the elements in his cosmology comprising what we would now call the Divine Theme; and he asked him to write a new story based on these ideas. Doubtless Vollmoeller's early draft forms the basis for the 44-page booklet version of *How It All Happened* published by Circle Productions the next year. If this identification is correct, then we can infer that Baba rejected the story in this published treatment for the purposes of his film almost at the outset of this phase of his film work.

Yet in addition to this main film that was the real center of Baba's interest, during Baba's European tour in June–July 1934, and during his subsequent visit to London and American the following December and January, other film projects were being mooted as well. Two of these in particular entered into discussions Baba conducted with Vollmoeller and Gabriel Pascal in Zurich in early July 1934, and with Vollmoeller and the well known Hollywood screenwriter H. S. Kraft in Hollywood the following December.[125] The first story, *Hell—Earth—Heaven,* concerns a group of characters who share an airplane flight from California to New York and later find themselves embroiled in a romantic melodrama culminating in a murder in a fashionable Park Avenue dress store. The other film narrative, *This Man David,* tells of David Lord, a mysterious stranger who unaccountably disembarks at the Middlesville train station, gets hired as the school teacher, transforms the small North Carolina town through the influence of his gentle love and moral character, awakens the ire and jealousy of the town's elite, and in the end gets lynched from a tree on a nearby hilltop. Both stories seem to have been drafted in their first forms by Vollmoeller. The story about the plane and garment shop got dropped in the course of 1934; but *This Man David* had a long afterlife, engaging the efforts of several other screenwriters over the next few years. Eventually this project too was abandoned.

In short, for various periods of time in 1934–35, a total of three film ideas had their briefs in the docket of active projects that Baba and his film team were contemplating. Since all three were written up as scenarios, and since none of this material is now available either in the form of a film or a published narrative treatment, below we provide plot synopses along with some history and information about manuscript sources. We conclude with some reflections as to the nature and depth of Baba's connection with these three stories. In particular we ask: to what extent, if at all, can Meher Baba be regarded as their author?

VOLLMOELLER'S *HOW IT ALL HAPPENED*

Vollmoeller's published scenario could be characterized as a politically inspired artistic contribution to the anti-war movement of the early 1930s. Though we do not know with certainty when he wrote it, the fact that it contains no trace of the material that Baba prepared at Meherabad in May 1934 supports the speculation this is the same script that, according to *Lord Meher,* he wrote before meeting Baba at the end of June and gave to him in a completed draft at that time. As we will see, several of its themes and narratives recur in other scenarios that Vollmoeller composed during this phase of Baba's work.

THE BOOKLET. Copies of Karl Vollmoeller's *How It All Happened* have, to date, surfaced only in the Elizabeth C. Patterson Archives in Myrtle Beach, South Carolina. Taking the form of a 44-page saddle-stitched pamphlet, it identifies its publisher as "Circle Production" [sic] and bears a 1935 copyright. On the title page it represents itself as a "revised version" and characterizes *How It All Happened* as a "tentative title." And indeed, though this title perfectly suits Baba's own narrative and cosmological rendering of the Divine Theme, it does not connect with Vollmoeller's story in any discernible way. Nonetheless, below the title and author, we find that the scenario is

Based on the Ideas of
Shri Meher Baba.

Moreover, at three points in the booklet (pp. 38, 42, and 44) one finds the parenthetical note: *"All this can be photographed under the supervision of Shri Meher Baba or his representative."* One gathers, then, that Vollmoeller himself conceived his treatment as an expression of Meher Baba's philosophy and mission to the world.

SUMMARY OF THE STORY. The published booklet divides somewhat confusingly into two parts. The first, prefaced by a full title page (p. 1), contains what seems to be a cinematic prologue. This is followed (on p. 11) by a new title page, identical to the first; and the remaining thirty-three pages of the script, divided into twenty-seven sub-sections, narrates the principal story line.

MAIN CHARACTERS

Sir Isaac Kayser—chairman of the World Armaments Trust which controls munitions plants throughout the world (in a previous lifetime he was the King)

Victoria—his daughter, who falls in love with Allan (in a previous lifetime she was the King's daughter)

Carter—Sir Isaac's son, in love with Iris (in a previous lifetime he was the King's son and a warrior)

Tibor Clark—Sir Isaac's right-hand assistant and vice president of the Trust (in a previous lifetime he was the King's advisor)

Allan—Sir Isaac's new pilot and a follower of John King (in a previous lifetime he was Arjuna, a disciple of the Master)

John King—Sir Isaac's new young personal attendant and, at the same time, the leader of the peace movement; a spiritual Master (in a previous lifetime he was the Master, an old man)

Iris—Carter's sweetheart (in a previous lifetime she was a young woman of the court)

Jeff—Allan's friend

Dudley—general manager of the Kayser Munition Plant

PLOT SYNOPSIS

A section entitled "Suggestion for Beginning—Continuity" opens with images of a "deadly void" from which music streams and slowly a revolving orb emerges. Gradually this globe comes into focus as an image of the earth, contoured by hills and forests and plains and mountains. A city swells into view, teeming with cars, trains, people, and all the restless agitation of modern life.

At the League of Nations, delegates at a conference for disarmament dilate on the imperative to achieve peace on earth. The camera cross-cuts to scenes of military preparation and war; munitions plants continue to pour out armaments, while protesters shout, "Stop wars! Disarm!"

The camera cross-cuts between the Kayser Munitions Company of Nemuria (a fictional country), the Kayser shipyards, and an airplane where Sir Isaac Kayser and his associates speak dismissively of the disarmament movement.

Here the prologue ends, and the script inserts a new title page.

The main action begins in one of Sir Isaac's munitions factories in the town of Kayser, where workers discuss the disarmament movement, arms production, Sir Isaac, and his assistant Tibor Clark. A cold, cunning, and ruthless man, Clark enters and converses with subordinates. He instructs them to use strong-armed tactics to break up the peace movement, led by a certain John King whose whereabouts no one seems to know.

Sir Isaac's second in command and designated successor, Clark is gradually taking over leadership of the World Armament Trust and Kayser's various industries. He is in love with Kayser's daughter, Victoria, and seeks her hand in marriage.

Clark, Sir Isaac, and Victoria all meet at the airport, where Victoria complains that her father has time only for his business and never for her. At her father's request she gives his new pilot, Allan, a ride into town, during the course of which she learns that the young man, despite a distinguished military record, has become disillusioned with war.

Meanwhile, on Clark's recommendation, Sir Isaac interviews a prospective replacement for his personal attendant, who has fallen ill. Although he comes to the job as an unknown with no written references, John King, the applicant, wields an extraordinary personal magnetism, and Sir Isaac, falling under his spell, decides to hire him. Sir Isaac and Clark proceed to a meeting of the representatives of the fourteen nations comprising the World Armament Trust. As a corrective to recently declining profits, Clark urges a covert operation against an aircraft carrier in the Nemurian navy, soon to dock in the port of Skodia; such an incident will precipitate a major conflict, improving the sales of weapons. Sir Isaacs disagrees, opining that the fear of war is more profitable than war itself.

Dropped off by Victoria at an obscure, rundown building, Allan in the stairwell happens upon a young man and woman (who turn out to be Carter and Iris). Escorted by the landlady to a room upstairs, Allan meets with his friend Jeff. Collaborators in a secret "Movement" headed by John King, whom they call "the Master," the two friends discuss progress in the movement's affairs.

Back at home, Victoria converses with her brother Carter, a second lieutenant in the naval aviation corps. Impulsively Carter confesses that he has fallen in love with a girl in town (i.e. Iris). Victoria, for her part, admits that she has invited Allan (the pilot) to the dinner party that they all plan to attend that night. Summoned by their father into his study, sister and brother briefly meet John King. Victoria tells her father that Carter is in love with a mystery girl, and in retaliation Carter says that Victoria is drawn to Allan. Sir Isaac leaves disgruntled on both accounts.

Through his intelligence service Clark has learned of Carter's infatuation with Iris but doesn't know where she has absconded to. He contrives to send Clark an urgent message to meet with her, planning to follow the young man to her door. Divining Clark's intention, John King warns Carter and thwarts the scheme. Meanwhile, the police, sent to investigate King's colony nestled among the sand dunes, are surprised and won over by the philosophical quietism and friendliness of the colonists.

At the dinner party Victoria and Allan dance. Jealous, Clark comments caustically, but Carter comes to Allan's defense. Suddenly the protesting workers outside hurl bricks through the window. John King addresses them and dispels the crowd. Impressed, Sir Isaac praises King and castigates Clark, whom he holds responsible for the demonstration.

In private conversation John King enlists the help of Allan and Victoria in protecting Iris from Clark's persecution. They visit her in her flat and surreptitiously remove her to Victoria's bedroom. Clark's detectives, breaking into her old room, find that she has escaped. (Later, we learn that Iris, a former prostitute, has been accepted by John King into his colony in the dunes.)

Enraged at the failure of his scheme, Clark reports to Sir Isaac what he knows of Allan and Victoria's budding romance. Sir Isaac promptly fires the pilot and orders his daughter to break relations with him. Clark makes advances towards Victoria, who angrily rebuffs him.

Still pursuing his plan to blow up the air craft carrier Dumont, Clark sends a message ordering the commandant at Skodia harbor to lay mines. Suspicious, Sir Isaac finds the message and realizes that his son, who has returned to duty aboard the Dumont, is in peril. The old munition magnate decides to fly to Skodia himself, since only through personal intervention can he save his son and prevent the war that would follow from the bombing of the ship. Though Sir Isaac fired Allan earlier in the day, King informs him that the pilot awaits him in the airport. Sir Isaac embarks, piloted by Allan and accompanied by Victoria and King.

En route, the plane is struck by lightning and bursts into flame. While others panic, John King remains calm and miraculously steadies the plane, enabling the passengers to bail out with parachutes.

Landing together in a river, Allan and Victoria flash back to the memory of a previous lifetime in India. In that incarnation Sir Isaac was a king, Victoria his daughter, Allan her impoverished and low-class suitor, Clark the king's evil adviser, Carter the king's son and warrior, and Iris an unidentified woman. At a court ball, the king, instigated by his advisor, disapproves of Allan's presence. At that moment a foreign army invades and overwhelms the King's defenses.

Just when all seems to be lost, the Master (an old man with John King's face) enters and repels the intruders simply through the force of his personal presence. When they leave, the king asks the Master to name his reward. The Master orders him to keep his army for defense only and inaugurate no further warfare.

In a later scene, however, we learn that the king has broken this promise and dispatched his advisor (Clark) at the head of an army. "All of us will suffer for this," the Master foretells.

Returning to the present, Allan finds himself back in the river. He saves Victoria from drowning and drags her to the river bank.

Parachuting together, Sir Isaac and King have landed in a desert. Sir Isaac supposes that his daughter has died; and although King knows the truth of the matter, he allows Sir Isaac to grieve for a time, knowing that this will purge and spiritualize him. Rescued a few days later and reunited with Victoria and Allan, Sir Isaac learns of the blowing up of the carrier Dumont, where his son was stationed. When this news reaches the colony, Iris, heart-broken, casts herself into the ocean.

John King, Sir Isaac, Victoria, and Allan visit her body, which the colonists have pulled up onto the beach. In another scene with special effects Iris in her astral body witnesses a "spirit dance" performed by ethereal figures. At its conclusion King touches her physical body, which comes back to life. King proclaims that the goal of life is to unite with the one, indivisible, infinite Truth, and that he is that Truth.

King informs Iris and Sir Isaac that Carter, though injured in the explosion on the Dumont, still lives. Sir Isaac, through prompt action within the World Armaments Trust, prevents war from breaking out and thereafter retires, joining Victoria, Allan, and Carter as new residents in the colony.

Now openly revealed as a Master, John King gives Victoria and Allan a mystical experience. First their astral bodies dissociate from their physical forms. Drawn towards the Truth, they experience the final snapping of all links with body, mind, universe, and energy. Rays of light from the two lovers merge into the luminous body of the Master, whose voice speaks of the annihilation of the ego in the infinite consciousness of the Divine Beloved.

Allans' and Victoria's astral bodies reunite with their physical forms; but now they been permanently endowed with the state of Superconsciousness.

This Man David

While the question of the original conception will be discussed more fully in due course, the first draft of *This Man David* seems to have been written by Karl Vollmoeller. Later, Vollmoeller and H. S. Kraft coauthored a narrative treatment (summarized below). *Lord Meher* relates that Mercedes de Acosta wrote a synopsis and that, when he first met Baba in London in November 1936, Alexander Markey was engaged to compose a complete treatment.[126] In addition, Garrett Fort, a friend of de Acosta and a prominent Hollywood screenwriter, may have tried his hand on this story at some stage in its evolution, as we will see presently. The fact is that our current information is fragmentary; a full and coherent history of this project cannot be formulated until more evidence comes to light. But this much at least we can say: that the germ of the story first took root in Karl Vollmoeller, and that he saw Meher Baba as the source of his inspiration.

The story descends to us in the form of two manuscripts, both of them preserved in the Archives of the Avatar Meher Baba Trust in Meherabad. Some description and comparison of these is offered below.

SURVEY OF THE MANUSCRIPTS. The two versions of *This Man David* differ from each other considerably both in their story lines and in their manuscript forms.

The shorter and perhaps more carefully wrought of the two treatments takes the form of a twenty-five page printed pamphlet whose title page identifies it as "*This Man David:* Outline of an Original Screen Play, inspired by Shri Meher Baba, written by Karl Vollmoeller and H. S. Kraft." A note on the next leaf reads:

This story is based on and inspired by
the Ideas of
Shri Meher Baba.

> *The Spiritual iscidents* [sic] *of this story will be photographed according to the instructions of Shri Meher Baba, and under the personal supervision of himself or his representative.*

The document bears a 1935 copyright notice in favor of Circle Production, [sic] Inc. (For more on Circle Productions, H. S. Kraft, and other elements in the history of this period, see the essay in the supplement, pp. 255–57).

The second version is a 102-page typed script with extensive dialogue, almost in the manner of a realistic novella. The first page carries the heading "This Man David by Karl Volmueller. [sic]" The preceding title page, however, identifies the work as "An Untitled Story by Karl Volmueller, [sic] based on the ideas of Shri Meher Baba." Below that, in an unidentified hand are written the words, "Long synopsis treatment by Garrett Fort."

Now as explained in the essay on historical and textual backgrounds, Garrett Fort did not meet Meher Baba until January 1935; since Baba's second visit to Hollywood came to an end on January 7, one doubts that Fort would have been able to involve himself in the creative work that had been ongoing through much of the preceding year, even if Vollmoeller were willing to admit a newcomer so late in the process. Since Fort kept up his association with Meher Baba for several years after that, even traveling to India to participate in the life of Baba's ashram for the Westerners at Nasik in late 1936 and early 1937, this long version might have been drafted by him sometime during this period, and perhaps even in India. But then again, were it not for this handwritten note, there would be no reason to associate Fort with *This Man David* at all, and one would have assumed without question that the long treatment had been composed by Vollmoeller, probably in 1934 or in early 1935 at the latest. For that matter, it is also possible that this long treatment was actually Alexander Markey's handiwork, since, as we have seen, Baba appears to have involved him in the project in late 1936. In short, the 102-page typescript remains a puzzle. Until new evidence surfaces, we cannot be sure who wrote it or which of the two treatments, the short and the long, was composed first and served as the source for the other.

A literary comparison of the two treatments reveals, however, considerable differences between them, in content, style, and sensibility. The shorter version names its characters (David Lord, William Greer, Eva Howell, Caleb Jackson, etc.) while the longer treatment identifies them through generic titles (the Stranger, the Boy, the Girl, the Editor). While the shorter version presents its action from a limited omniscient point of view, in the longer treatment the point of view identifies for the most part with the Boy. In its general outlines the same plot informs both treatments; but they diverge on many specific points, some major, some minor. For example, in the shorter version David is lynched from a maple tree on a hill, and afterwards, the profile of his face appears in the tree's branches. In the longer version, the crowd douses the Stranger with gasoline and lights him on fire before hanging him; and though no face appears in the tree, after his death the Stranger appears to the Boy in a mystical vision that fills several pages. Overall, the shorter version is more restrained stylistically and has been sorted out into main plot and subplots in a carefully wrought narrative structure, while the longer version is more linear in its narrative, colloquial in its dialogue, and emotive and psychological in its appeal. It is hard to believe that the same author would have written both.

SUMMARY OF THE STORY. This summary is based on the shorter treatment (by Karl Vollmoeller and H. S. Kraft), since its plot has been more clearly drawn and its characters given names.

MAIN CHARACTERS

Seth Gordon—the railway official at the Middlesville station

Caleb Jackson—publisher and editor of the *Middlesville Weekly*

David Lord—a mysterious stranger who disembarks from the Southern Flyer at Middlesville and becomes the school teacher

Jeff Mathews—owner of Mathews' General Store

Rufus Manning—president and cashier of the First National Bank

Duke Walker—the village "big shot"

Goofy—the "village idiot," without a home or known parents

Luther Greer—a poor farmer in whose attic David Lord lodges

Anna Greer—Luther's wife

Grandma Greer—Luther's mother

William Greer—Luther and Anna's son, the boyfriend of Eva Howell

Eva Howell—a young woman of twenty, William Greer's girlfriend, who works at the First National Bank

PLOT SYNOPSIS

Middlesville is a small farming town in North Carolina, sixty miles from Sumpter, the "big city." It boasts a few stores, a bank, a weekly newspaper, and little else. Most of the farmers in the vicinity eke out a marginal living with liens on their property. They sell their produce to Jeff Mathews, proprietor of Mathews' General Store and the community middle man, and they take out loans from Rufus Manning, the banker. Enjoying little social or economic mobility, the people are set in their ways. Children marry the sons and daughters of neighbors and die in the town of their birth. Few come, and few go.

One afternoon in November, the Southern Flyer stops at the Middlesville train station, and, to the surprise of all, a passenger disembarks. Since outsiders rarely visit, a small crowd gathers to greet him, including Seth Gordon and Caleb Jackson. Tall, gaunt, strong, in his mid-thirties, the mysterious newcomer identifies himself as David Lord. Though he comes from no recognizable background and professes no line of business, Caleb assumes that he must be the new school teacher that they have been expecting, and he escorts him into town. By prearrangement, the new school teacher is lodged with Luther Greer and his family.

That night, in David's honor, the townsfolk throw a "social," which consists of free refreshments and a dance to a home-grown four-piece orchestra at the school house. David meets the local community, where class distinctions are impressed upon him. When farmer Greer apologizes for his own lack of "ejication" and opines that better books are needed as a cure for the widespread unrest, David replies, "It isn't through books that we learn, but through the heart."

Away in a corner, William Greer and Eva Howell converse privately, and it emerges that William has gotten Eva pregnant. Meanwhile, the destitute and outcast Goofy is peering in through the school house window. David calls to him, befriends him, and invites him inside, despite Manning's warning that the derelict does not "belong." Duke, the town braggart, takes umbrage at Goofy's presence and starts to bully him, forcing him to crawl about on his hands and knees and bark like a dog. David intervenes and stops the sadistic game: "Goofy is a man, not a freak."

When Duke asks William if he can have a dance with his girlfriend, William takes Duke aside, gives a hint about Eva's condition, and lets him know that he plans to get out of town, since she is pressuring him to marry. Later, back at the Greer residence, David hears William absconding in the old Ford and challenges him with "running away." As William drives off angrily, David realizes that there is "great work to be done" in this "slumbering town."

At school the next morning, Manning delivers a long-winded speech before David Lord, Mathews, and a classroom of bored children. When David asks why half the seats are empty, Manning, embarrassed, replies that many of the parents are delinquent on school taxes, and others can't provide proper clothes or conveyance.

After Manning and Mathews leave, a mischievous boy shoots David Lord with a pea shooter and deposits the weapon in the lap of Tommy Greer. David nonetheless identifies the true culprit but declines to punish him. The children are favorably impressed. Later that day, when he observes Goofy gazing in longingly through the window, David invites him in, to the consternation of the class. After class is dismissed and Goofy tries to express his gratitude, David tells him, "Son, in this life you are born to suffer."

"Is there another life, Mr. David?" Goofy asks.

As David answers, the classroom dissolves and a new scene fills its place. In this vision Goofy is standing beside a Mohammedan Master, and William and Eva, dressed as Hindus, appear at the door. Despite Goofy's protest that these strangers "are not like us," the Master invites them in, explaining,

> When you meet the true Guru, he will awaken your heart. He will reveal to you the secret of love and detachment. Then you will know, indeed He transcends life.[127]

As this scene from the past fades, and we see Goofy and David again, walking arm in arm along a country road.

Back at the Greer farm, Eva begs an unsympathetic Anna Greer to tell her where William has gone. David consoles her and walks her back to her cottage.

Through a cold and snowy December, David often brings food and other necessities to poor children in the district. Manning and Mathews resent these acts of charity, and an opposition party forms. One night a half-drunken Duke makes advances on Eva, who manages to escape. The next day Duke gossips about her pregnancy, and Manning, her employer, calls her into his office. Manning explains that he is obligated to fire her, but he might do otherwise if she allows him to enjoy her favors. Eva angrily leaves the bank.

Friendless and jobless, Eva wants to die. David assures her that he will find William for her.

With Christmas approaching, Mathews' General Store has been decked out with a Christmas tree and a display of toys and decorations. Goofy covets the Christmas card, selling for a nickel. That night he stealthily climbs over the transom above the back door but falls to the floor noisily. Grabbing the card, Goofy flees into the night, while Mathews pursues him with a gun, firing buckshot. Goofy seeks sanctuary in David's room, explaining that it was for him that he stole the card. When Mathews barges in, David pays him the purchase price, but Mathews remains unappeased.

The next morning's newspaper carries the story. Manning sends a telegram to the State School Board, inquiring into David's antecedents.

Duke rabble rouses, urging that the disgraced Eva be tarred and feathered and David taught a lesson. With a dozen friends he forces entry into her cottage and finds her with David and Goofy. A ruckus ensues. When Duke prepares to strike Goofy (who is gallantly defending Eva), David restrains the young bully, holding his hand. David's sudden blazing brilliance and authoritative manner amazes and awes the crowd. He chastises them as children, not men; only cowards would persecute a helpless girl. Abashed, they prepare to leave.

Just then Mathews bursts in with a telegram from the State Board with the news that no teacher has been sent to Middlesville. David replies, "I did not come here to teach but to awaken."[128] Unimpressed, Mathews warns him henceforth to keep away from the school and its children. Duke threatens David, "You better watch out the next time."

Expelled from the Greer home, David takes up residence in a side room in Eva's cottage. Goofy stays with them, providing food, which he procures through odd jobs and occasional stealing.

One day David sets out for Sumpter with the undisclosed intention of locating William. In his absence Duke encounters Goofy, forces money on him, and intimidates him into agreeing to set fire to Mathews' store.

In Sumpter David finds William, who has secured a good job in a factory. David impresses upon him that the child soon to be born is his own and he should take up his responsibilities. At first antagonistic, William softens but refuses to make any promises. While leaving, David tells him, "When my voice ceases to speak, there will be a voice in your heart that will be stronger. You will come back, William."

The next day Middlesville is up in arms over the fire. David visits Eva, who is ashen white and breathing heavily. She dies, and her astral body rises. It joins with many other fluid forms in a chaotic but mesmerizing "Spirit Dance." This abruptly ends, and we find David with Eva, hand in hand. Her eyes open, and David tells Goofy, "She lives again."

Just then there is a pounding at the door. When he opens it, David finds Duke, Manning, Mathews, and an angry mob. Duke gloats, "We've come to get you."

Goofy protests that he, not David, was the arsonist, but no one listens. Refusing to convey David to the sheriff, the posse resolves to hang him from the nearest tree. Night has fallen, and the mob, most of them drunk on corn liquor, is incensed and bloodthirsty. They bring the unresisting David Lord to the old maple tree at the crown of a hill and fling a rope over its tallest branch. At first no one answers Duke's call to string him up, but eventually someone hauls on the rope, and David's body rises above the crowd.

At that moment William arrives. From a distance William finds a blessing in David's eyes, and a halo of light surrounds him. William experiences exaltation, and for a moment touches the Infinite. But then David's eyes close, and the light is extinguished.

But just as David dies, the child of William and Eva is being born, and it opens its eyes upon the world.

If you visit Middlesville today, you will see that maple tree on the hill with William, Eva, the baby, and Goofy seated beneath it. The branches of the tree, molded by some Great Sculptor, have "shaped themselves into a profile of the face of David Lord." And on a wooden tablet in Goofy's handwriting are the words,

I Come not to Teach but to Awaken.

A POSTSCRIPT. The final narrative element in this the short treatment of *This Man David* (it does not appear in the longer, 102-page version) deserves special comment, since it relates in a striking way to a poignant episode in real-life history.

The story runs thus. When Meher Baba dropped his body at Meherazad (ten miles north of the city of Ahmednagar) on January 31, 1969, Mehera, his closest female disciple, was distraught and inconsolable.

One day, looking out her bedroom window, to her amazement Mehera found an eye-level image of Baba's face in the umar tree that stood just a few feet away. Nature had molded this likeness in the bark; the interplay of projections and shadows there portrayed Baba's forehead, nose, eyes, and moustache with a great impressionistic vividness.

Mehera recalled that several years earlier, Baba had passed by this spot, placed his hand on the bark of the tree, and said, "I like this tree very much." At the time Mehera had been surprised, since the tree did not impress her as especially unusual or beautiful. But later she drew great comfort from this memory, which she took as a sign from her Beloved and token of his continuing presence in the depths of her grief.

Over the months and years that followed, thousands of pilgrims and other visitors were told this story and saw for themselves the remarkable formation in the bark of the umar tree. Though the likeness has faded with time, it can still be seen in photographs from 1969 and the early 1970s.

Many people have been struck by the applicability of this element in the *This Man David* story to this episode at the conclusion of Meher Baba's physical lifetime. Since we possess only limited information about the genesis of the film scenario, we do not know who came up with the idea of ending the movie in this unusual way.

Hell—Earth—Heaven

This story seems to have entered for only a brief moment into the planning and working of the creative team that Baba was assembling in 1934. Karl Vollmoeller apparently brought it into his discussion with Baba and Gabriel Pascal in Zurich on July 8, 1934; but by the time of Baba's next visit to the West in December, it had gone by the wayside. Vollmoeller was its author; we have no reason to suppose that Baba personally contributed to it in any identifiable way.

THE MANUSCRIPT. The fact that a 37-page typed manuscript found its way into the Archives of the Avatar Meher Baba Trust at Meherabad in itself constitutes strong evidence that this film treatment was at some stage under consideration by Baba and his creative cohorts as a possible part of his portfolio. It has no separate title page; page one has this heading:

HELL—EARTH—HEAVEN
A film idea
by
KARL VOLLMOELLER
(Changes in story suggested by
Anne Rowe.)

The treatment takes the form of a short story narrative (told by an omniscient narrator) interspersed with patches of dialogue presented in the manner of drama. The story has been sectionalized only to the extent that extra spacings between lines serve to mark segments and breaks in the action.

SUMMARY OF THE STORY. The plot has three main sections: an opening sequence in an airplane flying from California to New York; a flashback to the world of the ancient Incas thousands of years ago; and a conclusion and denouement playing itself out in a Park Avenue store. The characters in the modern American and ancient Incan settings are the same individuals in different incarnations.

MAIN CHARACTERS

Two airplane pilots and a hostess

Controller—an airline employee, who later in the story becomes the Silent Houseman (in a previous lifetime, he was the Holy Beggar)

Janet Keating—proprietor of Jeanette Inc., a Park Avenue dress shop (in a previous lifetime, she was the old Inca)

Barry Malcolm—a young man in his late twenties, head designer in Janet Keating's shop (in a previous lifetime, he was the Incan slave and rebel)

Senator Frank La Roche—New York Senator, father of Carter, and unacknowledged business associate of Janet Keating, secretly renting an apartment upstairs from her shop (in a previous lifetime, he was an Incan priest)

Carter—the senator's son, the spiritual type (in the previous lifetime, he was a young girl)

Myrna—the beautiful but cold and cynical sister (in the previous lifetime, the weaker and selfless twin daughter of the old Inca)

Mara—the shyer, more ordinary sister with poor health (in the previous lifetime, she was the more aggressive twin daughter of the old Inca)

PLOT SYNOPSIS

Four passengers have embarked on a flight from California to New York: Janet Keating; her chief designer and employee Barry Malcolm; Senator Frank La Roche; and the Senator's idealistic son Carter. As the scene progresses we learn that the Senator maintains a covert business relation with Janet: she sends girls for his enjoyment to the flat that he secretly rents upstairs from her shop. The high-minded Carter has no idea of this, but during the flight he is startled by the familiarity between his father and the vulgar Janet. For her own part, Janet is obviously infatuated with her employee Barry, who does not reciprocate her affections and is embarrassed by her public displays.

At an airport stop the sisters Myrna and Mara enter. As the flight resumes, lightning flickers ominously, and the passengers banter about the exigency of leaping from the plane with parachutes. Frightened, the shy and self-effacing Mara seeks reassurance from the Controller, a silent character who has been compassionately observing the action. He comforts her: "There is no end. Everything is a beginning." As the others sleep, Barry tries to flirt with Myrna, who responds with indifference and sarcasm.

The weather takes a turn for the worse, and suddenly the plane is struck by lightning. As fire breaks out and the plane reels out of control, a pilot orders the passengers to bail out and trust to their parachutes. Leaping through the open plane door tests and exhibits the character of the passengers: some do so with ease, and some with great difficulty. The Controller assists them and tells them not to fear.

Barry leaps, but his parachute malfunctions and won't open. As he falls, the scene before his eyes transforms into another landscape in another continent in the hoary, distant past.

The white clouds now change into snow-covered mountains. At an old Incan temple two thousand years ago, a human sacrificial rite is in progress.

An old Inca (Janet in a previous lifetime) is dedicating his two newly born twin daughters (Myrna and Mara in their previous lives) to the sun god. A Holy Beggar (who has the face of the Controller) gives a white flower to the infant Myrna, but Mara grabs it away.

Twenty years pass, and we find that a Slave (a previous incarnation of Barry) has been offering flowers to Myrna, in that lifetime the meek and loving sister; and this elicits the jealousy of the more self-assertive Mara. Meanwhile, a rebellion has broken out, in which the Slave proves to be a ringleader. He traps the old Inca in his palace but hesitates to kill him for fear of losing Myrna's affection. At that moment loyalists break in and subdue the rebels. The Slave is taken captive.

One by one, the rebels are forced to kill themselves by jumping over a cliff. The Holy Beggar watches compassionately, while a young girl (corresponding to Carter) crouches beside him. When the Slave's (Barry's) turn comes, Myrna pleads with her father on his behalf, but Mara cruelly calls for his death. The old Inca agrees to allow the slave to die unfettered, like a soldier. The moment the Slave is released, Myrna throws herself into his arms, and they step over the precipice together. Mara is horrified and blurts out her love for the Slave. The Holy Beggar consoles her: "There is no end; everything is a beginning."

The scene now returns to the present day, and the vision ends. Barry reappears, falling through the air head first. But suddenly his parachute opens, and he is saved. Meanwhile, back on the plane, the Controller miraculously extinguishes the flames, and with his help the pilot brings the plane to a glide. Carter, who remained aboard, is confirmed in his trust in the Controller.

All the parachuting passengers land uninjured, though Myrna, semiconscious, is carried onto the railway tracks with trains approaching. Barry saves her, and they smile at each other, he with love, she with irony.

They are still smiling in the next scene, now set in Janet's shop, where

Myrna has become the lead model. Janet enters, observes them, and flies into a jealous rage. Yet despite Myrna's irony and insolence, Janet cannot fire her, since Myrna is slated to star in the fashion show the next day. Mara enters with the former Controller, who has now become the Houseman for Jeannette Inc. La Roche enters through the secret stairway from his flat upstairs and conceives a lecherous attraction for Myrna.

Back at his penthouse, the Senator and Carter converse. Carter confesses his love for Myrna, and then proceeds to explain the doctrine of reincarnation, by which the sins of one lifetime are expiated in the next.

Mara's health is failing, and the Houseman takes her home. By his advice, Mara, whose feelings for Barry are true and selfless, decides to give her love to the heartless and soulless Myrna. In the remainder of the story, whenever Mara sincerely attempts to do this, Myrna awakens to her heart's deeper, suppressed feelings; but whenever Mara relapses into discouragement and self-pity, Myrna reverts to her old state of sardonic and emotionless unconcern.

Meanwhile, in the shop, Janet tries to win over Barry, who responds with disgust. Despairing, Janet informs him that Myrna, a slut, has sold herself to the La Roche and will visit him that very night. Infuriated, Barry gets his revolver. Meanwhile, Carter, who has overheard this exchange, is stunned with disillusionment. Myrna arrives, and when Barry pleads with her, she denies loving anyone and confesses to having no soul. But as Mara prays from afar, Myrna suddenly melts, and agrees to let Barry deal with La Roche for her. She prevails upon him to leave his gun behind on a table; and after he has departed, she observes Carter as he stealthily filches it from behind a curtain.

Barry and La Roche quarrel in the Senator's secret apartment. Reverting to form, Myrna makes her appearance and seems to be acceding to the Senator's desires; but unexpectedly repenting, she spurns him. When La Roche tries to force her, Barry intervenes, and the two men fight. Suddenly someone shoots the Senator through the heart, and he dies.

That night the murder goes undiscovered, and the next morning the fashion show gets under way swingingly. Meanwhile, the police detectives are informed, and they discover Barry's revolver. Barry is summoned. Although the distraught Janet pleads on his behalf, he cannot satisfactorily account for himself, and the police arrest him. The Houseman silently observes all, assisting when he is called upon to do so.

Meanwhile, Carter has entrained for California. But upon arrival, he discovers that an innocent man has been charged with the crime. Resolving to confess and surrender to the police, Carter tries to catch a return train for New York; but he trips, falls under the wheels, and dies.

With no evidence to acquit him, the trial progresses badly for Barry. Myrna, self-centered and indifferent, holds herself aloof and will not reveal what she knows. But just as she is called to testify as the star witness, back in her apartment Mara dies, praying on Barry's behalf. On the stand Myrna has disavowed any knowledge of who fired the shot. But at that moment she happens to glance at the Houseman among the courtroom audience, and she undergoes a change of heart. Repudiating her previous testimony, she admits that she saw Carter take the revolver: he is the murderer! Amid the pandemonium, she and Barry fall into each other's arms.

Meanwhile, the Houseman murmurs the words: "There is no end. Everything is a beginning."

Baba's Connection with the Three Stories: Literary Evidence

The moment has now arrived to inquire into the nature and extent of Meher Baba's own connection with these stories. He had involved himself in the world of moving pictures in the 1930s with a view towards making films that would convey his message to the world. We know that the material he gave for use in *How It All Happened* was meant to serve this purpose. To what extent can the same be said of the scripts that we have been reviewing—Volmoeller's

How It All Happened, his *Hell—Earth—Heaven,* and the two drafts of *This Man David?* Was Meher Baba an author or coauthor to all or most or any of the narrative ideas in these scenarios? Had he really taken these narratives on as vehicles for the expression of his message through the film medium? Or was he rather cultivating new associates in the film world by accommodating their pet notions, allowing them to believe that their narrative ideas served to express his own higher spiritual vision when in fact it was not so?

We do not at present have the historical and biographical evidence to answer these questions definitively. When the relevant archival material in collections around the world has been sorted and made available—and particularly relevant here is the correspondence between Baba, Vollmoeller, Norina, and other major players in this film work—we will know far more.

Yet even now, certain inferences can be drawn. It seems obvious, for example, that Volmoeller's *How It All Happened* stands as the German playwright's own brainchild, conceived and written without significant input from Baba. One indication of this is the story's political message. It openly champions the anti-war cause that enlisted widespread support among the European intelligentsia during the early 1930's. Indeed, the spiritual Master in Vollmoeller's story, John King, functions as a political activist, heading an underground, almost clandestine, disarmament movement. Yet Baba himself never mixed spirituality with politics in this way. Indeed, during this very period several times he explicitly dissociated himself from Gandhi's campaign of civil disobedience aimed at Indian independence. Rarely in history has a political movement achieved a level of idealism matching Gandhi's; and Gandhi's program featured non-violence in a manner that one imagines Vollmoeller would have approved of. The fact that Vollmoeller so freely attributed such political agendas to Baba suggests that, when he wrote this script, he did not yet know Baba well.

While Vollmoeller's unpublished script for *Hell—Earth—Heaven* does not impinge on the political domain in the way that his *How It All Happened* does, nothing in its story seems specially to register Baba's imprint, if one allows for certain elements that appear in all of Vollmoeller's scenarios, as we will detail below. Available evidence from *Lord Meher* and other sources suggests that *Hell—Earth—Heaven,* like Vollmoeller's *How It All Happened,* never gained any real traction in the unfoldment of Baba's film work and was quickly set aside. The manuscript names Vollmoeller as its author; we have no reason to suppose that Baba ever contributed materially to its conception and composition.

This Man David is another matter, however. For as has already been chronicled, it figured in several of the writing assignments that Baba gave to screen writers, even after Vollmoeller disappeared from the scene; and it descends to us in two very different drafts, suggesting, again, a considerable investment of creative labor on the part of Baba's film team. What, then, was Baba's relationship to this story? Did he contribute to it authorially? Did he truly embrace and accept it as one of his own film projects?

As to the authorship and origin of its narrative content, much can be gleaned through a comparison of *This Man David* with the other two stories. For certain motifs recur in all three; collectively these comprise a kind of Vollmoeller narrative and thematic thumbprint.

The most obvious commonality is the presence in each story of a spiritual Master. All three main characters in this mold—David Lord in *This Man David,* John King in *How It All Happened,* and, in *Hell—Earth—Heaven,* the Controller on the transcontinental plane flight (who later becomes the Houseman in the Park Avenue garment shop)—share certain characteristics. Of course the names "David Lord" and "John King" and the title "the Controller" all suggest an allegorical significance. Nonetheless, all three men belong vocationally to the middle or lower ranks of the social hierarchy in which they operate. All three appear to us unmarried and unencumbered by family ties; and if we make exception for John King's role as the leader of the disarmament movement and founder of the colony, none of them gives any indication as to his personal background or place of origin. They are, one might say, strangers in this world—David Lord and the Controller most markedly. Although they wield an extraordinary personal charisma that enables them to transform the lives of the people they meet, they act mildly and speak softly. Indeed, the Controller very nearly maintains silence, apart from an occasional "Don't be afraid" and, as his signature line, "There is no end; everything is a beginning." Though David Lord speaks more frequently and intervenes in the action more decisively, he pursues no personal agenda and exhibits no wants except to give comfort, spread peace, and awaken higher understanding. The most active and vocal of the three, John King, despite his political mission (and in this he differs from David Lord and the Controller), is like them in devoting much of his energy to fulfilling the legitimate desires and aspirations and imparting happiness to the people around him. Finally, all three men possess, and at key moments exhibit, miraculous powers—John King and David Lord by raising the dead. Overall, through these three portraits one gleans what was probably Vollmoeller's idea of a Christ-like modern-day Perfect Master. One suspects, further, that these three characters were modeled, to one degree or another, on Meher Baba as the German playwright saw him. In other words, Vollmoeller probably undertook to serve Baba's cause by putting Baba himself into his stories.

Another Vollmoeller trademark is the introduction, towards the middle or latter part of each scenario, of a flashback scene that shows the characters of the present story in a previous lifetime. In *This Man David* the past life memory arises as merely a passing glimpse. In *How It All Happened* the flashback is more developed, although the characters in their ancient Indian setting appear in family and social roles that are almost identical to those they occupy in modern Lemuria. This flashback is introduced in the course of an airplane accident caused by an electric storm; and *Hell—Earth—Heaven* employs exactly the same narrative device. In that script, however, the flashback-reincarnation digression has been most fully elaborated; the Incan episode has a complete plot line of its own and exhibits a developed system of correspondences and oppositions relative to the main story set in the airplane and the Park Avenue shop. In all three film narratives, by expressing the idea that the action of one lifetime derives from and fulfills the action of a previous one, Vollmoeller, doubtless in the understanding that reincarnation comprised an element in Baba's cosmology, was trying to introduce a metaphysics that was utterly foreign to the Western world at that time.

Finally, in all three stories the action turns, either in its main plot or major sub-plot, around romance. And here we can see perhaps most palpably the divergence between Vollmoeller's popular Hollywood orientation and Meher Baba's higher spiritual aim. For while Vollmoeller's scenarios depict certain inner struggles, calls for sacrifice, and personal transformations, the order of love that these stories portray cannot compare with the love dramatized in the great Middle Eastern saga of Majnun and Layla, in the story Baba gave to Bhau Kalchuri for use in the play "The Glory of Love," in the secret history behind the creation of the Taj Mahal that Eruch recounted to Baba during a seclusion in Mahabaleshwar, in the poignant legendary traditions about the princess Mirabai, and in other tales of divine romance that Baba was known to have liked. In *This Man David* and *Hell—Earth—Heaven* the silent sage figures seem to have no further spiritual mission beyond facilitating the consummation of man-woman romance in marriage. While John King, by contrast, has a greater political purpose to fulfill, the story ends with his imparting what we can only suppose to be Fana Fillah and Baqa Billah—God-realization and the return to creation consciousness—upon Allan and Victoria, the main romantic couple. By the measure of Meher Baba's message as we know it from other sources, all of this seems rather callow.

These major narrative themes—the presence of a sage figure, the reincarnation episode, and the romantic saga—appear in all three stories and probably derive, as one might say, from Volmoeller's personal creative portfolio. At the same time, one must acknowledge that *This Man David* contains distinctive elements. It brings a serious focus to spiritual themes, and in its overall effect rises above the level of political ideology, on the one hand, and sentimental romance and melodrama, on the other.

An important aspect of *This Man David* is its allegory. It its broad outlines (though one cannot press the analogy down to the level of details), it follows the Gospel narrative, all the way to David's death by lynching, which mirrors and evokes Christ's crucifixion. We should recall here that twenty years earlier Vollmoeller had written a play entitled *The Miracle* in which a statue of the Virgin Mary (enacted by his wife at the time, Norina Matchabelli) miraculously comes to life. The play had been a smashing success in London and America and was performed literally thousands of times. Like *The Miracle, This Man David* seems to emerge out of a culture and world of imagery and reference that is specifically Christian (one might even speculate, Christian socialist). It would have been natural for a man like Vollmoeller to see Meher Baba through this prism and frame of reference and to assume that a story of this type suitably expressed Baba's philosophy and message. And the fact that Baba apparently had several script writers apply their talents to the story, even after Vollmoeller himself had disappeared from the scene, suggests that Baba appreciated its qualities and saw its value for purposes of his work.

At the same time, one doubts that Meher Baba himself conceived and originated the story's central idea and plot line. For the universe of sensibility that it arises out of does not appear to be his. To be sure, Meher Baba's "teaching" embraced Christianity. Yet his own "culture" and "cosmology," that is to say, what Baba expressed of himself personally over the years, was consistently cosmopolitan and universal in its framing; it almost never exhibited a sectarian slant. His world of reference took in the Sufi and Vedantic and Hindu devotional and Zoroastrian as freely and naturally as the Christian. In short, the probability is that the story line in *This Man David,* like those in *Hell—Earth—Heaven* and *How It All Happened,* originated not with Meher Baba himself but with Vollmoeller, though doubtless a Vollmoeller influenced and enthused by his meetings with the Master. As they were collaborators in a common effort, it would have been natural for Meher Baba to encourage him; perhaps Baba even contributed with ideas and suggestions as the work progressed. The matter can best be summed up through reference to the title page cited above, where *This Man David* is said to have been "inspired" by Shri Meher Baba. This probably characterizes accurately the role in the conception of all three film scenarios that Meher Baba played.

Appendix 10.
A Summary of Meher Baba's Thirteen Western Tours

The following summary, intended as a quick reference and tool of convenience, draws its information from Bhau Kalchuri's *Lord Meher* (see p. 203, footnote 1). Readers interested in Meher Baba's work with the West should be aware that, during the period of the early- to mid-1930s that is the subject of this book, in addition to Meher Baba's own Western tours, groups of his Western disciples paid visits to his ashrams in India, first in April 1933, and then again for a period of six months or so starting in December 1936. Just before traveling to the West for the first time, Baba paid two visits to Persia, one in September-October-November 1929, and the other in June–July 1931. These two Persian trips, along with his thirteen Western tours, comprise the complete tally of Meher Baba's lifetime travels outside of India.

1. August 29, 1931 through January 1, 1932: England, Turkey, America, and France. Though he had cabled advance notice to Meredith Starr in England, Meher Baba effected a stealthy exit from the Indian subcontinent, informing virtually none of his close Indian disciples. On August 29, 1931, he embarked on the S. S. Rajputana from Bombay, accompanied by Chanji, Rustom, and Agha Ali (the former Prem Ashram student). On the last leg of the trip from Egypt, Mahatma Gandhi, traveling on the same boat to the Round Table Conference in London, learned of Meher Baba's presence and met with him several times. Disembarking in Marseilles, France on September 11, Baba traveled to London and on to Devonshire, where he stayed until September 24 at the ashram that Meredith Starr had created for him at East Challacombe near the village of Combe Martin. While during his first tour Meher Baba generally avoided the press and public meetings, in Devonshire and London he met many of those who proved to be his closest English disciples. On October 3 Baba departed for Istanbul, where he stayed for eight days. Embarking from Genoa on the S. S. Roma, Baba arrived in New York on November 6 and was received there by Malcolm and Jean Schloss. He stayed for a month at a house in Harmon, thirty miles up the Hudson River from New York City, visiting the city several times as well as Boston and New Hampshire. Avoiding public appearances, Baba held many personal interviews and met for the first time many of his close American disciples. He departed aboard the S. S. Bremen on December 5; after a few days in France, he departed from Marseilles on the S. S. Narkunda on December 18, arriving in port in Bombay on January 1, 1932.

2. March 24 through July 15, 1932: England, Switzerland, America, and China. On March 20, Meher Baba gave a twenty-five minute interview to a reporter from the Associated Press; the resulting article was carried in newspapers around the world. Traveling with six disciples (six others were dispatched to meet him in China), Baba embarked from Bombay on March 24 on the Conte Rosso, which docked in Venice on April 4. During his three-week stay in London and Devonshire from April 7, Baba was courted, pursued, and hounded by press representatives, who published a torrent of articles in the English newspapers. During this tour of England and America Baba gave to the general public a total of six major messages, in addition to a number of interviews. On April 27 Baba entrained with his disciples, Eastern and Western, for a ten-day stay in Lugano, Switzerland. Boarding the S. S. Bremen from London on May 14 with five of his Indian plus three of his new Western disciples, Baba arrived in New York on May 19, where his six-day visit received extensive press coverage. Traveling by train across the continent to Los Angeles, Baba was feted for a week (from May 29) by many of the leading celebrities in the Hollywood film world. Baba promised that he would return to Los Angeles on July 13 to break his silence in the Hollywood Bowl; but subsequently he broke that engagement. Departing from Monterey on June 4, Baba spent two days in

Hawaii, a few hours in Japan, and six days, from June 22–28, in Shanghai and Nanking, where he joined up with the disciples (including Herbert Davy) waiting for him there. Traveling on through Hong Kong, Singapore, and Colombo, Baba and his mandali landed in Bombay on July 15.

3. July 18 through September 5, 1932: Santa Margherita, Assisi, Venice, and Egypt. Just three days after returning from his previous world tour, on July 18 Baba embarked from Bombay on the Kaiser-i-Hind with Kaka Baria and Chanji. Arriving at Marseilles on July 29, Baba and party proceeded directly for Santa Margherita on the Italian Riviera where a villa had been rented for him. There for two weeks with a dozen of his new Western disciples Baba stayed in an intimate, holiday atmosphere. From August 5–8 Baba traveled with four of his disciples to Assisi, where, in a cave associated with Saint Francis, he carried out important spiritual work in seclusion. On August 17 Baba and party proceeded to Venice, where they stayed for three days. Boarding the Ausonia, Baba stopped for five days in Egypt, continuing his trip on the S. S. Victoria which reached Bombay on September 5.

4. November 21, 1932 through February 2, 1933: London, Zurich, Egypt, and Ceylon. Meher Baba embarked on the Conte Verde on November 21, 1932 with his brothers Jal and Adi Jr. and disciples Vishnu and Kaka Baria. Reaching port in Venice on December 2, he proceeded directly to London, where he renewed contact with his English disciples and met many newcomers. On December 14 he entrained with a small group of disciples for three days in Zurich. Setting out from Genoa on December 17 on the Esperia with his Indian mandali as well as Quentin Tod, Baba stopped for two weeks in Egypt (December 19 through January 2). Continuing on the S. S. Baloeran, Baba and party arrived at Colombo on January 12. After eighteen days in Ceylon, Baba and Kaka continued on by boat and train, reaching Bombay on February 2.

5. June 12 through August 4, 1933: Portofino. Sailing from Bombay on June 12 on the Victoria with Chanji, Pendu, brother Adi, Kaka Baria, and Dadu Abdulla (Ramjoo's son), Baba was met in Genoa and driven to the Villa Altachiara in Portofino, overlooking the Mediterranean Sea. In this idyllic setting he stayed for a month with some twenty of his disciples, cultivating an ease of intimacy, sharing in amusement and adventure, and training them in many kinds of work (including the literary). For two days (July 6–8) Baba took his group to Rome, for sightseeing and interviews with newcomers. On July 24 he embarked with his mandali on the Victoria in Genoa, reaching Bombay on August 4.

6. September 25 through November 14, 1933: London, Avila, Madrid, and Barcelona. Meher Baba set out from Bombay on September 25 aboard the Conte Verde with Chanji, Kaka Baria, and brother Adi. During the trip he had noteworthy interviews with Sir Akbar Hyderi and his wife and several other people. Arriving in Venice on October 6, Baba and party traveled by train to London. There, from October 9–22, Baba met with numerous visitors (including first-time meetings with William Donkin and Nonny and Rano Gayley) and strengthened ties with his older Western disciples. With a small group he entrained for Spain. Underscoring the spiritual significance of Avila, he carried out spiritual work there. Continuing for short stays in Madrid and Barcelona, Baba boarded the Viceroy of India in Marseilles on November 2, reaching Bombay on the 14th.

7. June 9 through August 2, 1934. Paris, London, and Zurich. After intensive work at Meherabad in the preparation of relevant materials, on June 9 Baba sailed from Bombay on the S. S. Mongolia with Chanji, Kaka Baria, and brother Adi in a trip ostensibly dedicated to Baba's work in the arena of moving pictures. Arriving in Marseilles on June 22, Baba traveled directly to Paris. There, among others, he met with Karl Vollmoeller and discussed the film projects under consideration. Continuing to London, on June 28 Baba became president of the newly created Circle Productions, Inc., a corporation intended to fundraise and otherwise to create a business framework for film production. Over a hectic eight days Baba held many interviews, including his first-time meeting with the celebrated Hungarian film director Gabriel Pascal, whom he enlisted in his film work. With a small group Baba traveled on to Switzerland, where he stayed from July 6–16. Continuing on for four days in Marseilles, Baba embarked on the S. S. Strathnaver, anchoring in Bombay on August 2.

8. November 15, 1934 through February 16, 1935: London, New York, California, and around the world. Again in pursuit of his work in the film arena, on November 15 Baba embarked from Bombay on S. S. Tuscania with Kaka Baria, Adi Sr., Chanji, and brother Jal, arriving in Marseilles thirteen days later. After a week in London meeting mostly with old followers and disciples, on December 5 he continued on his trip aboard the S. S. Majestic for New York. Still avoiding the press and most newcomers, during his ten days in New York Baba held another work meeting with screenwriter Karl Vollmoeller and director Gabriel Pascal, before entraining for Los Angeles on December 15. Though keeping a low profile, over his three weeks in Hollywood from December 18 Baba met daily with select business men and creative talents from the film industry. For two days in late December Baba visited a small spiritual-artistic community in Oceano, half way between Los Angeles and San Francisco. Although the film projects were still under discussion, on January 7 Baba set out by train for Vancouver; and from there, on January 12, he embarked on the Empress of Canada. After stops at Honolulu, Hong Kong, Singapore, and Colombo, Baba arrived by train in Ahmednagar on February 16.

9. October 20 through November 23, 1936: Baghdad, Paris, London, Zurich. A sizable group of Baba's American and European disciples were planning for a stay in Baba's ashram in Nasik during the first half of 1937. In anticipation of their visit, late in 1936 Baba traveled to Europe to meet them. Entraining from Bombay on October 20, Baba left Karachi with Chanji and Kaka Baria four days later, traveling by plane, and stopping for three days in Baghdad; continuing by train, Baba passed through Istanbul and Paris on the way to London on November 4. Visiting for three days with his old followers there, Baba continued on through Zurich and Paris, embarking from Marseilles on the Viceroy of India on November 12. Baba reached port in Bombay eleven days later.

10. July 31 through November 20, 1937: Cannes. Baba's tenth Western tour —and the last for fifteen years—was unusual in several ways. He brought with him from India a large party of disciples, both Eastern and Western; among them for the first time were Mehera and five other Eastern women mandali, who had been living for many years in strict seclusion. This group embarked on the Strathnaver from Bombay on July 31, arriving in Marseilles on August 13. Occupying several villas, Baba with a changing assortment of Western disciples and followers stayed in Cannes from August 15 through November 2, with various side trips, including four days in Paris. Maintaining large international households, Baba engaged in a wide variety of activities. During his stay he instructed several of his Indian mandali to bring Mohammed the mast from India, an arduous assignment; and in October Baba devoted much time to his spiritual work with him. Embarking with a diminished party of Easterners and Westerners on the S. S. Circassia from Marseilles on November 3, Baba interacted with the boat's passengers more than he usually had done. The boat docked in Bombay on November 20.

11. April 18 through August 22, 1952: New York, Myrtle Beach, Prague, London, Locarno. After an absence of almost fifteen years, Baba visited the West again during what he called the "Complicated Free Life" (from March 21) followed by the "Full Free Life" (from July 10). Departing from Bombay on April 18 on a TWA flight, Baba was accompanied by six of the women mandali and (on other flights) by six of the men. From New York Baba traveled by train and car to the newly created Meher Spiritual Center in Myrtle Beach, which he reached on April 21. He stayed there for a month, renewing old contacts and meeting many of his more recent followers. Sending the men mandali ahead to Ojai, California (which was Baba's own intended destination), Baba set out from Myrtle Beach by car on May 20. On May 24 he met with a severe automobile accident on Highway 62 ten miles west of Prague, Oklahoma. Baba broke bones in his lower left leg, his left shoulder, and the septum of his nose; Mehera, traveling in the same car, fractured her skull. After ten days in a clinic in Prague, Baba returned to Myrtle Beach by ambulance and stayed more than a month at Youpon Dunes, Elizabeth Patterson's house there. On July 14 Baba traveled by car and train to New York where he resided for two weeks at a house in Scarsdale. Departing from New York on a Pan Am flight, Baba arrived in London on July 31. On August 6 he continued on to Locarno, Switzerland, and two weeks later, to Bombay, arriving on August 22.

12. July 16 through August 17, 1956: London, New York, Myrtle Beach, Los Angeles, San Francisco, Sydney. Baba flew out of Bombay on July 16 with Eruch, Nilu, Adi Sr., and Meherjee via Air India. Greeted by his followers at the Zurich airport, Baba stayed three days in London, and then four days in New York, giving numerous interviews and attending receptions in his honor. On July 24 he flew to Wilmington and from there drove to Myrtle Beach, where he met with lovers and other visitors during a week's stay at the Meher Spiritual Center. On July 30 he continued on to Washington and thence to Los Angeles, where his three-day stay included a side trip to Meher Mount at Ojai. After a four-day visit to San Francisco, on August 7 Baba flew via Pan Am to Sydney, arriving August 9. Baba's five days in Australia included a side trip to Melbourne. On August 14 he departed from Sydney, flying via Qantas Airlines, and reached Bombay (after stops in Singapore and Colombo) on August 17.

13. May 16 through June 8, 1958: Myrtle Beach, Australia. As a continuation of the darshan he had given that February at Meherabad, on May 16, accompanied by Eruch, Adi Sr., Nariman, and Donkin, Baba flew out of Bombay on a TWA flight; from New York he proceeded directly on to Wilmington and Myrtle Beach, arriving at the Meher Spiritual Center on May 17. For ten days 225 of Baba's lovers from America and Europe enjoyed his intimate sahavas there. On May 30 he continued his trip on to San Francisco, and thence via Qantas Airlines to Australia. From June 3 to 7 he gave his sahavas to his Australian lovers at the newly established Avatar's Abode. Flying again out of Sydney, Baba brought his last world tour (the fourth in which he had encircled the globe) to a conclusion when he disembarked in Bombay on June 8.

Endnotes

Part One

1. The edited newsreel retained only a small portion of this message. For further discussion, see pp. 213–14. The date of April 10, 1932 given in *Messages of Meher Baba Delivered in the East and West* (Ahmednagar, India: Adi K. Irani for the Publication Committee, Meher Baba Universal Spiritual Centre, 1945), p. 83, appears to have been erroneous; the true date was April 8.

2. In *Messages of Meher Baba Delivered in the East and West,* p. 83, the text reads "catastrophes"; and Kitty Davy offers this reading in *Love Alone Prevails: A Story of Life with Meher Baba* (North Myrtle Beach, South Carolina: Sheriar Press, 1981), p. 42. On the other hand, Charles Purdom uses the word "crises" in "More About the Perfect Master," *Everyman,* April 21, 1932, p. 402; and one finds that word in the typed manuscript that we are calling A (see p. 269). In the absence of any obvious reason to prefer one word to the other, Charles Purdom's text, since it was the earliest, published just two weeks after the message was publicly delivered by him before the Paramount News cameras, makes the strongest claim. The text has been emended accordingly.

3. On this occasion Meher Baba declined to interview press representatives. The message was distributed in the form of a leaflet that had been printed on the ship's printing press.

4. The source text in *Messages,* p. 84, reads "touches." This seems to be an obvious error, a misreading or miscopying of "teaches"—which is the word in *Meher Gazette,* vol. 2, no. 2 (May–June 1932), p. 1; in Charles Purdom's *The Perfect Master: The Early Life of Meher Baba,* second edition (North Myrtle Beach, South Carolina: Sheriar Press, 1976), p. 165; and manuscripts A and C. (C is an early typed two-page document in the archival collection of the Avatar Meher Baba Trust that contains the entire text of Meher Baba's "Message to Reporters and Press Representatives"; for further details, see p. 269). Subsequent publications like *Lord Meher* have assumed the correctness of "teaches." I have emended accordingly.

5. The word "deeply" is missing from *Messages of Meher Baba,* p. 85, line 11. This omission appears to have been a transcription or typesetting error. "Deeply" appears in *Meher Gazette,* vol. 2, no. 2 (May–June 1933), p. 2; in Charles Purdom's *The Perfect Master* (p. 166); and manuscripts A and C. I have reinserted the word accordingly.

6. "Higher" occurs in *Messages of Meher Baba* (p. 85), manuscript A, and answer no. 10 in *Questions and Answers* (see p. 75). On the other hand, *Meher Gazette,* vol. 2, no. 3 (July–August 1933), p. 7, *The Perfect Master,* p. 167, and C all substitute the word "highest." The logic of the paragraph, however, appears to progress from the "lowest" (merely intellectual) understanding, to this the "higher" understanding of permanent illumination, to the "highest" understanding when the soul merges in the Ocean. The text of *Messages of Meher Baba* has accordingly been retained.

7. Two weeks earlier, *John Bull,* a British magazine, had published an unsigned exposé, "All Britain Duped by Sham Messiah" (*John Bull,* May 7, 1932, pp. 8–9). For further discussion, see pp. 222–23.

8. At this juncture the text of *Messages of Meher Baba* is severely defective, thirty words having been dropped out, no doubt through the error of a copyist. This corrupt passage reads thus:

   > In the beginning, before evolution began, we were united with the Source of All and a consequent conscious longing to return to it through a succession of lives and forms.

   Our emendation here follows primarily the text of manuscript A, which is virtually identical (except for some punctuation and capitalization) with that in *The Perfect Master*, p. 170.

   Probably the omission in the version in *Messages of Meher Baba* can be explained by the fact that, in the complete passage, the phrase "source of all" occurs twice. The text in *Messages* leaps from the first occurrence directly to the second, deleting all the words in between.

9. Baba wound up canceling this engagement; for further details, see p. 212.

10. Though at present we have no sure evidence as to how Meher Baba delivered this message, the Kitty Davy papers at Meher Spiritual Center contains a printed version—which we are calling B (see p. 269)—that is typeset with justified type. Perhaps Meher Baba had this message printed and distributed to reporters in Hollywood, just as he did upon his arrival in New York ten days earlier.

11. The comma appears in this position in *Messages of Meher Baba;* in the republication of this article in *Meher Gazette,* vol. 2, no. 1 (April 1933), p. 2; and in A. B, however, removes the comma after "spirituality" but inserts one after "moment," to read thus: "India, in spite of its high state of spirituality at the present moment, is very caste-ridden . . ." *The Perfect Master* does likewise. Since arguments could be advanced to support either meaning, I have kept to the reading that commands the greater number of these early sources.

12. I have inserted this paragraph break, following the practice of A. None of the other sources have a paragraph break here; but it should be added that the paragraphing in this particular message varies widely between one source and another.

13. *Messages of Meher Baba,* p. 92, reads "to the last." However, *The Perfect Master* (p. 173), the *Meher Gazette,* vol. 2, no. 1 (April 1933), p. 2, A, and B all contain the phrase "to the end"; and I have emended accordingly.

14. The text of *Messages of Meher Baba,* p. 92, reads: "Not till all the six, out of the seven, principal stages on the Path, culminating into one God-conscious state, are traversed, . . ." The punctuation of this sentence has been revised for clarity. Also, the phrase "into one God-conscious state" has been emended to the more idiomatic "in the God-conscious state," a reading that appears in the *Meher Gazette,* vol. 2, no. 1 (April 1933), p. 2.

15. *Messages of Meher Baba,* p. 92, deletes the word "and": "the Perfect One, an unflinching readiness . . ." I have preferred the text of *The Perfect Master* (pp. 173–74), the *Meher Gazette,* vol. 2, no. 1 (April 1933), p. 3, A, and B, all of which reinsert the conjunction, since this enunciates a more natural relationship between the two noun phrases and makes for grammatical agreement between the subject and verb.

16. *Messages of Meher Baba,* p. 93, uses the lower case: "self." I have emended to the upper case, however, since this usage comports with the "Divine Ego" earlier in this message. Meher Baba enunciated this distinction between the finite self (or ego) and the Real Self (or God) several times over the course of these six messages delivered during his 1932 tour.

17. This final paragraph, which replicates word for word the final paragraph that Baba gave to reporters aboard the S. S. Bremen on May 19, does not occur in the text of *The Perfect Master* (p. 174). We do find it, however, in *Messages* (p. 93); in the *Meher Gazette,* vol. 2, no. 2, p. 3; as well as in A. In B, that paragraph occurs at the bottom of the page, separated from the preceding paragraph by about twelve lines of blank space.

    Probably this paragraph was added to the message because the question of miracles kept arising during Meher Baba's 1932 world tour. Baba addressed this question in his message to press representatives upon his arrival in New York; and now again, in the same words, he spoke to the same question in his message to reporters on his arrival in Los Angeles.

18. In correlating the three bodies with the three conscious states, Meher Baba is expressing an idea that, in a somewhat different form, he developed at great length during the 1920s at Meherabad, as recorded in the two diaries (the "Intelligence Notebooks") that have been published under the title *Infinite Intelligence* (North Myrtle Beach, South Carolina: Sheriar Foundation, 2005).

    The difference between that account and this one is that, in *Infinite Intelligence,* sound sleep correlates not with the mental body but with what Meher Baba calls the *fine* body and the *fine* state. "Fine" describes sanskaras in complete latency during sound sleep. Strictly speaking, the sanskaras of the mental body remain in their fine state only so long as the individual sleeps dreamlessly. When the person dreams or wakes, however, the sanskaras of the mental body become active, and the correlation between "fine" and "mental body" breaks down.

    Obviously the mental body cannot always be associated with unconsciousness, as the passage in this present message indicates. The association does obtain, however, when the mental body is in its original state of quiescence. Presumably Meher Baba was expressing this correlation (between the three bodies and the three states) in a simplified form, in view of his Western audience's unfamiliarity with this kind of Vedanta-based mystical metaphysics.

19. Manuscript A reads "fundamental themes." Unfortunately *The Perfect Master* does not include this message and so provides no guidance. Since no obvious basis for emendation presents itself, the text of *Messages* has been allowed to stand.

Part Two

20. In a note at the end of the article Purdom describes this series of articles thus: *"This article forms part of a series "A Plan of Life," which started on July 9. The succeeding articles were: "Everyone asks, Who am I?" on July 16; "What Do We Mean by God?" on July 23; "The Task of Man," on July 30; "A First Sketch Plan," on August 6; "Morals, or How to Behave," on August 13; "The Value of Ambition," on August 20; "Work, or the Economics of Living," on August 27; "Joy in Work," on September 3; "Play and Leisure," on September 10; "Society, or Relations with Others," on September 17. Copies of* EVERYMAN *containing these articles may be obtained from the Publisher (3d. each, including postage),* EVERYMAN, *67–68, Chandos Street, Strand, London. W. C. 2."*

21. *Songs of Kabir,* translated by Rabindranath Tagore (New York: Macmillan, 1915), chapter 56, pp. 101–2. Purdom has slightly edited Tagore's translation. In what appears to be an error of transcription, line 2 in the text quoted here substitutes "the single way" in place of "the simple way" in the original.

22. The full original title, with its subtitles, is: "A Talk with a Strange Messiah. What He Told James Douglas in a Kensington Bedroom. 'My Mission Will Last for 33 Years.' Three Hours' Sleep a Day. Silent Interview with an Alphabet." For a facsimile reproduction of the original, see pp. 23 and 292.

23. This date is incorrect; the article was published on April 10, 1932, the day after the interview.

24. These quotations show a clear resemblance, though they frequently differ in small points of wording, with passages from answers nos. 29, 50, 16, and 51 in *Shri Meher Baba, the Perfect Master: Questions and Answers* (see pp. 88–89, 104, 79, and 104–5). Some of this content can also be found in Meher Baba's "Message to Reporters and Press Representatives" given in New York on May 19, 1932; but the relationship with *Questions and Answers* is closer and more pervasive. The quotation that follows, however, is unlike other known messages from Meher Baba during this period; it seems to be unique to Landau's account.

25. The original article has the subtitle "A Portrait of a Happy Man, Silent Seven Years, Who is Seeking to Right the World through Love"; its reading time is said to be 9 minutes 55 seconds. (For a facsimile reprint of the original article, see pp. 290–91.)

26. Collins unwittingly purveys misinformation here: the western part of the Deccan plateau on which Poona is situated is not generally regarded as "south India"; and Meher Baba was born in 1894, not 1895.

27. Ten days later, during his week-long visit to Hollywood, Meher Baba did indeed make arrangements to break his silence over the radio at the Hollywood Bowl. Subsequently he canceled this engagement, however. For further details, see p. 212.

28. For a fuller description of the content of the conversation between Humphreys and Meher Baba, see the account in *Lord Meher* (the specific reference appears in p. 226 note 35).

Part Three

29. For discussion of this citation, see p. 267.

30. The "English writer" was probably Charles Purdom; see note 43 below. Not only nos. 27 and 49, but also nos. 6, 12(b), 13, 26(a), and 26(c) seem to have been written in America. For further details, see note 35.

31. Here and throughout, quotations from the Bible are based on the King James Version. In addition to the other verses cited, the present quotation includes a phrase from Mark xiii.24.

32. This account appears in chapter 53 of *The Little Flowers of St. Francis.*

33. Literally a "place for alighting" or an inn, in Sufi spiritual parlance this Persian-Urdu term designates a state or station on the spiritual path.

34. Much of the answer to this question consists of phrases and sentences selected and adapted from Baba's "Message to Reporters in Hollywood" which he gave on May 29, 1932. For that full message, see pp. 12–14.

35. The is the first of several question-and-answer pairs that borrow heavily, or even repeat word for word, from a neatly typed two-page manuscript found among the papers of J. G. Phelps Stokes in the Columbia University Rare Book and Manuscript Library and supplied to the current editor by David Fenster. The document in question, neatly typed and formatted, conveys the impression of a circular. It identified its place of origin in a heading —Meherashram, Harmon, N.Y., with

telephone number and mailing address supplied; a handwritten note supplies the date, February 3, 1932. Probably it was prepared by Malcolm Schloss, who at that time was residing at and managing the Meherashram along with his wife Jean (later Jean Adriel). Meher Baba's first visit to America had concluded the preceding December; during January–February his second visit was under active planning. Presumably these typed sheets were used by Malcolm—formerly the proprietor of an occult book store in Manhattan—as a way of disseminating information to interested persons among his wide circle of acquaintances.

Other questions and answers that draw heavily on this Meherashram circular are nos. 12(b), 13, 26(a), and 27. An earlier two-page circular from the Meherashram, formatted identically and dated December 11, 1931, contains the substance of question-and-answer 26 (c)—along with other matter that does not purport to represent Meher Baba's own words but conveys the views and experiences of his followers.

36. These two or three sentences appear to derive from the fifth paragraph in the "Message to Reporters and Press Representatives" that Meher Baba gave on board the S. S. Bremen upon his arrival in New York on May 19, 1932. For the full text of this message, see pp. 6–8.

37. Some of the material in Baba's answer to this question has been selected and adapted from the "Message to Reporters and Press Representatives" that he gave on May 19, 1932.

38. The answer to this question is adapted from the "Message to Reporters and Press Representatives"; see p. 7.

39. On the source for this question and answer, see note 35.

40. On the source for this question and answer, see note 35.

41. In these two answers, and particularly in the "Editor's Note" at the bottom of the page, Baba does not appear to differentiate between the Perfect Master and the Avatar. In his early Western tours Meher Baba's followers characteristically referred to him as a Perfect Master; and while in several of his public messages Baba strongly implied that he was the Avatar, he did not say this openly. (The only point in *Questions and Answers* at which this assertion is explicitly made is in answer no. 37.) The distinction between the Avatar and Perfect Master was clearly spelled out in the discourse entitled "Avatar," published in the first issue of the *Meher Baba Journal* in 1938.

42. This content appears also in Rom Landau's account of his interview with Meher Baba in 1932 (in the book he published three years later); the relevant extract is reproduced here on p. 49. In both Landau's book and in this answer no. 16, the word "centrifugal" has been used incorrectly; the right word is "centripetal."

43. Tagore's celebrated translation was published under the title *Songs of Kabir* (see endnote 21); the two quotations here are from chapters 76 and 56 on pp. 118 and 101–02. Charles Purdom quoted this same passage from pp. 101–02 of Tagore's translation in the first article about Meher Baba that he wrote in *Everyman* (September 24, 1931, pp. 272 and 274), an article which has been reproduced here on pp. 28–32. The note on p. 66 earlier says that this answer no. 19 was "suggested by an English writer"; presumably that writer was Purdom.

44. These two sentences are taken from Meher Baba's "Message to Reporters and Press Representatives" given on board the S. S. Bremen in New York on May 19, 1932, and his subsequent "Message to Reporters in Hollywood," given upon Baba's arrival in Hollywood on May 29, 1932. See pp. 8 and 14.

45. In the early years Meher Baba used "astral" as a synonym for "subtle"; for another example of this, see the "Extract from Shri Meher Baba's Message to India" in answer no. 35 below. In later years, however, Baba distinguished between the astral and the subtle, characterizing the astral as a sheath between the subtle and the gross. (Baba seems to designate this astral sheath with the term "semi-subtle" in one of the sayings on p. 140.)

    While Baba does not define the "spiritual" body alluded to in this passage, it may correspond to what he called the "Universal Body" in *The Divine Theme,* reproduced in *God Speaks.* See *God Speaks: The Theme of Creation and Its Purpose,* ed. Ivy O. Duce and Don E. Stevens, 2nd ed. (Walnut Creek, California: Sufism Reoriented, 1973), 3rd printing (1997), pp. 220–28, and especially Chart X.

46. In its original publication this phrase read: "and, like him, to drink of the well of everlasting life." The revision here incorporates the change indicated in the original "Errata" list (see p. 344).

47. On the source for this question and answer, see note 35.

48. The original text (p. 33) reads "Self-interest." Yet clearly the capitalization of "Self" is in error, since the passage is talking about the false self and not the real Self. The distinction between self and Self is consistently recognized in *Questions and Answers.* The text has been emended accordingly.

49. This answer is based on Meher Baba's "Message to the West," London, April 8, 1932 (see p. 5).

50. On the source for this question and answer, see note 35.

51. On the source for this question and answer, see note 35.

52. Much of this answer is related to the answers to questions that Baba sent to Rom Landau; see p. 49.

53. This answer is based on the final paragraph in the "Message at the Residence of Mr. Graham Phelps Stokes" that Baba delivered May 22, 1932; see pp. 10–11.

54. The first paragraph of Baba's answer is taken from the fifth paragraph of the "Message to Reporters and Press Representatives" that he gave in New York on May 19, 132; see p. 6.

55. The original text (p. 38) reads "divinity" (lower case); it has been capitalized here to bring it into conformity with the general usage in *Questions and Answers.*

56. In the original text (p. 39) "consciousness" is in the lower case; it has been capitalized here to bring it into line with the form that this question takes in its other repetitions on pp. 7 and 49 of the original text (pp. 65 and 101 here), where both times it is capital.

57. The answer that follows, down as far as the *"Extract from Shri Meher Baba's Message to India,"* is based on the "Message at the Knickerbocker Hotel" that Meher Baba gave in Hollywood on May 31, 1932; see pp. 16–17 earlier. *See also* note 18 on the relation between the three bodies and the three conscious states.

58. The source for this "extract" remains a mystery; none of Meher Baba's known messages to India contain this material.

59. The original (p. 44) reads "either aware of." The emendation here incorporates the correction in the "Errata" list; see p. 344.

60. Elsewhere (see especially answers nos. 10, 18, and 43) "illumination" designates the state of the sixth plane; but here it refers to God-realization.

61. While many of the answers in *Questions and Answers* have implied that Meher Baba was the Avatar of the Age, this is the only point where it is explicitly asserted. *See also* note 41 earlier.

62. This answer reproduces four paragraphs from Meher Baba's "Message at the Knickerbocker Hotel," given in Hollywood May 31, 1932; see pp. 15–16.

63. The original text of *Questions and Answers,* answer no. 49, p. 53, reads: "security will replace certainty " Since the sense of security is the natural consequence of certainty, the idea that security should replace certainty makes no sense, particularly in the context of this sentence which, in a series of parallel clauses, accentuates how true values will replace false ones.

As indicated in the preceding endnote, this answer is directly based on Meher Baba's "Message at the Knickerbocker Hotel" (see p. 16), which at this juncture reads: "certainty will replace fear." Since this reading is manifestly superior, we have substituted it in place of the obviously erroneous phrase in the original answer no. 49.

64. The original (p. 54) reads "subsidiary to the primary, will . . ." The emendation incorporates the correction in the "Errata" list; see p. 344.

65. This answer is based on Meher Baba's "Message to Reporters and Press Representatives" on May 19, 1932. See p. 8.

66. Some of the phraseology in this answer appears to borrow from Baba's "Message to the West," delivered in London on April 8, 1932, and his "Message to Reporters and Press Representatives" given on the S. S. Bremen on May 19, 1932.

67. This answer uses material from Meher Baba's "Message at the Residence of Mr. Graham Phelps Stokes," New York, May 22, 1932. See p. 10.

68. In the original published text, these two paragraphs in (c) and (d) are presented in the opposite order. The "Errata" (see p. 344) call for their reversal; and I have emended accordingly.

69. Both the published text of the English translation in the *Meher Baba Journal,* vol. 2, no. 6 (April 1940), p. 353, and the unpublished typed manuscript in the Kitty Davy papers at the Meher Spiritual Center—which we are calling "D"—use this English word "Chance" to translate the French word "Chance" in *Shri Meher Baba, Le Maître Parfait: Questions et Réponses,* p. 53, reprinted in this appendix 6 on p. 347. (For convenience, all further citations to the French text will refer to appendix 6 of this book and not to the original 1934 publication.)

The problem here, as Françoise and Daniel Lemetais point out, is that the French word *Chance* is more accurately translated into English as "luck"; the English word "chance" would be better rendered into French as "hasard."

Since Herbert Davy's English draft (which must have served as the source for the French translation) has been lost, we cannot be completely sure whether "Chance" or "Luck" was the term employed in the original question and answer, as given to Baba and responded to by him.

In our opinion, it is more likely that the original question used the phrase "Destiny and Chance" than "Destiny and Luck." "Luck" might be conceived as chance seen through the lens of human subjectivity. "Luck" implies the alternatives of "good luck" and "bad luck," as determined by relation to human desire. "Chance" does not carry this connotation; and thus the dichotomy "Destiny and Chance" articulates a single philosophical opposition cleanly and clearly, as the phrase "Destiny and Luck" would not.

Accordingly, the word "Chance" has been retained from the translation in the *Meher Baba Journal.*

On the other hand, the *Awakener* records an answer given by Meher Baba on May 4, 1937 to the question, "What is destiny, luck, fate, etc.?" See *Awakener,* vol. 12, no. 2 (1964), pp. 22–23. The *Awakener* earlier published this same answer, without the accompanying information about context, in vol. 2, no. 1 (Summer 1954), p. 12.

70. In the text of the *Meher Baba Journal,* the words *"Karma," "Sanskaras,"* and *"Avatar"* have all been italicized. To bring usage into conformity with the main text of *Shri Meher Baba, the Perfect Master: Questions and Answers* (1933), we have changed all three into roman type; and "sanskaras" has been reduced to lower case.

71. See note 70.

72. We have retained this word from the English translation in the *Meher Baba Journal* (p. 353), despite the fact that the word in the French source, "actuellement," translates into English as "presently." Yet "actually" is clearly the correct meaning for this sentence; and we feel that this must have been the word used in Herbert Davy's original English draft. The fact that the French translation uses "actuellement" suggests that the French translator got taken in by a linguistic "false friend."

73. In question and answer 60 the text here departs from the text of the *Meher Baba Journal* (p. 354) in two significant ways.

First, the *Journal* translation uses the expression "exterior and interior work." This odd locution may represent an unduly slavish translation of the French (see p. 348), which reads "le travail intérieur et le travail extérieur." "Outer" and "inner work" are more idiomatic expressions in English, and we have substituted them in place of the awkward language of the *Journal.* Also, in the question, we have followed the order of the French by translating "inner and outer work," rather than "exterior and interior work" as in the *Journal,* since the answer that follows takes up the inner work first and then proceeds to the outer.

Second, the *Journal* translation breaks the last two sentences in a way that deviates from the French source and distorts its meaning. The *Journal* text reads as follows.

> The exterior work is accomplished through his physical body by personal contact with individuals. By passing through different countries, he turns their minds towards spirituality, he enhances their progression towards their [sic] subtle planes and from these towards the spiritual planes.

We have re-translated this passage so as to reincorporate the idea of the Avatar's passage through different countries back into the first sentence, as in the French source (for which, see p. 348).

74. The French text (see p. 348) spells the name of the Arabian prophet as "Mahomet"; the *Meher Baba Journal* uses the form "Mohomed." We have emended to "Mohammed," the form of the name used elsewhere in this book.

75. The French text here (see p. 349) indicates that Mohammed had six wives, and manuscript D says the same. But the *Meher Baba Journal,* p. 354, has changed the number to nine; and we have retained this reading. This is a rare example of a substantive difference between the *Journal* articles and D. Perhaps the editors of the *Journal,* in reviewing the manuscript or some copy thereof, corrected a number which they perceived as erroneous. (According to current opinion, Mohammad had either eleven or thirteen wives. But nine wives survived him. Perhaps this fact is what the text of the *Journal* refers to.)

76. The *Meher Baba Journal* reading, "were predominate" (p. 354), is ungrammatical, since "predominate" is a verb, not a predicate adjective. In the French (see p. 349), which reads "L'envie et l'avidité prédominaient," "prédominaient" is a verb. We have revised the translation accordingly.

77. Though this word does not appear in the *Meher Baba Journal*, we have inserted it in translation of the French word "Aussi" (see p. 349).

78. The translation in the *Meher Baba Journal* here uses the rather arcane English noun "renouncement" as a translation of the French "renoncement" (see p.349). We have retranslated the French, preferring "renunciation" as the far more idiomatic expression.

79. The article in the *Meher Baba Journal* here reads "humanity" (p. 355). In D, however, the corresponding word is "humility," which translates "humilité" in the French source (see p. 349).

Since D or some copy thereof probably served as the direct source for the *Journal* article, we think that "humanity" was an error of miscopying. We have corrected the *Journal* translation accordingly.

80. *The Meher Baba Journal* uses the plural "temptations" where D employs the singular form. We have selected the singular as more idiomatic in English.

81. The English text of these two questions comprising question 63 reproduces the text of D, which in turn closely translates the French (p. 350). In the *Meher Baba Journal*, vol. 2, no. 7, p. 415, on the other hand, the second part of the question—"What is his attitude regarding spiritualism?—has been deleted. Perhaps this omission was accidental; or perhaps the editors of the *Journal* did not want to highlight the theme of spiritualism. In any case, we have restored the second half of the question, since it accounts for part of Meher Baba's answer, and since it appears in the French source.

82. We retain this word from the text of the *Meher Baba Journal* (p. 416), even though the French word, "spirite," means "spiritualist." Yet clearly the text means to refer to communication with the spirits of dead persons; and so the English phrase "spirit communication" is best.

83. Following the French text (p. 351) as well as D, we have inserted a paragraph break here, even though the text in the *Meher Baba Journal* lacks it.

84. Once again, following the French text (p. 351) as well as D, we have inserted a paragraph break here, even though the text in the *Meher Baba Journal* lacks it.

85. This one-sentence final paragraph, which we translate directly from the French, is absent from both the *Meher Baba Journal* article and from D.

Both D and the French text (p. 351) contain the footnote; the version that we present here is a translation from the French. The French text refers to "Fragments Philosophiques," that is, "Philosophical Fragments" (called "Theosophical Fragments" in D). As noted elsewhere (see pp. 242–43), Herbert Davy appears to have used this as a designation for Ramjoo Abdulla's *Philosophy and Teachings* and for his own forthcoming edition of this same material. As the footnote suggests, much of the content of answer 63 does indeed appear in pp. 23–25 of Ramjoo's book.

Naturally the cross reference in the first line of the note has been updated to reflect the pagination of this present edition.

Part Four

86. In the 1920s, as represented (for example) in *Infinite Intelligence,* Meher Baba subdivided the world of God's creation into two spheres: the gross, which is the physical sphere that most people consciously inhabit and experience; and the subtle, which spans the six planes of the inner world. In later years, however, Meher Baba used the term "subtle sphere" to designate only the first four planes of the spiritual realm, and "mental sphere" to designate the fifth and sixth planes.

    The phraseology here seems to presuppose the earlier model, according to which there are two modes of consciousness, the gross and subtle, prior to the attainment of Superconsciousness. Curiously enough, the glossary at the end of *Sayings* defines three spheres—the gross, subtle, and "mind." Evidently an inconsistency regarding the number of bodies and spheres still persisted among Meher Baba's disciples at this time.

87. Baba's "Book" was actually written in 1925–26; Baba ceased writing with his own hand, except for the occasional signing of his signature, on January 2, 1927. As far as we know, "The Book" still remains lost. Baba gave only a few rare indications of its contents.

88. An annual holiday honoring the prophet Zoroaster. "Diso" means "day," and "Jarthoshtno" is a form of the name of Zoroaster.

89. As explained in the essay on "Historical and Textual Backgrounds" (pp. 239–40 and 273), all of the sayings in the 1933 Circle Editorial Committee booklet are also found in the *Meher Message* as well as in a manuscript entitled "Sayings of Shri Sadguru Meher Baba" among the Graham Phelps Stokes papers in the Columbia University Rare Book and Manuscript Library. In the case of this particular saying, in both the *Meher Message* and the Stokes Collection the first "self" is lower case: "to realize one's own self as the Universal Self." See *Meher Message,* vol. 1, no. 1 (January 1929), p. 1.

    Evidently the editors of *The Sayings* felt that the first "self" ought to be upper case, since the Self one realizes is not the false self (or ego) but the Real Self. Although this usage does not comport with what one ordinarily finds in phrases of this kind in the Meher Baba literature, the text of *The Sayings* has been reproduced here unemended, since it was the product of a deliberate and conscious editorial decision.

90. On the changing use of "astral" in Meher Baba's writings, see *Questions and Answers,* answer no. 24 and associated endnote no. 45.

91. The word that the footnote spells "Mun" is more commonly transliterated "man."

    That same note gives the word "anddhai" as a gloss for "intellect." Yet we can find no such word in Sanskrit, Hindi, or Marathi. Possibly the editor who wrote this footnote misspelled the Marathi word *andhar,* Hindi *andhakar,* darkness, which in *Infinite Intelligence* Baba had given as the opposite to *Prakash,* Light, which is another name for Intelligence. (See *Infinite Intelligence,* p. 71.)

    The best Indic word for "intellect" is *buddhi;* in Arabic and Persian, *aql* is the closest equivalent. Other words in the same general semantic domain are *pratibha, pragya,* and *dnyan.* In any event, "anddhai" appears to be the garbled form of some other word.

92. In the original booklet this phrase is spelled "tapa-yapa"; *Meher Message,* vol. 1, no. 11 (November 1929), p. 1, and the manuscript in the Stokes Collection give the same spelling. I have emended nonetheless, since the spelling *japa* is the more conventional and phonetically accurate.

93. The first three paragraphs in this note are based on answer no. 35 in *Questions and Answers*, p. 96, which in turn draws from the "Message at the Knickerbocker Hotel" that Meher Baba gave in Hollywood on May 31, 1932.

94. The footnote at the bottom of the page distinguishes between two kinds of miracles, *karamats* and *mojezas*. The glossary to the second edition of *God Speaks* defines a *karamat* as "a miracle performed by those on the fifth and sixth planes" (p. 289) and a *mojeza* as "A miracle performed by the *Avatar* or a *Qutub*" (p. 292). In light of how yogis and their powers are being discussed in this present series of sayings, however, it seems more likely that *karamat* is being used here to designate a miracle performed by a yogi of the fourth plane.

95. On this characterization of the universe as comprised of the gross and subtle, see endnote 86.

96. The content of this note exhibits a clear relationship to certain passages and sentences in Ramjoo Abdulla's *Shri Meher Baba: His Philosophy and Teaching*, pp. 1–7. Ramjoo's exposition, in turn, draws on an article entitled "What Is God?" in the *Meher Message*, vol. 1, no. 2 (February 1929), pp. 2–7. We do not have unequivocal evidence on what specific source Herbert Davy drew on in compiling this note—since these two published sources may or may not have been available to him when he was compiling *The Sayings of Shri Meher Baba;* but we do know that some certain body of literary-philosophical material was circulating among the English members of the Circle Editorial Committee at this time.

97. See endnote 91.

PART FIVE

98. "Nebula" is a general term for clouds of gas in interstellar space or for other galaxies outside the Milky Way. Baba intends to use this word in his own sense, to designate an infinitely fine, imperceptible gas prior to the origins of the gross sphere as we know it. His usage should not be confused with observable astronomical phenomena.

99. Though the word appears in the spelling "Bhan-Chava" at this point in the manuscript, we've chosen to follow the spelling in chapter 4, where the topic is explored more fully. In either form the word is something of a puzzle, eluding discovery in the Hindi, Urdu, Gujarati, and Sanskrit dictionaries that we have consulted. If we break the compound into its parts, the first element is probably *bhaan,* appearance, consciousness, while the second element, *chua,* may derive from the verb *choona,* to touch. By this explanation the compound would mean something like "touching consciousness," a sense suiting Baba's usage in this context.

100. This enormous chart, depicting the Divine Theme (that is, creation, evolution, reincarnation, and spiritual advancement to God-realization) was prepared at this time by Baba's mandali. It is reproduced on p. 194 and as an insert inside the back cover.

101. This language seems to imply that the subtle body perishes at death and that a new subtle body is created at the time of rebirth—an implication at odds with what Meher Baba has said elsewhere. This same issue arises in *Infinite Intelligence.* A footnote on p. 164 of that book provides an explanation that is applicable here: "In *God Speaks* and *Discourses,* Meher Baba clarifies that the soul does not actually drop the subtle body in the same way that it drops a physical body at the time of death.

The references in this present text to dissociation from and identification with subtle bodies refer to the shape or mold which the subtle body assumes for a given incarnation. In other words, this present text suggests that the sanskaras assume a certain shape or mold or pattern for the duration of an incarnation, and this pattern of sanskaras constitutes the subtle body. But after the physical body drops, the sanskaric pattern changes, and the subtle body changes accordingly. In this sense the subtle body assumes new forms, even though, really speaking, the subtle body never actually 'drops' in the way that the gross body does until the time of God-realization."

102. Though Meher Baba consistently subdivided evolution into seven stages, the seven identified here are not the same as he has specified elsewhere. In the Film Master Chart (p. 194), the seven named stages are stones, metals, vegetables, fish, reptiles, mammals, and humans. In part 3 of *God Speaks,* Baba characterized the "kingdoms" of evolution as consisting of stone and metals, vegetables, worms, fish, birds, animals, and humans. Quite frequently, however, Baba broke evolution into three major phases, the mineral, the vegetative, and the animal—as he has done in this text.

103. This section invites comparison with Meher Baba's handwritten text *In God's Hand: Explanations of Spirituality in Meher Baba's Own Hand* (East Windsor, New Jersey: Beloved Archives, 2000); see esp. Baba's page 18. That hierarchy of lights, however, which is ranged (in descending order) from Natural Light to Natural Darkness to unnatural darkness to unnatural light, differs from the hierarchy here, which descends from Infinite Light to Infinite Darkness to false light to false darkness.

104. "Space" and "Energy" are clearly English-language translations for the Indic words *Pran* and *Akash.* The interaction of *Pran* and *Akash,* an ancient theme in Indian cosmological texts, comes in for extensive discussion in *Infinite Intelligence* (see pp. 95–99 and elsewhere). Some of the content here is conveyed in the chapter "How It All Happened" (pp. 53–75) in Ramjoo Abdulla's *Shri Meher Baba: His Philosophy and Teachings;* see particularly pp. 60–62.

105. In the Indian numeric system a crore is ten million.

106. The original text reads: "So, we have the effect of the radiation of the earth in order of the crust, then the rocks and then the oceans." It is hard to make sense of the word "radiation" here; so I have emended it to "formation."

107. Literally *leel* (in Hindi and other Indic languages) means "blue." It is used as a general term for algae and other kinds of scum-like growth in the ocean. Perhaps Baba intended to refer to cyanobacteria, popularly known as blue-green algae.

108. *Infinite Intelligence* discusses chaitanya extensively in its connection with life and evolution; see, for example, pp. 22–41.

109. An ancient form of lizard extending back to the Mesozoic era, the sphenedon survives today only as the tuatara. An illustration of the sphenedon appears as figure 108 in the source book in use among Baba's mandali as he was preparing this material in 1934, reproduced here on p. 198.

110. The text below follows (with a few small corrections) Filis Frederick's version, "'A Touch of Maya': A Scenario by Meher Baba," *Awakener,* vol. 22, no. 1 (1986), pp. 1–4. For a review of the original source documents, see pp. 250–54 and 274–75.

111. Filis Frederick's text in the *Awakener* appears to have omitted a sentence of description that appears in the source manuscript. Her

text reads: "He sees other innumerable subtle bodies of other souls and also holds direct communication with the mental-bodied souls." Probably this deletion was unintentional. In any event, the omitted material has been reinstated in our text here.

112. The original text that Baba dictated to Margaret Mayo in 1931 here reads: "Insert sayings of Shri Meher Baba—see typed copy." This doubtless refers to a copy of the typed manuscript that is discussed in detail on pp. 239–40 and that served as the basis for the booklet *The Sayings of Shri Meher Baba* republished in this book.

113. See note 104.

114. The term "sub-Superconsciousness," as a designation for the states of spiritual advancement before Realization of God, appears in *Infinite Intelligence;* see pp. 402–04 and elsewhere.

Appendix 3

115. This number is erroneous: the original edition of *Questions and Answers* had fifty-eight questions and their responses from Baba; the second edition, ready for publication by the following December, had five more.

Appendix 4

116. A copy of this document in the collection of David Fenster inserts the following handwritten note: "Romanian, Russian, Spanish —(for 12 countries)."

117. David Fenster's copy has the following handwritten note at the bottom of the page: "Purdom has consented to write 'the Life.'"

118. It is not clear what piece of writing this "Life" of Meher Baba alludes to. As Herbert Davy notes in his letter of September 3, a "Biography" was already completed and available to him at that time; it could not refer, therefore, to Charles Purdom's undertaking that resulted in the publication of *The Perfect Master* four years later. During the mid-1930s the *Meher Gazette* published a biography serially. Though the magazine did not identify an author, conceivably it was written by Chanji, who indeed published a biography of Meher Baba in Gujarati in 1943.

119 Perhaps Stokes is alluding to the statement in answer no. 37 that, although Meher Baba appears not to keep "his promises about the dates of his speaking and healing, etc., in reality it is not so." Over the previous year newspapers had published predictions and promises about healing that were attributed to Baba and not kept; and during his 1932 world tour, spectacularly, Baba had canceled his highly publicized plans to break his silence over radio at the Hollywood Bowl.

120. For years Malcolm Schloss had operated an occult book store in Manhattan named The North Node; and although it had gone out of business, he had made his mailing list available for purposes of Meher Baba's work.

121.Probably the circular Elizabeth refers to is the October 1933 letter from the Circle Editorial Committee reproduced in Appendix 3.

122. Herbert doubtless refers here to articles in the *Meher Message,* including the series entitled "Fragments *from* Spiritual Speeches of His Divine Majesty Sadguru Meher Baba."

The fact that Herbert refers (awkwardly) to "Meher Articles" and does not mention the actual title of the *Meher Message* leads one to wonder whether he ever saw the published magazine itself. As is explained in "Historical and Textual Backgrounds" (pp. 242–44), Herbert seems to have had available to him all of this material from the *Meher Message* in the form of typed manuscripts.

123. As pointed out in the essay on historical and textual backgrounds (pp. 242–44), many of the notes in *The Sayings* are demonstrably based on "Baba's words" in the form that these were made available to Herbert Davy at this time. Herbert seems to have used the title "Philosophical Fragments" to refer both to Ramjoo Abdulla's *Shri Meher Baba: His Philosophy and Teachings,* published late in 1933, as well as to designate a forthcoming Western edition of this material that Herbert himself was working on at this time.

124. In the original letter the typed date "25th April 1934" has been crossed out and the date "May 6th" inserted in handwriting.

Appendix 9

125. See *LM* (Mownavani), vol. 3, pp. 1375–76 and 1407; *LM* (Manifestation), vol. 6, pp. 1890 and 1937.

126. *LM* (Mownavani), vol. 3, p. 1477; *LM* (Manifestation), vol. 6, pp. 2042–43.

127. This statement of David Lord's closely follows a passage from one of the *Songs of Kabir* that was quoted in *Questions and Answers* (see p. 82 earlier). Published in 1933, *Questions and Answers* was doubtless available to Vollmoeller and Kraft.

128. Meher Baba said these words at Meherabad on July 9, 1925, on the eve of the silence that he began the next day and maintained more than forty years until dropping his physical form in 1969. A version of this quotation appears in answer 26(a) in *Questions and Answers* (see p. 87); and it stands as the epigraph at the head of that book (p. 343).

Bibliography

A. Published Sources for the Primary Texts

Collins, Frederick. "I Can Hardly Believe It, Myself." *Liberty,* August 27, 1932, pp. 26–27.

Dadachanji, Framroze Hormusji. "Meher Baba, Part IV: The West Bows Down." *Glow International,* February 1980, pp. 3–30. This article concludes the four-part serial publication of *Meher Baba, Emnu Jivan-Charitra: Shikshan-Updesh, Sandesh. Bustak Pahelun* (Ahmednagar, India: Adi K. Irani for the Publication Committee, Meher Baba Universal Spiritual Centre, 1943), as translated in abridged form by Naosherwan Anzar. Chanji's account of James Douglas's interview with Meher Baba on May 9, 1932 (published in an abbreviated version in the *Sunday Express* the next day) appears in pp. 13–17 of the *Glow* issue (and is based on pp. 301–28 of the Gujarati original).

Douglas, James. "A Talk with the Strange Messiah." *Sunday Express* (England), April 10, 1932, p. 1.

Humphreys, Christmas. "The Man of Love." *Buddhism in England,* vol. 16, no. 4 (November–December 1941), p. 77.

Landau, Rom. "Portrait of a 'Perfect Master,' Shri Meher Baba." *God is My Adventure: A Book on Modern Mystics, Masters, and Teachers.* London: Ivor Nicholson and Watson, 1935, pp. 130–48 (pp. 131–34 comprise the selection reprinted in part two of this book). Rpt. New York: Alfred A. Knopf, 1936, pp. 126–43 (for the selection in part two, see pp. 127–30).

Meher Baba. "The Master's Message." *Meher Gazette,* vol. 2, no. 1 (April 1933), pp. 1–3. This article is the earliest known publication of Meher Baba's "Message to Reporters in Hollywood," May 29, 1932. Three successive articles, all published under the title "The Master's Message," in *Meher Gazette,* vol. 2, no. 2 (May–June 1933), pp. 1–2; vol. 2, no. 3 (July–August 1933), pp. 1–2; and vol. 2, no. 4 (September–October 1933), pp. 1–2 collectively reproduce the text of Meher Baba's "Message to Reporters and Press Representatives," May 19, 1932.

———. *Messages of Meher Baba Delivered in the East and West.* Ahmednagar, India: Adi K. Irani for the Publication Committee, Meher Baba Universal Spiritual Centre, 1945. "Messages of Meher Baba Delivered in the West," pp. 81–101, reproduces the six messages of Meher Baba's 1932 tour that in this present book we have entitled "Message to the West" (April 8, 1932), pp. 83–84 (in the 1934 publication); "Message to Reporters and Press Representatives" (May 19, 1932), pp. 84–87; "Message at the Residence of Mr. Graham Phelps Stokes" (May 22, 1932), pp. 88–90; "Message to Reporters in Hollywood" (May 29, 1932), pp. 90–93; "Message at the Knickerbocker Hotel" (May 31, 1932), pp. 94–97; and "Message at Pickfair House" (June 1, 1932), pp. 97–101.

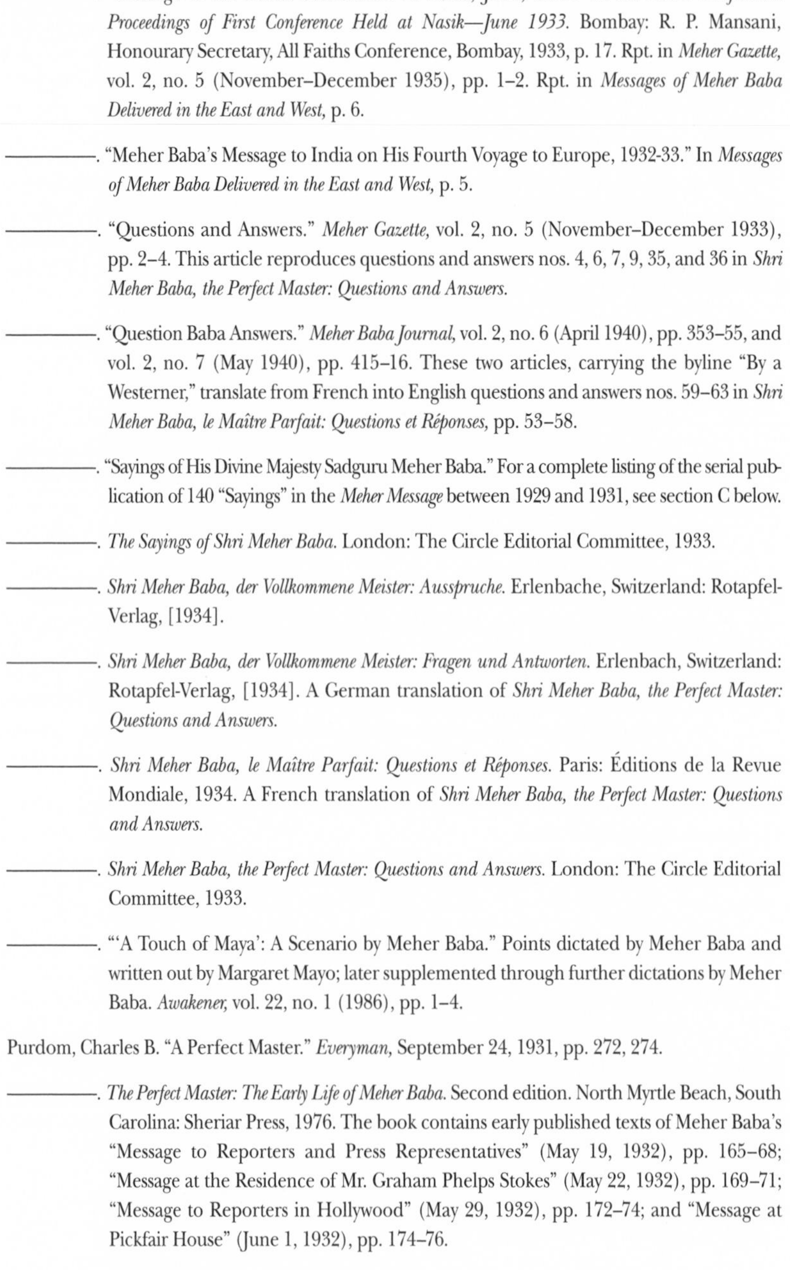

————. "Message to All Faiths Conference in Nasik, June, 1933." In *All Faiths Conference: Proceedings of First Conference Held at Nasik—June 1933.* Bombay: R. P. Mansani, Honourary Secretary, All Faiths Conference, Bombay, 1933, p. 17. Rpt. in *Meher Gazette,* vol. 2, no. 5 (November–December 1935), pp. 1–2. Rpt. in *Messages of Meher Baba Delivered in the East and West,* p. 6.

————. "Meher Baba's Message to India on His Fourth Voyage to Europe, 1932-33." In *Messages of Meher Baba Delivered in the East and West,* p. 5.

————. "Questions and Answers." *Meher Gazette,* vol. 2, no. 5 (November–December 1933), pp. 2–4. This article reproduces questions and answers nos. 4, 6, 7, 9, 35, and 36 in *Shri Meher Baba, the Perfect Master: Questions and Answers.*

————. "Question Baba Answers." *Meher Baba Journal,* vol. 2, no. 6 (April 1940), pp. 353–55, and vol. 2, no. 7 (May 1940), pp. 415–16. These two articles, carrying the byline "By a Westerner," translate from French into English questions and answers nos. 59–63 in *Shri Meher Baba, le Maître Parfait: Questions et Réponses,* pp. 53–58.

————. "Sayings of His Divine Majesty Sadguru Meher Baba." For a complete listing of the serial publication of 140 "Sayings" in the *Meher Message* between 1929 and 1931, see section C below.

————. *The Sayings of Shri Meher Baba.* London: The Circle Editorial Committee, 1933.

————. *Shri Meher Baba, der Vollkommene Meister: Ausspruche.* Erlenbache, Switzerland: Rotapfel-Verlag, [1934].

————. *Shri Meher Baba, der Vollkommene Meister: Fragen und Antworten.* Erlenbach, Switzerland: Rotapfel-Verlag, [1934]. A German translation of *Shri Meher Baba, the Perfect Master: Questions and Answers.*

————. *Shri Meher Baba, le Maître Parfait: Questions et Réponses.* Paris: Éditions de la Revue Mondiale, 1934. A French translation of *Shri Meher Baba, the Perfect Master: Questions and Answers.*

————. *Shri Meher Baba, the Perfect Master: Questions and Answers.* London: The Circle Editorial Committee, 1933.

————. "'A Touch of Maya': A Scenario by Meher Baba." Points dictated by Meher Baba and written out by Margaret Mayo; later supplemented through further dictations by Meher Baba. *Awakener,* vol. 22, no. 1 (1986), pp. 1–4.

Purdom, Charles B. "A Perfect Master." *Everyman,* September 24, 1931, pp. 272, 274.

————. *The Perfect Master: The Early Life of Meher Baba.* Second edition. North Myrtle Beach, South Carolina: Sheriar Press, 1976. The book contains early published texts of Meher Baba's "Message to Reporters and Press Representatives" (May 19, 1932), pp. 165–68; "Message at the Residence of Mr. Graham Phelps Stokes" (May 22, 1932), pp. 169–71; "Message to Reporters in Hollywood" (May 29, 1932), pp. 172–74; and "Message at Pickfair House" (June 1, 1932), pp. 174–76.

B. Books and Pamphlets

Abdulla, A[bdul] K[areem] (Ramjoo). *Shri Meher Baba: His Philosophy and Teachings.* "Compiled from His Own Dictations." Nasik, India: Rustom K. Sarosh Irani, 1933. Rpt. in the *Awakener,* vol. 15, nos. 1 and 2, pp. 1–27.

———. *Sobs and Throbs, or, Some Spiritual Sidelights: A Real Romance about the Meherashram Institute, and the Living Miracles of Hazarat Qibla Meher Baba.* Meherabad, Ahmednagar, India: N. N. Satha, 1929. Rpt. in a slightly edited form in *Ramjoo's Diaries, 1922–1929: A Personal Account of Meher Baba's Early Work.* Edited by Ira G. Deitrick. Walnut Creek, California: Sufism Reoriented, 1979, pp. 403–511.

Adriel, Jean. *Avatar: The Life Story of Avatar Meher Baba.* 1947; rpt. Berkeley: John F. Kennedy University Press, 1971.

Brunton, Paul. *A Search in Secret India.* Third edition. London: Random House, 1983. See esp. chapter 4, "I Meet a Messiah," pp. 46–65, and chapter 14, "At the Parsee Messiah's Headquarters," pp. 253–62. Originally published in London: Rider, 1934.

Craske, Margaret. *The Dance of Love: My Life with Meher Baba.* North Myrtle Beach, South Carolina: Sheriar Press, 1980.

———. *Still Dancing with Love: More Stories of Life with Meher Baba.* Myrtle Beach, South Carolina: Sheriar Press, 1990.

Dadachanji, Framroze Hormusji (Chanji). *Meher Baba, Emnu Jivan-Charitra: Shikshan-Updesh, Sandesh. Bustak Pahelun [Biography of Meher Baba: His Teachings, Discourses, and Messages. Book One].* By "Manzil." Ahmednagar, India: Adi K. Irani for the Publication Committee, Meher Baba Universal Spiritual Centre, 1943.

Davy, Kitty. *Love Alone Prevails: A Story of Life with Meher Baba.* North Myrtle Beach, South Carolina: Sheriar Press, 1981.

DeLeon, Delia. *The Ocean of Love.* Myrtle Beach, South Carolina: Sheriar Press, 1991.

Gayley, Rano. *Because of Love: My Life and Art with Meher Baba.* Edited by Ann Conlon. North Myrtle Beach, South Carolina: Sheriar Press, 1983.

His Eastern and Western Disciples. *Meher Baba.* Bangalore: Publication Committee for Meher Baba, Universal Spiritual Centre, 1939.

Kabir. *Songs of Kabir.* Translated by Rabindranath Tagore. New York: Macmillan, 1915.

Kalchuri, V. S. *Lord Meher: The Biography of Avatar Meher Baba.* 20 vols. North Myrtle Beach, South Carolina: Manifestation, 1986–2001.

———. *Lord Meher: The Biography of the Avatar of the Age, Meher Baba.* 8 vols. Hyderabad, A.P., India: Meher Mownavani Publications, 2005.

Meher Baba. *84 Questions and Answers on Avatar Meher Baba.* Enlarged second edition. New Delhi: A. C. S. Chari for Avatar Meher Baba Centre [1969]. The original edition was entitled

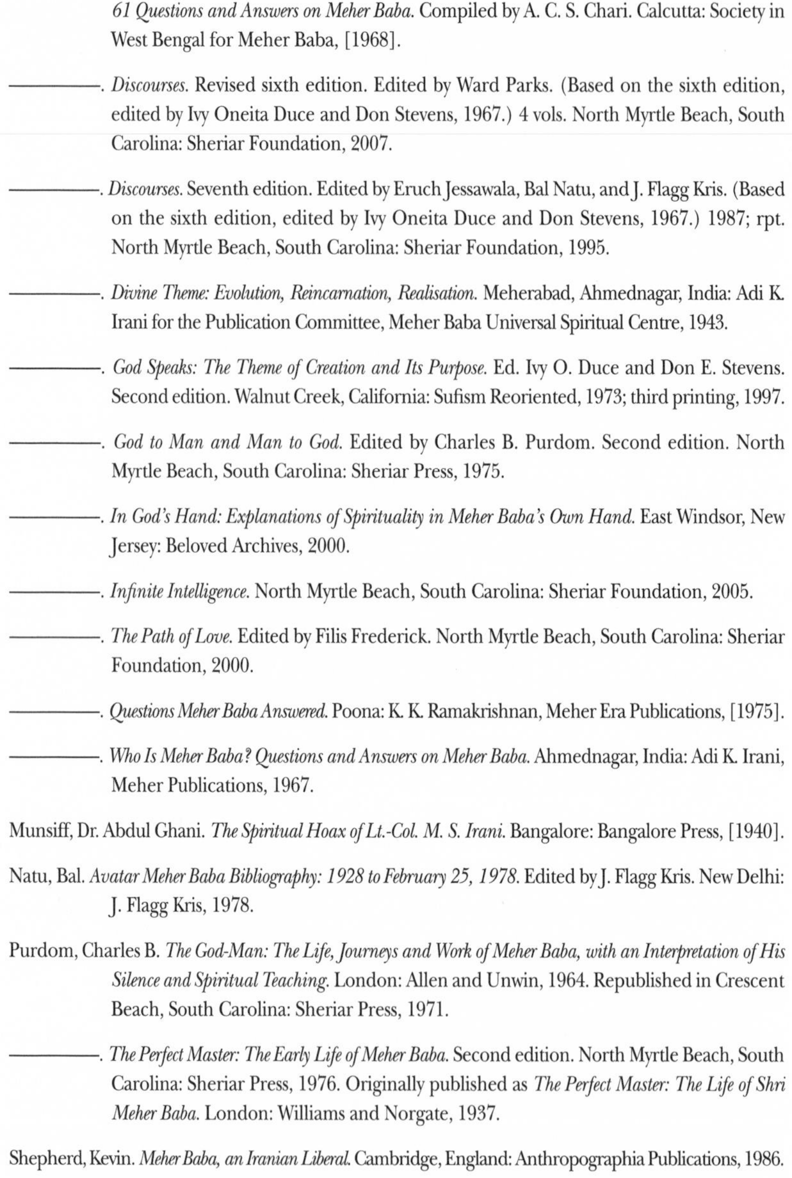

61 Questions and Answers on Meher Baba. Compiled by A. C. S. Chari. Calcutta: Society in West Bengal for Meher Baba, [1968].

————. *Discourses.* Revised sixth edition. Edited by Ward Parks. (Based on the sixth edition, edited by Ivy Oneita Duce and Don Stevens, 1967.) 4 vols. North Myrtle Beach, South Carolina: Sheriar Foundation, 2007.

————. *Discourses.* Seventh edition. Edited by Eruch Jessawala, Bal Natu, and J. Flagg Kris. (Based on the sixth edition, edited by Ivy Oneita Duce and Don Stevens, 1967.) 1987; rpt. North Myrtle Beach, South Carolina: Sheriar Foundation, 1995.

————. *Divine Theme: Evolution, Reincarnation, Realisation.* Meherabad, Ahmednagar, India: Adi K. Irani for the Publication Committee, Meher Baba Universal Spiritual Centre, 1943.

————. *God Speaks: The Theme of Creation and Its Purpose.* Ed. Ivy O. Duce and Don E. Stevens. Second edition. Walnut Creek, California: Sufism Reoriented, 1973; third printing, 1997.

————. *God to Man and Man to God.* Edited by Charles B. Purdom. Second edition. North Myrtle Beach, South Carolina: Sheriar Press, 1975.

————. *In God's Hand: Explanations of Spirituality in Meher Baba's Own Hand.* East Windsor, New Jersey: Beloved Archives, 2000.

————. *Infinite Intelligence.* North Myrtle Beach, South Carolina: Sheriar Foundation, 2005.

————. *The Path of Love.* Edited by Filis Frederick. North Myrtle Beach, South Carolina: Sheriar Foundation, 2000.

————. *Questions Meher Baba Answered.* Poona: K. K. Ramakrishnan, Meher Era Publications, [1975].

————. *Who Is Meher Baba? Questions and Answers on Meher Baba.* Ahmednagar, India: Adi K. Irani, Meher Publications, 1967.

Munsiff, Dr. Abdul Ghani. *The Spiritual Hoax of Lt.-Col. M. S. Irani.* Bangalore: Bangalore Press, [1940].

Natu, Bal. *Avatar Meher Baba Bibliography: 1928 to February 25, 1978.* Edited by J. Flagg Kris. New Delhi: J. Flagg Kris, 1978.

Purdom, Charles B. *The God-Man: The Life, Journeys and Work of Meher Baba, with an Interpretation of His Silence and Spiritual Teaching.* London: Allen and Unwin, 1964. Republished in Crescent Beach, South Carolina: Sheriar Press, 1971.

————. *The Perfect Master: The Early Life of Meher Baba.* Second edition. North Myrtle Beach, South Carolina: Sheriar Press, 1976. Originally published as *The Perfect Master: The Life of Shri Meher Baba.* London: Williams and Norgate, 1937.

Shepherd, Kevin. *Meher Baba, an Iranian Liberal.* Cambridge, England: Anthropographia Publications, 1986.

Vollmoeller, Karl. *How It All Happened.* "Based on the ideas of Shri Meher Baba." New York: Circle Productions, 1935.

Vollmoeller, Karl and H. S. Kraft. *This Man David: Outline of an Original Screen Play.* "Based on and inspired by the ideas of Shri Meher Baba." New York: Circle Productions, 1935.

C. Articles in Meher Baba Publications

Abdulla, A. K. (Ramjoo)."Meher Baba—His Philosophy and Mysticism." Based on A. K. Abdulla, *Shri Meher Baba: His Philosophy and Teaching*. Revised and enlarged by Abdul Ghani Munsiff. *Meher Baba Journal*, vol. 4, no. 1 (November 1941), pp. 41–51; vol. 4, no. 2 (December 1941), pp. 69–75; vol. 4, no. 3 (January 1942), pp. 133–43; vol. 4, no. 4 (February 1942), pp. 211–21; vol. 4, no. 6 (April 1942), pp. 289–93; vol. 4, no. 7 (May 1942), pp. 353–65; vol. 4, no. 8 (June 1942), pp. 422–34; vol. 4, no. 9 (July 1942), pp. 454–63; and vol. 4, no. 10 (August 1942), pp. 503–13.

Backett, William. "Impressions." *Meher Baba Journal*, vol. 1, no. 6 (April 1939), pp. 43–45.

————. "Incidents from the Master's Work at 50, Charing Cross, London (1933–37) and Elsewhere in London." *Meher Baba Journal*, vol. 3, no. 1 (November 1940), pp. 31–40.

Bogislav, Ruano. "Facts." *Meher Baba Journal*, vol. 2, no. 8 (June 1940), pp. 465–70. Rpt. as "How I Met Meher Baba." *Awakener*, vol. 3, no. 3 (Winter 1956), pp. 1–6.

Dadachanji, Framroze Hormusji (Chanji). The 1943 Gujarati biography entitled *Meher Baba* (see section B), published serially in four parts in its abridged English translation by Naosherwan Anzar. "Meher Baba, Part I: His Life and Work," *Glow International*, May 1979, pp. 6–11. "Meher Baba, Part II: The Preparation," *Glow International*, August 1979, pp. 3–24. "Meher Baba, Part III: Travels," *Glow International*, November 1979, pp. 4–23. "Meher Baba, Part IV: The West Bows Down," *Glow International*, February 1980, pp. 3–30.

Davy, Kitty. "Baba's First World Tour, 1932." Part 1, *Awakener*, vol. 12, no. 1 (Winter 1967), pp. 1–34. Part 2, *Awakener*, vol. 12, no. 3 (Summer 1968), pp. 1–21. Part 3, *Awakener*, vol. 14, no. 1 (1971), pp. 19–36.

Gayley, Rano. "An Awakening." *Meher Baba Journal*, vol. 1, no. 7 (May 1939), pp. 14–16.

Irani, Adi K. "Diary of a Disciple." *Glow International*, February 1993, pp. 5–9.

Matchabelli, Norina, Kitty Davy, Herbert Davy, and Will Backett. "Minutes of Meeting of Circle Editorial Committee," October 18, 1933. The original five-page handwritten manuscript is reproduced in facsimile as display insets on pp. 9–13 and 15 (the second page of the memorandum is repeated on pp. 10 and 11) in "Answers: The True Messiah." *Glow International*, Spring 2009, pp. 3–15.

Meher Baba. "Answers: The True Messiah." *Glow International*, Spring 2009, pp. 3–15. Reproduces most of the content in *Shri Meher Baba, the Perfect Master: Questions and Answers*.

————. "God, Creator and Creation." *Meher Message*, vol. 1, no. 4 (April 1929), pp. 2–7; vol. 1, no. 5 (May 1929), pp. 2–5; vol. 1, no. 6 (June 1929), pp. 2–6; vol. 1, no. 7 (July 1929), pp. 2–6; vol. 1, no. 8 (August 1929), pp. 2–8; vol. 1, no. 9 (September 1929), pp. 2–7; vol. 1, no. 10 (October 1929), pp. 2–6; vol. 1, no. 11 (November 1929), pp. 2–5; vol. 1, no. 12 (December 1929), pp. 2–5.

————. "My Message Is . . ." *Awakener*, vol. 18, no. 1, pp. 26–31. The texts of the messages that Meher Baba gave on May 22, May 29, May 31, and June 1 of his 1932 Western tour.

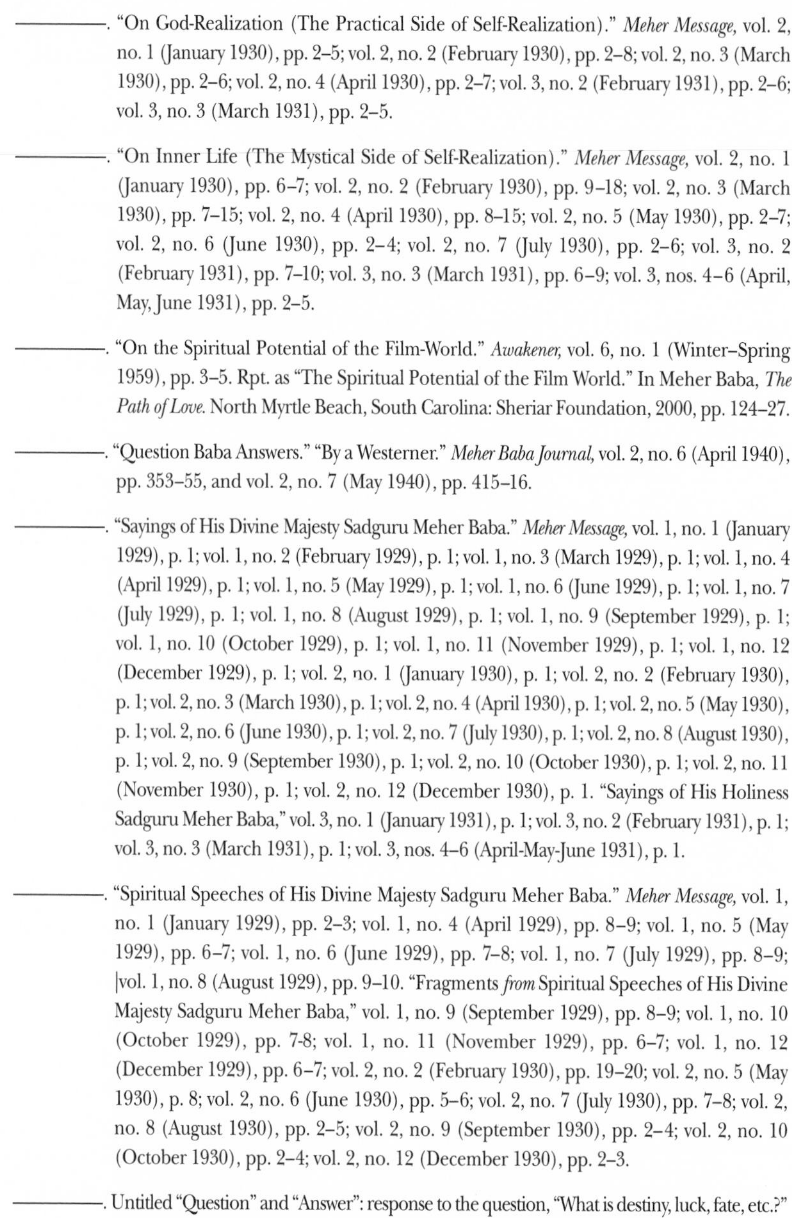

———. "On God-Realization (The Practical Side of Self-Realization)." *Meher Message,* vol. 2, no. 1 (January 1930), pp. 2–5; vol. 2, no. 2 (February 1930), pp. 2–8; vol. 2, no. 3 (March 1930), pp. 2–6; vol. 2, no. 4 (April 1930), pp. 2–7; vol. 3, no. 2 (February 1931), pp. 2–6; vol. 3, no. 3 (March 1931), pp. 2–5.

———. "On Inner Life (The Mystical Side of Self-Realization)." *Meher Message,* vol. 2, no. 1 (January 1930), pp. 6–7; vol. 2, no. 2 (February 1930), pp. 9–18; vol. 2, no. 3 (March 1930), pp. 7–15; vol. 2, no. 4 (April 1930), pp. 8–15; vol. 2, no. 5 (May 1930), pp. 2–7; vol. 2, no. 6 (June 1930), pp. 2–4; vol. 2, no. 7 (July 1930), pp. 2–6; vol. 3, no. 2 (February 1931), pp. 7–10; vol. 3, no. 3 (March 1931), pp. 6–9; vol. 3, nos. 4–6 (April, May, June 1931), pp. 2–5.

———. "On the Spiritual Potential of the Film-World." *Awakener,* vol. 6, no. 1 (Winter–Spring 1959), pp. 3–5. Rpt. as "The Spiritual Potential of the Film World." In Meher Baba, *The Path of Love.* North Myrtle Beach, South Carolina: Sheriar Foundation, 2000, pp. 124–27.

———. "Question Baba Answers." "By a Westerner." *Meher Baba Journal,* vol. 2, no. 6 (April 1940), pp. 353–55, and vol. 2, no. 7 (May 1940), pp. 415–16.

———. "Sayings of His Divine Majesty Sadguru Meher Baba." *Meher Message,* vol. 1, no. 1 (January 1929), p. 1; vol. 1, no. 2 (February 1929), p. 1; vol. 1, no. 3 (March 1929), p. 1; vol. 1, no. 4 (April 1929), p. 1; vol. 1, no. 5 (May 1929), p. 1; vol. 1, no. 6 (June 1929), p. 1; vol. 1, no. 7 (July 1929), p. 1; vol. 1, no. 8 (August 1929), p. 1; vol. 1, no. 9 (September 1929), p. 1; vol. 1, no. 10 (October 1929), p. 1; vol. 1, no. 11 (November 1929), p. 1; vol. 1, no. 12 (December 1929), p. 1; vol. 2, no. 1 (January 1930), p. 1; vol. 2, no. 2 (February 1930), p. 1; vol. 2, no. 3 (March 1930), p. 1; vol. 2, no. 4 (April 1930), p. 1; vol. 2, no. 5 (May 1930), p. 1; vol. 2, no. 6 (June 1930), p. 1; vol. 2, no. 7 (July 1930), p. 1; vol. 2, no. 8 (August 1930), p. 1; vol. 2, no. 9 (September 1930), p. 1; vol. 2, no. 10 (October 1930), p. 1; vol. 2, no. 11 (November 1930), p. 1; vol. 2, no. 12 (December 1930), p. 1. "Sayings of His Holiness Sadguru Meher Baba," vol. 3, no. 1 (January 1931), p. 1; vol. 3, no. 2 (February 1931), p. 1; vol. 3, no. 3 (March 1931), p. 1; vol. 3, nos. 4–6 (April-May-June 1931), p. 1.

———. "Spiritual Speeches of His Divine Majesty Sadguru Meher Baba." *Meher Message,* vol. 1, no. 1 (January 1929), pp. 2–3; vol. 1, no. 4 (April 1929), pp. 8–9; vol. 1, no. 5 (May 1929), pp. 6–7; vol. 1, no. 6 (June 1929), pp. 7–8; vol. 1, no. 7 (July 1929), pp. 8–9; vol. 1, no. 8 (August 1929), pp. 9–10. "Fragments *from* Spiritual Speeches of His Divine Majesty Sadguru Meher Baba," vol. 1, no. 9 (September 1929), pp. 8–9; vol. 1, no. 10 (October 1929), pp. 7-8; vol. 1, no. 11 (November 1929), pp. 6–7; vol. 1, no. 12 (December 1929), pp. 6–7; vol. 2, no. 2 (February 1930), pp. 19–20; vol. 2, no. 5 (May 1930), p. 8; vol. 2, no. 6 (June 1930), pp. 5–6; vol. 2, no. 7 (July 1930), pp. 7–8; vol. 2, no. 8 (August 1930), pp. 2–5; vol. 2, no. 9 (September 1930), pp. 2–4; vol. 2, no. 10 (October 1930), pp. 2–4; vol. 2, no. 12 (December 1930), pp. 2–3.

———. Untitled "Question" and "Answer": response to the question, "What is destiny, luck, fate, etc.?" *Awakener,* vol. 2, no. 1 (Summer 1954), p. 12; rpt. *Awakener,* vol. 12, no. 2 (1964), pp. 22–23.

[Parks, Ward.] "Trust Embraces Editorial Policy" and "The *Discourses,* Copyright, and the Preservation of Meher Baba's Words." *In His Service,* July 2006, pp. 2 and 3.

Patterson, Elizabeth C. "A Meeting of Master and Chela." *Meher Baba Journal,* vol. 2, no. 4 (February 1940), pp. 237–45. Originally published as "A Modern Meeting of Master and Chel." *Occult Review,* vol. 60, September 1934, pp. 186–192.

[Powell, Ann]. "Impressions: Ann Powell (Welsh) Meets Shri Meher Baba." *Meher Baba Journal,* vol. 2, no. 10 (August 1940), pp. 615–19.

Purdom, Charles B. "More about the Perfect Master." In *Meher Baba,* by His Eastern and Western Disciples. Bangalore: Publication Committee for Meher Baba Universal Spiritual Centre, 1939, pp. 9–13. Originally published in *Everyman,* April 21, 1932, pp. 400, 402. Includes Purdom's edited version of Meher Baba's "Message to the West," dictated in London on April 8, 1932.

————. "The Need of a Teacher." In *Meher Baba,* by His Eastern and Western Disciples, pp. 1–5. Originally published in *Everyman,* February 11, 1932, pp. 80, 82.

————. "A Perfect Master." In *Meher Baba,* by His Eastern and Western Disciples, pp. 5–9. Originally published in *Everyman,* September 24, 1931, pp. 272, 274.

Ross, Josephine Grabau. "Here Was the Christ." *Glow International,* November 1991, p. 23.

Schloss, Malcolm. "America Welcomes Meher Baba in 1931." *Glow International,* November 1991, pp. 3–22.

————. "When the Master Is Ready." Part 1 in the *Awakener,* vol. 19, no. 1 (1980), pp. 45–59. Part 2 in the *Awakener,* vol. 19, no. 2 (1981), pp. 39–54.

Tod, Quentin. "Meher Baba in America, 1932." *Glow,* November 1972 (vol. 7, no. 4), pp. 3–8.

————. "When I Saw Him." *Glow,* May 1970 (vol. 5, no. 2), p. 13.

Tolstoy, Countess Nadine. "Meher Baba and My Spiritual Path." *Meher Baba Journal,* vol. 3, no. 8 (June 1941), pp. 447–57; vol. 3, no. 9 (July 1941), pp. 507–15; vol. 3, no. 10 (August 1941), pp. 563–73; vol. 3, no. 11 (September 1941), pp. 619–26; and vol. 3, no. 12 (October 1941), pp. 679–85.

D. Mainstream Newspaper and Magazine Articles

August 1929. "His Holiness Sadguru Meher Bàbà." By Kaikhushru Jamshedji Dastur. *Occult Review,* vol. 50, pp. 175-78.

September 24, 1931. "A Perfect Master." By Charles B. Purdom. *Everyman,* pp. 272, 274.

February 11, 1932. "The Need of a Teacher." By Charles B. Purdom. *Everyman,* pp. 80, 82.

March 25, 1932. "Baba Coming to United States. Indian Spiritual Leader Proposes to Break Down All Religious Barriers." By James A. Mills. *Centralia Daily Chronicle* (Centralia,Washington) p. 8. From the Associated Press.

March 25, 1932. "Hindu 'Messiah' Plans Religious Crusade in U.S." *Kingsport Times* (Tennessee), p. 7. From the Associated Press.

March 25, 1932. "Indian 'Messiah' Sails for Crusade in America." *Appleton Post-Crescent* (Wisconsin), pp. 1, 11. From the Associated Press.

March 25, 1932. "Indian Religious Leader Will Establish Retreat in New York." By James A. Mills. *Santa Fe New Mexican,* p. 3. From the Associated Press.

March 25, 1932. "Indian Seer Leaves for Crusade in U. S." *Bismarck Tribune* (North Dakota), p. 1. From the Associated Press.

March 25, 1932. "Indian Spiritual Leader Coming to United States." *Daily Inter Lake* (Kalispell, Montana), p. 1. From the Associated Press.

March 25, 1932. "Indian Spiritual Leader Plans to Tour Nation. Meher Baba, Called 'The Messiah' by His Indian Disciples, Says He Hopes to Bring Love to America." By James A. Mills. *Jefferson City Post-Tribune* (Missouri), p. 5. From the Associated Press.

March 25, 1932. "India's God Man Coming to America." *Muscatine Journal and News-Tribune* (Iowa), p. 2. From the Associated Press.

March 25, 1932. "India's Messiah Leaves Bombay for Tour of U.S. Disciples Declare Priest has Performed Many Miracles." *Alton Evening Telegraph* (Illinois), p. 1. From the Associated Press.

March 25, 1932. "Man from India Would Amalgamate All Creeds." *Evening News Journal* (Clovis, New Mexico), p. 1. From the Associated Press.

March 25, 1932. "Materialism Is Target. Indian Leader, Confidant of Gandhi, Discloses Plans for Trip to U.S." *Fairbanks Daily News-Miner* (Alaska), p. 1. From the Associated Press.

March 25, 1932. "New Crusade in U. S. Plan of 'Messiah.' Meher Baba, Indian 'God-Man,' Would Amalgamate All Creeds. Has Gandhi's Aid. Spiritual Retreat at Harmon Would Also Draw Mahatma." *Syracuse Herald* (New York). From the Associated Press.

March 26, 1932. "Indian Priest Coming to U.S. Expects to Make Convert. Healing of Ill through Faith." By James A. Mills. *Ogden Standard-Examiner* (Utah), p. 2. From the Associated Press.

March 26, 1932. "Indian Seer Starts for American Tour. Meher Baba Hopes to Elevate People Here to 'Infinite State' He Enjoys. To Break Vow of Silence. He Will Establish Spiritual Retreat at Harmon, N.Y., and Seek to Break Religious Barriers." *New York Times,* p. 5. From the Associated Press.

March 26, 1932. "Noted Indian Zoroastrian Follower Leaves for U.S." By James A. Mills. *Billings Gazette* (Montana), p. 2. From the Associated Press.

March 26, 1932. "Too Large a Contract." *Reno Evening Gazette* (Nevada), p. 4.

March 29, 1932. "Meher Baba Plans Crusade in U.S. Spiritual Leader Leaves India for America to Establish a Retreat at Harmon." *Daily Gleaner* (Kingston, Jamaica), p. 15. By Air Mail to the *Gleaner.*

March 30, 1932. "On Way to U.S." *Chicago Daily Tribune,* p. 9.

March 31, 1932. "'God Man.'" *North Adams Evening Transcript* (Massachusetts), p. 9.

April 7, 1932. "Indian 'Messiah' Visiting England. To 'Raise the Dead' If Necessary." *Daily Mirror* (England), p. 1.

April 8, 1932. "Indian 'Miracle Man' Arrives in England. Welcome by Devotees. Devon Colony Awaits 'The New Messiah.' 7 Years' Silence." *Daily Mirror* (England), p. 2.

April 8, 1932. "Indian Mystic's Silence Vow Delays His Entry at Dover." *New York Times,* p. 7. From the Associated Press.

April 8, 1932. "Leader of Indian Cult Leaves Ship in England." *Washington Post,* p. 3. From the Associated Press.

April 9, 1932. "London Guard for Messiah." *Daily Herald* (England), p. 3.

April 9, 1932. "'Miracle Man' Talks to 'Daily Mirror.' Indian Mystic's Finger Signals to Preserve Seven Years' Silence. His Message to the World. Waiting for Spirit to Move Him to Revelation —Miracles Performed 'If Necessary.'" *Daily Mirror* (England), p. 3.

April 9, 1932. "'Miraculous Cure.'" *Daily Mirror* (England), p. 6.

April 9, 1932. "Silent Indian Messiah." *Daily Mirror* (England), p. 1.

April 9, 1932. "To Lead Western World. Shri Meher Baba on His Plans During Visit to England." *Daily Mirror* (England), pp. 3, 6.

April 10, 1932. "'New Messiah' Here. Claim to 'Master Mankind.' English Followers Prepare for 'Greatest Being of All Time.'" *The People,* p. 3.

April 10, 1932. "A Talk with the Strange Messiah. What He Told James Douglas in a Kensington Bedroom. 'My Mission Will Last for 33 Years.' Three Hours Sleep a Day. Silent Interview with an Alphabet." By James Douglas. *Sunday Express* (England), p. 1.

April 11, 1932. "Baba's Children's Party. Tiddley Winks with His Ten Disciples." *Daily Herald* (England), p. 3.

April 11, 1932. "Baba Wears a Paper Cap! Indian Miracle Man Joins Party Fun. Strange Music." *Daily Mirror* (England), p. 2.

April 11, 1932. "The New Messiah." *Evening Standard* (England), p 6.

April 11, 1932. "Waiting for the New 'Messiah.'" *Daily Sketch* (England), p. 1.

April 11, 1932. "White-Robed Prophet Tells How a Kiss Inspired Him." *Daily Express* (England), p. 3.

April 12, 1932. "Indian 'Messiah's' Vow of Miracles. To Heal the Sick and Restore Sight When He Visits America." *Daily Sketch* (England), p. 4.

April 12, 1932. "Prophet Tells of 'Divine' Kiss." *Daily Sketch* (England), p. 1.

April 13, 1932. "Baba Makes a Prophecy. Incurable Child to Be Well in August. Parents' Appeal." *Daily Mirror* (England), pp. 2, 4.

April 13, 1932. "A Messiah Sits for a Sculptor. Chat with the Silent Indian Mystic." *Daily Sketch* (England), p. 5.

April 16, 1932. "Indian Mystic and Devon. Arrival Expected at Week-end. May Spend Some Days at Combe Martin." *Western Morning News and Daily Gazette* (Devon and Cornwall, England), p. 6.

April 17, 1932. "'Messiah' Advent. Expected To-day to Join Disciples." *Empire News* (England), p. 1.

April 18, 1932. "Indian Mystic in Devon. Bagpipes Greeting at Challacombe. Discord through Materialism." *Western Morning News and Daily Gazette* (Devon and Cornwall, England), p. 4.

April 18, 1932. "The New Indian Teacher. Meher Baba's Message." From a correspondent. *Manchester Guardian* (Manchester, England), p. 16.

April 19, 1932. "Bagpipes for the Indian 'Messiah.' His Arrival at the Retreat at Devon." *Daily Sketch* (England), p. 11.

April 19, 1932. "The New Messiah." *Daily Herald* (England), p. 9.

April 21, 1932. "More about the Perfect Master." By Charles B. Purdom. *Everyman,* April 21, 1932, pp. 400, 402.

April 21, 1932. "Shri Meher Baba. Pressman's Visit to East Challacombe." *North Devon Herald* (Devon, England), p. 3.

April 22, 1932. "Biblical Scene. Indian Mystic Arrives at Combe Martin. Meher Baba's Message." *Ilfracombe Chronicle and North Devon News* (Devon, England), p. 1.

April 22, 1932. "Mystic's Retreat. Indian Visitor Leaving North Devon." *Western Morning News and Daily Gazette* (Devon and Cornwall, England), p. 4.

April 22, 1932. "The New Messiah in Devon. Meher Baba's Message in England. Greeted by Indians. Sightseers Avoided at Combe Martin." *Western Times* (Devon, England), p. 11.

April 22, 1932. "The 'New Messiah' in North Devon." *Western Times* (Devon, England), p. 5.

April 22, 1932. "The New 'Messiah's' Retreat in North Devon." By our own correspondent. *Western Times* (Devon, England), p. 11.

April 24, 1932. "'Miracles.' Sad Scenes at School of 'Messiah.'" From our Correspondent. *Empire News* (England), p. 1.

April 24, 1932. "Proxy Hands of the Mystic. 2,000 Models for His Disciples to Kiss." *Sunday Dispatch* (England), p. 11.

April 24, 1932. "Shri Meher Baba." *Western Independent* (west England), p. 15.

April 24, 1932. "A Silent Seer Comes to Arouse Americans. Shri Meher Baba, Who has Lived Seven Years Plunged in Thought, Teaches Disciples by Means of Signs." By Henry James Foreman. *New York Times,* p. XX7.

April 26, 1932. "A Great Prophet." *Charleston Daily Mail* (Western Virginia), p. 6.

April 28, 1932. "Meher Baba's Farewell." *North Devon Herald* (Devon, England), p. 3.

April 28, 1932. "The New 'Messiah' Mentioned at Barnstable R.D.C. Meeting." *North Devon Herald* (Devon, England), p. 3.

April 29, 1932. "Combe Martin." *Ilfracombe Chronicle and North Devon News* (Devon, England), p. 3.

April 29, 1932. "Indian Mystic's Retreat at Combe Martin. Complaint Regarding Condition of Lane." *Ilfracombe Chronicle and North Devon News* (Devon, England), p. 1.

April 29, 1932. "New Messiah's Abode." *Western Times* (Devon, England), p. 9.

April 30, 1932. "Hindu Philosopher to Break 7-Year Silence in U.S." *Huntington Daily News* (Pennsylvania).

May 2, 1932. "God on the Hudson." *Time* magazine, p. 22.

May 7, 1932. "All Britain Duped by Sham Messiah." *John Bull* magazine, pp. 8–9.

May 8, 1932. "The 'Messiah' of India Coming. Meher Baba, Holy Man of the Hindu Yogis, Who Hasn't Spoken a Word in Eight Years and Claims He Can Perform Miracles, Will Try to Start a Colony of Mystics in America." *San Antonio Light* (Texas), p. 7.

May 8, 1932. "Mystic 'Redeemer' Awaited at Crofton. Meher Baba, Who has Kept Vow of Silence for 7 Years, Expected at Retreat about May 15. Plans to End Spell Here. Aides [sic] Prepare a House of Margaret Mayo, for Use as 'Peaceful Meherashram.'" *New York Times*, p. N2.

May 16, 1932. "God Man of India to Reach New York May 19." *Wisconsin State Journal* (Madison, Wisconsin), p. 16.

May 19, 1932. "Indian, Mute 7 Years, Arrives Here Today. Shri Sadguru Meher Baba, the Prophet, Coming on the Bremen with Nine Disciples." *New York Times*, p. 18.

May 19, 1932. "On Broadway." By Walter Winchell. *Wisconsin State Journal* (Madison, Wisconsin), p. 3.

May 19, 1932. "Silent Hindu Messiah Arrives." *New York Journal American.*

May 20, 1932. "God-Man Here." *Waterloo Daily Courier* (Iowa), p. 1.

May 20, 1932. "Hindu 'Messiah' Lands in East. Shri Meher Baba to Conduct Campaign in America. Indian Coming to Hollywood and May Enter Films. Long Silence to be Broken with World Message." *Los Angeles Times*, p. 3. From the Associated Press.

May 20, 1932. "India 'Messiah,' Silent 7 Years, to Speak Here. Shri Meher Baba Arrives on Way to California, Where He Will Give World Message." *New York Journal American*, p.15.

May 20, 1932. "Indian Mystic Arrives to Break 7-Year Silence." *Fitchburg Sentinel* (Massachusetts), p. 15. From the Associated Press.

May 20, 1932. "Indian Mystic Comes with Message for US. Indian Who has been Silent for 7 Years Here. Shri Meher Baba Will Break His Seven-Year Silence on Visit to Harmon, N.Y." *New York Times*, p. 17.

May 20, 1932. "Indian Mystic in New York. Shri Meher Baba Calls Self 'The Infinite Source of Everything.'" *Lowell Sun* (Massachusetts), p. 15. From the Associated Press.

May 20, 1932. "Indian Mystic Will Break Long Silence. 'One with Infinite Source of Everything' Comes to America." *Rhinelander Daily News* (Wisconsin), p. 9. From the Associated Press.

May 20, 1932. "India's Silent 'God-Man' Arrives in America." *Edwardsville Intelligencer* (Illinois), p. 1.

May 20, 1932. "In U.S. to Break 7-Years Silence. Indian Mystic Says 'My First Message to World Will Have to Be Accepted." *Greensburg Daily News* (Indiana), p. 4. From the Associated Press.

May 20, 1932. "Messiah, Hollywood Bound, Keeps His 7 Year Silence." *Chicago Daily Tribune,* p. 27.

May 20, 1932. "'Sphinx of India' to End 7-Yr. Silence. Arrives to Address His Followers at Harmon, N.Y." By Dorothy Kilgallen. *New York Evening Journal.*

May 21, 1932. "He Will Speak." *Daily News* (Huntington, Pennsylvania).

May 21, 1932. "Will Break Silence of Seven Years." *Stevens Point Daily Journal* (Wisconsin), p. 5. From the Associated Press.

May 23, 1932. "He'll Talk to Us. MUST He Really Do That?" *New York Evening Journal.* Rpt. May 26, 1932, *Chicago American.*

May 23, 1932. "Indian Prophet Will Break Long Silence in U.S." *San Antonio Light* (Texas), p. 7-B.

May 23, 1932. "To Convert U.S." *Circleville Herald* (Ohio), p. 2.

May 24, 1932. "Silence, Please!" *Clearfield Progress* (Pennsylvania), p. 4.

May 24, 1932. "U.S. Disciples Are Waiting for First Word of 'Perfect Master' after a Silence of Seven Years." *Lubbock Morning Avalanche* (Texas), pp. 1, 5. By the NEA Service.

May 25, 1932. "Indian 'Messiah' to Lead America from Materialism." *Daily Independent* (Monessen, Pennsylvania), p. 5.

May 26, 1932. "Indian 'Messiah' to Lead America from Materialism." *Tipton Daily Tribune* (Indiana), p. 6.

May 26, 1932. "Indian Mystic Arrives Soon." *Los Angeles Times,* p. 7. From the Associated Press.

May 27, 1932. "Baba to Give Up His 'Uh.' A Few More Months and 7-Year Silence Will End. He'll Become a Messiah in Hollywood Then and His Fingers Will Get a Rest." *Kansas City Star,* pp. 1, 3.

May 27, 1932. "To Convert U.S." *Albuquerque Journal* (New Mexico), p. 5.

May 27, 1932. Untitled. *Van Wert Daily Bulletin* (Ohio), p. 6.

May 29, 1932. "Silent Mystic of India to Arrive Here Today." *Los Angeles Times,* pp. A1, A2.

May 30, 1932. "Indian Mystic Arrives for Visit in Hollywood." *Los Angeles Times,* p. 14.

May 30, 1932. "'Perfect Master' Has Been Silent for 7-Year Period." *Appleton Post-Crescent* (Wisconsin), p. 2.

May 30, 1932, 1932. "To Convert U.S." *Tipton Daily Tribune* (Indiana), p. 6.

June 3, 1932. "Indian Mystic Plans to View 'Grand Hotel.'" *Los Angeles Times,* p. 14.

June 3, 1932. "What Do You Think of Keeping Silent for Seven Years?" By Manthei Howe. *Ironwood Times* (Michigan), p. 3.

June 4, 1932. "Shri Meher Baba Sails for China on One-Day Visit." *Los Angeles Times.*

June 4, 1932. "Silence, Please!" *Ames Daily Tribune-Times* (Iowa), p. 8.

June 5, 1932. "Ruth E. Chew Will Discuss New India Mystic on Sunday." *Helena Daily Independent* (Montana) p. 2.

June 5, 1932. "Silent Mystic Off for China. Shri Meher Baba Embarks on Shanghai Trip. 'Holy Man' Declares British Fail to Upset Him. Hollywood Followers Wait Radio Talk on Return." *Los Angeles Times.*

June 9, 1932. "Hollywood." By Cecil Cable. *Emporia Daily Gazette* (Illinois), p. 3.

June 12, 1932. "The Barrymores in Hollywood. Ethel, Lionel and John Preparing to Act in 'Rasputin —Chain Gang and Action Pictures—Further Items." *New York Times,* p. X3.

June 23, 1932. Untitled. *Beverly Hills Citizen* (California), p. 14.

July 2, 1932. "A Persian Mystic. Meher Baba Passing through Colony. Message for the World." *South China Morning Post* (Hong Kong), p. 12.

July 10, 1932. "Hindu Philosopher to Break 7-Year Silence in U.S." *Galveston Daily News* (Texas), p. 3.

July 10, 1932. "The Long-Haired 'Messiah' Who Seeks to Save the World with a 'Ouija' Board. He Is Shri Sadguru Meher Baba Who Threatens to Break His Seven Years' Silence for the Benefit of Mankind." By Arthur Mefford. *Daily Mirror* (England), p. 18.

July 13, 1932. "Baba Will Continue to Keep Silent. 'Holy Man' Changes Mind on Radio Talk Here Today as Time's Not Ripe." *Los Angeles Times.*

July 14, 1932. "Mystic Will Not Break Long Period Silence." *Bluefield Daily Telegraph* (West Virginia), p. 11. From the Associated Press.

July 14, 1932. "Silent Hindu Defers Radio Talk." *New York Times,* p. 21. From the Associated Press.

July 14, 1932. "Today." By Arthur Brisbane. *Logansport Pharos-Tribune* (Indiana), p. 4.

July 16, 1932. "Today." By Arthur Brisbane. *Ogden Standard-Examiner* (Utah), p. 4.

July 25, 1932. "God Man Still Silent." *Time* magazine, p. 32.

August 27, 1932. "I Can Hardly Believe it Myself. A Portrait of a Happy Man, Silent Seven Years, Who is Seeking to Right the World through Love." By Frederick L. Collins. *Liberty* magazine, pp. 26–27.

September 15, 1932. "India's 'Messiah' to Break Seven-Year-Silence in U.S. Pent Up Thoughts to See Light on Coast in February." *New York Journal American.*

November 2, 1932. "The Eastern 'Messiah' from India, and a Western Type." *New York Evening Journal.*

November 19, 1932. "'God-Man' of India to Break Silence. Doctors Fear His Vocal Chords are Dead." *Charleroi Mail* (Pennsylvania), p. 2.

November 28, 1932. "'God-Man' of India to Break Silence. Doctors Fear His Vocal Chords Are Dead." *Republican Press* (Salamanca, New York), p. 2.

April 11, 1933. "Baba's Rich Women Disciples. London Pilgrims in India. New 'Messiah' to Break Silence." *Daily Mirror* (England), pp. 1–2.

May 9, 1933. "'Messiah' Coming Here to End Silence. Girl Disciples Lead Way. Message to be Given to World." *Daily Herald* (England), p. 9.

May 14, 1933. "His Seven-Year Silence. Mystic Wants to Talk Again." From our own correspondent. *Sunday Dispatch* (England), p. 15.

May 14, 1933. "'The New Messiah.'" *Sunday Graphic* (England), p. 1.

May 14, 1933. "Silent Mystic's Disciple Speaks." From our own correspondent. *The People* (England), p. 10.

May 23, 1933. "Meher Baba's Disciples." *Daily Herald* (England), p. 9.

May 23, 1933. "'Messiah's' Girl Disciples Reveal their Plans. Colony to be Formed in London. Mystic's Retinue of Twenty-Five Followers. World Message in July." *Daily Express* (England), p. 3.

May 23, 1933. "Mystic's Girl Followers Home Again. His Love of Films. Admirer of Greta Garbo." *Daily Mail* (England), p. 9.

August 10, 1933. "World Fellowship." *San Antonio Express* (Texas).

October 12, 1933. "The Master Calls." *Daily Express* (England), p. 1.

October 12, 1933. "Princess Leaves her Husband to Follow Indian 'Messiah.' Sacrifice of Stage Madonna. Across World through Faith in Dumb Man. Disciples Await His Speech." By Winifred Lorraine. *Daily Express* (England), p. 11.

November 4, 1933. "Prince Matchabelli Confirms Divorce. Indicates Interest of Wife in Indian Cult Led to Rift—Keeps Details Secret." *New York Times,* p. 13.

November 7, 1933. "Who's Who in News of Today." By Lemuel F. Parton. *Altoona Mirror* (Pennsylvania).

November 17, 1933. "'Nun' Turns Parsee." *Wisconsin State Journal* (Madison, Wisconsin), p. 10.

November 22, 1933. "Nun in 'Miracle' Turns Parsee." *Evening Gazette* (Xenia, Ohio), p. 2.

December 17, 1933. "The Troubles of a Modern 'Messiah.' One Widely Acclaimed Holy Man Refuses to Play the Part any Longer and Another, Who Hasn't Spoken a Word in Eight Years, Still Declines to Give the World His Promised Message." *San Antonio Light* (Texas), p. 8.

September 1934. "A Modern Meeting of Master and Chela." By Elizabeth C. Patterson. *Occult Review,* vol. 60, pp. 186–192.

November 15, 1934. "'Messiah' to Break Seven Years' Silence Here. Meher Baba Coming from India for Talking Film." *New York Evening Journal.* From the International News Service.

November 16, 1934. "7 Years of Silence." *New York Evening Journal*

December 13, 1934. "Imported Silence. Meher Baba Bound for California." *New York Journal American.*

December 15, 1934. "Sphinx-Like Messiah Off to Save Hollywood Souls." By Lady Terrington. *Daily Mirror* (England), pp. 4, 9.

September 15, 1935. "The Wonders of Eastern Mysticism." By Edward Frank Allen. A review of Paul Brunton's *A Search in Secret India. New York Times,* p. BR12.

February 27, 1936. "Book Notes." Includes publication announcement review of Rom Landau's *God Is My Adventure. New York Times,* p. 17.

March 7, 1937. "Had to Flee his Frankensteins! Garrett Fort's Dramatic Escape from the Appalling Effects of Monsters He Created for the Movies." By Marjorie Driscoll. *Salt Lake Review* (Utah), p. 2. Also published on March 7, 1937 in *Port Arthur News* (Texas); on March 7, 1937 in *Albuquerque Journal* (New Mexico); and on March 14, 1937 in *Portsmouth Times* (Ohio).

April 24, 1937. "Self-Styled Indian Prophet Is Silent." Review of *The Perfect Master* by C. B. Purdom. *Winnipeg Free Press* (Canada), p. 17.

E. Unpublished Books and Manuscripts

"A." A thirteen-page typed manuscript containing the complete text of the Meher Baba's six major messages given during his 1932 world tour. Kitty Davy's papers at the Meher Spiritual Center, Myrtle Beach, South Carolina.

"B." A one-page, two-column printed sheet containing the text of Meher Baba's "Message to Reporters in Hollywood" (May 29, 1932). Kitty Davy's papers at the Meher Spiritual Center, Myrtle Beach, South Carolina.

"C." A two-page typed manuscript containing the text of Baba's "Message to Reporters and Press Representatives" (May 19, 1932). Kitty Davy's papers at the Meher Spiritual Center, Myrtle Beach, South Carolina.

"Creation and Evolution." An untitled, eighteen-page typed manuscript with an introduction and four chapters (the source for the "Introduction" and "First Movement" in *How It All Happened*). Probably based in part on the dictations of Meher Baba. Archives of the Avatar Meher Baba P. P. C. Trust, Ahmednagar, India.

"The Combined Diary." 1924–27. 2 vols. Kept by Faredoon N. Driver ("Padri"), Gangaran L. Pawar, Pandurang S. Deshmukh ("Pandoba"), Nadirsha N. Dastur, and Framroze H. Dadachanji ("Chanji"). Archives of the Avatar Meher Baba P. P. C. Trust, Ahmednagar, India.

"D." A four-page typed manuscript translating into English questions and answers nos. 59–63 in *Shri Meher Baba, le Maître Parfait: Questions et Réponses.* Kitty Davy's papers at the Meher Spiritual Center, Myrtle Beach, South Carolina.

"Hell—Earth—Heaven: A Film Idea." By Karl Vollmoeller. A 37-page typed manuscript. Archives of the Avatar Meher Baba P. P. C. Trust, Ahmednagar, India.

"Introduction to Planes and Reincarnation." A four-page typed document containing content that is reproduced verbatim (though reordered in its paragraphing) in A. K. (Ramjoo) Abdulla, *Shri Meher Baba: His Philosophy and Teachings*, pp. 19–25. Archives of the Avatar Meher Baba P. P. C. Trust, Ahmednagar, India.

"Introduction to the Planes." A four-page typed document containing a rough draft version of the description of the experiences of the planes in pages 2–5 of "Scenario." Archives of the Avatar Meher Baba P. P. C. Trust, Ahmednagar, India.

Lord Meher: The Biography of the Avatar of the Age, Meher Baba. By V. S. Kalchuri. Digital text, under editorial revision by David Fenster, January 2009.

"Points for Shri Meher Baba's Film." A four-page typed document containing Margaret Mayo's write-up of points Meher Baba dictated to her on December 3, 1931 (the first draft of "A Touch of Maya"). Archives of the Avatar Meher Baba P. P. C. Trust, Ahmednagar, India.

"Scenario." A five-page typed document fragment containing (on p. 1) a complete outline of *How It All Happened* and (on pp. 2–5) a revised draft of the experiences of the planes of consciousness (incorporated into "A Touch of Maya"). Archives of the Avatar Meher Baba P. P. C. Trust, Ahmednagar, India.

"This Man David." By Karl Volmueller [sic]. A 102-page typed manuscript recounting a version of the story related by Karl Vollmoeller and H. S. Kraft in *This Man David* (1935). Archives of the Avatar Meher Baba P. P. C. Trust, Ahmednagar, India.

"Tiffin Lectures." Unpublished manuscript of lectures delivered by Meher Baba between April 19, 1926 and August 30, 1927. Compiled and edited by Framroze Dadachanji. Archives of the Avatar Meher Baba P. P. C. Trust, Ahmednagar, India.

F. Films

Meher Baba at the Davy residence in Kensington, London, April 8, 1932. Captioned "India's Mute Messiah," this Paramount Newsreel, about 75 seconds in length, presents Meher Baba as he dictates through Charles B. Purdom his "Message to the West." Live audio with Charles Purdom's voice. Hollywood, California: Paramount Pictures.

Meher Baba in New York Harbor, May 19, 1932. Captioned "Universal Newspaper Newsreel," this 45-second film clip shows Meher Baba on board the S. S. Bremen upon its arrival from London. Voiceover audio from the original newsreel. College Park, Maryland: National Archives and Records Administration.

Meher Baba Baba at the residence of Graham Phelps Stokes in Grenwich Village, New York sometime between May 19 and May 23, 1932. Six minutes fifteen seconds in length, this film, made by Fox Movietone News, contains live audio of Meher Baba dictating a message through Meredith Starr. Columbia, South Carolina: University of South Carolina Newsfilm Library.

Meher Baba at Harmon, New York, May 24–25, 1932. Captioned "Mystic Visits U.S.!" this one-minute twenty-second newsreel of Meher Baba probably at the Meherashram in Harmon contains live audio of Malcolm Schloss's voice reading out a message from Meher Baba. New York: Sherman Grindberg Library.

Meher Baba in Nasik, India, April 1933, and Portofino, Italy, July–July 1933. Entitled "I Am the One Reality," this recently produced forty-minute video contains slightly under two minutes of original footage from the period of Meher Baba's Western disciples' visit to his ashram in Nasik, India, in April 1933, and from Baba's sojourn in Portofino, Italy in June–July, 1933. Myrtle Beach, South Carolina: EliNor Publications Inc., forthcoming 2010.

Register of Editorial Alterations

In keeping with the editorial policy of the Avatar Meher Baba Trust (described on pp. 263–66), we provide here a register of emendations in Meher Baba's "published words" as presented in this book. The expression "published words" refers to books and messages that were published during Meher Baba's lifetime, with his evident knowledge and approval, and with his name as author. The phrase does not extend to cover records of Meher Baba's dictations, accounts of his words by disciples in notebooks and diaries, and other manuscripts that went unpublished during his lifetime. These are eligible for editing, and the editorial emendations are not recorded here.

The task of this present register is complicated by the fact that several of the messages republished in this book were, during Meher Baba's lifetime, published several times, and occasionally these versions differ from each other, usually in small ways. Moreover, we have been able to locate original manuscripts that sometimes provide clues as to the original form and intention of the messages.

In view of this multiplicity of sources, the general editorial procedure has been to select, in the case of each message or book, a primary source text, and to characterize as emendations any variations from that primary source. Certain categories of editorial emendation are allowable under Trust policy, as enumerated below. Other editorial emendations have been introduced because some source other than that which we have selected as the primary source offers a superior reading. These edits we call "source-based emendations." (Certain special problems have been presented by "Five Additional Questions and Answers," pp. 110–14, since that text has two primary sources, one in French and the other in English. For further explanation, see pp. 234–36 and 272–73.)

In the register below, the first column lists, by page number, paragraph number, and line number (in parentheses), where *in this book* the emendation has been introduced. The second column refers in the same way to the corresponding spot in the primary source text. The third column quotes the emended phrase or passage, and the fourth column quotes that phrase or passage in its unemended original form. The fifth column cites the Trust editorial policy under which the emendation has been allowed. The sixth (far right hand) column cites (when relevant) the alternate source texts that have been used as sources or supports for the emendations.

The fifth column, "Edit. Policy," and the sixth column, "Textual Sources for Emendation," use the following abbreviations.

Abbreviations for Editorial Policies

Ed (a) = spelling
Ed (b) = capitalization
Ed (c) = punctuation
Ed (d) = font
Ed (e) = lineation and paragraphing
Ed (f) = change in cross-reference necessitated by the new pagination in a new edition
Ed (g) = erroneous word repetition (such as "and and")
Ed (h) = grammatical agreement (as between subject and verb or pronoun and referent) or faulty parallelism
Ed (i) = mistakes evidently resulting from typesetting and other print production errors

Abbreviations for Published Texts or Manuscript Sources

A = A thirteen-page typed manuscript among Kitty Davy's papers at the Meher Spiritual Center in Myrtle Beach, South Carolina containing the complete text of the six major messages of Meher Baba's 1932 world tour (for further details see p. 269).

AF = *All Faiths Conference: Proceedings of First Conference Held at Nasik—June 1933.* Bombay: R. P. Mansani, Honourary Secretary, All Faiths Conference, Bombay, 1933.

B = The one-page typeset and fully justified two-column sheet among Kitty Davy's papers at the Meher Spiritual Center in Myrtle Beach, South Carolina containing the text of Meher Baba's "Message to Reporters in Hollywood" given at a press conference on May 29, 1932 (see p. 269).

C = A two-page typed manuscript among Kitty Davy's papers at the Meher Spiritual Center in Myrtle Beach, South Carolina that contains the text of Baba's "Message to Reporters and Press Representatives" given when the S. S. Bremen arrived in the port of New York on May 19, 1932 (see p. 269).

D = A four-page typed manuscript among Kitty Davy's papers at the Meher Spiritual Center in Myrtle Beach, South Carolina translating into English questions and answers nos. 59–63 in *Shri Meher Baba, le Maître Parfait: Questions et Réponses,* pp. 53–58 (see pp. 272–73).

EMW = *Early Messages to the West.* By Meher Baba. North Myrtle Beach, South Carolina: Sheriar Foundation, 2009.

LAP = *Love Alone Prevails: A Story of Life with Meher Baba.* By Kitty Davy. North Myrtle Beach, South Carolina: Sheriar Press, 1981.

M = *Messages of Meher Baba Delivered in the East and West.* By Meher Baba. Ahmednagar, India: Adi K. Irani for the Publication Committee, Meher Baba Universal Spiritual Centre, 1945.

MG = *Meher Gazette.*

MBJ = *Meher Baba Journal.*
MM = *Meher Message.*
MPM = "More about the Perfect Master." By Charles Purdom. *Everyman,* April 21, 1932, pp. 400, 402.
QA = *Shri Meher Baba, the Perfect Master: Questions and Answers.* London: The Circle Editorial Committee, 1933.
QR = *Shri Meher Baba, le Maître Parfait: Questions et Réponses.* Paris: Éditions de la Revue Mondiale, 1934.
PM = *The Perfect Master: The Early Life of Meher Baba.* By Charles B. Purdom. Second edition. North Myrtle Beach, South Carolina: Sheriar Press, 1976.
S = *The Sayings of Shri Meher Baba.* London: The Circle Editorial Committee, 1933.
TM = "A Touch of Maya: A Scenario by Meher Baba." Points dictated by Meher Baba and written out by Margaret Mayo. *Awakener,* vol. 22, no. 1 (1986), pp. 1–4.

Register of Editorial Alterations in Early Messages to the West

WHERE In EMW	WHERE IN PRIMARY SOURCE	CHANGED TO	CHANGED FROM	EDIT. POLICY	TEXTUAL SOURCES
p. 5 byline	M p.83 byline	*Everyman*	*EVERY MAN*	Ed (a)	
p. 5 ¶2 (2)	M p.83 ¶1 (2–3)	organizations,	organisations;	Ed (a), Ed (c)	LAP p. 42; MPM p. 402
p.5 ¶1–2	M p.83 ¶1 (4)	. . . sense. True . . .	. . . sense. True . . .	Ed (e)	A
p. 5 ¶3 (4)	M p. 83 ¶2 (5)	crises.	catastrophes.	source-based emendation	LAP p. 42; MPM p. 402
p.5 ¶4 (1)	M p.83 ¶3 (1)	Organized	Organised	Ed (a)	
p.5 ¶4 (2)	M p.83 ¶3 (3)	millennium	millenium	Ed (a)	
p.5 ¶5 (2)	M p.84 ¶1 (3)	revitalizing	re-vitalize	Ed (a); Ed (h)	LAP, p. 42; MPM p. 402
p. 5 ¶5 (3)	M p.84 ¶1 (4)	mission to	mission in	source-based emendation	MPM p. 402; A
p.6 ¶2 (1)	M p.84 ¶3 (1)	teaches	touches	source-based emendation	MG vol. 2, no. 1, p.1; PM p.165; A
p. 5 ¶5 (3)	M p.84 ¶1 (4)	mission to	mission to	source-based emendation	MPM p. 402; A

WHERE In EMW	WHERE IN PRIMARY SOURCE	CHANGED TO	CHANGED FROM	EDIT. POLICY	TEXTUAL SOURCES FOR EMENDATION
p.6 ¶2 (3)	M p.84 ¶3 (4)	mystery of life	Mystery of Life	Ed (b)	MG vol. 2, no. 2, p. 1; PM p.166; A
p.6 ¶4 (2)	M p.84 ¶5 (3)	within	with	source-based emendation	MG vol. 2, no. 2, p. 2; PM p.166; A
p.6 ¶4 (4)	M p.84 ¶5–6	. . . assumes. His . . .	. . . assumes. His . . .	Ed (e)	MG vol. 2, no. 2, p. 2; PM p.166
p.6¶4–5	M p.84 ¶6 (2)	. . . personal contact. The . . .	. . . personal contact. The . . .	. Ed (e)	MG vol. 2, no. 2, p. 2; A
p.6 ¶5 (2)	M p.84 ¶6 (4)	spiritual Master	Spiritual Master	Ed (b)	MG vol. 2, no. 2, p. 2; PM p.166; A
p.6 ¶5 (10)	M p.85 ¶1 (11)	more deeply into	more into	source-based emendation	MG vol. 2, no. 2, p. 2; PM p.166; A; C
p.7 ¶1 (2)	M p.85 ¶2 (3)	"Avataric"	'Avataric'	Ed (c)	
p.7 ¶5 (6)	M p.86 ¶1 (4)	life, and	life and	Ed (c)	MG vol. 2, no. 3, p. 2; PM p. 167
p.7 ¶5 (13)	M p.86 ¶1 (14-15)	visualize	visualise	Ed (a)	
p.7 ¶5 (17)	M p.86 ¶1 (20)	ideal if	ideal, if	Ed (c)	MG vol. 2, no. 3, p. 2; PM p.167; A
p.7 ¶5 (19)	M p.86 ¶1 (23)	problems such	problems, such	Ed (c)	MG vol. 2, no. 3, p. 2; PM p.167; A
p.8 ¶2 (7-8)	M p.87 ¶1 (3–4)	spiritual manifestation	Spiritual Manifestation	Ed (b)	PM p.168
p.8 ¶3 (2)	M p.87 ¶2 (3)	Savior	Saviour	Ed (a)	
p.8 ¶4 (7)	M p.87 ¶3 (9)	everyone but	everyone, but	Ed (c)	A
p.9 ¶3 (4)	M p.88 ¶3 (5-6)	practice, between	practice and between	source-based emendation	PM p.169; A
p.9 ¶5 (1)	M p.89 ¶1 (1)	truth	Truth	Ed (b)	PM p.170; A
p.9 ¶5 (1)	M p.89 ¶1 (2)	knowledge	Knowledge	Ed (b)	PM p.170; A
p.9 ¶5 (2)	M p.89 ¶1 (2)	illumination.	Illumination.	Ed (b)	PM p.170; A

WHERE In EMW	WHERE IN PRIMARY SOURCE	CHANGED TO	CHANGED FROM	EDIT. POLICY	TEXTUAL SOURCES FOR EMENDATION
p.10 ¶1 (2)	M p.89 ¶2 (3)	"sanskaras."	'sanskaras'.	Ed (c)	
p.10 ¶2 (2–4)	M p.89 ¶3 (2)	source of all, but unconsciously, as the fish lives in the sea without being aware of the sea, because it has never left it. Evolution involved a separation from the source of all and a consequent	Source of All and a consequent	source-based emendation	A; PM p.170
p.10 ¶3 (1)	M p.89 ¶4 (1)	vanguard and synthesis	vanguard and the synthesis	source-based emendation	PM p.170; A
p.10 ¶5 (2)	M p.89 ¶6 (2)	illumination.	Illumination.	Ed (b)	PM p.171; A
p.10 ¶5 (3)	M p.90 ¶1 (1-2)	source of all love and existence,	Source of All Love and Existence,	Ed (b)	A
p.12 ¶1 (5)	M p.90 ¶4 (6-7)	highest state of consciousness	Highest State of Consciousness	Ed (b)	PM p.172; A; B
p.12 ¶1 (7)	M p.90 ¶4 (9)	consciousness	Consciousness	Ed (b)	PM p.172; A; B
p.12 ¶2 (5)	M p.91 ¶2 (7-8)	ceremonies, which	ceremonies which	Ed (c)	MG vol. 2, no. 1, p.2; PM p.172; A; B
p.12 ¶2 (9)	M p.91 ¶2 (12-14)	"I am in the right," "I am the favored one," "I only have the right to live,"	"I am in the right", "I am the favoured one", "I only have the right to live",	Ed (a), Ed (c)	
p.12 ¶2 (11)	M p.91 ¶2 (16)	commandment	Commandment	Ed (b)	MG vol. 2, no. 1, p.2; PM p.172; A; B
p.12 ¶2-3	M p.91 ¶2 (18)	. . . by the ego. In the . . .	. . . by the ego. In the . . .	Ed (e)	A
p.13 ¶1 (4)	M p.91 ¶2 (28)	the "I,"	the 'I',	Ed (c)	
p.13 ¶2 (13)	M p.92 ¶1 (16)	The ego persists to the end.	Tho ego persists to the last.	Ed (a) and source-based emendation	MG vol. 2, no. 1, p.2; PM p.173; A; B

WHERE In EMW	WHERE IN PRIMARY SOURCE	CHANGED TO	CHANGED FROM	EDIT. POLICY	TEXTUAL SOURCES FOR EMENDATION
p.13 ¶2 (13–15)	M p.92 ¶1 (16–19)	the six out of the seven principal stages on the Path (culminating in the God-conscious state) are traversed is the ego completely eliminated, to reappear	the six, out of the seven, principal stages on the Path, culminating into one God-conscious state, are traversed, is the ego completely eliminated to re-appear	Ed (c)	
p.13 ¶2 (14)	M p.92 ¶1 (18)	in the God-conscious state)	into one God-conscious state,	source-based emendation	MG vol. 2, no. 1, p.2; B
p.13 ¶ (16)	M p.92 ¶1 (20)	"I,"	"I",	Ed (c)	
p.13 ¶ 2 (17)	M p.92 ¶1 (21-22)	"I and my Father are One," and	"I and my Father are one" and	Ed (b), Ed (c)	
p.13 ¶4 (1)	M p.92 ¶3 (2)	One, and an	One, an	Ed (c)	MG vol. 2, no. 1, p.2; PM pp.173–74; A; B
p.14 ¶1 (3)	M p.93 ¶1 (6)	humor.	humour.	Ed (a)	
p.14 ¶2 (2)	M p.93 ¶2 (3)	Self.	self.	Ed (b)	A
p.15 ¶1 (2)	M p.94 ¶1 (3)	you—what	you, —what	Ed (c)	PM p.174
p.15 ¶1 (3–4)	M p.94 ¶1 (5)	crime—that	crime, —that	Ed (c)	PM p.174
p.15 ¶3 (5)	M p.94 ¶ 3 (7)	connive,	connive	Ed (c)	PM p.174; A
p.16 ¶1 (5)	M p.95 ¶2 (6)	Self, and	Self and	Ed (c)	PM p.175; A
p.16 ¶2 (3)	M p. 95 ¶3 (3)	disappear, and	disappear and	Ed (c)	PM p.175; A
p.16 ¶4 (6–7)	M p.96 ¶1 (1)	Subtle or the Desire Body,	Subtle, or the Desire, Body,	Ed (c)	PM p.176
p.16 ¶4 (9)	M p.96 ¶1 (5)	Body, with	Body with	Ed (c)	PM p.176; A
p.16 ¶5 (3–4)	M p.96 ¶2 (5)	desires, and	desires and	Ed (c)	
p.16 ¶6 (2)	M p.96 ¶3 (2)	expression may	expression, may	Ed (c)	A
p.17 ¶1 (2)	M p.96 ¶4 (3)	clear, and	clear and	Ed (c)	PM p.176; A

WHERE In EMW	WHERE IN PRIMARY SOURCE	CHANGED TO	CHANGED FROM	EDIT. POLICY	TEXTUAL SOURCES FOR EMENDATION
p.17 ¶2 (2–3)	M p.96 ¶5 (3–4)	spiritual body, which in the ordinary human being is	spiritual body which, in the ordinary human being, is	Ed (c)	PM p.176; A
p.17 ¶3 (2)	M p.96 ¶6 (3)	or in	or, in	Ed (c)	
p.17 ¶5 (2)	M p.97 ¶2 (3)	Avatars	'Avataras'	Ed (a), Ed (c)	PM p. 176
p.19 ¶2 (7)	M p.99 ¶1 (10)	Self,	self	Ed (b)	
p.19 ¶3 (4)	M p.99 ¶2 (5)	then, for	then for	Ed (c)	A
p.20 ¶3 (8)	M p.100 ¶3 (11)	Once one	Once, one	Ed (c)	A
p.21 ¶1 (3)	M p.101 ¶2 (6)	inspiring.	inspiring	Ed (c)	A
p.73 no. 7 ¶2 (4)	QA p.16 no.7 ¶2 (5)	Sanskrit*)	Sanskrit)[1]	Ed (c)	
p.85 (no. 24) ¶1 (2)	QA p.30 (no. 24) ¶3 (11)	and drink of the well	and, like him, to drink of the well	source-based emendation	QA p.8 "Errata" list (see EMW p. 344)
p.87 no. 26 (a) ¶1 (2)	QA p.33 no.26 (a) ¶1 (3)	self-interest.	Self-interest.	Ed (b)	
p.87 bottom right	QA p. 33 bottom right		C	Ed (i)	
p.90 no. 33 ¶4 (8)	QA p.38 no. 33 ¶1 (7)	Divinity,	divinity,	Ed (b)	
p.92 no. 44	QA p.39 no. 44	Christ Consciousness?	Christ consciousness?	Ed (b)	
p.95 (no. 34 (a)) ¶2 (1)	QA p.41 (no. 34(a)) ¶3 (2)	Western-trained	Western trained	Ed (c)	
p.97 (no. 35) ¶6 (1)	QA p.44 (no. 35) ¶6 (1)	unaware of either	either unaware of	source-based emendation	QA p.8 "Errata" list (see EMW p. 344)
p.98 (no. 35) ¶2 (6)	QA p.45 (no. 35) ¶2 (6)	universal	univeral	Ed (a)	
p.98 (no. 35) ¶3 (2)	QA p.45 (no. 35) ¶3 (2)	nor	not	Ed (a)	

WHERE In EMW	WHERE IN PRIMARY SOURCE	CHANGED TO	CHANGED FROM	EDIT. POLICY	TEXTUAL SOURCES FOR EMENDATION
p. 101 bottom right	QA p.49 bottom right		D	Ed (i)	
p.103 no. 49 ¶1 (12)	QA p.53 (no.49) ¶1 (2)	equipment; which,	equipment, which,	Ed (c)	M p.94
p.104 (no. 49)¶4 (4)	QA p.53 (no. 49) ¶4 (5-6)	certainty will replace fear;	security will replace certainty;	source-based emendation	M p.95
p.104 no. 50 ¶1 (2–3)	QA p.54 (no. 50) ¶1 (2)	the primary purpose, will	the primary, will	source-based emendation	QA p.8 "Errata" list (see EMW p. 344)
p.107 no. 56 ¶4 and ¶5	QA p.58 no. 56 ¶2 and ¶3	*(c)* The *mind* is the medium by which the spirit's experiences of matter are expressed. *(d)* The *body* is the medium through which the *mind* puts its desires, emotions and thoughts into action on the physical plane.	*(c)* The *body* is the medium through which the *mind* puts its desires, emotions, and thoughts into action on the physical plane. *(d)* The *mind* is the medium by which the spirit's experiences of matter are expressed.	source-based emendation	QA p.8 "Errata" list (see EMW p. 344)
p.110 no. 59 ¶1 (2)	MBJ vol.2 no. 6 p.353 col. 1 ¶2 (5)	unhappiness,	unahappiness	Ed (a)	D
p.110 no. 59 ¶1 (3)	MBJ vol.2 no. 6 p.353 col. 1 ¶2 (7)	up to	upto	Ed (a)	D
p.110 no. 59 ¶2 (1)	MBJ vol.2 no. 6 p.353 col. 1 ¶3 (1)	Karma,	*Karma;*	Ed (c), Ed (d)	
p.110 no. 59 ¶2 (4)	MBJ vol.2 no. 6 p.353 col. 2 ¶1 (2)	sanskaras.	*Sanskaras.*	Ed (b), Ed (d)	
p.110 no. 59 ¶2 (12)	MBJ vol.2 no. 6 p.354 col. 1 ¶1 (6–7)	sanskaras	*Sanskaras*	Ed (b), Ed (d)	
p.111 no. 61 ¶1 (1)	MBJ vol.2 no. 6 p.354 col. 1 ¶5 (2)	Avatar	*Avatar*	Ed (d)	

WHERE In EMW	WHERE IN PRIMARY SOURCE	CHANGED TO	CHANGED FROM	EDIT. POLICY	TEXTUAL SOURCES FOR EMENDATION
p.111 no. 61 ¶1 (3)	MBJ vol.2 no. 6 p.354 col. 2 ¶1 (5)	Avatars	Avatars	Ed (d)	
p.111 no. 61 ¶1 (4, 9)	MBJ vol.2 no. 6 p.354 col. 2 ¶1 (7, 20)	Mohammed	Mohomed	Ed (a)	D
p.111 no. 61 ¶1 (6)	MBJ vol.2 no. 6 p.354 col. 2 ¶1 (10–11)	If, like Jesus,	If like Jesus	Ed (c)	D
p.111 no. 61 ¶1 (9)	MBJ vol.2 no. 6 p.354 col. 2 ¶1 (19)	towards	toward	Ed (a)	
p.111 no. 61 ¶2 (2)	MBJ vol.2 no. 6 p.354 col. 2 ¶2 (4)	predominated;	were predominate;	source-based emendation	QR p. 55, and endnote 76 in EMW
p.112 (no. 61) ¶1 (1)	MBJ vol.2 no. 6 p.355 col. 1 ¶1 (13)	actions."	actions".	Ed (c)	
p.112 (no. 61) ¶3 (4)	MBJ vol.2 no. 6 p.355 col. 2 ¶2 (10)	humility,	humanity,	source-based emendation	QR p. 56, D, and endnote 79 in EMW
p.112 (no. 61) ¶3 (7)	MBJ vol.2 no. 6 p.355 col. 2 ¶2 (17)	temptation;	temptations,	Ed (c) and source-based emendation	D, and endnote 80 in EMW
p.112 no. 62 ¶1 (1)	MBJ vol.2 no.7 p.415 col.1 ¶2 (1)	Avatars	*Avatars*	Ed (d)	
p.112 no. 62 ¶1 (3)	MBJ vol.2 no.7 p.415 col. 1 ¶2 (7)	Avatar	*Avatar*	Ed (d)	
p.112 no. 62 ¶1 (6)	MBJ vol.2 no.7 p.415 col.1 ¶2 (13)	pigs'	pigs	Ed (c)	
p.112 no. 62 ¶1 (6)	MBJ vol.2 no.7 p.415 col.1 ¶2 (15)	cows'	cows	Ed (c)	
p.112 no. 62 ¶1 (10)	MBJ vol.2 no.7 p.415 col.2 ¶1 (9–10)	Avatar of different periods,	*Avatar* of different periods	Ed (d), Ed (c)	
p.113 no. 63 ¶2 (3)	MBJ vol.2 no.7 p.416 col.1 ¶2 (7)	sanskaras	*Sanskaras*	Ed (b), Ed (d)	D, QR p. 57

WHERE In EMW	WHERE IN PRIMARY SOURCE	CHANGED TO	CHANGED FROM	EDIT. POLICY	TEXTUAL SOURCES FOR EMENDATION
p.113 no. 63 ¶2 (4), ¶3 (1)	MBJ vol.2 no.7 p.416 col.1 ¶2 (8), col.2 ¶1 (15)	"heaven"	'heaven'	Ed (c)	
p.113 no. 63 ¶2 (4), ¶3 (1)	MBJ vol.2 no.7 p.416 col.1 ¶2 (8), col. 2 ¶1 (16)	"hell,"	'hell',	Ed (c)	
p.113 no. 63 ¶2 (10)	MBJ vol.2 no.7 p.416 col.1 ¶2 (14)	"heaven"	'Heaven'	Ed (b), Ed (c)	
p.113 no. 63 ¶2 (10)	MBJ vol.2 no.7 p.416 col. 2 ¶1 (14)	"hell."	'hell'.	Ed (c)	
p.113 no. 63 ¶3 (2)	MBJ vol.2 no.7 p.416 col.2 ¶1 (17)	no reality;	no reality,	Ed (c)	
p.120 ¶2 (4)	S p.5 ¶2 (6)	Sakori	Sakora	Ed (a)	
p.121 footnote *	S p.7 footnote 1	"Self"	self	Ed (b), Ed (c)	
p.127 saying 4 (1)	S p.15 saying 2 (1)	practicing,	practising,	Ed (a)	
p.129 bottom right	S p.17 bottom right		B	Ed (i)	
p.132 saying 2 (2)	S p.20 saying 4 (3)	posture[*] which you find most convenient should	posture,[2] which you find most convenient, should	Ed (c)	
p.132 footnote †	S p.21 footnote 1	attained as	attained a	Ed (a)	
p.136 saying 4 (2)	S p.26 saying 5 (3)	tapa-japa[*]	tapa-yapa[1]	Ed (a)	
p.138 ¶5 (4)	S p. 29 ¶5 (6)	Illumination,	*Illumination,*	Ed (d)	
p.140 footnote *	S p.32 footnote 1	heaven, hell,	Heaven, Hell,	Ed (b)	
p.140 saying 5 (1)	S p.32 saying 4 (1)	Yogis,	yogis,	Ed (b)	
p.141 saying 3 (1)	S p.33 saying 3 (1)	Miracles[†]	[1]Miracles	Ed (c)	

WHERE In EMW	WHERE IN PRIMARY SOURCE	CHANGED TO	CHANGED FROM	EDIT. POLICY	TEXTUAL SOURCES FOR EMENDATION
p.141 saying 3 (2)	S p.33 saying 3 (3)	Miracles[‡]	[2]miracles	Ed (c)	
p.142 saying 1 (1)	S p.34 saying 1 (1)	Yoga Samadhi	Yoga-Samadhi	Ed (c)	
p.142 saying 1 (3)	S p.34 saying 1 (4)	Samadhi	samadhi	Ed (b)	
p.142 saying 1 (4)	S p.34 saying 1 (6)	Yoga Samadhi.	Yogi Samadhi.	Ed (a)	
p.142 saying 5 (3)	S p.35 saying 2 (5)	practice	practise	Ed (a)	
p.153 (under the entry Soul) (1)	S p.47 (under the entry Soul) (1)	infinite Self	infinite self	Ed (b)	
p.153 (under the entry Spirit) (7)	S p.48 (under the entry Spirit) (2)	infinite Self	infinite self	Ed (b)	
p.153 (under the entry Spirit) (8)	S p.48 (under the entry Spirit) (5)	Spirit	spirit	Ed (b)	
p.153 (entry word)	S p.48 (entry word)	Yoga	-Yoga	Ed (c)	
p.153 (entry word)	S p.48 (entry word)	Yogi	-Yogi	Ed (c)	
p.308 ¶4 (2)	M p.5 ¶1 (3)	Masters	masters	Ed (b)	
p.309 ¶2 (2–3)	AF p.17	principle—faith	principle,—faith	Ed (c)	M p.6
p.309 ¶2 (12)	AF p. 17	realized,	Realized,	Ed (b)	MG vol. 2, no. 5, p. 2; M p.6
p.309 ¶4 (3)	MG Birthday Supp. 1934 p.1 ¶1 (3)	irresistibly	irresistably	Ed (a)	
p.310 ¶1 (2)	MG Birthday Supp. 1934 p.1 ¶1 (5)	yogas	Yogas	Ed (b)	
p.310 ¶2 (7)	MG Birthday Supp. 1934 p.1 ¶2 (7)	eye-opener	eyeopener	Ed (a)	

WHERE In EMW	WHERE IN PRIMARY SOURCE	CHANGED TO	CHANGED FROM	EDIT. POLICY	TEXTUAL SOURCES FOR EMENDATION
p.310 ¶3 (3)	MG Birthday Supp. 1934 p.1 ¶3 (2–3)	as, under this law, the	as under this law the	Ed (c)	M p.7
p.310 ¶3 (3)	MG Birthday Supp. 1934 p.1 ¶3 (3)	at all times	for all times	source-based emendation	M p.7
p.351 saying 2 (2)	MM vol. 2 no. 6 p. 1 saying 88	importance	importnnce	Ed (a)	

Index

Acknowledgments

Early Messages to the West has been edited for publication under the auspices of the Avatar Meher Baba Perpetual Public Charitable Trust in Ahmednagar, India. It continues the Trust's work of trying to help spread Avatar Meher Baba's message of Love and Truth to the world by making available authentic, reliable, and well-researched texts of his words and messages.

This book was edited by Ward Parks with the advice and guidance of Meherwan B. Jessawala. It was designed by Sheila Krynski.

Many other people contributed to this edition in many ways. The tasks of typing out, proofreading, and correcting the text were assisted at various stages by Chitra Alverado, Kendra Crossen Borroughs, Jack Burke, Becky Kent, Jean McKinney, Susan McKendree, Larry Nessly, Ken Neunzig, Alicia Rivero, Steve Sakellarios, and Darryl and Susan Smith.

Meher Baba's lovers from all over the world assisted enormously in the research and collection of materials. Special thanks is due to David Fenster, for the sharing of rare documents and astute critique and guidance in the history of Meher Baba's life. The Archives teams of the Avatar Meher Baba Trust, notably Meg DeLoe, Patrick Finley, Janet Judson, Meredith Klein, Jessica Mednick, and William Ward, along with other Trust workers Martin and Christine Cook, Bob Street, Frank Bloise, and Ted Judson, made an extraordinary effort in providing the original materials for part five. And also Meredith Klein, Jessica Mednick, and others in locating and providing high quality digital scans that appear in many places in the book. and helping in the research in other ways. Heather Nadel shared copies of film-related material originally made available to her by Eruch Jessawala. The Meher Spiritual Center in Myrtle Beach, South Carolina most generously gave access to and allowed publication of selections from Kitty Davy's papers, particularly as pertaining to the work of Herbert Davy. Buz and Wendy Connor provided rare material from the Elizabeth C. Patterson Archives relating to Meher Baba's work in film. Dot Lesnik helped in locating many critical research materials. Françoise and Daniel Lemetais helped with the translation from the French in "Five Additional Questions and Answers." Thanks are due to Naosherwan Anzar for allowing the republication of his translation of Chanji's originals Gujarati account of Meher Baba's 1932 interview with James Douglas.

The discovery and compilation of newspaper and magazine articles represented in appendix 1 and other parts of this book was accomplished by various persons, notably Keith Miles, Jamie and Zo

Newell, Dru Swinson, Valerie McKean, James and Elaine Miller, Tian Gunther, Ken Coleman, and others. Among those who helped in finding photographs, we specially thank Sarah McNeill (in England), Victor Seckelor and Diane Snow (of Sufism Reoriented), and Charles Haynes. Tips and guidance in other areas of research were given at various times by Peter Ravazza, Philip Creager, Hank Mindlin, Peter Nordeen, Gokaran Shrivastava, Jal Dastur, and Ellen Kimball.

Our special appreciations to our beloved friend Eric Nadel, who over many years, and in his own inimitable ways, contributed enormously to the Trust publications program.

Finally, we wish to thank Jim Wrobel and Andy Lesnik for their continuing support and many contributions.